P9-BVC-122

The Voice of Anna Julia Cooper

LEGACIES OF SOCIAL THOUGHT

Charles Lemert, Series Editor

Roads from Past to Future (1997), by Charles Tilly

The Voice of Anna Julia Cooper, including A Voice from the South *and Other Essays, Papers, and Letters* (1998), edited by Charles Lemert and Esme Bhan

The Voice of Anna Julia Cooper

Including *A Voice from the South* and Other Important Essays, Papers, and Letters

edited by
Charles Lemert
and
Esme Bhan

975.04
C776 L

ROWMAN & LITTLEFIELD PUBLISHERS, INC.
Lanham • Boulder • New York • Oxford

Alverno College
Library Media Center
Milwaukee, Wisconsin

ROWMAN & LITTLEFIELD PUBLISHERS, INC.

Published in the United States of America
by Rowman & Littlefield Publishers, Inc.
4720 Boston Way, Lanham, Maryland 20706

12 Hid's Copse Road
Cumnor Hill, Oxford OX2 9JJ, England

Copyright © 1998 by Rowman & Littlefield Publishers, Inc.
Introduction copyright © 1998 by Charles Lemert

All rights reserved. No part of this publication may be reproduced,
stored in a retrieval system, or transmitted in any form or by any
means, electronic, mechanical, photocopying, recording, or otherwise,
without the prior permission of the publisher.

British Library Cataloguing in Publication Information Available

Library of Congress Cataloging-in-Publication Data

Cooper, Anna J. (Anna Julia), 1858–1964.
    The voice of Anna Julia Cooper : including a voice from the south
and other important essays, papers, and letters / [edited by]
Charles Lemert and Esme Bhan.
      p. cm.
    Includes bibliographical references and index.
    ISBN 0-8476-8407-5 (cloth). — ISBN 0-8476-8408-3 (pbk.)
    1. Afro-American women—Southern States—History—19th century.
2. Southern States—Race relations. 3. Cooper, Anna J. (Anna
Julia), 1858–1964—Archives. I. Lemert, Charles C., 1937– .
II. Bhan, Esme, 1947– . III. Cooper, Anna J. (Anna Julia),
1858–1964. Voice from the South. IV. Title.
E185.86.C58214 1998
975'.00496073—dc21   97-37767
                                        CIP
ISBN 0-8476-8407-5-1 (cloth : alk. paper)
ISBN 0-8476-8408-3 (pbk. : alk. paper)

Printed in the United States of America

⊖™ The paper used in this publication meets the minimum requirements of American National
Standard for Information Sciences—Permanence of Paper for Printed Library Materials, ANSI
Z39.48–1984.

to Julie Doar

—C.L.

to my husband, Chander

—E.B.

Contents

IV. World Politics, Race, and Slavery: The Historical Studies

V. Reflections on Her Life: Memoirs, Occasional Writings, Letters: 1925–1958

Acknowledgments

We appreciate the invaluable support of all those who shared our enthusiasm for this project and encouraged us in our efforts to bring Anna Julia Cooper's writings to a wider audience. Because we both believe that Cooper's voice deserves to be heard, we decided to embark upon this work almost as soon as we met in June 1994. Cooper's quest for knowledge and learning, her zest for social justice and fairness, her race pride, and especially her uncompromising commitment to women's rights more than justify this long overdue project.

The editors wish to express their respect and gratitude for the pioneering work of Louise Daniel Hutchinson, author of the indispensable *Anna Julia Cooper: A Voice from the South,* published by the Smithsonian Institution Press in conjunction with the Anacostia Neighborhood Museum exhibition on Cooper's life. While we have collected from and drawn on other sources than those presented by Louise Hutchinson's efforts, we often returned to check our facts against hers.

We thank the staff of the Moorland-Spingarn Research Center of Howard University for assistance in our work and Larry Fields for translating Cooper's introduction to *Le Pèlerinage de Charlemagne* on very short notice. We also thank Dean Birkenkamp and his editorial colleagues at Rowman & Littlefield, who so patiently worked the magic that caused photocopies, manuscript copy, and page proofs to fly about the continent in sufficient time to meet a very unforgiving production schedule.

Charles dedicates his efforts in this project to Julie Doar, a friend of many years, who today is following in Anna Julia Cooper's footsteps by teaching high school in the Washington area while keeping an ever vigilant eye on the current prospects of the colored woman's office. He also thanks his wife, Geri Thoma, for more than could or should be said.

Esme dedicates her efforts to Chander, her partner and husband for over twenty years, for his unfailing support, continuous encouragement, and even for occasional, but always well-meaning, criticism. His enthusiasm showed through when he accompanied her to archives and took notes for her on picture-perfect golf days.

The editors and the publisher gratefully acknowledge permission from the Moorland-Spingarn Research Center, Howard University, to reprint chapters 12, 14, 17, 18, 19; from the NAACP to reprint chapter 20; and from Frances Richardson Keller and the Mellen Press to reprint chapters 22 and 23.

The following were privately printed, or appear to have been privately printed, and we have been unable to find a rights-holder: chapters 21 and 24, both of which the Moorland-Spingarn Research Center has graciously allowed us to photocopy from its files, and chapters 2, 3, 4, 5, 6, 7, 8, 9, 10, 13, 26, and 27 and the souvenir in chapter 28.

We also thank the Moorland-Spingarn Research Center for providing photocopies from its files, most particularly of chapter 25 and of the following materials in chapter 28: the autobiographical fragment, all the letters except Cooper's to Du Bois, and the poem "No Flowers Please." For none of these have we been able to find a rights-holder.

Chapter 16 is used courtesy of the NAACP; the letter to Du Bois in chapter 28, courtesy of the Du Bois Archive, University of Massachusetts.

The newspaper contributions in chapter 28 appear to have been printed in the *Washington Tribune,* which has been out of publication since 1935.

Charles Lemert, Killingworth, Connecticut
Esme Bhan, Annapolis, Maryland

· 1 ·

Anna Julia Cooper:
The Colored Woman's Office

Charles Lemert

$\mathcal{A}$nna Julia Cooper is one of the most distinctly recognizable of those powerful and influential American black women whose lineage goes back, at least, to Sojourner Truth and Harriet Tubman in the nineteenth century and Phillis Wheatley in the eighteenth century. Yet, Anna Cooper's reputation as a foundational figure among black feminists in America, in contrast to those of other notable women in the tradition, is fraught with ambiguity. What is striking about her, both visually and personally, shines against the ambiguities without always illuminating them. She is venerated for her heroic life. But Cooper is also, and regularly, the subject of controversy today, as she was in her lifetime. As a result, both the striking and the ambiguous must be considered if we are to understand and take with full seriousness Cooper's exceptional place in American history.

The ready recognizability of Anna Julia Cooper owes at least partly to a beauty so commanding that she has become a virtual emblem of the "Black Woman of America" (to use Cooper's own distinctive phrase). A familiar photograph of Cooper in early midlife was selected for the jacket of *Black Women of America*—the most important and most comprehensive encyclopedia of writings by and about black women in American history.[1] In the photograph, Cooper faces the light that shades her face and shoulders. The image is of her profile, and the photographer's front-lighting

---

1. Darlene Clark Hine, with Elsa Barkley Brown and Rosalyn Terborg-Penn, eds., *Black Women of America* (Brooklyn, N.Y.: Carlson, 1993). The same photo appears on the covers of two important biographical studies of Cooper: Louise Daniel Hutchinson, *Anna Julia Cooper: A Voice from the South* (Washington, D.C.: Anacostia Neighborhood Museum and Smithsonian Press, 1981), and Leona C. Gabel, *From Slavery to the Sorbonne and Beyond: The Life and Writings of Anna J. Cooper* (Northampton, Mass.: Smith College Studies in History, 1982).

accentuates enough of the physical reminders of her slaveholding father to encourage among the innocent an illusion as to the subject's race. Cooper's dress is adorned by a generous, but modest and delicate, jabot that comes to her neck in a white lace collar neat to the throat. Cooper's eyes are fixed, firm, and unwavering; her jaw set, but relaxed; her hair drawn up as if to add substance to the jabot's already discreet Victorian fringe. Her lighted visage is framed against a darkened background, often set as though she were the classic figure of a cameo. Cooper is thus portrayed very much as she was: entirely ready for business, yet composed, dignified, and slightly superior.

Some white people coming upon this image out of context, with no prior knowledge of its subject, do not at first realize that she was black. At the same time, those already familiar with Cooper's important contributions to American social thought might well be reminded of several of her most elegant lines, appearing at the end of chapter 6, "The Status of Woman in America":

> What a responsibility then to have the sole management of the primal lights and shadows! Such is the colored woman's office. She must stamp weal or woe on the coming history of this people. May she see her opportunity and vindicate her high prerogative. (P. 117[2])

Still, even those who are wise to Cooper may well be puzzled by these words, if not by the photograph. To whom does she refer? Which is "this people" upon whom the colored women must stamp weal or woe? Is it "her people" (an expression she hated)[3]? Or is it the whole of the American people, whose "primal lights and shadows" are to be managed by the colored woman? On the one hand, the essay in which these lines appear makes it clear that Cooper was a race-woman who believed deeply in the unique vocation of black women. She defined that vocation, in part, by the black woman's moral superiority to white civilization, whose "*blasé* world-weary look," as she put it, "characterize[d] the old washed out and worn out races which ha[d] already, so to speak, seen their best days" (p. 117). On the other hand, elsewhere Cooper made it clear that she did not believe any less seriously in the West and American civilization: "But there can be no doubt that here in America is the arena in which the next triumph of

---

2. Throughout this book, unless otherwise indicated, page numbers mentioned by editors refer to Cooper's works as they appear herein.

3. See p. 102 for an example of her disdain for the expression.

civilization is to be won; and here too we find promise abundant and possibilities infinite" (p. 54). How could a fin de siècle schoolteacher who would serve the famous M Street (colloquially, the "Colored," later officially changed to Dunbar) High School in the District of Columbia for more than forty years believe otherwise?

Cooper did, in fact, sustain all at once many different ideas, values, and commitments—not all of which settle into clarifying focus. To understand Cooper is to come face-to-face with a woman who lived with heroic dignity while refusing all along to be exactly what others would have her be. As a result, even those who are drawn to the influential ideas of Cooper's most famous book, *A Voice from the South,* may well express certain reservations.

One of the most frequently held reservations toward Cooper is that she all too comfortably accepted the white pieties of the true womanhood ideal, in particular those emphasizing a woman's duty to establish the domestic circle.[4] And there are grounds for the suspicion in Cooper's own words, written late in life but recalling the beginnings of her enriching domestic life in Washington, D.C.:

---

4. The first, and still well-regarded, scholarly discussion of the idea of the cult of true womanhood is Barbara Welter, *Dimity Convictions: The American Woman in the Nineteenth Century* (Athens: Ohio University Press, 1976). A famous recent use of the idea is Ann duCille, "The Occult of True Black Womanhood: Critical Demeanor and Black Feminist Studies," *Signs* 19, no. 3 (1994): 591–629, reprinted in duCille, *Skin Trade* (Cambridge, Mass.: Harvard University Press, 1996).

It should be said that since Barbara Welter's original presentation of the true womanhood ideal in 1976, subsequent scholarship has shown that, among white southern women, especially in the antebellum period and during the Civil War, responsibility for moral and domestic culture was always painfully bound up with the economics and politics of the plantation system. See, for example, Drew Gilpin Faust, *Mothers of Invention: Women of the Slaveholding South in the American Civil War* (Chapel Hill: University of North Carolina Press, 1996). Just the same, the concept as Welter described it remains a central issue in interpretations of Cooper, and rightly so.

Most prominent among those who consider Cooper too indulgent of true womanhood doctrines is Mary Helen Washington in her introduction to the Oxford-Schomburg Library edition of Cooper's *Voice from the South* (New York: Oxford University Press, 1988), p. xlvi. Notable among others who question Cooper on this score is Karen Baker-Fletcher, "A 'Singing Something': The Literature of Anna Julia Cooper as a Resource for a Theological Anthropology of Voice" (doctoral thesis, Harvard University, 1991), ch. 5. Baker-Fletcher's thesis has been published in substantially revised form as *A Singing Something: Womanist Reflections on Anna Julia Cooper* (New York: Crossroad, 1994). References to Baker-Fletcher's work will be to the unpublished thesis unless otherwise indicated. Somewhat less persuasive is Jesse Michael Lang's discussion of this theme in Cooper's writings: *Anticipations of the Booker T. Washington–W. E. B. Du Bois Dialectic in the Writings of Frances E. W. Harper, Ida B. Wells, and Anna Julia Cooper* (master's thesis, Georgetown University, 1992). The most demanding argument on the other side is Hazel Carby's in *Reconstructing Womanhood: The Emergence of the Afro-American Woman Novelist* (New York: Oxford University Press, 1987), ch. 5.

> The very next year [1888] I had planted my little North Carolina colony on Seventeenth street where I immediately began, like the proverbial beaver to build a home, not merely a house to shelter the body, but a home to sustain and refresh the mind, a home where friends foregather for interchange of ideas and agreeable association of sympathetic spirits. (P. 310)

The life Anna Julia Cooper built and lived from her birth in North Carolina, probably in 1858, until her death in Washington, D.C., in 1964, was one centered deeply in the virtues of home, religion, and proper public conduct. How, indeed, could a woman of such classically southern virtues have become one of the most widely recognized symbols of the new black woman?

Whatever is to be made of the ambiguities created by the image and writings of Anna Julia Cooper, they are surely not confusions arising from an uncertain identity. It is impossible to read even a few paragraphs of any of Cooper's writings without knowing that this was a woman who knew exactly who she was. And who she was was someone who kept nothing within her conscious grasp in the dark. In contrast to writers of a later and culturally more complicated time and place, Cooper gave not the least thought to shading the public presentation of her racial or gender natures and convictions.

The years of Cooper's most important productivity as a writer and scholar (roughly 1886 to 1930) were anything but uncomplicated. She began her work barely twenty years after Emancipation and a short decade after the collapse of Reconstruction in 1877. She continued it through the rise of Jim Crow; through the era of the northern and urban migrations, of which she herself was a pioneer; through the early-twentieth-century struggles between Booker T. Washington and W. E. B. Du Bois, of which she was a more or less innocent victim; and through the Harlem Renaissance, in respect to which she took a generally marginal, occasionally dim view. She died in 1964, just when the Civil Rights Movement was turning toward its final agonal transformation into the Black Power phase, of which she would have surely approved for its power while disapproving of its manners. Still, though Cooper, a woman of the South, lived through all this history, her views were, if not simple, at least uncomplicated by the troubles the urban North could invite. Quite by contrast to the culturally and politically more fractious movements that took shape with the Harlem

Renaissance in the 1920s, Cooper saw the issues of race and culture in very straightforward terms. Unlike, for example, Harlem Renaissance writer Nella Larsen,[5] Cooper gave not the least thought to passing—either as an option for herself or for others in her circumstances. In this sense, but only in this sense, she remained true to the title of her great book. She was a black woman of the rural South, one who brought the gentle manners of her mother to the near North, from where she cultured a life's work that led her across the seas.

Cooper herself was anything but uncertain as to her own true nature and purposes in life. In this, as in other respects, she was like the great race-women who were her contemporaries and colleagues in the race politics of the day: Mary Church Terrell and Ida B. Wells-Barnett.[6] Save for her close friendship in the early years with Charlotte Forten Grimké,[7] Cooper was never personally close to the other race-women with whom she shared so much—politically, morally, and personally. Though in many ways an isolated figure, Cooper was an uncommonly self-assured person, not one to be easily shaken by what others thought of her. As a consequence, her self-certainty issued in good works covering a breathtaking range and number of areas of professional and intellectual accomplishment.

She was, for one, a colleague and high school teacher of the classics, the modern and ancient languages, literature, mathematics, and the sciences. Her teaching career began, by some indications, when she was scarcely ten years old and continued until she was well into her eighties.[8]

---

5. Larsen (1891–1964) published two important novels, *Quicksand* (1928) and *Passing* (1929), both involving the theme of passing. See Deborah McDowell, ed., *Quicksand and Passing* (Trenton, N.J.: Rutgers University Press, 1988).

6. Mary Eliza Church Terrell (1863–1954) was Cooper's classmate at Oberlin in the 1880s and her colleague at the M Street High School—about whom more in a moment. Ida Bell Wells-Barnett (1862–1931), the antilynching campaigner and black women's suffragist, was not personally close to Cooper, though they shared many causes, including opposition to Booker T. Washington. Fanny Jackson Coppin (1837–1913) of an earlier generation preceded Cooper and Mary Church at Oberlin by twenty years. Yet in 1893, Cooper and Coppin shared the platform at the women's congress of the Chicago World's Fair (see chapter 11). There is a photograph of Cooper, Terrell, and Ida Wells-Barnett (their classmate at Oberlin) in their later years in Hutchinson, *Anna Julia Cooper*, p. 187.

7. Charlotte Forten Grimké (1837–1914), more the contemporary of Fanny Jackson Coppin, was Cooper's closest friend among the politically active black women of her day (see chapter 26).

8. When still a child, she assisted in the instruction of mathematics at St. Augustine's College in Raleigh, North Carolina, from which she herself eventually graduated. Many of the much older students, especially those in the seminary, were from backward rural areas with no benefit of prior education. Cooper's service as a teacher of mathematics was, in effect, a kind of work-study arrangement. In her days at St. Augustine's, faculty and other resources were limited, as her own call to the teaching ranks as a child indicates. As a result, Cooper herself felt the need of a "northern" college education, which she later pursued at Oberlin.

But, of all the subjects she mastered, it was in the languages and history that she made her reputation as a scholar. After more than thirty-five years as a high school teacher, Cooper's translation of *Le Pèlerinage de Charlemagne* from old to modern French won her professional recognition while advancing her graduate studies at Columbia University. And, at the age of no less than sixty-six years, she completed her doctoral thesis at the Sorbonne on the subject of French attitudes toward slavery during the French Revolution. Her thesis defense in Paris on 23 March 1925 offered one of the surest proofs of her strong and courageous character. On her examining committee was the prominent and notorious Célestin Bouglé, a leader of the post-Durkheimian sociologists and an academic force to be reckoned with. Bouglé had previously written a book Cooper considered not so subtly racist. Rather than evade the subject, Cooper firmly took Bouglé to task and won his approval.[9]

But these endeavors of the academic life were but a part of a long life of more than a century (and lasting more than a decade longer than that of Du Bois, her younger contemporary). Through much of her active life, Cooper was a popular public speaker. One of her best-known speeches was delivered in 1886, when she was just two years out of Oberlin College and not yet thirty, to a meeting of the exclusively male, black clergy of the Protestant Episcopal Church. The talk, "Womanhood: A Vital Element in the Regeneration and Progress of a Race," later published as the first chapter of Cooper's *Voice from the South* (chapter 3 of this book), must have stirred some considerable controversy. In it she uttered the most famous of all her lines declaiming, in effect, the black woman's moral superiority to the black man.

> Only the BLACK WOMAN can say "when and where I enter, in the quiet, undisputed dignity of my womanhood, without violence and without suing or special patronage, then and there the whole *Negro race enters with me.*" (P. 63)

These words are a play on what Cooper took to be the vanity of one of the great race-men of the mid-nineteenth century, Martin R. Delany,

---

The date of her teaching experience at this early age is entered in her report in Charles Johnson's 1930 "Occupational History" survey in the Moorland-Spingarn Research Center archive at Howard University.

At the other end of her life, after retiring from public school teaching in 1930, when she was seventy-two, Cooper assumed the presidency of Frelinghuysen University, where she continued to teach well into her eighties.

9. See chapter 24 for Cooper's response to Bouglé.

whom she characterized as "an unadulterated black man" (p. 63). The gentlemen clergy addressed by this young woman must have taken her meaning with some discomfort. This was Cooper's way—direct, eloquent, ever dignified, never obsequious; thus, disturbing, but convincing. Surely one of the reasons she could speak and write so powerfully was the moral force deep in her character, which was usually evident in her public discourse, notably in an address delivered before the General Conference of the Society of Friends in 1902 on "The Ethics of the Negro Question" (chapter 12). *A Voice from the South* arose from a moral and religious depth that inspired her work not only as a public intellectual but also as an activist.[10]

Yet Anna Julia Cooper's activism was never as widely recognized as Mary Church Terrell's or Ida B. Wells-Barnett's. Nor were her writings as numerous or as well known as Du Bois's. Cooper was the more quiet leader of social programs and causes for the poor in her home city, the District of Columbia. She was active in establishing a local branch of the YWCA and was an early and lifelong leader in the social settlement movement. She was also a leader in the Negro Women's Club Movement and a regular contributor of agitating letters and columns to newspapers like the *Washington Post* and magazines like *Crisis*.

Though Cooper's professional activities and public speaking took her around the country and the world, the force of her social activism was local. She was a woman who knew how to put down roots in the city of her adult life where, but for five years in the Midwest, she lived from 1887 until her death. Even after retiring from teaching in 1930 when she was in her seventies, Cooper took over the presidency of Frelinghuysen University, a school organized to provide educational opportunities to the working poor in Washington's black community. She held the last position well into her ninth decade of life. At one point she literally took the financially struggling school into her own home.

Everything she did seemed always to issue from or return to her homes. Nothing better expresses Cooper's sense of her life's work than the ways she used and effectively redefined her home. Her first Washington home, on Seventeenth Street, N.W., from which she moved into her local life as a member of Washington's black cultural elite, was a figurative as well as literal hearth of domestic warmth for a cosmopolitan life of many

---

10. For example, see chapters 11, 12, 17, and 20. Karen Baker-Fletcher's "A 'Singing Something' " (1991) is the most thorough, if occasionally unconvincing, interpretation of the religious and moral aspects of, in Baker-Fletcher's words, Cooper's "theological voice."

accomplishments.[11] She was always ready to bring others into her homes, and not just the poor students of her night school late in life. Over the years Cooper reared seven children—two foster children when she was young and the five orphans she adopted just shy of her sixtieth year. Yet she cared for these children on a teacher's salary while, among so much else, commuting to New York City and Paris in pursuit of her doctoral degree.

The ambiguity of Cooper's public image, as well as the seeming contradictions of her writings, may owe as much to her personal character as to the conflicting demands of her times.[12] In her day, as in today's attempts to understand her, Cooper stood out among others for the way her personal character allowed her to speak to her complicated times with, precisely, the quiet, undisputed dignity of her womanhood. These qualities are evident in all of her writings and activities. But they were conveyed with striking poignancy on 29 December 1925 when she addressed the Washington Chapter of the Alpha Kappa Alpha Sorority as it honored her for the doctorate from the University of Paris. Cooper began with an affirmation of faith in human progress:

> The impulse of humanity toward social progress is like the movement in the currents of a great water system, from myriad sources and under myriad circumstances and conditions, beating onward, ever onward toward its eternity, the Ocean. (P. 339)

Then, later in the speech, she referred more to herself in relation to the conditions of her race:

> And now, if I may be pardoned a personal word on an occasion so provocative of pride and vainglory, I may say honestly and truthfully that my one aim is and has always been so far as I may, to hold a torch for the children of a group too long exploited and too frequently disparaged in its struggling for the light. I have not made capital of my race, have paid my own way and have never asked a concession or claimed a gratuity. Nor on the other hand have I ever denied identification in every handicap and every limitation that the checkered history of our native land imposes. In the simple words of the Master, spoken for another nameless

---

11. After 1916, she built the home of her later years at 201 T St., N.W., in the District of Columbia.

12. See chapter 26. Paula Giddings offers a particularly balanced discussion of the personal politics of women like Cooper in *When and Where I Enter: The Impact of Black Women on Race and Sex in America* (New York: William Morrow, 1984), especially pp. 108–17.

one, my humble career may be summed up to date—"She hath done what she could." (P. 340)

Some time after the speech, Cooper added to her partial souvenir of the occasion, in her own steady, teacher's handwriting, the following note, set in the third person:

> The most significant fact, perhaps, in Mrs. Cooper's contributions to Education in Washington and certainly the most directly provocative of the cause of her own segregated group is the courageous revolt she waged against a lower "colored" curriculum for M St school.[13]

The belated note has several meanings, one less obvious than the others. In one sense, Cooper is referring to her life's work as a teacher in which she pursued a strategy of racial uplift close to that of Du Bois's Talented Tenth principle. Cooper was a brilliant teacher and an effective school leader. While principal of M Street High School from 1901 to 1906, she so strengthened its curriculum in classical subjects that a markedly greater number of its graduates were accepted to elite colleges like Harvard. But, in a deeper sense, there is a distant, wistful air to Cooper's handwritten note—one that suggests that in 1925 she had in mind events from twenty years earlier, events so painful that, even during her finest moment of academic triumph, she could not have kept them out of her private thoughts. Indeed, it would not be far-fetched to assume that her pursuit of the French doctorate, when she was already at normal retirement age, was itself partly an attempt to redeem a public disgrace visited upon her in 1906 for having done nothing worse than succeeding as a teacher and school leader.

The reference Cooper makes to her "courageous revolt" is undoubtedly an allusion to her stewardship of the curriculum at the M Street High School, which ended in what was certainly the most decisive public moment in her younger life. In 1906, after five years of distinguished service, Cooper was dismissed from the principalship of the school and forced, for want of work, into a five-year exile at Lincoln University in Jefferson City, Missouri. The action taken against her was clearly prompted by agents of one of the two unadulterated race-men of that day, Booker T. Washington. Washington was, of course, the founding principal of the Tuskegee

---

13. Since it is probable that she did not have her remarks printed until the mid-1940s, the added note may have been quite late in Cooper's life. The note is on the file copy of the souvenir in Box 23–4, folder 28, Moorland-Spingarn Manuscript Collection.

Institute, from which he reinforced his position as the leader of the industrial education strategy of racial uplift. At the dawn of the twentieth century, his strategy appealed to the white politicians and philanthropists who controlled what remained of the dominant society's post-Reconstruction outreach to the nation's black population. Washington's Tuskegee Machine, as it was known by its opponents, worked hard to exercise its control wherever in the nation the industrial education strategy was opposed—in fact or in the imagination. Cooper was a prime target of the Tuskegee's hostility, notwithstanding her strong commitments to the industrial education program at M Street, because she was herself so obviously well educated and so effective a model to her pupils.

For a full year, beginning in 1905, the white members of the District of Columbia's board of education joined, actively or passively, in the conspiracy to ruin Cooper's reputation and force her from the principal's office. The false complaints against her did not, of course, show the hand of the Tuskegee forces. They complained not of her curricular philosophy but against her alleged failures as an administrator. When these carpings proved insufficient, the Tuskegee operatives turned to the ultimate dirty trick—absurdly accusing Cooper of a sexual liaison with John Love, one of her (then young adult) foster children. The controversy was played out in public for a long year, often reported in detail in the *Washington Post*. It is not hard to imagine the mortification such preposterous charges must have caused in a woman of Cooper's work ethic and impeccable morals. In the end, she was dismissed in the fashion to which school administrators still resort. They simply did not renew her contract at the end of the 1905–1906 school year.[14]

In the M Street High School controversy, Cooper's life was drawn into the battle between Booker T. Washington and his archrival in American racial politics, W. E. B. Du Bois. The struggle between these two men had been gathering force for a number of years since Du Bois's first public attack on Washington in 1901.[15] Yet, even before their differences broke into the open, Du Bois himself had fallen victim to Booker T. Washington's power in an episode that, harbinger of things to come, also involved the colored schools in the District of Columbia. In 1900, Du Bois suffered

---

14. The most thorough report on the controversy, as in many other matters, is Hutchinson, *Anna Julia Cooper,* ch. 4.

15. Du Bois's first shot was "The Evolution of Negro Leadership," published in the *Dial* in 1901 and revised in 1903 as "Of Mr. Booker T. Washington and Others," ch. 3 of *The Souls of Black Folk* (New York: Bantam, 1989).

the indignity of rejection for a post for which he was overqualified. He had applied, with some encouragement from Washington himself, for the post of assistant superintendent of the colored schools in the nation's capital. Upon seeing what was at stake in the earliest days of his rivalry with the younger Du Bois, Washington abruptly withdrew his support. The post was denied Du Bois. Though Du Bois had been ambivalent about a position that would have left him less time for his scholarly pursuits, he was disappointed. But, of course, he went on to other things.[16]

Cooper, too, went on after her dismissal. From 1906 to 1911, she taught college courses at Lincoln University in Missouri. Then, when her enemies in the Washington, D.C., school administration had left office, she returned to the M Street High School, where she taught until her retirement in 1930. As in everything else, Cooper suffered the dismissal and its humiliations with tough moral fortitude. Even so, she was left to suffer for her convictions without the active support of those upon whom she might reasonably have counted. To be sure, she was not left utterly alone. During the year-long siege in 1905–1906, Cooper was actively supported by many in the community, especially by her friend the Reverend Francis Grimké.[17] On the other hand, among those who were notably silent was her classmate at Oberlin and colleague at M Street, Mary Church Terrell, as was W. E. B. Du Bois. It is, perhaps, less remarkable that Du Bois, already a national and international figure, did not lift hand or voice in support of Cooper in 1905. But the Mary Church Terrell story is intriguing.

Why did Cooper not have a closer relation to Mary Church Terrell? Not only had they been college classmates at Oberlin, but, after graduation in 1884, they had both settled in Washington, D.C., where their lives were closely connected as teachers at the M Street High School and colleagues in many causes such as the local social settlement movement. Yet Mary Church Terrell kept her distance from Cooper during the M Street controversy and, even harder to explain, for years after. Though Cooper refers often to Terrell, Terrell's 1940 autobiography, *A Colored Woman in a White World,* mentions Cooper not at all.[18] Perhaps the explanation of Terrell's silence in the 1905 affair is rather straightforward in that she and her

---

16. The most reliable and complete discussion of the 1900 incident is David Levering Lewis's in *W. E. B. Du Bois: Biography of a Race* (New York: Henry Holt, 1993), ch. 10.

17. See Cooper's and Grimké's letters in chapter 28 and her reminiscences in chapter 26.

18. Terrell, *A Colored Woman in a White World* (1940; reprinted by New York: G. K. Hall, 1996). See also, Beverly Washington Jones, ed., *Quest for Equality: The Life and Writings of Mary Eliza Church Terrell: 1863–1954* (Brooklyn, N.Y.: Carlson Publishing, 1990).

husband, Robert H. Terrell (himself a former principal at M Street), were at the time beholden to Booker T. Washington for Robert's appointments to the District of Columbia's school board and, later, its judiciary. But Mary eventually broke with the Tuskegee group in 1910 when she joined in the founding of the NAACP, which adds to the intrigue. Why, so many years later, in 1940, did Terrell still have nothing to say of Cooper, with whom she had worked in such proximity for over sixty years?

And why, also, were Cooper and Du Bois not closer? Though there were differences of an obvious sort between the two, Cooper had nonetheless been in close contact with him from the earliest years. She had been with him at the 1900 Pan African Congress in London and, over the years, had corresponded with him over several notable race matters.[19] But Du Bois, who had many good relations with women, seemed never to pay Cooper more than passing acknowledgment. Cooper's isolation from Terrell and Du Bois, when considered alongside their respective involvements in the M Street controversy, adds to the mysterious impression of Cooper as a solitary woman in the history of her time.

The facts of Cooper's life as a solitary figure are consistent with her theoretical views on the black woman in America, such as those expressed in "The Status of Woman in America," which is part of *A Voice from the South* (chapter 6 in this volume):

> The colored woman of to-day occupies, one may say, a unique position in this country. In a period of itself transitional and unsettled, her status seems one of the least ascertainable and definitive of all the forces which make for our civilization. (P. 112)

This is one of the most assured statements in Cooper's black feminist theory. She means precisely to argue that in the "transitional and unsettled" times at the end of the nineteenth century, the black woman was "unique," but unique in a particular way. For she alone, being "least ascertainable," was the most "definitive of all the forces" then at play. The intended primary sense of "unique" here is political and historical. The statement comes just after an appreciative, but uninflected, commentary on what some interpreters see as the "feminine principle"[20] at work in Cooper's thinking: "in a reign of moral ideas she [woman] is easily queen" (p. 112).

---

19. See Cooper's letter to Du Bois in chapter 28.
20. bell hooks, *Ain't I a Woman: Black Women and Feminism* (Boston: South End Press, 1981), p. 167.

But, then, as she often does, Cooper sets in rhetorical motion an abrupt shift to a disjunctive point, which here means, in effect: Though in prior times woman as such had a moral responsibility, now it is the black woman who has the unique responsibility. She alone, the black woman, is the sole manager of the primal lights and shadows. So, for Cooper to have been a black woman in her times was to be unique in the sense of being subject to a distinctive historical calling.

Yet it is impossible to escape a second, entailed meaning of such vocation: unique in the sense of being solitary, alone in bearing one's moral obligations. Indeed, she was. Cooper had married while still a young woman teaching at St. Augustine's College in 1877. Her older husband, George Cooper, a priest in the Protestant Episcopal Church, was very well regarded. But the marriage ended with his death two years later. She never remarried. And, though sexual scandal was used against her by the forces seeking her dismissal from the M Street High School, there is no evidence of any desire on her part to remarry. Nor is there, in the available record, even a hint of romantic or sexual involvement thereafter.[21] Cooper lived without a domestic partner from the age of twenty-one until her death nearly eighty-five years later. Though, in addition to her foster and adopted children, she enjoyed a rich social life, especially with the family of her older and dearest friend, Charlotte Forten Grimké, Cooper lived all those years as a single, widowed woman.[22] Yet there is no sign of complaint on her part; nor, importantly, of loneliness.

Cooper appropriated the solitary life as part of her vocation. The homes she built in houses at 1706 Seventeenth Street, N.W., and later (after 1916) at 201 T Street, N.W., were the foundations for a wide domestic circle into which she brought foster children, the Grimkés and other friends, and the working poor of the District of Columbia. When asked in 1930 to describe her vocation, she answered simply: "The Education of neglected people."[23] In *A Voice from the South,* shortly after the statement on the unique position of the black woman, Cooper reiterated the idea of uniqueness, now with a stronger hint of this second meaning of the term "unique":

---

21. There are indications that, before the 1906 controversy, her foster child John Love, when he was an adult, may have proposed marriage to Cooper and that she promptly declined.

22. Among Cooper's papers in the Moorland-Spingarn Collection at Howard University there is a bulky file of greeting cards from friends and family, which she kept until the end of her life.

23. The line appears in Cooper's 1930 response to the Charles Johnson survey, a selection from which appears as chapter 17.

The colored woman, then, should not be ignored because her bark is resting in the silent waters of the sheltered cove. She is watching the movements of the contestants none the less and is all the better qualified, perhaps, to weigh and judge and advise because not herself in the excitement of the race. Her voice, too, has always been heard in clear, unfaltering tones, ringing the changes on those deeper interests which make for permanent good. (P. 114)

Thus, again, one thinks of the photographic image of this woman: solitary, though not alone; quiet, but not voiceless; dignified, but attentive to the permanent good.

Cooper's Unique, Isolating Theoretical Position

What set Cooper apart from others who were engaged at the time in a similar sort of work was that she, virtually alone, gave precise and unflinching voice to a theoretical attitude that today is very well known. Inasmuch as she was herself unexceptionably concrete, it may seem a bit formal to refer to her work as "theoretical." Just the same, Cooper's ideas, though simply put, were an important link in the more-than-a-century-long evolution of black feminist social theory from Sojourner Truth's legendary "Arn't I a Woman?" speech in the mid–nineteenth century to the full expression of black feminist thought in the 1980s. In a language that was surely invented by reporters on the speech, Truth is said to have uttered the powerful idea in 1851: "I tink dat 'twixt de niggers of the Souf and the womin at the Norf, all talkin' 'bout rights, de white men will be in a fix pretty soon." Truth, even less theoretical than Cooper, was one of the first to speak about her position as a black woman as a reason for calling into question the assumption that race ("de niggers of the Souf") and, to use today's word, gender ("the womin at the Norf") can be held as though they were separable categories of social thought.[24]

Though today Sojourner Truth's idea is well understood, Cooper's *Voice from the South* was the first *systematic* working out of the insistence that no one social category can capture the reality of the colored woman. In

---

24. The lines quoted are found in Nell Irvin Painter, "Sojourner Truth," in *Black Women of America,* ed. by Hine, Brown, and Terborg-Penn, p. 1173. In her recent biography of Truth, Painter shows that the "Arn't I a Woman?" line may well have been a later invention by Frances Dana Gage, who also is likely to have composed the dialect of the lines quoted. See Painter, *Sojourner Truth: A Life, A Symbol* (W.W. Norton, 1996).

the sentence immediately following the passage describing the colored woman's unique position, Cooper adds that the colored woman "is confronted by both a woman question and a race problem" (p. 112).[25]

At first, one might be concerned about the precise meaning of the expression "colored woman." Generally, when Cooper used the expression, she meant it as an alternative to "Negro" and in preference to, say, Truth's alleged use of "nigger." But here it is possible that she also used "colored woman" in a sense closer to today's expression "women of color"—referring, that is, to all women whose racial and social situations set them off from generically universal, or white, women. This interpretation is encouraged because the passage referring to the colored woman's unique position occurs in a chapter Cooper placed strategically just after her most carefully worked-through statement of black feminist theory, the famous essay attacking white feminists. In " 'Woman versus the Indian' " (chapter 5 in this volume), whose title is taken from a talk given by a leading white feminist, the Reverend Anna Shaw, Cooper offers an early statement of what today would be recognized as a social theory of the woman of color. Though some would not agree,[26] it is hard to imagine what else Cooper might have had in mind when she asked, against Shaw's careless opposition of woman to the Indian, "Why should woman become plaintiff in a suit versus the Indian, or the Negro or any other race or class who have been crushed under the iron heel of Anglo-Saxon power and selfishness?" (p. 107).

At an earlier but crucial historical time, Cooper focused the terms of debates occurring today. Many of the concepts at issue in black-feminist and women-of-color social theory can be traced, even if indirectly, to Cooper. In fact, one of the most urgent debates among feminists today bears on the central point in Cooper's thinking in *A Voice from the South.* Cooper anticipated by nearly a century today's debates over the insufficiency of such categories as race or gender, even class, to capture, by themselves,

---

25. hooks, *Ain't I a Woman,* p. 166, cites this passage at the crucial place. Collins, *Black Feminist Thought* (Boston: Unwin Hyman, 1990), p. 37, cites a related passage from Cooper's 1893 speech to the Women's Congress of the Chicago World's Fair (chapter 11). But neither works out the implications of Cooper's idea.

26. Ann duCille, referring to a talk by Louise Newman, seems to share the conclusion that Cooper's Christian "ethnocentrism" (Newman's word) "led her to marginalize Asian and non-Christian women" (duCille's words): duCille, *The Coupling Convention* (New York: Oxford University Press, 1993), p. 53. On the other hand, Hazel Carby stops just short of declaring Cooper a forerunner of postcolonial thinking when she credits Cooper with "a perspective which gave insight into the plight of all oppressed peoples." See Carby, *Reconstructing Womanhood,* p. 103.

the complexities of a woman's social experiences. What Susan Bordo calls "gender skepticism," what Donna Haraway means by "fractured identities," and what Judith Butler views as the necessary trouble of analytic categories (among many possible examples) are all concerned with the most difficult question, How are we to think about the varieties of social experiences that may affect many people, perhaps all, but most dramatically women of color?[27]

In the critical literature on Cooper, the uniqueness of her personal politics in the history of black feminist thought is widely recognized. In addition to the symbolic use of her portrait in *Black Women of America,* Cooper's most famous line furnishes the title of Paula Giddings's history of black women in America, *When and Where I Enter,* just as the most powerful phrase in that line, "In the Quiet, Undisputed Dignity of My Womanhood," serves as the title for Hazel Carby's important discussion of black feminism after Emancipation. More importantly, beyond the symbolic value of Cooper's words and image, there is ample and sometimes extravagant praise for Cooper. In Cooper's own day, Gertrude Bustill Mossell, author of *The Work of the Afro-American Woman* (1894), recognized Cooper's *A Voice from the South* "as one of the strongest pleas for the race and sex of the writer that ha[d] ever appeared." Recently, Claudia Tate, in *Domestic Allegories of Political Desire: The Black Heroine's Text at the Turn of the Century,* considers both Mossell herself and Cooper so important as to have been to the ideal of black womanhood what their contemporaries, Booker T. Washington and W. E. B. Du Bois, were to popular ideals of black manhood. Tate goes so far as to state, as though it were self-evident, that "it is important to remember . . . that Cooper and Mossell were probably real-life models for many of the exemplary heroines of black women's domestic novels." In a similarly grand historical claim, Jacqueline Jones, in her prize-winning study, *Labor of Love, Labor of Sorrow,* puts Cooper on a short list of black feminist writers whose "critique of black womanhood marked the emergence of the 'black matriarchy thesis,' for they suggest that

---

27. Bordo, "Feminism, Postmodernism, and Gender-Skepticism," in *Feminism/Postmodernism,* ed. by Linda Nicholson (New York: Routledge, 1990), ch. 6; Haraway, "A Cyborg Manifesto," in *Simians, Cyborgs, and Women: The Reinvention of Nature* (New York: Routledge, 1991), ch. 8; Butler, *Gender Trouble: Feminism and the Subversion of Identity* (New York: Routledge, 1990). For a particularly interesting discussion of the Sojourner Truth line, see Donna Haraway, "Ecce Homo, Ain't (Arn't) I a Woman, and Inappropriate/d Others: The Human in a Posthumanist Landscape," in *Feminists Theorize the Political,* ed. by Judith Butler and Joan W. Scott (New York: Routledge, 1991), ch. 5.

the main problem in Afro-American family was an 'irresponsible' father who took advantage of his 'faithful, hardworking womenfolks.' "[28]

Even critics who harbor reservations about Cooper's alleged inability to escape the true womanhood ideal give strong testimony to her importance. Ann duCille identifies Cooper, along with Mary Church Terrell and Ida B. Wells-Barnett, as among those women who knew the legacy of the black woman born to slavery but, in giving "voice to the unspoken," *were* in fact that legacy to subsequent generations.[29] Even Mary Helen Washington, the most prominent critic of Cooper's supposed adherence to true womanhood virtues, concludes in the end that *A Voice from the South* "is the most precise, forceful, well-argued statement of black feminist thought to come out of the nineteenth century."[30]

Yet, for all this recognition, Cooper remains an essentially isolated figure in the history of black feminist thought. To date, there are few studies devoted exclusively to Cooper's feminism. Both of the currently available biographies of Cooper tend to underexamine her ideas relative to the details of her life.[31] And the most serious scholarly works on the emergence of black feminist thought and fiction at the turn of century tend to leave readers somewhat in the dark with respect to Cooper's specific contributions to black feminist theory.[32]

---

28. Giddings, *When and Where I Enter: The Impact of Black Women on Race and Sex in America* (New York: William Morrow, 1984); Carby, *Reconstructing Womanhood,* ch. 5; Mossell, *The Work of the Afro-American Woman* (1894; reprint, New York: Oxford University Press, 1988), p. 61; Tate, *Domestic Allegories of Political Desire: The Black Heroine's Text at the Turn of the Century* (New York: Oxford University Press, 1992), p. 128; Jones, *Labor of Love, Labor of Sorrow: Black Women, Work, and the Family, from Slavery to the Present* (New York: Random House, 1986), p. 104.

29. duCille, *The Coupling Convention,* p. 53. duCille is in error to include Mary Church Terrell as the daughter of a slave. Terrell was born in 1863 to parents of the black elite in Memphis. Cooper and Wells-Barnett were born to slaves. Still, in its broader meaning, the point is well taken.

30. Washington, Introduction, p. li. Karen Baker-Fletcher, in *A Singing Something* (1994), similarly has reservations about the true womanhood issue but is just as affirming of Cooper's importance in black womanist thought (as she puts it). Another recent affirmation of Cooper's importance is Elizabeth Alexander, " 'We Must Be about Our Father's Business': Anna Julia Cooper and the In-Corporation of the Nineteenth-Century African-American Woman Intellectual," *Signs* 20, no. 2 (1995): 336–56.

31. Hutchinson, *Anna Julia Cooper,* and Gabel, *From Slavery to the Sorbonne* are, for the moment, the two leading biographies. Hutchinson's is the more complete, though Gabel includes some interesting details omitted by Hutchinson. Many of the subsequent biographical commentaries (including ours, and Karen Baker-Fletcher's) rely on Hutchinson along with the archival sources (many of which are published here for the first time).

32. Even Hazel Carby, though the most important of these sources, tends to present Cooper more as a sociological theorist of postslavery America than as a feminist. Ann duCille

This relative neglect might be due in some part to the nature of the theoretical position Cooper defined so precisely but wrote up so episodically. Though she was clear as to her convictions, Cooper's main work of feminist theory, *A Voice from the South,* was a composition after the fact, drawing as it did on occasional essays and public lectures.

As Karen Baker-Fletcher points out, *A Voice from the South* is structured into two distinct parts: a first that brings forth the solo voice of the black woman; and a second that is more broadly expressive of the concerns of the racial and cultural community.[33] Most of the critical discussion of Cooper's book is devoted to the first, black feminist part, in which are found Cooper's most familiar statements and ideas. This part comprises four essays, each (one assumes) originally a public lecture: (1) "Womanhood: A Vital Element in the Regeneration and Progress of a Race" (the talk delivered before the clergymen in 1886), (2) "The Higher Education of Women" (an 1890 talk to the American Conference of Educators), (3) " 'Woman versus the Indian' " (the well-known reply to Anna Shaw probably in late 1891), and finally, (4) "The Status of Woman in America" (an essay of unknown origins, perhaps written for *Voice*).

Of the four essays in the first part (chapters 3, 4, 5, and 6 here), "Womanhood: A Vital Element" (chapter 3) and " 'Woman versus the Indian' " (chapter 5) are the heart of the social theory for which Cooper is best known because it is in these two that Cooper most daringly challenges, first, the black man and, then, the white feminist. Yet, even though she is in places quite severe in her references to both, Cooper is much more intent on defining the unique position of the black woman in human history than on dismissing the men of her race and feminists not of her race—with both of whom she had something in common, politically as well as

---

and Claudia Tate tend to understate the complexities of Cooper's feminism. Though a somewhat incomplete examination of Cooper's feminist social theory is perfectly understandable when the subject is the literary tradition (as it is in all three of these sources), it is somewhat more surprising when the subject is black feminist thought as such. The most important systematic work on the latter subject recognizes Cooper but does not analyze her theory, in spite of its convergence with the author's own theoretical scheme—see Patricia Hill Collins, *Black Feminist Thought* (Boston: Unwin Hyman, 1990); compare Collins, *Fighting Words* (Minneapolis: University of Minnesota Press, 1998).

33. Baker-Fletcher, in *A Singing Something* (1994), p. 136, understands the division of *A Voice from the South* as a self-conscious use of the voice metaphor in its musical sense: the first part as a solo performance, the second more as a chorus of the black community. Somewhat of the same view, though a little more convincing, is Alexander's interpretation of the voice theme (in " 'Father's Business' ") as an expression of Cooper's voice as a political, as well as cultural, representative of the black woman's social position. Still, Baker-Fletcher's idea of the second part as a chorus is not without its merits.

socially. Whatever is found elsewhere in her writings, Cooper's unique theoretical contribution rests largely on the delicacy with which she handled the other two figures—and it was the social figures as much as the real individuals that interested her. Her respectful, if firm, critiques of the black man and the white woman served her primary purpose, to give voice to the black woman.

Cooper pursued her literary purposes in *A Voice from the South,* as she conducted her long life after its publication in 1892, with reference to an acutely self-conscious understanding of the importance of the black woman in American political and cultural life. One might say today that she was intent upon inventing the discursive space of the black woman. And it may well be that the importance of her theory is underestimated because her language is so practical, so direct to a reading public that was not primarily academic. Still, long before anyone had formulated the notion that intellectual work ought to be an archaeological discovery of the unique in social life, Cooper did just that. When reading her elegant language, one must continually pause to ask, Who was this woman? How did her social circumstances affect her social ideas?

The brilliance of her academic accomplishments, and the polish of her culture, might all too easily blind the reader to the most fundamental economic fact of Cooper's life. Though she lived well, she lived frugally and was never a woman of means. She chose and furnished her homes, traveled to Europe, and raised her foster children as a single woman whose annual income never much exceeded eighteen hundred dollars. While in the 1930s this sum (her retirement benefit) would have put her in the modest middle class, it was hardly a substantial income. What is more, Cooper pursued her intellectual and teaching work throughout her life with none of the financial or domestic supports a spouse (even then) would have provided. On the contrary, she was forced to fight against the continuous opposition of her school supervisor for the most meager pay increments and the right to pursue her academic work. Her doctoral studies, for example, were subjected to mean-spirited interference by school administrators who continued to hound her more than twenty years after the M Street High School dismissal.[34] To be sure, she enjoyed certain class advantages, but ones she earned, protected, and nurtured entirely on her own. But,

---

34. They threatened to fire her in 1924 if she did not return from a research trip to Paris, tried to block her trip in 1925 to defend the thesis, and later actually dared to fail her on the teacher's examination that would have allowed a pay raise (see chapter 27 and the Wilkinson letter in chapter 28). She defied them at every turn.

winning the advantages of class culture is an entirely different matter from the reality of economic security. Cooper was, after all, a black woman in a border city during the Jim Crow era, and she was a woman who devoted her life to, as she put it, "neglected people"—her pupils, the young women at the YWCA, the struggling families of the social settlement house.

Cooper was, in this sense, a very solitary voice. If not poor, at least constantly at economic risk; if cultured and learned, ever attentive to the needs of the poor. Compared with others, even other black women in her day—like Mary Church Terrell, who came from a family of means (and had a successful husband), or Ida B. Wells-Barnett, who in spite of her birth to slavery was married throughout much of her antilynching work— Cooper earned for herself every penny she had, just as she alone designed, maintained, and decorated her lovely home on T Street. Cooper herself is somewhat responsible for the illusion that she lived a life of privilege. One of the effects of her deep religious belief was the conviction that her life was a calling to which she responded and that even the suffering we endure is a matter of choice.[35]

The facts of Cooper's unique personal attitudes and position in life are of vital importance to the interpretation of her life and theory, in three respects: (1) as to the broader circumstances of her relative isolation in her day, (2) as to the confusions in the critical literature, in particular about her attitudes toward the true womanhood ideal, and (3) as to the distinctive literary, as well as theoretical, voice she claimed. Each merits its own consideration.

The Quiet, Undisputed Dignity of Her Womanhood

Though Cooper enjoyed good friends and warm recognition in her time, she also suffered severe embarrassments to her natural desire for human companionship and cooperation. After the effects of her birth in slavery (and their enduring consequences for her mother and brothers), the loss of her husband was the next of such blows, but not the last.

---

35. A poignant illustration of this belief is found in one of her friendly disputes with her friend, the Reverend Francis Grimké. Grimké, a strict fundamentalist as to biblical interpretation, objected to the license Cooper took in her poem on the theme of Simon of Cyrene, the black man who is said to have borne Christ's cross. Cooper had it that Simon had chosen this calling. Grimké, the more puritanical as well as the more fundamentalist, insisted that the duty had been imposed on Simon because that is what the Bible says. See chapter 26 for her account of the argument and for the poem.

Four years after George Cooper's death in 1877, Anna pursued her education at Oberlin, where, because she had no financial resources of her own, she lived at the home of Professor Charles H. Churchill. Though this was an entirely satisfying arrangement for all concerned, it nonetheless served, it seems, to widen the social distance between Cooper and her classmates, a distance already significant because of her older age and her race.[36] Though Cooper kept up a lifelong correspondence with members of the class of 1884, the puzzling absence of any lasting ties with her two black classmates, Mary Church and Ida Gibbs Hunt (who were roommates at Oberlin), was certainly due in part to the economic necessity of Cooper's off-campus housing. As we know, more than twenty years after their graduation, the separation from Mary Church Terrell would be a factor of some importance in the events leading up to Cooper's dismissal from M Street High School in 1906.

At the most desperate moment in her life, a person whom a feminist in Cooper's position would normally have had every reason to count on left her (or was forced to leave her) without help. It is true, of course, that Mary Terrell was not free to act, even if she had wanted to, because of her husband's political entanglements as a virtual delegate of the Tuskegee machine in the District of Columbia. Race politics surely played their role. But there was another more subtle, but telling, difference between the two Oberlin schoolmates, one likely to be the better explanation for Terrell's lifelong social distance from Cooper.

They were of different social classes, both by birth and in adult life. Cooper was born in slavery; Terrell, to a life of means. Cooper was a widow on a teacher's salary; Terrell was married to a Harvard graduate and prominent lawyer in Washington. Neither was poor, not by any means. But this does not mean that differences in class standing between Cooper and Terrell might not have played the decisive role in the mysterious social distance the one kept from the other. Then, as now, class differences could wedge their way between people of otherwise similar social position. Clearly, it was Terrell, if anyone, who, especially in the early years in Washington, lived the life of devotion to the "cardinal virtues—piety, purity, submissiveness, and domesticity," as Barbara Welter defined the principles of nineteenth-century true womanhood.[37] It was the young Mary Church

---

36. Cooper began her undergraduate studies at Oberlin at age twenty-three, then, as now, older than the average freshman. Her classmate Mary Church, for example, was five years younger than Cooper.

37. Welter, *Dimity Convictions*, p. 21.

whose heart fluttered upon seeing the handsome Robert Terrell (and who, later in life, was not embarrassed to recount the episode), and she who left her teaching post first to travel at her leisure, then to marry.[38] And, most important to the life of Cooper, it was Mary Terrell who was beholden and, thus, "submissive," not just to her politically obliged husband but, at the time of Cooper's trouble, directly to Booker T. Washington himself.

There is more than one cause of the uncertainties in Cooper's incomplete, nearly lifelong relationship with Terrell. The early differences of race politics were also differences of class politics. The local story of these two great women leaders was part of the national debate between the then increasingly divergent philosophies of the two great race-men of the first decade of the twentieth century. The positions of both men involved subtle but important connections between race and class. To be sure, Booker T. Washington's philosophy, whatever its merits, was nothing if not a race philosophy of submissiveness, most famously expressed in his notorious 1895 Atlanta Compromise.[39] But, just as importantly, it was the power of this philosophy in the hands of Washington and his agents that aggravated class differences within black communities across the nation. Washington's dispute with Du Bois, which led eventually to the founding of the NAACP, was not, of course, simply about class differences. It involved, centrally, a fundamental divergence of opinion as to the importance of higher education to racial uplift, which, in turn, entailed disagreement over the class advantages that American blacks could hope to gain. In reality, at the turn of the century, the actual class gains from higher education (as opposed to industrial education) were meager in relative terms, as is evidenced by the economic uncertainties that beset both Du Bois and Cooper throughout their active lives. But there were advantages if not always those one might suppose. The cultural achievements of Du Bois and Cooper usually softened the blows of economic uncertainty.

The principals in the national debate, as well as those in the M Street School controversy, well illustrate this complex, and sometimes counterintuitive, play of class and race. It was Washington and, in our story, the Terrells who, though they openly or tacitly sponsored a philosophy of in-

---

38. See Terrell, *A Colored Woman in a White World*.
39. The Atlanta Compromise refers to the speech in which Washington proposed the hand-and-fingers analogy for racial cooperation. To paraphrase, he proposed that, in all things economic, the races should be one as the hand, but in all things social, they should be as separate as the fingers. See Cooper's "Angry Saxons and Negro Education" (chapter 20) for her views on this.

dustrial education, nonetheless enjoyed the considerable blessing of class privilege. By contrast, Du Bois and Cooper, though they believed in what is usually considered an elitist philosophy, suffered relative economic marginality. Though neither side was poor in fact, the relative differences of actual class position ran counter to the assumptions of the ideals themselves in more than these few cases, if not as a general rule. Yet Tuskegee did, in fact, serve the poor, and Du Bois, no less than Washington, enjoyed the support of men and women of considerable wealth, many of them white. Whatever the contradictions on either side in the national debate between Washington and Du Bois and its effects on the school politics at M Street, the nasty web of class differences trapped Cooper in an impossible situation she could not control. Whatever the Terrells might have felt at being forced in 1905–1906 to abandon their former teaching colleague, the more terrible contradictions were Cooper's.

Critics who would take Cooper's high moral values as a sign of indifference to the poor may be right that she did not suffer poverty after the Oberlin years. But they would be wrong to think that, in other ways, she did not suffer as the weak and poor most often do—by being unable in the face of attack to control one's own destiny. Again, relative to Mary Terrell and the others, white and black, who forced Cooper out of the position at the M Street High School, she was abused in 1906, not alone because of her race or gender but just as much, if only indirectly, because of her economic and political marginality. Her values led her to the Du Bois side of the national debate, as they inspired her brilliant teaching and leadership in the school. But, having chosen her side, as if she had a choice, Cooper was ultimately defenseless. And the reason she had no choice as to the values was that she never lost her sense of identification with the neglected people from whose circles she, and her mother, had come. Neither Washington nor Du Bois, not to mention the Terrells, lived and worked for so long in daily contact with the poor.

All the principals in the great and local struggles went on their ways after 1906. Washington headed eventually to decline, and death in 1915, while Du Bois joined Mary Terrell and others in the founding of the NAACP in 1910, which led to his launching *Crisis* magazine, by which Du Bois solidified his position as the leading intellectual spokesman for American blacks in the period between Washington's decline and the Harlem Renaissance in the 1920s. By the time Washington passed from the scene, the Terrells had passed to the Du Bois side. And Cooper, after the five years in Missouri, returned to Washington, D.C., in 1911, thence to reknit her family and domestic circle and enjoy another half century of success and life. But it is unlikely that the pain of the dismissal ever left her, as it is probable that she was driven to pursue the doctorate (which, after all, was not necessary in any way to her work) in order to compensate for the loss of face the public controversy had caused her. If this is even remotely so, as the witness of Cooper's wistful note appended to the printed souvenir of her most proud moment in 1925 suggests, then it is also so that she was, at least in part, driven ever more to direct her energies after 1911 to her work—with students and the poor, primarily; but also toward the graduate degrees that set her even farther apart from others. Whichever direction she turned, and no matter how well she enjoyed the particulars of her social and intellectual life, Cooper's life turned more and more to isolation. If her successes put her *above* in some respects, they did as compensation for the *belows* of other moments of her life.

No one aspect of Cooper's experience explains her unique and solitary position. Not even the injuries of the 1906 dismissal are as important as the effective force of her moral and religious ideas, which surely were the energizing source of her unusually focused personal life. But even a woman of "quiet, undisputed dignity" can suffer injury and seek to heal it by her own constructive means. The best interpretation is, I think, that Cooper was indeed forced into a position of relative isolation by *all* the circumstances of her life—her widowhood, the poverty of her young adult life, the economic and political uncertainties of her position in the Washington school system, and her desire to clear the public record of the stigma by which she was marked in 1906.

Cooper was an individual of such deep moral resources that she understood her *own* womanhood quite uniquely. If the dismissal did lead to the scholarly life that accentuated an already isolated position, then it led by passage through the character of a person who was not defeated by bitterness and who converted her pain into a significant intellectual accomplishment. Her 1925 doctoral thesis (see chapters 22 and 23), while different in every way from the book of her youth, confirms the wisdom and intellectual acuity already apparent in 1892 in *A Voice from the South*. She was not just a good and unique woman; she was a superior intellect.

Critical Confusions

The facts of Cooper's personal life shed clarifying light on the critical confusions in the secondary interpretations of her ideas—especially her ideas with respect, first, to womanhood and, second, to men. The two, of course, are related. Too soft on the men is too true to pious womanhood. As I have said, Cooper's avowed religious piety, her high-minded morals, and her evident devotion to home and hearth lend reason to the critical rumor that she was old-fashioned. But the rumor persists in spite of the evidence that she was just as much a tough-minded fighter who permitted no insult to her dignity to go unanswered. Even her affirmation of the colored woman's office was not satisfied her critics.

The strongest and most frequently made criticism of Cooper is, in the words of Mary Helen Washington, that she "is never able to discard totally the ethics of true womanhood, and except for the one passage about black laundry women, she does not imagine ordinary black working women as the basis of her feminist politics."[40] Karen Baker-Fletcher generally shares Washington's view: "What is problematic in Cooper's text is the lack of self-criticism regarding the degree to which the black middle class could speak on behalf of working and poor black people."[41] On the level of Cooper's language, her literary style and allusions, this is clearly so. Though Washington, as I will try to show, overstates her case, on the matter of literary voice she and Baker-Fletcher are not wrong. There was, to be sure, a considerable piety in Cooper's language, most notably in her address to the colored clergy:

> We need men and women who do not exhaust their genius splitting hairs on aristocratic distinctions and thanking God they are not as others; but earnest, unselfish souls, who can go into the highways and byways, lifting up and leading, advising and encouraging with the truly catholic benevolences of the Gospel of Christ. (P. 64)

Cooper was at least a believer in the virtues of piety and purity and, as we have seen, domesticity. These values were basic to her nature and, thus, could not but have influenced Cooper's social thought, including, as bell hooks observes, those statements that seem to suggest a belief in a universal "feminine principle."[42] While it remains to be seen if hooks is right, it is incontestably true that Cooper's moral values affect her notably less harsh views toward men. Though Cooper could be biting in her criticism of

---

40. Washington, Introduction, p. xlvi.
41. Baker-Fletcher, "A Singing Something," p. 247; compare ch. 6 of this same thesis, especially p. 214. See also ch. 6 of Baker-Fletcher's book *A Singing Something*.
42. hooks, *Ain't I a Woman*, p. 157.

men, including men in general, she does frequently display a striking reluctance to denounce them altogether.[43] On the contrary, she thought in the manner of the times, as the passage just quoted reveals. She believed that men and women, by their different complementary geniuses, could "lift and lead" together. Cooper's famous rebuke of Martin Delany for his use of the "when and where I enter" line was generally as harsh as her attacks on men got.

It is also true that the very language she used opens doubts as to her ability to see the black woman of the South as culturally and politically different from the pious white women to whom she was for so long subjected. In "The Status of Woman in America" (chapter 6), for example, Cooper juxtaposed the great black women of the century—Sojourner Truth, Frances Watkins Harper, Charlotte Forten Grimké, among others (pp. 115–16)—to the great white women to whom she had referred at the beginning of the chapter—Dorothea Dix, Helen Hunt Jackson, Lucretia Mott (pp. 109–10). The comparison serves, no doubt, to shift the rhetorical advantage by asserting the equality of the former to the latter. Yet Mary Helen Washington is not wrong to question Cooper's use of words like "pleasing," "sweet," "gentle," "charming," and "matchless and irresistible personality" to describe the black woman's special virtues.[44] But Washington does not press this point, perhaps because she understands that what is at work here is Cooper's use of the rhetorical device of contrasting by simple comparison. By the use of such a classically "feminine" vocabulary, Cooper means to suggest not just that black women are equal to the whites but that in their equivalency they are superior. This, remember, is the chapter that concludes with her affirmation of the colored woman's office. There is something to Washington's criticism, though perhaps not as much as it may seem.

Ann duCille takes a somewhat more nuanced view. She sees Cooper's position on the womanhood ideal as conflicted and contradictory. On the one hand "Cooper's feminist vision may have roved beyond the immediate material conditions of her constituency" in overestimating what was realistically possible for poor women. At the same time, duCille thinks, Cooper developed a strong critique of the prevailing ideology on sex and marriage and was among those who "laid siege to womanhood." Still, duCille main-

---

43. For example, in the striking passage in which she replies to a white woman's assumption that, in her experience, men of "your" [Cooper's] race "outstrip" women, Cooper refrains from contradicting the beliefs behind the intrusive question (p. 85).

44. Washington, Introduction, p. xlvi.

tains the reservation that, "while [Cooper] had a finely honed sense of the imperialist impulse and its power to colonize the female mind and body, she never quite managed to fully extricate her own mind from the tenets of true womanhood."[45]

Claudia Tate seems at first to take a view similar to duCille's, that Cooper was of two minds. Tate, like bell hooks, takes Cooper's version of a universal feminine principle seriously, but she attributes to it the force of a double-edged sword—cutting one way against the domination of men, cutting another against the all too cautious reformism of white feminists. Tate's position seems to be that Cooper knew just what she was doing; that is, Cooper used the *language* of true womanhood[46] to establish a point of communication with those to whom she spoke (white and black alike) in order to isolate and define the political position of the black woman. Tate understands Cooper's opening chapter, "Womanhood: A Vital Element in the Regeneration and Progress of a Race" (chapter 3 here), along with Mossell's introductory chapter in *The Work of the Afro-American Woman*, as strategic transformations of the true womanhood doctrine:

> In these chapters as well as throughout their works, we find the construction of black womanhood in an enlarged intraracial domesticity as the signifier for enlightened, politicized black self-authority, self-interest, and self-development.[47]

The least ambivalent defender of Cooper on this score is Hazel Carby, who sees Cooper's understanding of what duCille calls the "imperialist impulse" in clear and unqualified terms. Carby believes that Cooper held a structural theory of women's power that allowed her to criticize "the intimate link between internal and external colonialization, between domestic racial oppression and imperialism." In contrast to others (even to duCille and Tate), Carby interprets Cooper as an explicit, knowing, and unambivalent critic of the true womanhood idea:

> Black women, [Cooper] argued, could not retreat into an abstraction of womanhood dissociated from the oppression of their whole people; their

---

45. duCille, *The Coupling Convention*, pp. 52 (where her view on Cooper's contradictions is also found), 53, 144.

46. See Tate, *Domestic Allegories of Political Desire*, pp. 156–57. The issue here is the value of higher education. Tate is calling attention to Cooper's ability to appreciate, and use, learning, both to maintain domestic values and to criticize some black men's patriarchal attitudes.

47. Ibid., p. 132; compare p. 152.

everyday lives were a confrontation of the division between the inviolability of elitist conceptions of womanhood and that which it denied.[48]

Were these critical confusions simply a matter of the textual evidence,
it would seem to me that Tate's position, though not fully developed, is
the more compelling on the literary facts. While I believe that Carby is
closer on Cooper's ultimate political attitude, Tate seems to have got Cooper's literary method exactly right.

As a writer, not to mention as an actor in a dangerous world, Cooper
was perfectly capable of catching her readers, or opponents, off guard. She
used seemingly gentle means to draw those she addressed into rhetorical
traps of frequently harsh and challenging proportions.[49] At no place is this
tactic more powerfully executed than in " 'Woman versus the Indian' "
(chapter 5), which happens, also, to be the chapter that lends strongest
support to Carby's reading of Cooper as a social theoretical critic of imperialism.

The Voice of the Black Woman of the South

" 'Woman versus the Indian' " opens with a simple, uninflected mention
of the speech of that title delivered by the Reverend Anna Shaw to the
National Woman's Council in February 1891. Cooper's readiness to deceive for good purpose is evident from her beginning compliment that
Shaw's paper was "among a number of thoughtful and suggestive papers
read by eminent women." She continues in this vein: "That Miss Shaw is
broad and just and liberal in principle is proved beyond contradiction"
(p. 88). Cooper goes on to document the broad, just, and liberal spirit of
Miss Shaw and of Susan B. Anthony by reference to an episode involving
Wimodaughsis, a national white women's literary club.[50]

---

48. Carby, *Reconstructing Womanhood*, p. 101. See pp. 98–101 for Carby's general discussion.

49. The following section, "The Voice of the Black Woman of the South," will document this point with respect to Cooper's literary methods, but for an illustration of it at work
in her practical politics, see her 1926 letter to Wilkinson in chapter 28.

50. "Wimodaughsis," that is, *wi*ves, *mo*thers, *daugh*ters, *sis*ters. It is hard to imagine that
Cooper is not joking here, either by making up the ridiculous acronym or, if it was indeed
the name of a club, by using it without comment. In either case, it would be harder still to
invent a better target at which to aim a criticism of the true womanhood values.

Anthony and Shaw were joined in many causes, including the National Woman Suffrage
Association (NWSA). It is possible that Cooper's reference to the "National Woman's Council" could have been a mistaken allusion to the NWSA before which Shaw was a prominent
lecturer in 1891.

Then Cooper tells a story, one so archetypical as to invite the impression that it comes from collective, rather than personal, experience: A colored woman applies, in writing, for membership in the club. When the color of the applicant comes to light, a certain "Kentucky secretary, a lady zealous in good works" denies admission for the now obvious reason (p. 88). Miss Shaw and, by implication, Miss Anthony promptly overrule the lady's officious good work, admit the applicant, and dismiss the secretary. Cooper comments on the story and on the character of the Kentucky secretary with biting sarcasm:

> I can't help imagining [that she] belongs to that estimable class who daily thank the Lord that He made the earth that they may have the job of superintending its rotations, and who really would like to help "elevate" the colored people (in her own way of course and so long as they understand their places) [and that she] is filled with grief and horror that any persons of Negro extraction should aspire to learn type-writing or languages or to enjoy any other advantages offered in the sacred halls of Wimodaughsis. (P. 88)

The tone of the chapter changes. At the very least, these are not the words of a blind adherent to the pious submissiveness of the classic, true woman.

Cooper here makes a series of rhetorical moves by which the reader is abruptly brought into the author's way of thinking. The first of these is the establishment of a strategic uncertainty. Assuming the story is true in all its details, the reader is left to wonder, Was the rejected colored woman Cooper herself? Cooper suggests this possibility by the use of a direct narrative voice. But she withholds confirmation by assuming the third person: "Accordingly the Kentucky secretary took the cream-colored applicant aside, and, with emotions befitting such an epoch-making crisis, told her, 'as kindly as she could,' that colored people were not admitted to the classes." (p. 89). The text creates the impression of a first-hand account, yet it is only an impression. Cooper might have been the applicant, though it is hard to say why she would have been interested in joining a whites-only literary group. By 1892, Cooper had been long committed to a literary circle with the Grimkés, which met twice weekly. In addition, she was already deeply involved with black women's groups such as the Colored Women's League in Washington, which she was to cofound in 1894—not to mention her involvements in the national Negro Women's Club

Movement,[51] to say nothing of her habit of keeping her distance from white people.[52] It is more than possible that Cooper is here retelling a story so frequently heard that she does not hesitate to use it, perhaps to fictionalize it, for her own purposes. Though it is impossible to know for certain, this probability is supported by the larger intent of the story itself.

Just after the recounting of this episode, Cooper again praises Shaw and Anthony, but now with a slight, but noticeable, hint of the attitude she presents toward the Kentucky lady: "Susan B. Anthony and Anna Shaw are evidently too noble to be held in thrall by the provincialisms of women who seem never to have breathed the atmosphere beyond the confines of their grandfathers' plantations" (p. 89). She is clearly affirming the just liberality of the white feminists, but the use of "noble" seems to play uncertainly with the obnoxious *noblesse oblige* of the Kentucky secretary. Cooper used words with precision and care. Was the "noble" in contrast to the false nobility of the southern lady, as if to affirm the good whites against the bad? Not likely. Cooper was far too subtle for such a move. It is more likely that she means to distinguish the white feminists neatly but not completely. This, as we shall see, is more than evident from the major point of the chapter, which she defers until much later in this, the longest of her published essays.

The overall structure of the chapter evolves from this introduction. Here Cooper is teasing. She opens to her theme, but without developing it in so many words. She thus imposes another element of ambiguity. What does she think of Miss Shaw, really? And why is she interested at all in her "Woman versus the Indian" talk? The reader must wait for answers. The uncertainty in these opening pages is easily overlooked, inviting a hasty reading. Mary Helen Washington, for example, takes the description of the applicant to be further indication of Cooper's inability to escape the reaching force of the very cultural ideas Cooper so openly despises in the southern lady: "Although her sympathies were with the poor and uneducated, Cooper's images in *A Voice* are almost entirely of privileged women: the struggling, ambitious intellectual, those fatally beautiful Southern mulatto women, a 'cream-colored' aspirant to a white culture club."[53] Washington

---

51. Hutchinson, *Anna Julia Cooper,* p. 93. See also, in the same place, Hutchinson's discussion of Cooper's work with the Colored Women's League of Washington, D.C. as well as the national movement. For example, Cooper's "Higher Education of Women" (chapter 4) was originally a speech at Howard University before a precursor meeting of the Colored Women's League.

52. See "My Racial Philosophy" (chapter 17).

53. Washington, Introduction, p. xlix. Note also that, in her complaint about Cooper's use of benign descriptors for the black woman, Washington marks "cream-colored" as if it

does not say that she takes Cooper as that aspirant, but she does believe that Cooper, if not fully identified with such a type, was at least unable to separate herself from it. Like Baker-Fletcher and others who remain skeptical of Cooper's rejection of the true womanhood ideal, Washington takes the author's verbal imagery as of greater interpretive importance than the substance of Cooper's actual argument as it unfolds, and she ignores altogether the testimony of Cooper's life.

How Cooper unfolds that argument is telling. Just after she returns to Miss Shaw's nobility, Cooper makes the all-important distinction that governs everything following in the chapter: that between the black woman and the southern woman (later transposed with all due sarcasm into southern "lady"). Here she is making a self-conscious distinction that was already set up by the biting sarcasm directed at the Kentucky secretary. But, importantly, she is quick to say that, though the difference between the southern lady and the black woman is confusing, the black woman knows the difference:

> The black woman and the southern woman, I imagine, often get them into the predicament of the befuddled man who had to take singly across a stream a bag of corn, a fox and a goose. There was no one to help, and to leave the goose with the fox was death—with the corn, destruction. To re-christen the animals, the lion could not be induced to lie down with the lamb unless the lamb would take the inside berth.
>
> The black woman appreciates the situation and can even sympathize with the actors in the serio-comic dilemma. (Pp. 89–90)

Is it likely, therefore, that the black woman who is able to appreciate the confusion could lie down with such a lion? Cooper understands the trap of true womanhood and, though she uses its language, it seems to me improbable that she would take an inner berth with it without some broader purpose.[54]

The narrative line of " 'Woman versus the Indian' " then moves to other subjects—principally to a complicated theory of race and sex caste in American society, which Cooper states as a general theory of Western civilization. She now shifts momentarily from the southern lady to "the American woman . . . [who] is responsible for American manners" (p. 90), of whom she says:

---

belonged to the same series as "pleasing," "sweet," and "gentle" in reference to real, black heroines. In the text, however, Cooper is clearly setting "cream-colored" against, one might say, the sugar-coated manners of the Kentucky secretary.

54. This, if I understand Claudia Tate correctly, is the implication of her interpretation of Cooper.

> With all her vaunted independence, the American woman of to-day is as
> fearful of losing caste as a Brahmin in India. That is the law under which
> she lives. . . .
>   The queen of the drawing room is absolute ruler under this law.
> (P. 91)

The southern lady *and* the American woman? Why the shift in terms? Does
Cooper mean now to put the liberal feminist in the same ethical category
with the Kentucky secretary? Again, uncertainty is her method. She shifts
to "American woman" but leaves her meaning open, nagging. Still, there
is no doubt she is attacking something very much like the true womanhood
ideal.

When Cooper turns back to the black woman, she again shifts, as if to
emphasize the distinction. Now, suddenly, "black woman" becomes the
"Black Woman," capitalized and personified: "It was the good fortune of
the Black Woman of the South to spend some weeks, not long since, in a
land over which floated the Union Jack" (p. 92). The reader again won-
ders, Is Cooper here speaking for herself even if she was not the cream-
colored applicant? Again, the answer is as unsure as the question is interesting. What is likely is that now Cooper is speaking for herself but through
the means of creating a new social figure. This figure is none other than
the pseudonymous author, who, in effect, becomes the figurative person
age of the book's subtitle: *A Voice from the South: By a Black Woman of the
South*. Here, after three long chapters, Cooper returns to a theme that
appeared briefly in the book's preface, significantly titled "Our Raison
d'Être" (chapter 2). In the preface, she introduced the Black Woman (with
unexplained capital letters) as the only figure of importance in American
culture who had not been heard. Only she, the "Black Woman," can give
voice to the "Silent South" (p. 51). Neither "our Caucasian barristers"
nor the "dark man" should be "wholly expected fully and adequately to
reproduce the exact Voice of the Black Woman" (p. 52). Hence, the preface, which is set in the impersonal third person, is recalled at a crucial
juncture in the key chapter where Cooper herself becomes the personifi-
cation of that Voice.

As Karen Baker-Fletcher, Claudia Tate, and Elizabeth Alexander have
all said in different ways, Cooper possessed a very self-conscious theory of
her voice. That theory is, in one respect, a literary device, but it is also

what Baker-Fletcher calls Cooper's "theological anthropology."[55] If, by this, one can also mean a general social theory of voice, then I would agree with Baker-Fletcher. Yet the surprising thing is that, in the end, Baker-Fletcher imposes an unnecessary limit on her own interpretation. She is among those with reservations about Cooper's continuing submissiveness to the ideal of true womanhood, which supposedly interferes with her ability to speak for the poor, black woman.[56] How, it might be asked, could a black woman of the South like Cooper have a theological anthropology, or any other kind of social theory, without speaking for the poor?

How does a voice become a representative Voice? How does a writer or speaker, to use the expression Baker-Fletcher takes from Cooper, become the "Singing Something" of a people?[57] In the broadest sense, this is the familiar problem of the representative intellectual that is at least as old as Marx. But, in the more immediate context, this is the question of the provocative limitedness of language. If one is to sing the voice of an oppressed people, must the song come forth in the language of that people? Today much more is known about this, but we must take Cooper on her terms, those prevalent in her day. As a teacher of languages, she surely understood the problems of the translatability of voice and language generally. She, after all, taught poor children for whom Latin and Greek were more than simply foreign and ancient. By the cultural standards of the elite public education to which Cooper held her pupils, the mastery of Latin and Greek, while valuable in its own right, was also, and urgently, the price of admission to Harvard and Yale, and thus to the prospect of class advantage. She could hardly be expected to have appreciated today's debates over the cultural values of nonstandard English usages. Her own language, especially in *A Voice from the South,* has to be understood in this context.

---

55. In Baker-Fletcher's 1991 thesis, the theological anthropology theme is more pronounced, while in its revision in the 1994 book, Cooper's feminism is more at issue. See note 4 this chapter.

56. And, in spite of (or because of) Baker-Fletcher's shift in themes from the thesis to the book (see previous note), she fails, in my opinion, to stress that Cooper's voice is in fact a strategic (hence, political) voice.

57. Though Elizabeth Alexander does not refer to the phrase, her excellent essay " 'Fothe's Business' " is on the same idea. The "Singing Something" is most explicitly developed by Cooper at the time of her 1925 thesis defense (see chapter 24). In the key passage (pp. 293–94), Cooper is defending her thesis against Célestin Bouglé's idea that the democratic principle is restricted to the northern regions of the world. Cooper argues that this principle is universal because it is, in effect, the divine spark in all human beings—thus leaving open the question as to whether it is the divine or the human that sings (hence the point of Baker-Fletcher's theological interpretation).

Today, it is well understood that whenever voice is seized by a formerly silent people, the terms of political representation in the social whole
also change. Both liberal and Left ideals of democratic participation have
been severely challenged in the past quarter century, mostly by the emergence of formerly colonized peoples in the arena once controlled univo-
cally by the Euro-American dominant classes. While Cooper could not
have had access to our understandings, she was in her day, at the end of the
nineteenth century, attempting to do just what the decolonizing and related
social movements have done in the last generations of the twentieth—and
this is surely what Hazel Carby is driving at in her interpretation of Cooper
as a virtual decolonizer before the fact. Cooper was, most self-consciously,
seeking to give voice to black women in America by creating, then assuming, the representative position of the Black Woman of the South. To be
sure, in *A Voice from the South* she did not very often employ the language
of the poor.[58] Still, there is no good reason to doubt the stated purpose of
the preface, much less the argument as it develops in " 'Woman versus the
Indian.' " She knew exactly what she was doing all along, and what she
was doing was what she always did. She was one who worked for "neglected people."

In several previously unpublished writings, Cooper did in fact address
the question of the language of the poor. Her much later essay "Sketches
from a Teacher's Notebook: Loss of Speech through Isolation" (chapter
14) drew upon her experiences during and after World War I as director of
War Camp community service programs. This quietly brilliant and touch-
ing essay is shorn of lofty ideals and fancy ideas. Here Cooper is speaking
from the heart of life with the most poor. The essay tells the story of her
encounter with the Berry family, a desperately poor, isolated, and broken
rural family. Years before Cooper knew them, the father had been lynched.
Though the locals realized that a mistake had been made, the family was
irreparably damaged. The mother had chosen to keep herself, and particularly her child Walter in as complete as possible isolation from the cruel,
wider world. As a result, the boy spoke in a strange, near incoherent idio-
lect. Slowly Cooper coaxed the boy into a tentative relationship.

"Mith Coo' show—*I* make bick *too!*"
"Why certainly, Walter," I said with ready comprehension. "I'll be glad

---

58. Though she did on occasion. Also, her 1893 speech to the Women's Congress of
the Chicago World's Fair is often cited as evidence that she did in fact, even in the early years,
have the poor very clearly in mind (see chapter 11).

to show you how to make a bas–ket," speaking very distinctly and letting him observe the motion of my lips in pronouncing "bas–ket." (P. 227)

Can there be any doubt from this that Mrs. Cooper (Mith Coo'), even though proud of her "ready comprehension," knew how to give, and was committed to giving, voice to the poor in their language?

Importantly, the story makes its point about the defeating effects of social isolation with simple reference to, exactly, the naivete of bourgeois ideals of home and family life:

> And I wondered what our brand of education, what our smug injunction that the home "is expected" to cooperate with the school will find or create for the help and guidance of such a home, a type as truly evolved from American environmental conditions as are the blind fish in the Mammoth Cave or the bronchos of the western plains. (P. 229)

If, then, Cooper could speak and comprehend the language of the poor, why did she not do so in *A Voice from the South*? One answer, as I have said, is that she was above all else a teacher. But a different one is found in another previously unpublished essay, "The Negro's Dialect" (chapter 18). Here, she takes up the question of public abuses of Negro dialect. Her purpose is to demonstrate that popular culture's caricatures of Negro dialect are, with rare exceptions, linguistically (that is, phonetically) impossible—made-up, foolish images of "colored people." Cooper applies her considerable skill as a linguist in order to demystify popular perversions of black language and culture in such media as the *Amos 'n Andy* radio program. This later essay suggests that, even much earlier when she wrote *A Voice from the South*, Cooper was not the sort of person who was willing, even remotely, to give comfort to the worse white images of black culture. She understood her work to be the lifting of the culture and its language. Whatever else she was, Cooper was a leader among the first generation of black women in America struggling to make the cultural, as well as social and economic, transition from the rural South to the cosmopolitan and urban North.[59] Everything they had, such as it precariously was, owed to their hard-won ability to work out from slavery—from the South into the middle-class life won by education and learning.

What choice is there but to understand Cooper's ideas in context—the

---

59. And this, too, is a point Hazel Carby makes so well. See ch. 5 of her *Reconstructing Womanhood*.

context of her times, and of her life? Whatever the lingering effects of the
true womanhood doctrine, they are at best, as Claudia Tate implies, a kind
of literary slate on which is written the voice of the black woman by a
Black Woman of the South. Cooper's book is about nothing if it is not
about voice in this sense, and this becomes overwhelmingly clear as the
narrative in " 'Woman versus the Indian' " moves toward its conclusion.
After the introduction of herself as the Black Woman, Cooper presents a
version of her implicit theory of oppression, as Carby refers to it. But
Cooper does so, again, by an odd path. She cites a then popular book by
the astronomer and writer Percival Lowell. In *Soul of the Far East,* Lowell
proposed that "personality" and "sense of self" decline in inverse relation
to "manners." In simple terms, the theory is that the West is more "personal" than the East. Accordingly, it has fewer manners. America, being
the most Western, is "the least courteous nation on the globe" (p. 96).
But,in Cooper's hands, Lowell's not very convincing claim becomes an
implicit theory of Western culture with quite a different meaning from
Lowell's.[60]

Just before these remarks, Cooper tells a story (to which I shall return)
in which she, the Black Woman, while a passenger on a train in the South,
was exposed to the worst sort of rude and crude abuse. She uses, here, the
common language:

> "Here gurl," (I am past thirty) "you better git out 'n dis kyar 'f yer don't,
> I'll put yer out,"—my mental annotation is *Here's an American citizen who
> has been badly trained. He is sadly lacking in both 'sweetness' and 'light.'* (P. 95)

At first, it would seem that this is an instance in which Cooper is calling
her racist tormentor to the account of true womanhood values by judging
his inferior (typically American) manners. The impression is heightened
when she adds:

> But since Mr. Lowell shows so conclusively that the entire Land of
> the West is a *mannerless continent,* I have determined to plead with our
> women, the mannerless sex on this mannerless continent, to institute a
> reform by placing immediately in our national curricula a department for
> teaching GOOD MANNERS. (P. 96)

---

60. Cooper develops this idea in part 2 of *A Voice from the South* in "Has America a Race
Problem?" (chapter 7 of this book).

But read the text closely. The American woman is "the mannerless sex on this mannerless continent." Does Cooper mean to put her in the same category as the ill-mannered men—as Lowell's Americans? Not at all. She is toying with Lowell's odd idea that manners decline in inverse proportion to a "sense of self." Though she *seems* to be calling for greater courtesy, she is actually demanding a better sense of "self," of personhood—one might even say of womanhood. Cooper capitalizes "good manners" perhaps to be ironic, as if to say: Against the personless, sterile manners, can we not *at least* have good manners? She means, I think, to trifle with a then popular writer's half-baked theory of good manners in order subtly to emphasize the deeper values of personal character (with which, of course, her work as a teacher was preoccupied).

Though this is a tricky passage to understand, my interpretation is further supported by Cooper's return, in the pages following, to the distinction between the southern lady and the Black Woman (pp. 97–100). The former, being the bearer of all virtue and "manners" (not necessarily good ones), is again subjected to Cooper's own brand of verbal abuse, after which Cooper carefully turns back to the white feminist movement:

> Lately a great national and international movement characteristic of this age and country, a movement based on the inherent right of every soul to its own highest development, I mean the movement making for Woman's full, free, and complete emancipation, has, after much courting, obtained the gracious smile of the Southern woman—I beg her pardon—the Southern *lady*. (P. 100)

Earlier, under the metonymic guise of Miss Shaw, Cooper has rebuked the Kentucky secretary and chided her precisely for her figurative liaisons with the true southern lady. Here, it seems, the muted praise of Anthony and Shaw (with their liberal and noble virtues) takes on its true meaning. Cooper does not condemn the white feminists to mere equivalency with the southern lady, even though she does rebuke them for their recent courtings of the original true woman. This is evident from what follows in Cooper's discussion.

The true woman, the southern lady, does not care about manners. Her concern is with the terrifying prospect of *social* equality with Negroes who have a quite different idea of civility from hers. The southern lady fears that "civility to the Negro implies social equality," which to her means forced association between the races (p. 101). But quickly Cooper distinguishes the southern lady's fear from the Black Woman's (her own) idea that social equality means nothing necessarily more than a simple, human identity of needs and interests—in particular, the normal necessity of people of both races to move at will through the public sphere and its accommodations, there to buy and sell according to one's means and desires. The Black Woman of the South then declaims any particular or necessary desire for enforced association with anyone, whether colored or white.[61]

This would seem to be a regressive statement, a recourse to what would become the Tuskegee idea of race relations—of the common economic hand with separate social fingers. The difference, however, is that Cooper is writing here from a position of avowed moral and cultural *superiority*—to the crude man on the train, to the Kentucky secretary, to the mannerless West, and to the mannerless woman. Whereupon Cooper introduces her version of what bell hooks has called her "feminine principle":

> And this is why, as it appears to me, woman in her lately acquired vantage ground for speaking an earnest helpful word, can do this country no deeper and truer and more lasting good than by bending all her energies to thus broadening, humanizing, and civilizing her native land. (P. 104)

But, as I have been suggesting, this is not quite what it seems. Cooper's feminine principle, such as it is, is always qualified, as it is here, most dramatically.

Two paragraphs after the above statement of this apparently seamless and universalistic gender principle, Cooper returns (at long last) to Miss Shaw and her paper "Woman versus the Indian." This occurs nearly seventeen pages later, as the chapter draws to its conclusion, and its main point. Cooper, aware of what she has been doing, but sensitive to the likelihood that the reader could be lost in the studied uncertainty projected over such a long intervening space, lets Miss Shaw back in gently: "This, too, is why I conceive the subject to have been unfortunately worded which was chosen by Miss Shaw at the Woman's Council and which stands at the head of this chapter" (p. 105). Now Cooper speaks of Shaw's voice, from which she draws her concern for the unfortunate title:

> Miss Shaw is one of the most powerful of our leaders, and we feel her voice should give no uncertain note. Woman should not, even by infer-

---

61. See pp. 102–03 for Cooper's views on "forced association." Though its purposes were different, Cooper's idea was not entirely free of the implications of Booker T. Washington's yet-to-be pronounced Atlanta Compromise.

ence, or for the sake of argument, seem to disparage what is weak. For woman's cause is the cause of the weak; and when all the weak shall have received their due consideration, then woman will have her "rights," and the Indian will have his rights, and the Negro will have his rights, and all the strong will have learned at last to deal justly, to love mercy, and to walk humbly; and our fair land will have been taught the secret of universal courtesy which is after all nothing but the art, the science, and the religion of regarding one's neighbor as one's self, and do for him as we would, were conditions swapped, that he do for us. (P. 105)

The invocation of biblical language[62] at the end fulfills the uncertain meaning of "GOOD MANNERS." As Cooper puts it here, "the secret of universal courtesy" is a simple morality of public, reciprocal regard. Good manners, therefore, are something quite different form the false social virtues of the true southern lady. "All prejudices, whether of race, sect or sex, class pride and caste distinctions are the belittling inheritance and badge of snobs and prigs" (p. 105).

More to the point of the entire chapter, however, Cooper finally begins to make herself more explicit, less indefinite with respect to white feminists. Cooper does possess a sort of fractured principle of universal womanhood, but the Black Woman's relation to womanhood is certainly not through the southern lady. Instead, Cooper's figure of the Black Woman claims its representative power by relation to another—the no less idealized American woman, who had been mentioned earlier and dropped, only to reappear ever so necessarily at the crucial moment in Cooper's unfolding idea. If the Black Woman is to have her voice in the construction of the American woman, she must be able to set the white feminist straight on the terms of her own white, if feminist, moral courtesy. We see now that Cooper's purpose in rebuking the feminist metonym, Miss Shaw, can only be that of encouraging her, the white feminist, toward a greater appreciation of the secret of universal courtesy, as Cooper defines it. This Cooper pursues at the conclusion of the long chapter by describing, with notable precision, the error of Shaw's title. That error is not, of course, bad manners, or political insensitivity, but that of ignoring woman's sense of unity and identification with the weak. The problem is that the white feminist, like the American woman, is in the same social and economic position as are the poor and thus is the natural ally with those who are weak. The idea quoted in full:

---

62. Language, by the way, that, not incidentally, does communicate to great numbers of the poor.

Why should woman become plaintiff in a suit versus the Indian, or the Negro or any other race or class who have been crushed under the iron heel of Anglo-Saxon power and selfishness? If the Indian has been wronged and cheated by the puissance of this American government, it is woman's mission to plead with her country to cease to do evil and to pay its honest debts. If the Negro has been deceitfully cajoled or inhumanly cuffed according to selfish expediency or capricious antipathy, let it be woman's mission to plead that he be met as a man and honestly given half the road. If woman's own happiness has been ignored or misunderstood in our country's legislating for bread winners, for rum sellers, for property holders, for the family relations, for any or all the interests that touch her vitality, let her rest her plea, not on Indian inferiority, nor on Negro depravity, but on the obligation of legislators to do for her as they would have others do for them were relations reversed. (p. 108)[63]

The golden rule of courtesy is, thus, the foundational principle of Cooper's feminist politics. Those, like bell hooks, who divine a universal principle of the feminine in Cooper are not wrong. And, to be sure, Cooper's feminist politics would not be considered revolutionary by today's standards. But neither is Cooper's feminism even remotely a knee-jerk version of the true womanhood ideal. Nor is Cooper politically naive, which is why Claudia Tate and, more tentatively, Ann duCille see in Cooper versions of Hazel Carby's strong interpretation of her as a self-conscious social critic of internal colonization. Some might be more cautious, but Carby is close to Cooper's thinking. Cooper may have grounded her feminism in moral and religious principles that seem remote today, but her politics were a far cry from the true womanhood manners of the southern lady.

For Cooper, who lived a largely solitary life in service of the poor, the domestic ideal was anything but ladylike submissiveness. It was, quite to the contrary, the practical form of that service and the expression of the moral culture from which she believed it must issue.

Anna Julia Cooper's Signs

In the story of her confrontation with ill-mannered whites, mentioned earlier, the reader comes upon another of Cooper's more memorable state-

---

63. Here, importantly, Cooper returns to the judicial motif that appeared first in her preface, "Our Raison d'Être" (p. 51). The preface also used the capitalized expression "Black Woman." That both usages appear in the preface suggests that Cooper herself thought of " 'Woman versus the Indian' " as the most important chapter in the book.

ments, one that brings all the more clarity to her theory of the Black Woman. Cooper continues the story of what transpired during her—that is, the Black Woman's—train trip in the South:

> And when farther on in the same section our train stops at a dilapidated station, rendered yet more unsightly by dozens of loafers with their hands in their pockets while a productive soil and inviting climate beckon in vain to industry; and when, looking a little more closely, I see two dingy little rooms with "FOR LADIES" swinging over one and "FOR COL-ORED PEOPLE" over the other; . . . [I wonder] under which head I come. (P. 95)

Though understated, these few lines express most elegantly Anna Julia Cooper's unique position in the social theory of America and of American women at another time in history.

Just as Cooper's personal life was one of solitary—often isolated—purpose, her most impressive theoretical statements drew upon her personal experience in order to define the unique and univocal position of the Black Woman in those times. The 1890s in the urban North were an historical moment when, for the first time, black women in America were rising in significant numbers to positions of prominence and relative power.

In 1895, three years after *A Voice from the South* was published, Frederick Douglass died late in the evening after he had addressed a meeting of the National Woman's Council convening just four years after Miss Shaw's address to the same group. Though his relations with feminists, notably with Sojourner Truth, were not always easy, more than any black man of the nineteenth century Douglass had tried somehow to align issues of the race with those of women's rights. He did not succeed, and no man after, including Du Bois, did better than he. These differences were, very probably, unbridgeable by any man, even if, in Cooper's view, the solution must not exclude men.

In an exact historical sense, the end of the nineteenth century was indeed an exceptional moment for the black woman. On the surface, the United States was in a time of change, hope, and progress. But under the surface of white, dominant, and male culture, there lay unsettled discontents. The failure of Reconstruction and the rise of Jim Crow made the color line a virtual wall of political regression against which, in particular, the new class of urban blacks would struggle, preparing the way for the transitions from the rural South to the urban North, from the culture of southern folkways to the urban ways of the new middle classes—transitions that gathered force after World War I. At the same time, the end of the nineteenth century was a period of still significant feminist struggle, which would achieve a definite, though incomplete, political success in the 1920s.

More generally, the 1890s was that crucial moment in American history when the new industrial order was coming into its own. The older feudal system of the South, which had bred both the slave economy and the culture of true womanhood, lay in ruins. Since the Civil War, it had been clear that industrialization meant that the economic future lay in the North. It would take the better part of the century following for the South to shed its past and enter this new order. In the retrospect of many years, we can see today just to what extent the new economic arrangements changed the class system, and how these changes brought instabilities in the caste systems governing race and sex, instabilities that, by shaking the South and the North differently, made the central point of Cooper's thinking evident to anyone willing to see. Hence, the historical principle we are only today beginning to understand: Race and sex can never be reliably thought-through apart from each other because neither, in its turn, is ever free of the causes and effects of class relations.

Amid this larger social business, it was, at the time Cooper wrote *A Voice from the South,* impossible that either the white woman, however good her manners, or a man of any race, however close one might be tied to him, could resolve the underlying structural tensions. Structural instabilities never arise along any one fault line—not of race alone, nor of gender, nor of class. But insofar as the emerging economic order would come in a degree and kind of industrial growth never before experienced, it was already impossible that America's refusal to acknowledge its own moral contradictions with respect to the castelike exclusions of blacks, women, and (in Cooper's essay) Indians would not begin to break into the yield.

As a result, only someone like Anna Julia Cooper could read the signs for what they meant. In a society in which the Black Woman has no place to go—where she encounters two signs, "FOR LADIES" and "FOR COLORED PEOPLE," neither of which defines her properly—then that Black Woman is uniquely situated to understand the larger structural situation. Cooper was not, by any means, the only social critical to grasp the situation. But she may have put it with such simple integrity and clarity because of the unique position into which life had forced her. She knew where she did not belong. Just the same, she knew how to live and serve with moral purpose. Being able, perhaps more than others, to tolerate the solitary position, she could read the signs for what they meant.

Ironically, Cooper's ability to tolerate and draw upon the uniqueness of her social experience may also account for her extreme faith in the American future, a surprising faith she expressed, at the conclusion of her four-chapter black feminist manifesto, in "The Status of Woman in America" (chapter 6). There, remember, she had said:

> What a responsibility then to have the sole management of the primal lights and shadows! Such is the colored woman's office. She must stamp weal or woe on the coming history of this people. (P. 117)

Who is "this people"? Evidently she did mean to embrace the American people, and to claim for the Black Woman of America the unique office of moral responsibility for the future of the society as a whole. Just before this benedictory conclusion, Cooper also said:

> But to be a woman of the Negro race in America, and to be able to grasp the deep significance of the possibilities of the crisis, is to have a heritage, it seems to me, unique in the ages. (P. 117)

Only she who could read the signs could have understood the possibilities that then lay ahead at the end of the previous century.

If only others had read them so well.

· I ·

The Colored Woman's Office:
A Voice from the South, Part 1

A Voice from the South *is a remarkable book for reasons other than its powerful ideas. Just as striking is that it was composed by a still very young woman, just out of college and beginning her career as a public school teacher. More significant still is that the book comprises essays and talks in which Cooper delivers her graceful and convincing judgments on some of the most urgent issues of her day—race, womanhood, higher education, and racial uplift. These concerns, among others, turned on the foremost social conflict besetting an otherwise upbeat, industrializing America at the end of the nineteenth century: What shall be the future of this ethically minded republic in the face of the failure of Reconstruction and the rise of Jim Crow segregation?*

The papers that Cooper collected for the 1892 book were of different origins. The earliest, we assume, is "Womanhood: A Vital Element in the Regeneration and Progress of a Race" (chapter 3), a speech given to an assembly of Episcopal clergy in 1886 (before she had begun her life and work in Washington, D.C.). The only other that we know for certain to have been a public speech is "The Higher Education of Women" (chapter 4), a presentation to a convention of the American Conference of Educators in 1890 and published in Southland *in 1891. Beyond these two, Cooper did not provide information as to the origin of the papers in* A Voice from the South, *and none is discernible in the archives. Each chapter, however, reads as though it were written for a special occasion or in response to a particular problem of the day. The famous " 'Woman versus the Indian' " (chapter 5) was clearly written in reply to Anna Shaw's February 1891 speech at the National Woman's Council meeting in Washington, D.C. Cooper may well have been present at this meeting and is likely to have written her response sometime in late 1891 or early 1892. She was not one to let sleeping dogs lie. All of the papers out of which Cooper composed this book were written in the earliest stage of her public career—probably all between 1884 (the year she graduated from Oberlin and began her teaching career) and 1892. Most, it seems, are from the end of this period, and some may have been written expressly for the book.*

Whatever the origins of these papers, Cooper clearly intended to fashion them into a coherent book. As Karen Baker-Fletcher observes in A Singing Something: Womanist Reflections on Anna Julia Cooper, *Cooper divided the chapters into two parts, each scored under a musical notation. The first part (here chapters 3 through 6) was marked "Soprano Obligato" and is clearly meant to represent the solitary, discordant voice from the South—the voice of the black woman in the affairs of her race and of American civil society. We have labeled this part "The Colored Woman's Office," thus drawing upon the powerful figure of speech with which Cooper brings this half of her book to conclusion.*

46

Cooper scored the second part under the notation *"Tutti ad Libitum"* (chapters 7 through 10 in this volume). Baker-Fletcher, keeping to the musical figure, interprets this section as an improvisational reference to the *"black community as a whole."* This is an entirely plausible interpretation inasmuch as Cooper, especially in the early years in Washington, joined a small circle of friends who, in addition to being as committed as she was to the black community, were devoted to the study of classical music and art. Cooper's memoir of life with the Grimkés (chapter 26) gives a sense of her love of music. Baker-Fletcher is well justified in tying her interpretation to Cooper's own musical framing of the book.

Yet, our purposes are to set Cooper's work in the broader frame of her life as a whole. We have therefore chosen to describe the second part of A Voice from the South as a contribution to the study of Race and Culture. While it is true that the second part is less well integrated than the first, it is far from being merely improvisational. As a lifelong teacher of students from the most meager of economic conditions, Cooper sought to provide them with the pleasures and educational opportunities associated with knowledge of the higher culture of the West. Cooper's idea of racial uplift was not expressly the same as Du Bois's famous Talented Tenth doctrine, but it was surely akin. While Du Bois eventually passed on to a more Marxist and global theory of race, Cooper kept her eye on the importance of culture. Yet except at the end, Du Bois always remained a devotee of Western culture, even in his most bitter rage at its politics (as Cooper turned to a more overtly political point of view in her 1925 doctoral thesis on the global politics of French attitudes toward slavery [chapters 22–24]). Still, especially in their earliest works, the emphasis on culture is notably similar. As Cooper scored her Voice from the South, taking seriously the *"singing something"* figure of speech that would reemerge in her 1925 defense of her thesis (chapter 24), so Du Bois memorably introduced each of the chapters in his Souls of Black Folk with a quotation from the poetry of Western civilization and an unscored bar of music from the Negro sorrow songs. Voice was a serious matter to them both, as it still is to those today in their traditions.

Yet our view is that, though voice was important, perhaps even central, to Cooper's intentions in organizing her book, she always had the political and legal circumstances of her race well in mind. Thus, in her short preface, *"Our Raison d'Être"* (chapter 2), Cooper uses a more formal, even legal expression to introduce the book itself. The voice figure is set against one taken from the courtroom and legal proceedings. She opens by defining her problem in this book; *"In the clash and clatter of our American Conflict, it has been said that the South remains Silent"* (p. 51). She continues, then, to explain by way of introduction that this book will give voice to the Black Woman, who is here presented less as a *"singing something"* than as a trial witness: *"One important witness has not yet been heard from. The summing up of the evidence deposed, and the charge to the jury have been made— but no word from the Black Woman"* (p. 51). *Clearly, Cooper wants as much to situate the Black Woman in the political clashes and conflicts as to raise the Black Woman's moral voice over the din.*

It should be noted also that the major theme of Cooper's black feminism, and the signature for the original 1892 edition of A Voice from the South, *is taken respectfully from Alexander Crummell's 1883 speech before the Freedom's Aid Society, "The Black Woman of the South: Her Neglects and Her Needs." In chapter 3, Cooper turns Crummell's idea to an even more affirming description of the black woman's position. The 1892 edition is, thus, signed "By a Black Woman of the South." Though the copyright is listed in the name of Anna Julia Cooper, our copy of the original gives no other indication of Cooper's authorship. It is plain as Lemert's introduction explains, that she had the most explicit of theoretical and political intentions in her presentation of this book. Her decision not to sign her book was anything but false modesty or some other empty virtue. In* A Voice from the South *Cooper dared to assert that the moral office of the Black Woman possessed the most powerful political authority in the land. She very likely used the signature of the "Black Woman of the South" instead of her own, because she was so very well aware of the power that could move the society when individuals assume so potent a collective office.*

A Voice from the South

With regret
I forget
If the song be living yet,
    Yet remember, vaguely now,
    It was honest, anyhow.

Anna Julia Cooper's copyright has expired, and, so far as our research has been able to determine, it has not been renewed in her name by Cooper's last surviving family members. The book was privately printed by the Aldine Printing House in Xenia, Ohio, which claims no rights to the book.

Part I: Soprano Obligato

For they the *Royal-hearted Women* are
Who nobly love the noblest, yet have grace
For needy, suffering lives in lowliest place;
Carrying a choicer sunlight in their smile,
The heavenliest ray that pitieth the vile.

    ★   ★   ★

Though I were happy, throned beside the king,
I should be tender to each little thing
With hurt warm breast, that had no speech to tell
Its inward pangs; and I would soothe it well
With tender touch and with a low, soft moan
For company.

                  —*George Eliot*★

★George Eliot is the pen name of Mary Ann Evans (1819–1880), an English novelist best known for *Middlemarch*.

· *2* ·

Our Raison d'Être (1892)

$\mathcal{I}$n the clash and clatter of our American Conflict, it has been said that the South remains Silent. Like the Sphinx she inspires vociferous disputation, but herself takes little part in the noisy controversy. One muffled strain in the Silent South, a jarring chord and a vague and uncomprehended cadenza has been and still is the Negro. And of that muffled chord, the one mute and voiceless note has been the sadly expectant Black Woman,

> An infant crying in the night,
> An infant crying for the light;
> And with *no language—but a cry.*

The colored man's inheritance and apportionment is still the sombre crux, the perplexing *cul de sac* of the nation,—the dumb skeleton in the closet provoking ceaseless harangues, indeed, but little understood and seldom consulted. Attorneys for the plaintiff and attorneys for the defendant, with bungling *gaucherie* have analyzed and dissected, theorized and synthesized with sublime ignorance or pathetic misapprehension of counsel from the black client. One important witness has not yet been heard from. The summing up of the evidence deposed, and the charge to the jury have been made—but no word from the Black Woman.

It is because I believe the American people to be conscientiously committed to a fair trial and ungarbled evidence, and because I feel it essential to a perfect understanding and an equitable verdict that truth from *each* standpoint be presented at the bar,—that this little Voice has been added to the already full chorus. The "other side" has not been represented by one who "lives there." And not many can more sensibly realize and more accurately tell the weight and the fret of the "long dull pain" than the open-eyed but hitherto voiceless Black Woman of America.

The feverish agitation, the perfervid energy, the busy objectivity of the

51

more turbulent life of our men serves, it may be, at once to cloud or color their vision somewhat, and as well to relieve the smart and deaden the pain for them. Their voice is in consequence not always temperate and calm, and at the same time radically corrective and sanatory. At any rate, as our Caucasian barristers are not to blame if they cannot *quite* put themselves in the dark man's place, neither should the dark man be wholly expected fully and adequately to reproduce the exact Voice of the Black Woman.

Delicately sensitive at every pore to social atmospheric conditions, her calorimeter may well be studied in the interest of accuracy and fairness in diagnosing what is often conceded to be a "puzzling" case. If these broken utterances can in any way help to a clearer vision and a truer pulse-beat in studying our Nation's Problem, this Voice by a Black Woman of the South will not have been raised in vain.

TAWAWA CHIMNEY CORNER,
SEPT. 17, 1892.

· 3 ·

Womanhood: A Vital Element in the Regeneration and Progress of a Race (1886)

$\mathscr{T}$he two sources from which, perhaps, modern civilization has derived its noble and ennobling ideal of woman are Christianity and the Feudal System.

In Oriental countries woman has been uniformly devoted to a life of ignorance, infamy, and complete stagnation. The Chinese shoe of to-day does not more entirely dwarf, cramp, and destroy her physical powers, than have the customs, laws, and social instincts, which from remotest ages have governed our Sister of the East, enervated and blighted her mental and moral life.

Mahomet[1] makes no account of woman whatever in his polity. The Koran, which, unlike our Bible, was a product and not a growth, tried to address itself to the needs of Arabian civilization as Mahomet with his circumscribed powers saw them. The Arab was a nomad. Home to him meant his present camping place. That deity who, according to our western ideals, makes and sanctifies the home, was to him a transient bauble to be toyed with so long as it gave pleasure and then to be thrown aside for a new one. As a personality, an individual soul, capable of eternal growth and unlimited development, and destined to mould and shape the civilization of the future to an incalculable extent, Mahomet did not know woman. There was no hereafter, no paradise for her. The heaven of the Mussulman[2] is peopled and made gladsome not by the departed wife, or sister, or

---

Read before the convocation of colored clergy of the Protestant Episcopal Church at Washington, D.C., 1886. *AJC*. Throughout this book, the abbreviation "*AJC*" identifies Cooper's notes. All other notes have been added by the editors, who have attempted to identify the more important sources and quotes. Some, unfortunately, they were unable to identify.

1. Archaic spelling of Mohammed (A.D. 570–632), founder of Islam. The Koran mentioned below is the sacred book of the Islamic religion.

2. Archaic spelling of Muslim, a follower of Mohammed and member of the Islamic faith.

mother, but by *houri*—a figment of Mahomet's brain, partaking of the ethereal qualities of angels, yet imbued with all the vices and inanity of Oriental women. The harem here, and—"dust to dust" hereafter, this was the hope, the inspiration, the *summum bonum* of the Eastern woman's life! With what result on the life of the nation, the "Unspeakable Turk," the "sick man" of modern Europe can to-day exemplify.

Says a certain writer: "The private life of the Turk is vilest of the vile, unprogressive, unambitious, and inconceivably low." And yet Turkey is not without her great men. She has produced most brilliant minds; men skilled in all the intricacies of diplomacy and statesmanship; men whose intellects could grapple with the deep problems of empire and manipulate the subtle agencies which check-mate kings. But these minds were not the normal outgrowth of a healthy trunk. They seemed rather ephemeral excrescencies which shoot far out with all the vigor and promise, apparently, of strong branches; but soon alas fall into decay and ugliness because there is no soundness in the root, no life-giving sap, permeating, strengthening and perpetuating the whole. There is a worm at the core! The home-life is impure! and when we look for fruit, like apples of Sodom, it crumbles within our grasp into dust and ashes.

It is pleasing to turn from this effete and immobile civilization to a society still fresh and vigorous, whose seed is in itself, and whose very name is synonymous with all that is progressive, elevating and inspiring, viz., the European bud and the American flower of modern civilization.

And here let me say parenthetically that our satisfaction in American institutions rests not on the fruition we now enjoy, but springs rather from the possibilities and promise that are inherent in the system, though as yet, perhaps, far in the future.

"Happiness," says Madame de Staël,[3] "consists not in perfections attained, but in a sense of progress, the result of our own endeavor under conspiring circumstances *toward* a goal which continually advances and broadens and deepens till it is swallowed up in the Infinite." Such conditions in embryo are all that we claim for the land of the West. We have not yet reached our ideal in American civilization. The pessimists even declare that we are not marching in that direction. But there can be no doubt that here in America is the arena in which the next triumph of civilization is to be won; and here too we find promise abundant and possibilities infinite.

Now let us see on what basis this hope for our country primarily and

---

3. Madame de Staël (1766–1817): French writer at the time of the French Revolution.

fundamentally rests. Can any one doubt that it is chiefly on the homelife and on the influence of good women in those homes? Says Macaulay:[4] "You may judge a nation's rank in the scale of civilization from the way they treat their women." And Emerson,[5] "I have thought that a sufficient measure of civilization is the influence of good women." Now this high regard for woman, this germ of a prolific idea which in our own day is bearing such rich and varied fruit, was ingrafted into European civilization, we have said, from two sources, the Christian Church and the Feudal System. For although the Feudal System can in no sense be said to have originated the idea, yet there can be no doubt that the habits of life and modes of thought to which Feudalism gave rise, materially fostered and developed it; for they gave us chivalry, than which no institution has more sensibly magnified and elevated woman's position in society.

Tacitus[6] dwells on the tender regard for woman entertained by these rugged barbarians before they left their northern homes to overrun Europe. Old Norse legends too, and primitive poems, all breathe the same spirit of love of home and veneration for the pure and noble influence there presiding—the wife, the sister, the mother.

And when later on we see the settled life of the Middle Ages "oozing out," as M. Guizot[7] expresses it, from the plundering and pillaging life of barbarism and crystallizing into the Feudal System, the tiger of the field is brought once more within the charmed circle of the goddesses of his castle, and his imagination weaves around them a halo whose reflection possibly has not yet altogether vanished.

It is true the spirit of Christianity had not yet put the seal of catholicity on this sentiment. Chivalry, according to Bascom,[8] was but the toning down and softening of a rough and lawless period. It gave a roseate glow to a bitter winter's day. Those who looked out from castle windows revelled in its "amethyst tints." But God's poor, the weak, the unlovely, the commonplace were still freezing and starving none the less in unpitied, unrelieved loneliness.

Respect for woman, the much lauded chivalry of the Middle Ages, meant what I fear it still means to some men in our own day—respect for the elect few among whom they expect to consort.

---

4. Thomas Babington Macaulay (1800–1859): English historian and writer.
5. Ralph Waldo Emerson (1803–1882): New England Transcendentalist.
6. Tacitus (A.D. 56–120): Roman historian.
7. François-Pierre-Guillaume Guizot (1787–1874): French historian and politician.
8. Henry Bidleman Bascom (1796–1850): Methodist bishop.

The idea of the radical amelioration of womankind, reverence for woman as woman regardless of rank, wealth, or culture, was to come from that rich and bounteous fountain from which flow all our liberal and universal ideas—the Gospel of Jesus Christ.

And yet the Christian Church at the time of which we have been speaking would seem to have been doing even less to protect and elevate woman than the little done by secular society. The Church as an organization committed a double offense against woman in the Middle Ages. Making of marriage a sacrament and at the same time insisting on the celibacy of the clergy and other religious orders, she gave an inferior if not an impure character to the marriage relation, especially fitted to reflect discredit on woman. Would this were all or the worst! but the Church by the licentiousness of its chosen servants invaded the household and established too often as vicious connections those relations which it forbade to assume openly and in good faith. "Thus," to use the words of our authority,[9] "the religious corps became as numerous, as searching, and as unclean as the frogs of Egypt, which penetrated into all quarters, into the ovens and kneading troughs, leaving their filthy trail wherever they went." Says Chaucer with characteristic satire, speaking of the Friars:

> Women may now go safely up and doun,
> In every bush, and under every tree,
> Ther is non other incubus but he,
> And he ne will don hem no dishonour.

Henry, Bishop of Liege, could unblushingly boast the birth of twenty-two children in fourteen years.[10]

It may help us under some of the perplexities which beset our way in "the one Catholic and Apostolic Church" to-day, to recall some of the corruptions and incongruities against which the Bride of Christ has had to struggle in her past history and in spite of which she has kept, through many vicissitudes, the faith once delivered to the saints. Individuals, organizations, whole sections of the Church militant may outrage the Christ whom they profess, may ruthlessly trample under foot both the spirit and the letter of his precepts, yet not till we hear the voices audibly saying "Come let us depart hence," shall we cease to believe and cling to the promise, *"I am with you to the end of the world."*

---

9. Presumably Bascom.
10. Bascom. *AJC.*

Yet saints their watch are keeping,
The cry goes up "How long!"
And soon the night of weeping
Shall be the morn of song.

However much then the facts of any particular period of history may seem to deny it, I for one do not doubt that the source of the vitalizing principle of woman's development and amelioration is the Christian Church, so far as that church is coincident with Christianity.

Christ gave ideals not formulae. The Gospel is a germ requiring millennia for its growth and ripening. It needs and at the same time helps to form around itself a soil enriched in civilization, and perfected in culture and insight without which the embryo can neither be unfolded or comprehended. With all the strides our civilization has made from the first to the nineteenth century, we can boast not an idea, not a principle of action, not a progressive social force but was already mutely foreshadowed, or directly enjoined in that simple tale of a meek and lowly life. The quiet face of the Nazarene is ever seen a little way ahead, never too far to come down to and touch the life of the lowest in days the darkest, yet ever leading onward, still onward, the tottering childish feet of our strangely boastful civilization.

By laying down for woman the same code of morality, the same standard of purity, as for man; by refusing to countenance the shameless and equally guilty monsters who were gloating over her fall,—graciously stooping in all the majesty of his own spotlessness to wipe away the filth and grime of her guilty past and bid her go in peace and sin no more; and again in the moments of his own careworn and footsore dejection, turning trustfully and lovingly, away from the heartless snubbing and sneers, away from the cruel malignity of mobs and prelates in the dusty marts of Jerusalem to the ready sympathy, loving appreciation and unfaltering friendship of that quiet home at Bethany; and even at the last, by his dying bequest to the disciple whom he loved, signifying the protection and tender regard to be extended to that sorrowing mother and ever afterward to the sex she represented;—throughout his life and in his death he has given to men a rule and guide for the estimation of woman as an equal, as a helper, as a friend, and as a sacred charge to be sheltered and cared for with a brother's love and sympathy, lessons which nineteen centuries' gigantic strides in knowledge, arts, and sciences, in social and ethical principles have not been able to probe to their depth or to exhaust in practice.

It seems not too much to say then of the vitalizing, regenerating, and progressive influence of womanhood on the civilization of to-day, that, while it was foreshadowed among Germanic nations in the far away dawn of their history as a narrow, sickly and stunted growth, it yet owes its catholicity and power, the deepening of its roots and broadening of its branches to Christianity.

The union of these two forces, the Barbaric and the Christian, was not long delayed after the Fall of the Empire. The Church, which fell with Rome, finding herself in danger of being swallowed up by barbarism, with characteristic vigor and fertility of resources, addressed herself immediately to the task of conquering her conquerors. The means chosen does credit to her power of penetration and adaptability, as well as to her profound, unerring, all-compassing diplomacy; and makes us even now wonder if aught human can successfully and ultimately withstand her far-seeing designs and brilliant policy, or gainsay her well-earned claim to the word *Catholic.*

She saw the barbarian, little more developed than a wild beast. She forbore to antagonize and mystify his warlike nature by a full blaze of the heartsearching and humanizing tenets of her great Head. She said little of the rule "If thy brother smite thee on one cheek, turn to him the other also"; but thought it sufficient for the needs of those times, to establish the so-called "Truce of God" under which men were bound to abstain from butchering one another for three days of each week and on Church festivals. In other words, she respected their individuality: non-resistance pure and simple being for them an utter impossibility, she contented herself with less radical measures calculated to lead up finally to the full measure of the benevolence of Christ.

Next she took advantage of the barbarian's sensuous love of gaudy display and put all her magnificent garments on. She could not capture him by physical force, she would dazzle him by gorgeous spectacles. It is said that Romanism[11] gained more in pomp and ritual during this trying period of the Dark Ages than throughout all her former history.

The result was she carried her point. Once more Rome laid her ambitious hand on the temporal power, and allied with Charlemagne, aspired to rule the world through a civilization dominated by Christianity and permeated by the traditions and instincts of those sturdy barbarians.

Here was the confluence of the two streams we have been tracing, which, united now, stretch before us as a broad majestic river. In regard to

---

11. By Romanism, Cooper means Roman Catholicism.

woman it was the meeting of two noble and ennobling forces, two kindred ideas the resultant of which, we doubt not, is destined to be a potent force in the betterment of the world.

Now after our appeal to history comparing nations destitute of this force and so destitute also of the principle of progress, with other nations among whom the influence of woman is prominent coupled with a brisk, progressive, satisfying civilization,—if in addition we find this strong presumptive evidence corroborated by reason and experience, we may conclude that these two equally varying concomitants are linked as cause and effect; in other words, that the position of woman in society determines the vital elements of its regeneration and progress.

Now that this is so on *a priori* grounds all must admit. And this not because woman is better or stronger or wiser than man, but from the nature of the case, because it is she who must first form the man by directing the earliest impulses of his character.

Byron and Wordsworth were both geniuses and would have stamped themselves on the thought of their age under any circumstances; and yet we find the one a savor of life unto life, the other of death into death. "Byron, like a rocket, shot his way upward with scorn and repulsion, flamed out in wild, explosive, brilliant excesses and disappeared in darkness made all the more palpable."[12]

Wordsworth lent of his gifts to reinforce that "power in the Universe which makes for righteousness" by taking the harp handed him from Heaven and using it to swell the strains of angelic choirs. Two locomotives equally mighty stand facing opposite tracks; the one to rush headlong to destruction with all its precious freight, the other to toil grandly and gloriously up the steep embattlements to Heaven and to God. Who—who can say what a world of consequences hung on the first placing and starting of these enormous forces!

Woman, Mother,—your responsibility is one that might make angels tremble and fear to take hold! To trifle with it, to ignore or misuse it, is to treat lightly the most sacred and solemn trust ever confided by God to human kind. The training of children is a task on which an infinity of weal or woe depends. Who does not covet it? Yet who does not stand awestruck before its momentous issues! It is a matter of small moment, it seems to me, whether that lovely girl in whose accomplishments you take such pride and delight, can enter the gay and crowded salon with the ease and

---

12. Bascom's Eng. Lit. p. 253. *AJC.*

elegance of this or that French or English gentlewoman, compared with the decision as to whether her individuality is going to reinforce the good or the evil elements of the world. The lace and the diamonds, the dance and the theater, gain a new significance when scanned in their bearings on such issues. Their influence on the individual personality, and through her on the society and civilization which she vitalizes and inspires—all this and more must be weighed in the balance before the jury can return a just and intelligent verdict as to the innocence or banefulness of these apparently simple amusements.

Now the fact of woman's influence on society being granted, what are its practical bearings on the work which brought together this conference of colored clergy and laymen in Washington? "We come not here to talk." Life is too busy, too pregnant with meaning and far reaching consequences to allow you to come this far for mere intellectual entertainment.

The vital agency of womanhood in the regeneration and progress of a race, as a general question, is conceded almost before it is fairly stated. I confess one of the difficulties for me in the subject assigned lay in its obviousness. The plea is taken away by the opposite attorney's granting the whole question.

"Woman's influence on social progress"—who in Christendom doubts or questions it? One may as well be called on to prove that the sun is the source of light and heat and energy to this many-sided little world.

Nor, on the other hand, could it have been intended that I should apply the position when taken and proven, to the needs and responsibilities of the women of our race in the South. For is it not written, "Cursed is he that cometh after the king?" and has not the King already preceded me in "The Black Woman of the South"?[13]

They have had both Moses and the Prophets in Dr. Crummell and if they hear not him, neither would they be persuaded though one came up from the South.

I would beg, however, with the Doctor's permission, to add my plea for the *Colored Girls* of the South:—that large, bright, promising fatally beautiful class that stand shivering like a delicate plantlet before the fury of tempestuous elements, so full of promise and possibilities, yet so sure of

---

13. Cooper refers to a notable speech, "The Black Woman of the South: Her Neglects and Her Needs," by Dr. Alexander Crummell (1819–1898) on 15 August 1883. Crummell, an Episcopal clergyman, was one of the nineteenth century's prominent race-men. Cooper lived with the Crummell family in Washington, D.C., the year after she wrote the present chapter.

destruction; often without a father to whom they dare apply the loving term, often without a stronger brother to espouse their cause and defend their honor with his life's blood; in the midst of pitfalls and snares, waylaid by the lower classes of white men, with no shelter, no protection nearer than the great blue vault above, which half conceals and half reveals the one Care-Taker they know so little of. Oh, save them, help them, shield, train, develop, teach, inspire them! Snatch them, in God's name, as brands from the burning! There is material in them well worth your while, the hope in germ of a staunch, helpful, regenerating womanhood on which, primarily, rests the foundation stones of our future as a race.

It is absurd to quote statistics showing the Negro's bank account and rent rolls, to point to the hundreds of newspapers edited by colored men and lists of lawyers, doctors, professors, D.D.'s, LL.D.'s, etc., etc., etc., while the source from which the life-blood of the race is to flow is subject to taint and corruption in the enemy's camp.

True progress is never made by spasms. Real progress is growth. It must begin in the seed. Then, "first the blade, then the ear, after that the full corn in the ear." There is something to encourage and inspire us in the advancement of individuals since their emancipation from slavery. It at least proves that there is nothing irretrievably wrong in the shape of the black man's skull, and that under given circumstances his development, downward or upward, will be similar to that of other average human beings.

But there is no time to be wasted in mere felicitation. That the Negro has his niche in the infinite purposes of the Eternal, no one who has studied the history of the last fifty years in America will deny. That much depends on his own right comprehension of his responsibility and rising to the demands of the hour, it will be good for him to see; and how best to use his present so that the structure of the future shall be stronger and higher and brighter and nobler and holier than that of the past, is a question to be decided each day by every one of us.

The race is just twenty-one years removed from the conception and experience of a chattel, just at the age of ruddy manhood. It is well enough to pause a moment for retrospection, introspection, and prospection. We look back, not to become inflated with conceit because of the depths from which we have arisen, but that we may learn wisdom from experience. We look within that we may gather together once more our forces, and, by improved and more practical methods, address ourselves to the tasks before us. We look forward with hope and trust that the same God whose guiding hand led our fathers through and out of the gall and bitterness of oppression, will still lead and direct their children, to the honor of His name, and for their ultimate salvation.

But this survey of the failures or achievements of the past, the difficulties and embarrassments of the present, and the mingled hopes and fears for the future, must not degenerate into mere dreaming nor consume the time which belongs to the practical and effective handling of the crucial questions of the hour; and there can be no issue more vital and momentous than this of the womanhood of the race.

Here is the vulnerable point, not in the heel, but at the heart of the young Achilles; and here must the defenses be strengthened and the watch redoubled.

We are the heirs of a past which was not our fathers' moulding. "Every man the arbiter of his own destiny" was not true for the American Negro of the past: and it is no fault of his that he finds himself to-day the inheritor of a manhood and womanhood impoverished and debased by two centuries and more of compression and degradation.

But weaknesses and malformations, which to-day are attributable to a vicious schoolmaster and a pernicious system, will a century hence be rightly regarded as proofs of innate corruptness and radical incurability.

Now the fundamental agency under God in the regeneration, the retraining of the race, as well as the ground work and starting point of its progress upward, must be the *black woman.*

With all the wrongs and neglects of her past, with all the weakness, the debasement, the moral thralldom of her present, the black woman of to-day stands mute and wondering at the Herculean task devolving upon her. But the cycles wait for her. No other hand can move the lever. She must be loosed from her hands and set to work.

Our meager and superficial results from past efforts prove their futility; and every attempt to elevate the Negro, whether undertaken by himself or through the philanthropy of others, cannot but prove abortive unless so directed as to utilize the indispensable agency of an elevated and trained womanhood.

A race cannot be purified from without. Preachers and teachers are helps, and stimulants and conditions as necessary as the gracious rain and sunshine are to plant growth. But what are rain and dew and sunshine and cloud if there be no life in the plant germ? We must go to the root and see that that is sound and healthy and vigorous; and not deceive ourselves with waxen flowers and painted leaves of mock chlorophyll.

We too often mistake individuals' honor for race development and so are ready to substitute pretty accomplishments for sound sense and earnest purpose.

A stream cannot rise higher than its source. The atmosphere of homes is no rarer and purer and sweeter than are the mothers in those homes. A race is but a total of families. The nation is the aggregate of its homes. As the whole is sum of all its parts, so the character of the parts will determine the characteristics of the whole. These are all axioms and so evident that it seems gratuitous to remark it; and yet, unless I am greatly mistaken, most of the unsatisfaction from our past results arises from just such a radical and palpable error, as much almost on our own part as on that of our benevolent white friends.

The Negro is constitutionally hopeful and proverbially irrepressible; and naturally stands in danger of being dazzled by the shimmer and tinsel of superficials. We often mistake foliage for fruit and overestimate or wrongly estimate brilliant results.

The late Martin R. Delany,[14] who was an unadulterated black man, used to say when honors of state fell upon him, that when he entered the council of kings the black race entered with him; meaning, I suppose, that there was no discounting his race identity and attributing his achievements to some admixture of Saxon blood. But our present record of eminent men, when placed beside the actual status of the race in America to-day, proves that no man can represent the race. Whatever the attainments of the individual may be, unless his home has moved on *pari passu,* he can never be regarded as identical with or representative of the whole.

Not by pointing to sun-bathed mountain tops do we prove that Phoebus warms the valleys. We must point to homes, average homes, homes of the rank and file of horny handed toiling men and women of the South (where the masses are) lighted and cheered by the good, the beautiful, and the true,—then and not till then will the whole plateau be lifted into the sunlight.

Only the BLACK WOMAN can say "when and where I enter, in the quiet, undisputed dignity of my womanhood, without violence and without suing or special patronage, then and there the whole *Negro race enters with me.*" Is it not evident then that as individual workers for this race we must address ourselves with no half-hearted zeal to this feature of our mission. The need is felt and must be recognized by all. There is a call for

---

14. Martin R. Delany (1812–1885): physician, editor, and soldier. Along with Crummell, Delany was a proponent of emigration to Africa as a solution to slavery.

workers, for missionaries, for men and women with the double consecration of a fundamental love of humanity and a desire for its melioration through the Gospel; but superadded to this we demanded an intelligent and sympathetic comprehension of the interests and special needs of the Negro.

I see not why there should not be an organized effort for the protection and elevation of our girls such as the White Cross League in England. English women are strengthened and protected by more than twelve centuries of Christian influences, freedom and civilization; English girls are dispirited and crushed down by no such all-leveling prejudice as that supercilious caste spirit in America which cynically assumes "A Negro woman cannot be a lady." English womanhood is beset by no such snares and traps as betray the unprotected, untrained colored girl of the South, whose only crime and dire destruction often is her unconscious and marvelous beauty. Surely then if English indignation is aroused and English manhood thrilled under the leadership of a Bishop of the English church to build up bulwarks around their wronged sisters, Negro sentiment cannot remain callous and Negro efforts nerveless in view of the imminent peril of the mothers of the next generation. *"I am my Sister's keeper!"* should be the hearty response of every man and woman of the race, and this conviction should purify and exalt the narrow, selfish and petty personal aims of life into a noble and sacred purpose.

We need men who can let their interest and gallantry extend outside the circle of their aesthetic appreciation; men who can be a father, a brother, a friend to every weak, struggling unshielded girl. We need women who are so sure of their own social footing that they need not fear leaning to lend a hand to a fallen or falling sister. We need men and women who do not exhaust their genius splitting hairs on aristocratic distinctions and thanking God they are not as others; but earnest, unselfish souls, who can go into the highways and byways, lifting up and leading, advising and encouraging with the truly catholic benevolence of the Gospel of Christ.

As Church workers we must confess our path of duty is less obvious; or rather our ability to adapt our machinery to our conception of the peculiar exigencies of this work as taught by experience and our own consciousness of the needs of the Negro, is as yet not demonstrable. Flexibility and aggressiveness are not such strong characteristics of the Church to-day as in the Dark Ages.

As a Mission field for the Church the Southern Negro is in some aspects most promising; in others, perplexing. Aliens neither in language and customs, nor in associations and sympathies, naturally of deeply rooted religious instincts and taking most readily and kindly to the worship and teachings of the Church, surely the task of proselytizing the American Negro is infinitely less formidable than that which confronted the Church in the Barbarians of Europe. Besides, this people already look to the Church as the hope of their race. Thinking colored men almost uniformly admit that the Protestant Episcopal Church with its quiet, chaste dignity and decorous solemnity, its instructive and elevating ritual, its bright chanting and joyous hymning, is eminently fitted to correct the peculiar faults of worship—the rank exuberance and often ludicrous demonstrativeness of their people. Yet, strange to say, the Church, claiming to be missionary and Catholic, urging that schism is sin and denominationalism inexcusable, has made in all these years almost no inroads upon this semi-civilized regionalism.

Harvests from this over ripe field of home missions have been gathered in by Methodists, Baptists, and not least by Congregationalists, who were unknown to the Freedmen before their emancipation.

Our clergy numbers less than two dozen[15] priests of Negro blood and we have hardly more than one self-supporting colored congregation in the entire Southland. While the organization known as the A. M. E. Church[16] has 14,063 ministers, itinerant and local, 4,069 self-supporting churches, 4,275 Sunday-schools, with property valued at $7,772,284, raising yearly for church purposes $1,427,000.

Stranger and more significant than all, the leading men of this race (I do not mean demagogues and politicians, but men of intellect, heart, and race devotion, men to whom the elevation of their people means more than personal ambition and sordid gain—and the men of that stamp have not all died yet) the Christian workers for the race, of younger and more cultured growth, are noticeably drifting into sectarian churches, many of them declaring all the time that they acknowledge the historic claims of the Church, believe her apostolicity, and would experience greater personal comfort, spiritual and intellectual, in her revered communion. It is a fact which any one may verify for himself, that representative colored men, professing that in their heart of hearts they are Episcopalians, are actually working in Methodist and Baptist pulpits; while the ranks of the Episcopal

---

15. The published report of [18]91 shows 26 priests for the entire country, including one not engaged in work and one a professor in a non-sectarian school, since made Dean of an Episcopal Annex to Howard University known as King Hall. *AJC.*

16. African Methodist Episcopal Church.

clergy are left to be filled largely by men who certainly suggest the propriety of a "*perpetual* Diaconate" if they cannot be said to have created the necessity for it.

Now where is the trouble? Something must be wrong. What is it?

A certain Southern Bishop of our Church reviewing the situation, whether in Godly anxiety or in "Gothic antipathy" I know not, deprecates the fact that the colored people do not seem *drawn* to the Episcopal Church, and comes to the sage conclusion that the Church is not adapted to the rude untutored minds of the Freedmen, and that they may be left to go to the Methodists and Baptists whither their racial proclivities undeniably tend. How the good Bishop can agree that all-foreseeing Wisdom, and Catholic Love would have framed his Church as typified in his seamless garment and unbroken body, and yet not leave it broad enough and deep enough and loving enough to seek and save and hold seven millions of God's poor, I cannot see.

But the doctors while discussing their scientifically conclusive diagnosis of the disease, will perhaps not think it presumptuous in the patient if he dares to suggest where at least the pain is. If this be allowed, a *Black woman of the South* would beg to point out two possible oversights in this southern work which may indicate in part both a cause and a remedy for some failure. The first is *not calculating for the Black man's personality;* not having respect, if I may so express it, to his manhood or deferring at all to his conceptions of the needs of his people. When colored persons have been employed it was too often as machines or as manikins. There has been no disposition, generally, to get the black man's ideal or to let his individuality work by its own gravity, as it were. A conference of earnest Christian men have met at regular intervals for some years past to discuss the best methods of promoting the welfare and development of colored people in this country. Yet, strange as it may seem, they have never invited a colored man or even intimated that one would be welcome to take part in their deliberations. Their remedial contrivances are purely theoretical or empirical, therefore, and the whole machinery devoid of soul.

The second important oversight in my judgment is closely allied to this and probably grows out of it, and that is not developing Negro womanhood as an essential fundamental for the elevation of the race, and utilizing this agency in extending the work of the Church.

Of the first I have possibly already presumed to say too much since it does not strictly come within the province of my subject. However, Macaulay somewhere criticises the Church of England as not knowing how to use fanatics, and declares that had Ignatius Loyola been in the Anglican instead of the Roman communion, the Jesuits would have been schismatics instead of Catholics; and if the religious awakenings of the Wesleys had been in Rome, she would have shaven their heads, tied ropes around their waists, and sent them out under her own banner and blessing. Whether this be true or not, there is certainly a vast amount of force potential for Negro evangelization rendered latent, or worse, antagonistic by the halting, uncertain, I had almost said, *trimming* policy of the Church in the South. This may sound both presumptuous and ungrateful. It is mortifying, I know, to benevolent wisdom, after having spent itself in the execution of well conned theories for the ideal development of a particular work, to hear perhaps the weakest and humblest element of that work asking "what doest thou?"

Yet so it will be in life. The "thus far and no further" pattern cannot be fitted to any growth in God's kingdom. The universal law of development is "onward and upward." It is God-given and inviolable. From the unfolding of the germ in the acorn to reach the sturdy oak, to the growth of a human soul into the full knowledge and likeness of its Creator, the breadth and scope of the movement in each and all are too grand, too mysterious, too like God himself, to be encompassed and locked down in human molds.

After all the Southern slave owners were right: either the very alphabet of intellectual growth must be forbidden and the Negro dealt with absolutely as a chattel having neither rights nor sensibilities; or else the clamps and irons of mental and moral, as well as civil compression must be riven asunder and the truly enfranchised soul led to the entrance of that boundless vista through which it is to toil upwards to its beckoning God as the buried seed germ to meet the sun.

A perpetual colored diaconate, carefully and kindly superintended by the white clergy; congregations of shiny faced peasants with their clean white aprons and sunbonnets catechised at regular intervals and taught to recite the creed, the Lord's prayer and the ten commandments—duty towards God and duty towards neighbor, surely such well tended sheep ought to be grateful to their shepherds and content in that station of life to which it pleased God to call them. True, like the old professor lecturing to his solitary student, we make no provisions here for irregularities. "Questions must be kept till after class," or dispensed with altogether. That some do ask questions and insist on answers, in class too, must be both impertinent and annoying. Let not our spiritual pastors and masters however be grieved at such self-assertion as merely signifies we have a destiny to fulfill and as men and women we must *be about our Father's business.*

It is a mistake to suppose that the Negro is prejudiced against a white ministry. Naturally there is not a more kindly and implicit follower of a white man's guidance than the average colored peasant. What would to others be an ordinary act of friendly or pastoral interest he would be more inclined to regard gratefully as a condescension. And he never forgets such kindness. Could the Negro be brought near to his white priest or bishop, he is not suspicious. He is not only willing but often longs to unburden his soul to this intelligent guide. There are no reservations when he is convinced that you are his friend. It is a saddening satire on American history and manners that it takes something to convince him.

That our people are not "drawn" to a church whose chief dignitaries they see only in the chancel, and whom they reverence as they would a painting or an angel, whose life never comes down to and touches theirs with the inspiration of an objective reality, may be "perplexing" truly (American caste and American Christianity both being facts) but it need not be surprising. There must be something of human nature in it, the same as that which brought about that "the Word was made flesh and dwelt among us" that He might "draw" us towards God.

Men are not "drawn" by abstractions. Only sympathy and love can draw, and until our Church in America realizes this and provides a clergy that can come in touch with our life and have a fellow feeling for our woes, without being imbedded and frozen up in their "Gothic antipathies," the good bishops are likely to continue "perplexed" by the sparsity of colored Episcopalians.

A colored priest of my acquaintance recently related to me, with tears in his eyes, how his reverend Father in God, the Bishop who had ordained him, had met him on the cars on his way to the diocesan convention and warned him, not unkindly, not to take a seat in the body of the convention with the white clergy. To avoid disturbance of their godly placidity he would of course please sit back and somewhat apart. I do not imagine that that clergyman had very much heart for the Christly (!) deliberations of that convention.

To return, however, it is not on this broader view of Church work, which I mentioned as a primary cause of its halting progress with the colored people, that I am to speak. My proper theme is the second oversight of which in my judgment our Christian propagandists have been guilty:

or, the necessity of church training, protecting and uplifting our colored womanhood as indispensable to the evangelization of the race.

Apelles[17] did not disdain even that criticism of his lofty art which came from an uncouth cobbler; and may I not hope that the writer's oneness with her subject both in feeling and in being may palliate undue obtrusiveness of opinions here. That the race cannot be effectually lifted up till its women are truly elevated we take as proven. It is not for us to dwell on the needs, the neglects, and the ways of succor, pertaining to the black woman of the South. The ground has been ably discussed and an admirable and practical plan proposed by the oldest Negro priest in America, advising and urging that special organizations such as Church Sisterhoods and industrial schools be advised to meet her pressing needs in the Southland. That some such movements are vital to the life of this people and the extension of the Church among them, is not hard to see. Yet the pamphlet fell stillborn from the press. So far as I am informed the Church has made no motion towards carrying out Dr. Crummell's suggestion.

The denomination which comes next [to] our own in opposing the proverbial emotionalism of Negro worship in the South, and which in consequence like ours receives the cold shoulder from the old heads, resting as we do under the charge of not "having religion" and not believing in conversion—the Congregationalists—have quietly gone to work on the young, have established industrial and training schools, and now almost every community in the South is yearly enriched by a fresh infusion of vigorous young hearts, cultivated heads, and helpful hands that have been trained at Fisk, at Hampton, in Atlanta University, and in Tuskegee, Alabama.

These young people are missionaries actual or virtual both here and in Africa. They have learned to love the methods and doctrines of the Church which trained and educated them; and so Congregationalism surely and steadily progresses.

Need I compare these well known facts with results shown by the Church in the same field and during the same or even a longer time.

The institution of the Church in the South to which she mainly looks for the training of her colored clergy and for the help of the "Black Woman" and "Colored Girl" of the South, has graduated since the year 1868, when the school was founded, *five young women,*[18] and while yearly

---

17. Appelles (fourth century B.C.): Greek painter.
18. Five have been graduated since [18]86, two in [18]91, two in [18]92. *AJC.*

numerous young men have been kept and trained for the ministry by the charities of the Church, the number of indigent females who have here been supported, sheltered and trained, is phenomenally small. Indeed, to my mind, the attitude of the Church toward this feature of her work is as if the solution of the problem of Negro missions depended solely on sending a quota of deacons and priests into the field, girls being a sort of *tertium quid* whose development may be promoted if they can pay their way and fall in with the plans mapped out for the training of the other sex. Now I would ask in all earnestness, does not this force potential deserve by education and stimulus to be made dynamic? Is it not a solemn duty incumbent on all colored churchmen to make it so? Will not the aid of the Church be given to prepare our girls in head, heart, and hand for the duties and responsibilities that await the intelligent wife, the Christian mother, the earnest, virtuous, helpful woman, at once both the lever and the fulcrum for uplifting the race.

As Negroes and churchmen we cannot be indifferent to these questions. They touch us most vitally on both sides. We believe in the Holy Catholic Church. We believe that however gigantic and apparently remote the consummation, the Church will go on conquering and to conquer till the kingdoms of this world, not excepting the black man and the black woman of the South, shall have become the kingdoms of the Lord and of his Christ.

That past work in this direction has been unsatisfactory we must admit. That without a change of policy results in the future will be as meagre, we greatly fear. Our life as a race is at stake. The dearest interests of our hearts are in the scale. We must either break away from dear old landmarks and plunge out in any line and every line that enables us to meet the pressing need of our people, or we must ask the Church to allow and help us, untrammelled by the prejudices and theories of individuals, to work aggressively under her direction as we alone can, with God's help, for the salvation of our people.

The time is ripe for action. Self-seeking and ambition must be laid on the altar. The battle is one of sacrifice and hardship, but our duty is plain. We have been recipients of missionary bounty in some sort for twenty-one years. Not even the senseless vegetable is content to be a mere reservoir. Receiving without giving is an anomaly in nature. Nature's cells are all little workshops for manufacturing sunbeams, the product to be *given out* to earth's inhabitants in warmth, energy, thought, action. Inanimate creation always pays back an equivalent.

Now, *How much owest thou my Lord?* Will his account be overdrawn if he call for singleness of purpose and self-sacrificing labor for your brethren? Having passed through your drill school, will you refuse a general's commission even if it entail responsibility, risk and anxiety, with possibly some adverse criticism? Is it too much to ask you to step forward and direct the work for your race along those lines which you know to be of first and vital importance?

Will you allow these words of Ralph Waldo Emerson? "In ordinary," says he,

we have a snappish criticism which watches and contradicts the opposite party. We want the will which advances and dictates [acts]. Nature has made up her mind that what cannot defend itself, shall not be defended. Complaining never so loud and with never so much reason, is of no use. What cannot stand must fall; *and the measure of our sincerity and therefore of the respect of men is the amount of health and wealth we will hazard in the defense of our right.*

· 4 ·

The Higher Education of Women
(1890–1891)

 $\mathcal{I}$ n the very first year of our century, the year 1801, there appeared in Paris a book by Silvain Marechal, entitled *Shall Woman Learn the Alphabet.* The book proposes a law prohibiting the alphabet to women, and quotes authorities weighty and various, to prove that the woman who knows the alphabet has already lost part of her womanliness. The author declares that women can use the alphabet only as Molière predicted they would, in spelling out the verb *amo;* that they have no occasion to peruse Ovid's *Ars Amoris,* since that is already the ground and limit of their intuitive furnishing; that Madame Guion would have been far more adorable had she remained a beautiful ignoramus as nature made her; that Ruth, Naomi, and Spartan woman, the Amazons, Penelope, Andromache, Lucretia, Joan of Arc, Petrarch's Laura, the daughters of Charlemagne, could not spell their names; while Sappho, Aspasia, Madame de Maintenon, and Madame de Staël could read altogether too well for their good; finally, that if women were once permitted to read Sophocles and work with logarithms, or to nibble at any side of the apple of knowledge, there would be an end forever to their sewing on buttons and embroidering slippers.

Please remember this book was published at the *beginning* of the Nineteenth Century. At the end of its first third, (in the year 1833) one solitary college in America decided to admit women within its sacred precincts, and organized what was called a "Ladies' Course" as well as the regular B.A. or Gentlemen's course.

It was felt to be an experiment—a rather dangerous experiment—and was adopted with fear and trembling by the good fathers, who looked as if they had been caught secretly mixing explosive compounds and were guiltily expecting every moment to see the foundations under them shaken and rent and their fair superstructure shattered into fragments.

But the girls came, and there was no upheaval. They performed their

72

tasks modestly and intelligently. Once in a while one or two were found choosing the gentlemen's course. Still no collapse; and the dear, careful, scrupulous, frightened old professors were just getting their hearts out of their throats and preparing to draw one good free breath, when they found they would have to change the names of those courses; for there were as many ladies in the gentlemen's course as in the ladies', and a distinctively Ladies's Course, inferior in scope and aim to the regular classical course, did not and could not exist.

Other colleges gradually fell into line, and to-day there are one hundred and ninety-eight colleges for women, and two hundred and seven coeducational colleges and universities in the United States alone offering the degree of B.A. to women, and sending out yearly into the arteries of this nation a warm, rich flood of strong, brave, active, energetic, well-equipped, thoughtful women—women quick to see and eager to help the needs of this needy world—women who can think as well as feel, and who feel none the less because they think—women who are none the less tender and true for the parchment scroll they bear in their hands—women who have given a deeper, richer, nobler and grander meaning to the word "womanly" than any one-sided masculine definition could ever have suggested or inspired—women whom the world has long waited for in pain and anguish till there should be at last added to its forces and allowed to permeate its thought the complement of that masculine influence which has dominated it for fourteen centuries.

Since the idea of order and subordination succumbed to barbarian brawn and brutality in the fifth century, the civilized world has been like a child brought up by his father. It has needed the great mother heart to teach it to be pitiful, to love mercy, to succor the weak and care for the lowly.

Whence came this apotheosis of greed and cruelty? Whence this sneaking admiration we all have for bullies and prize-fighters? Whence the self-congratulation of "dominant" races, as if "dominant" meant "righteous" and carried with it a title to inherit the earth? Whence the scorn of so-called weak or unwarlike races and individuals, and the very comfortable assurance that it is their manifest destiny to be wiped out as vermin before this advancing civilization? As if the possession of the Christian graces of meekness, nonresistance and forgiveness, were incompatible with the civilization professedly based on Christianity, the religion of love! Just listen to this little bit of Barbarian brag:

As for Far Orientals, they are not of those who will survive. Artistic attractive people that they are, their civilization is like their own tree flowers, beautiful blossoms destined never to bear fruit. If these people continue in their old course, their earthly career is closed. Just as surely as morning passes into afternoon, so surely are these races of the Far East, if unchanged, destined to disappear before the advancing nations of the West. Vanish, they will, off the face of the earth, and leave our planet the eventual possession of the dwellers where the day declines. Unless their newly imported ideas really take root, it is from this whole world that Japanese and Koreans, as well as Chinese, will inevitably be excluded. Their Nirvana is already being realized; already, it has wrapped Far Eastern Asia in its winding sheet.[1]

Delightful reflection for "the dwellers where day declines." A spectacle to make the gods laugh, truly, to see the scion of an upstart race by one sweep of his generalizing pen consigning to annihilation one-third the inhabitants of the globe—a people whose civilization was hoary headed before the parent elements that begot his race had advanced beyond nebulosity.

How like Longfellow's Iagoo, we Westerners are, to be sure! In the few hundred years . . . we have had to strut across our allotted territory and bask in the afternoon sun, we imagine we have exhausted the possibilities of humanity. Verily, we are the people, and after us there is none other. Our God is power; strength, our standard of excellence, inherited from barbarian ancestors through a long line of male progenitors, the Law Salic permitting no feminine modifications.

Says one, "The Chinaman is not popular with us, and we do not like the Negro. It is not that the eyes of the one are set bias, and the other is dark-skinned; but the Chinaman, the Negro is weak—*and Anglo Saxons don't like weakness.*"

The world of thought under the predominant man-influence, unmollified and unrestrained by its complementary force, would become like Daniel's fourth beast: "dreadful and terrible, and *strong* exceedingly"; "it had great iron teeth; it devoured and brake in pieces, and stamped the residue with the feet of it"; and the most independent of us find ourselves ready at times to fall down and worship this incarnation of power.

Mrs. Mary A. Livermore,[2] a woman whom I can mention only to

---

1. Percival Lowell, *Soul of the Far East.* Lowell (1855–1916): American astronomer best known for predicting the existence of the planet Pluto, also traveled in China and Japan.

2. Mary A. Livermore (1820–1905): American suffragist and reformer, editor of the *Agitator.* Probably the source of ". . . Anglo Saxons don't like weakness," above. See also p. 162.

admire, came near shaking my faith a few weeks ago in my theory of the thinking woman's mission to put in the tender and sympathetic chord in nature's grand symphony, and counteract, or better, harmonize the diapason of mere strength and might.

She was dwelling on the Anglo-Saxon genius for power and his contempt for weakness, and described a scene in San Francisco which she had witnessed.

The incorrigible animal known as the American small-boy, had pounced upon a simple, unoffending Chinaman, who was taking home his work, and had emptied the beautifully laundried contents of his basket into the ditch. "And," said she, "when that great man stood there and blubbered before that crowd of lawless urchins, to any one of whom he might have taught a lesson with his two fists, *I didn't much care.*"

This is said like a man! It grates harshly. It smacks of the worship of the beast. It is contempt for weakness, and taken out of its setting it seems to contradict my theory. It either shows that one of the highest exponents of the Higher Education can be at times untrue to the instincts I have ascribed to the thinking woman and to the contribution she is to add to the civilized world, or else the influence she wields upon our civilization may be potent without being necessarily and always direct and conscious. The latter is the case. Her voice may strike a false note, but her whole being is musical with vibrations of human suffering. Her tongue may parrot over the cold conceits that some man has taught her, but her heart is aglow with sympathy and loving kindness, and she cannot be true to her real self without giving out these elements into the forces of the world.

No one is in any danger of imagining Mark Antony "a plain blunt man," nor Cassius a sincere one—whatever the speeches they may make.

As individuals, we are constantly and inevitably, whether we are conscious of it or not, giving out our real selves into our several little worlds, inexorably adding our own true ray to the flood of starlight, quite independently of our professions and our masquerading; and so in the world of thought, the influence of thinking woman far transcends her feeble declamation and may seem at times even opposed to it.

A visitor in Oberlin once said to the lady principal, "Have you no rabble in Oberlin? How is it I see no police here, and yet the streets are as quiet and orderly as if there were an officer of the law standing on every corner."

Mrs. Johnston replied, "Oh, yes; there are vicious persons in Oberlin just as in other towns—*but our girls are our police.*"

With from five to ten hundred pure-minded young women threading the streets of the village every evening unattended, vice must slink away, like frost before the rising sun: and yet I venture to say there was not one in a hundred of those girls who would not have run from a street brawl as she would from a mouse, and who would not have declared she could never stand the sight of blood and pistols.

There is, then, a real and special influence of woman. An influence subtle and often involuntary, an influence so intimately interwoven in, so intricately interpenetrated by the masculine influence of the time that it is often difficult to extricate the delicate meshes and analyze and identify the closely clinging fibers. And yet, without this influence—so long as woman sat with bandaged eyes and manacled hands, fast bound in the clamps of ignorance and inaction, the world of thought moved in its orbit like the revolutions of the moon; with one face (the man's face) always out, so that the spectator could not distinguish whether it was disc or sphere.

Now I claim that it is the prevalence of the Higher Education among women, the making it a common everyday affair for women to reason and think and express their thought, the training and stimulus which enable and encourage women to administer to the world the bread it needs as well as the sugar it cries for; in short it is the transmitting the potential forces of her soul into dynamic factors that has given symmetry and completeness to the world's agencies. So only could it be consummated that Mercy, the lesson she teaches, and Truth, the task man has set himself, should meet together: that righteousness, or *rightness,* man's ideal,—and *peace,* its necessary "other half," should kiss each other.

We must thank the general enlightenment and independence of woman (which we may now regard as a *fait accompli*) that both these forces are now at work in the world, and it is fair to demand from them for the twentieth century a higher type of civilization than any attained in the nineteenth. Religion, science, art, economics, have all needed the feminine flavor; and literature, the expression of what is permanent and best in all of these, may be gauged at any time to measure the strength of the feminine ingredient. You will not find theology consigning infants to lakes of unquenchable fire long after women have had a chance to grasp, master, and wield its dogmas. You will not find science annihilating personality from the government of the Universe and making of God an ungovernable, unintelligible, blind, often destructive physical force; you will not find jurisprudence formulating as an axiom the absurdity that man and wife are one, and that one the man—that the married woman may not hold or bequeath her own property save as subject to her husband's direction; you will not find political economists declaring that the only possible adjustment between laborers and capitalists is that of selfishness and rapacity—that each must get all he can and keep all that he gets, while the world cries *laissez-faire* and the lawyers explain, "it is the beautiful working of the law of supply and demand"; in fine, you will not find the law of love shut out from the affairs of men after the feminine half of the world's truth is completed.

Nay, put your ear now close to the pulse of the time. What is the keynote of the literature of these days? What is the banner cry of all the activities of the last half decade? What is the dominant seventh which is to add richness and tone to the final cadences of this century and lead by a grand modulation into the triumphant harmonies of the next? It is not compassion for the poor and unfortunate, and, as Bellamy[3] has expressed it, "indignant outcry against the failure of the social machinery as it is, to ameliorate the miseries of men!" Even Christianity is being brought to the bar of humanity and tried by the standard of its ability to alleviate the world's suffering and lighten and brighten its woe. What else can be the meaning of Matthew Arnold's[4] saddening protest, "We cannot do without Christianity," cried he, "and we cannot endure it as it is."

When went there by an age, when so much time and thought, so much money and labor were given to God's poor and God's invalids, the lowly and unlovely, the sinning as well as the suffering—homes for inebriates and homes for lunatics, shelter for the aged and shelter for babes, hospitals for the sick, props and braces for the falling, reformatory prisons and prison reformatories, all show that a "mothering" influence from some source is leavening the nation.

Now please understand me. I do not ask you to admit that these benefactions and virtues are the exclusive possession of women, or even that women are their chief and only advocates. It may be a man who formulates and makes them vocal. It may be, and often is, a man who weeps over the wrongs and struggles for the amelioration: but that man has imbibed those impulses from a mother rather than from a father and is simply materializing and giving back to the world in tangible form the ideal love and tenderness, devotion and care that have cherished and nourished the helpless period of his own existence.

---

3. Edward Bellamy (1850–1898): author of the utopian novel *Looking Backward*.
4. Matthew Arnold (1822–1888): English poet and critic.

All I claim is that there is a feminine as well as a masculine side to truth; that these are related not as inferior and superior, not as better and worse, not as weaker and stronger, but as complements—complements in one necessary and symmetric whole. That as the man is more noble in reason, so the woman is more quick in sympathy. That as he is indefatigable in pursuit of abstract truth, so is she in caring for the interests by the way—striving tenderly and lovingly that not one of the least of these "little ones" should perish. That while we not unfrequently see women who reason, we say, with the coolness and precision of a man, and men as considerate of helplessness as a woman, still there is a general consensus of mankind that the one trait is essentially masculine and the other is peculiarly feminine. That both are needed to be worked into the training of children, in order that our boys may supplement their virility by tenderness and sensibility, and our girls may round out their gentleness by strength and self-reliance. That, as both are alike necessary in giving symmetry to the individual, so a nation or a race will degenerate into mere emotionalism on the one hand, or bullyism on the other, if dominated by either exclusively; lastly, and most emphatically, that the feminine factor can have its proper effect only through women's development and education so that she may fitly and intelligently stamp her force on the forces of her day, and add her modicum to the riches of the world's thought.

> For woman's cause is man's: they rise or sink
> Together, dwarfed or godlike, bond or free:
> For she that out of Lethe scales with man
> The shining steps of nature, shares with man
> His nights, his days, moves with him to one goal.
> If she be small, slight-natured, miserable,
> How shall men grow?
> ★ ★ ★ Let her make herself her own
> To give or keep, to live and learn and be
> All that not harms distinctive womanhood.
> For woman is not undeveloped man
> But diverse: could we make her as the man
> Sweet love were slain; his dearest bond is this,
> Not like to like, but like in difference.
> Yet in the long years liker must they grow;
> The man be more of woman, she of man;
> He gain in sweetness and in moral height,
> Nor lose the wrestling thews that throw the world;

> She mental breadth, nor fail in childward care,
> Nor lose the childlike in the larger mind;
> Till at the last she set herself to man,
> Like perfect music unto noble words.

Now you will argue, perhaps, and rightly, that higher education for women is not a modern idea, and that, if that is the means of setting free and invigorating the long desired feminine force in the world, it has already had a trial and should, in the past, have produced some of these glowing effects. Sappho,[5] the bright, sweet singer of Lesbos, "the violet-crowned, pure, sweetly smiling Sappho" as Alcaeus calls her, chanted her lyrics and poured forth her soul nearly six centuries before Christ, in notes as full and free, as passionate and eloquent as did ever Archilochus or Anacreon.

Aspasia,[6] that earliest queen of the drawing-room, a century later ministered to the intellectual entertainment of Socrates and the leading wits and philosophers of her time. Indeed, to her is attributed, by the best critics, the authorship of one of the most noted speeches ever delivered by Pericles.

Later on, during the Renaissance period, women were professors in mathematics, physics, metaphysics, and the classic languages in Bologna, Pavia, Padua, and Brescia. Olympia Fulvia Morata, of Ferrara, a most interesting character, whose magnificent library was destroyed in 1553 in the invasion of Schweinfurt by Albert of Brandenburg, had acquired a most extensive education. It is said that this wonderful girl gave lectures on classical subjects in her sixteenth year, and had even before that written several very remarkable Greek and Latin poems, and what is also to the point, she married a professor at Heidelberg, and became a *help-meet for him.*

It is true then that the higher education for women—in fact, the highest that the world has ever witnessed—belongs to the past; but we must remember that it was possible, down to the middle or our own century, only to a select few; and that the fashions and traditions of the times were before that all against it. There were not only no stimuli to encourage women to make the most of their powers and to welcome their development as a helpful agency in the progress of civilization, but their little aspirations, when they had any, were chilled and snubbed in embryo, and any attempt at thought was received as a monstrous usurpation of man's prerogative.

---

5. Sappho (610–580 B.C.): Greek lyric poet.
6. Aspasia (fifth century B.C.): mistress of Pericles of Athens.

Lessing declared that "the woman who thinks is like the man who puts on rouge—ridiculous"; and Voltaire in his coarse, flippant way used to say, "Ideas are like beards—women and boys have none." Dr. Maginn remarked, "We like to hear a few words of sense from a woman sometimes, as we do from a parrot—they are so unexpected!" and even the pious Fénelon[7] taught that virgin delicacy is almost as incompatible with learning as with vice.

That the average woman retired before these shafts of wit and ridicule and even gloried in her ignorance is not surprising. The Abbé Choisi, it is said, praised the Duchesse de Fontanges as being pretty as an angel and silly as a goose, and all the young ladies of the court strove to make up in folly what they lacked in charms. The ideal of the day was that "woman must be pretty, dress prettily, flirt prettily, and not be too well informed"; that it was the *summum bonum* of her early hopes to have, as Thackeray puts it, "all the fellows battling to dance with her"; that she had no God-given destiny, no soul with unquenchable longings and inexhaustible possibilities—no work of her own to do and give to the world—no absolute and inherent value, no duty to self, transcending all pleasure-giving that may be demanded of a mere toy; but that her value was purely a relative one and to be estimated as are the fine arts—by the pleasure they give. "Woman, wine and song," as "the world's best gifts to man," were linked together in praise with as little thought of the first saying, "What doest thou," as that the wine and the song should declare, "We must be about our Father's business."

Men believed, or pretended to believe, that the great law of self development was obligatory on their half of the human family only; that while it was the chief end of man to glorify God and put his five talents to the exchangers, gaining thereby other five, it was, or ought to be, the sole end of woman to glorify man and wrap her one talent decently away in a napkin, retiring into "Hezekiah Smith's lady during her natural life and Hezekiah Smith's relict on her tombstone"; that higher education was incompatible with the shape of the female cerebrum, and that even if it could be acquired it must inevitably unsex woman destroying the lisping, clinging, tenderly helpless, and beautifully dependent creatures whom men would so heroically think for and so gallantly fight for, and giving in their stead a formidable race of blue stockings with corkscrew ringlets and other spinster propensities.

---

7. François de Salignac de la Mothe Fénelon (1651–1715): French Catholic theologian.

But these are eighteenth century ideas.

We have seen how the pendulum has swung across our present century. The men of our time have asked with Emerson, "that woman only show us how she can best be served"; and woman has replied: the chance of the seedling and of the animalcule is all I ask—the chance for growth and self development, the permission to be true to the aspirations of my soul without incurring the blight of your censure and ridicule. "Audet viris concurrere virgo."

In soul-culture woman at last dares to contend with men, and we may cite Grant Allen (who certainly cannot be suspected of advocating the unsexing of woman) as an example of the broadening effect of this contest on the ideas at least of the men of the day. He says in his *Plain Words on the Woman Question,* recently published:

> The position of women was not [in the past a] position which could bear the test of nineteenth-century scrutiny. Their education was inadequate, their social status was humiliating, their political power was nil, their practical and personal grievances were innumerable; above all, their relations to the family—to their husbands, their children, their friends, their property—were simply insupportable.

And again:

> As a body we "Advanced men" are, I think, prepared to reconsider, and to reconsider fundamentally, without prejudice or misconception, the entire question of the relation between the sexes. We are ready to make any modifications in those relations which will satisfy the woman's just aspiration for personal independence, for intellectual and moral development, for physical culture, for political activity, and for a voice in the arrangement of her own affairs, both domestic and national.

Now this is magnanimous enough, surely; and quite a step from eighteenth century preaching, is it not? The higher education of Woman has certainly developed the men;—let us see what it has done for the women.

Matthew Arnold during his last visit to America in [18]82 or [18]83, lectured before a certain co-educational college in the West. After the lecture he remarked, with some surprise, to a lady professor, that the young women in his audience, he noticed, "paid as close attention as the men, *all the way through.*" This led, of course, to a spirited discussion of the higher education for women, during which he said to his enthusiastic interlocutor, eyeing her philosophically through his English eyeglass: "But—eh—don't you think it—eh—spoils their *chawnces,* you know!"

Now, as to the result to women, this is the most serious argument ever used against the higher education. If it interferes with marriage, classical training has a grave objection to weigh and answer.

For I agree with Mr. Allen[8] at least on this one point, that there must be marrying and giving in marriage even till the end of time.

I grant you that intellectual development, with the self-reliance and capacity for earning a livelihood which it gives, renders woman less dependent on the marriage relation for physical support (which, by the way, does not always accompany it). Neither is she compelled to look to sexual love as the one sensation capable of giving tone and relish, movement and vim to the life she leads. Her horizon is extended. Her sympathies are broadened and deepened and multiplied. She is in closer touch with nature. Not a bud that opens, not a dew drop, not a ray of light, not a cloud-burst or a thunderbolt, but adds to the expansiveness and zest of her soul. And if the sun of an absorbing passion be gone down, still 'tis night that brings the stars. She has remaining the mellow, less obtrusive, but none the less enchanting and inspiring light of friendship, and into its charmed circle she may gather the best the world has known. She can commune with Socrates about the *daimon* he knew and to which she too can bear witness; she can revel in the majesty of Dante, the sweetness of Virgil, the simplicity of Homer, and strength of Milton. She can listen to the pulsing heart throbs of passionate Sappho's encaged soul, as she beats her bruised wings against her prison bars and struggles to flutter out into Heaven's aether, and the fires of her own soul cry back as she listens. "Yes; Sappho, I know it all; I know it all." Here, at last, can be communion without suspicion; friendship without misunderstanding; love without jealousy.

We must admit then that Byron's picture, whether a thing of beauty or not, has faded from the canvas of to-day. "Man's love," he wrote,

> is of man's life a thing apart,
> 'Tis woman's whole existence.
> Man may range the court, camp, church, the vessel and the mart,
> Sword, gown, gain, glory offer in exchange.
> Pride, fame, ambition, to fill up his heart—
> And few there are whom these cannot estrange.

---

8. Reference to Grant Allen, author of *Plain Words on the Woman Question,* quoted on page 81.

Men have all these resources, we *but one*—
To love again and be again undone.

This may have been true when written. *It is not true to-day.* The old, subjective, stagnant, indolent and wretched life for woman has gone. She has as many resources as men, as many activities beckon her on. As large possibilities swell and inspire her heart.

Now, then, does it destroy or diminish her capacity for loving?

Her standards have undoubtedly gone up. The necessity of speculating in "chawnces" has probably shifted. The question is not now with the woman "How shall I so cramp, stunt, simplify and nullify myself as to make me eligible to the honor of being swallowed up into some little man?" but the problem, I trow, now rests with the man as to how he can so develop his God-given powers as to reach the ideal of a generation of women who demand the noblest, grandest and best achievements of which he is capable; and this surely is the only fair and natural adjustment of the chances. Nature never meant that the ideals and standards of the world should be dwarfing and minimizing ones, and the men should thank us for requiring of them the richest fruits which they can grow. If it makes them work, all the better for them.

As to the adaptability of the educated woman to the marriage relation, I shall simply quote from that excellent symposium of learned women that appeared recently under Mrs. Armstrong's signature in answer to the *Plain Words* of Mr. Allen,[9] already referred to.

> Admitting no longer any question as to their intellectual equality with the men whom they meet, with the simplicity of conscious strength, they take their place beside the men who challenge them, and fearlessly face the result of their actions. They deny that their education in any way unfits them for the duty of wifehood and maternity or primarily renders these conditions any less attractive to them than to the domestic type of woman. On the contrary, they hold that their knowledge of physiology makes them better mothers and housekeepers; their knowledge of chemistry makes them better cooks; while from their training in other natural sciences and in mathematics, they obtain an accuracy and fair-mindedness which is of great value to them in dealing with their children or employees.

---

9. See note 8. Cooper is quoting Allen extensively in the previous three pages.

So much for their willingness. Now the apple may be good for food and pleasant to the eyes, and a fruit to be desired to make one wise. Nay, it may even assure you that it has no aversion whatever to being tasted. Still, if you do not like the flavor all these recommendations are nothing. Is the intellectual woman *desirable* in the matrimonial market?

This I cannot answer. I confess my ignorance. I am no judge of such things. I have been told that strong-minded women could be, when they thought it worth their while, quite endurable, and, judging from the number of female names I find in college catalogues among the alumnae with double patronymics, I surmise that quite a number of men are willing to put up with them.

Now I would that my task ended here. Having shown that a great want of the world in the past has been a feminine force; that that force can have its full effect only through the untrammelled development of woman; that such development, while it gives her to the world and to civilization, does not necessarily remove her from the home and fireside; finally, that while past centuries have witnessed sporadic instances of this higher growth, still it was reserved for the latter half of the nineteenth century to render it common and general enough to be effective; I might close with a glowing prediction of what the twentieth century may expect from this heritage of twin forces—the masculine battered and toil-worn as a grim veteran after centuries of warfare, but still strong, active, and vigorous, ready to help with his hard-won experience the young recruit rejoicing in her newly found freedom, who so confidently places her hand in his with mutual pledges to redeem the ages.

> And so the twain upon the skirts of Time,
> Sit side by side, full-summed in all their powers,
> Dispensing harvest, sowing the To-be,
> Self-reverent each and reverencing each.

Fain would I follow them, but duty is nearer home. The high ground of generalities is alluring but my pen is devoted to a special cause: and with a view to further enlightenment on the achievements of the century for THE HIGHER EDUCATION OF COLORED WOMEN, I wrote a few days ago to the colleges which admit women and asked how many colored women had completed the B.A. course in each during its entire history. These are the figures returned: Fisk leads the way with twelve; Oberlin next with five; Wilberforcè, four; Ann Arbor and Wellesley three each, Livingstone two, Atlanta one, Howard, as yet, none.

I then asked the principal of the Washington High School how many out of a large number of female graduates from his school had chosen to go forward and take a collegiate course. He replied that but one had ever done so, and she was then in Cornell.[10]

Others ask questions too, sometimes, and I was asked a few years ago by a white friend, "How is it that the men of your race seem to outstrip the women in mental attainment?" "Oh," I said, "so far as it is true, the men, I suppose, from the life they lead, gain more by contact; and so far as it is only apparent, I think the women are more quiet. They don't feel called to mount a barrel and harangue by the hour every time they imagine they have produced an idea."

But I am sure there is another reason which I did not at that time see fit to give. The atmosphere, the standards, the requirements of our little world do not afford any special stimulus to female development.

It seems hardly a gracious thing to say, but it strikes me as true, that while our men seem thoroughly abreast of the times on almost every other subject, when they strike the woman question they drop back into sixteenth century logic. They leave nothing to be desired generally in regard to gallantry and chivalry, but they actually do not seem sometimes to have outgrown that old contemporary of chivalry—the idea that women may stand on pedestals or live in doll houses, (if they happen to have them) but they must not furrow their brows with thought or attempt to help men tug at the great questions of the world. I fear the majority of colored men do not yet think it worth while that women aspire to higher education. Not many will subscribe to the "advanced" ideas of Grant Allen already quoted. The three R's, a little music and a good deal of dancing, a first rate dressmaker and a bottle of magnolia balm, are quite enough generally to render charming any woman possessed of tact and the capacity for worshiping masculinity.

My readers will pardon my illustrating my point and also giving a reason for the fear that is in me, by a little bit of personal experience. When a child I was put into a school near home that professed to be normal and collegiate, i.e. to prepare teachers for colored youth, furnish candidates for the ministry, and offer collegiate training for those who should be ready for it. Well, I found after a while that I had a good deal of time on my hands. I had devoured what was put before me, and, like Oliver Twist, was look-

---

10. Graduated from Scientific Course, June, 1890, the first colored woman to graduate from Cornell. *AJC.*

ing around to ask for more. I constantly felt (as I suppose many an ambitious girl has felt) a thumping from within unanswered by any beckoning from without. Class after class was organized for these ministerial candidates (many of them men who had been preaching before I was born). Into every one of these classes I was expected to go, with the sole intent, I thought at the time, of enabling the dear old principal, as he looked from the vacant countenances of his sleepy old class over to where I sat, to get off his solitary pun—his never-failing pleasantry, especially in hot weather—which was, as he called out "Any one!" to the effect that "*any* one" then meant "*Annie* one."

Finally a Greek class was to be formed. My inspiring preceptor informed me that Greek had never been taught in the school, but that he was going to form a class *for the candidates for the ministry,* and if I liked I might join it. I replied—humbly I hope, as became a female of the human species—that I would like very much to study Greek, and that I was thankful for the opportunity, and so it went on. A boy, however meager his equipment and shallow his pretentions, had only to declare a floating intention to study theology and he could get all the support, encouragement and stimulus he needed, be absolved from work and invested beforehand with all the dignity of his far away office. While a self-supporting girl had to struggle on by teaching in the summer and working after school hours to keep up with her board bills, and actually to fight her way against positive discouragements to the higher education; till one such girl one day flared out and told the principal "the only mission opening before a girl in his school was to marry one of those candidates." He said he didn't know but it was. And when at last that same girl announced her desire and intention to go to college it was received with about the same incredulity and dismay as if a brass button on one of those candidate's coats had propounded a new method for squaring the circle or trisecting the arc.

Now this is not fancy. It is a simple unvarnished photograph, and what I believe was not in those days exceptional in colored schools, and I ask the men and women who are teachers and co-workers for the highest interests of the race, that they give the girls a chance! We might as well expect to grow trees from leaves as hope to build up a civilization or a manhood without taking into consideration our women and the home life made by them, which must be the root and ground of the whole matter. Let us insist then on special encouragement for the education of our women and special care in their training. Let our girls feel that we expect something more of them than that they merely look pretty and appear well in society. Teach them that there is a race with special needs which they and only they can help; that the world needs and is already asking for their trained, efficient forces. Finally, if there is an ambitious girl with pluck and brain to take the higher education, encourage her to make the most of it. Let there be the same flourish of trumpets and clapping of hands as when a boy announces his determination to enter the lists; and then, as you know that she is physically the weaker of the two, don't stand from under and leave her to buffet the waves alone. Let her know that your heart is following her, that your hand, though she sees it not, is ready to support her. To be plain, I mean let money be raised and scholarships be founded in our colleges and universities for self-supporting, worthy young women, to offset and balance the aid that can always be found for boys who will take theology.

The earnest well trained Christian young woman, as a teacher, as a home-maker, as wife, mother, or silent influence even, is as potent a missionary agency among our people as is the theologian; and I claim that at the present stage of our development in the South she is ever more important and necessary.

Let us then, here and now, recognize this force and resolve to make the most of it—not the boys less, but the girls more.

· 5 ·

"Woman versus the Indian" (1891–1892)

 $\mathcal{W}$ hen the National Woman's Council convened at Washington in February 1891, among a number of thoughtful and suggestive papers read by eminent women, was one by the Rev. Anna Shaw,[1] bearing the above title.

That Miss Shaw is broad and just and liberal in principal is proved beyond contradiction. Her noble generosity and womanly firmness are unimpeachable. The unwavering stand taken by herself and Miss Anthony[2] in the subsequent color ripple in Wimodaughsis ought to be sufficient to allay forever any doubts as to the pure gold of these two women.

Of Wimodaughsis (which, being interpreted for the uninitiated, is a woman's culture club whose name is made up of the first few letters of the four words wives, mothers, daughters, and sisters) Miss Shaw is president, and a lady from the Blue Grass State *was* secretary.

Pandora's box is opened in the ideal harmony of this modern Eden without an Adam when a colored lady, a teacher in one of our schools, applies for admission to its privileges and opportunities.

The Kentucky secretary, a lady zealous in good works and one who, I can't help imagining, belongs to that estimable class who daily thank the Lord that He made the earth that they may have the job of superintending its rotations, and who really would like to help "elevate" the colored people (in her own way of course and so long as they understand their places) is filled with grief and horror that any persons of Negro extraction should aspire to learn type-writing or languages or to enjoy any other advantages offered in the sacred halls of Wimodaughsis. Indeed, she had not calculated that there were any wives, mothers, daughters, and sisters, except white ones; and she is really convinced that *Whimodaughsis* would sound just as well, and then it need mean just *white mothers, daughters and sisters*. In fact, so far as there is anything in a name, nothing would be lost by omitting for

---

1. The Reverend Anna Shaw (1847–1919): suffragist and Methodist preacher.
2. Susan B. Anthony (1820–1906): American suffragist.

the sake of euphony, from this unique mosaic, the letters that represent wives. *Whiwimodaughsis* might be a little startling, and on the whole wives would better yield to white; since clearly all women are not wives, while surely all wives are daughters. The daughters therefore could represent the wives and this immaculate assembly for propagating liberal and progressive ideas and disseminating a broad and humanizing culture might be spared the painful possibility of the sight of a black man coming in the future to escort from an evening class this solitary cream-colored applicant. Accordingly the Kentucky secretary took the cream-colored applicant aside, and, with emotions befitting such an epoch-making crisis, told her, "as kindly as she could," that colored people were not admitted to the classes, at the same time refunding the money which said cream-colored applicant had paid for lessons in type-writing.

When this little incident came to the knowledge of Miss Shaw, she said firmly and emphatically, NO. As a minister of the gospel and as a Christian woman, she could not lend her influence to such unreasonable and uncharitable discrimination; and she must resign the honor or president of Wimodaughsis if persons were to be proscribed solely on account of their color.

To the honor of the board of managers, be it said, they sustained Miss Shaw; and the Kentucky secretary, and those whom she succeeded in inoculating with her prejudices, resigned.

'Twas only a ripple,—some bewailing of lost opportunity on the part of those who could not or would not seize God's opportunity for broadening and enlarging their own souls—and then the work flowed on as before.

Susan B. Anthony and Anna Shaw are evidently too noble to be held in thrall by the provincialisms of women who seem never to have breathed the atmosphere beyond the confines of their grandfathers' plantations. It is only from the broad plateau of light and love that one can see petty prejudice and narrow priggishness in their true perspective; and it is on this high ground, as I sincerely believe, these two grand women stand.

As leaders in the woman's movement of today, they have need of clearness of vision as well as firmness of soul in adjusting recalcitrant forces, and wheeling into line the thousand and one none-such, never-to-be-modified, won't-be-dictated-to banners of their somewhat mottled array.

The black woman and the southern woman, I imagine, often get them into the predicament of the befuddled man who had to take singly across a stream a bag of corn, a fox and a goose. There was no one to help, and to leave the goose with the fox was death—with the corn, destruction. To rechristen the animals, the lion could not be induced to lie down with the lamb unless the lamb would take the inside berth.

The black woman appreciates the situation and can even sympathize with the actors in the serio-comic dilemma.

But, may it not be that, as women, the very lessons which seem hardest to master now, are possibly the ones most essential for our promotion to a higher grade of work?

We assume to be leaders of thought and guardians of society. Our country's manners and morals are under our tutoring. Our standards are law in our several little worlds. However tenaciously men may guard some prerogatives, they are our willing slaves in that sphere which they have always conceded to be woman's. Here, no one dares demur when her fiat has gone forth. The man would be mad who presumed, however inexplicable and past finding out any reason for her action might be, to attempt to open a door in her kingdom officially closed and regally sealed by her.

The American woman of to-day not only gives tone directly to her immediate world, but her tiniest pulsation ripples out and out, down and down, till the outermost circles and the deepest layers of society feel the vibrations. It is pre-eminently an age of organizations. The "leading woman," the preacher, the reformer, the organizer "enthuses" her lieutenants and captains, the literary women, the thinking women, the strong, earnest, irresistible women; these in turn touch their myriads of church clubs, social clubs, culture clubs, pleasure clubs and charitable clubs, till the same lecture has been duly administered to every married man in the land (not to speak of sons and brothers) from the President in the White House to the stone-splitter of the ditches. And so woman's lightest whisper is heard as in Dionysius' ear, by quick relays and endless reproductions, through every recess and cavern as well as on every hilltop and mountain in her vast domain. And her mandates are obeyed. When she says "thumbs up," woe to the luckless thumb that falters in its rising. They may be little things, the amenities of life, the little nothings which cost nothing and come to nothing, and yet can make a sentient being so comfortable or so miserable in this life, and oil of social machinery, which we call the courtesies of life, all are under the magic key of woman's permit.

The American woman then is responsible for American manners. Not merely the right ascension and declination of the satellites of her own drawing room; but the rising and the setting of the pestilential or life-giving orbs which seem to wander afar in space, all are governed almost wholly through her magnetic polarity. The atmosphere of street cars and parks and boulevards, of cafes and hotels and steamboats is charged and surcharged with her sentiments and restrictions. Shop girls and serving maids, cashiers and accountant clerks, scribblers and drummers, whether wage earner, salaried toiler, or proprietress, whether laboring to instruct minds, to save souls, to delight fancies, or to win bread,—the working women of America in whatever station or calling they may be found, are subjects, officers, or rulers of a strong centralized government, and bound together by a system of codes and countersigns, which, though unwritten, forms a network of perfect subordination and unquestioning obedience as marvelous as that of the Jesuits. At the head and center in this regime stands the Leading Woman in the principality. The one talismanic word that plays along the wires from palace to cook-shop, from imperial Congress to the distant plain, is *Caste*. With all her vaunted independence, the American woman of to-day is as fearful of losing caste as a Brahmin in India. That is the law under which she lives, the precepts which she binds as frontlets between her eyes and writes on the door-posts of her homes, the lesson which she instils into her children with their first baby breakfasts, the injunction she lays upon husband and lover with direst penalties attached.

The queen of the drawing room is absolute ruler under this law. Her pose gives the cue. The microscopic angle at which her pencilled brows are elevated, signifies who may be recognized and who are beyond the pale. The delicate intimation is, quick as electricity, telegraphed down. Like the wonderful transformation in the House that Jack Built (or regions thereabouts) when the rat began to gnaw the rope, the rope to hang the butcher, the butcher to kill the ox, the ox to drink the water, the water to quench the fire, the fire to burn the stick, the stick to beat the dog, and the dog to worry the cat, and on, and on, and on,—when milady causes the inner arch over her matchless orbs to ascend the merest trifle, *presto!* the Miss at the notions counter grows curt and pert, the dress goods clerk becomes indifferent and taciturn, hotel waiters and ticket dispensers look the other way, the Irish street laborer snarls and scowls, conductors, policemen and park superintendents jostle and push and threaten, and society suddenly seems transformed into a band of organized adders, snapping, and striking and hissing just because they like it on general principles. The tune set by the head singer, sung through all keys and registers, with all qualities of tone,—the smooth, flowing, and gentle, the creaking, whizzing, grating, screeching, growling—according to ability, taste, and temperament of the singers. Another application of like master, like man. In this case, like mistress, like nation.

It was the good fortune of the Black Woman of the South to spend some weeks, not long since, in a land over which floated the Union Jack. The Stars and Stripes were not the only familiar experiences missed. A uniform, matter-of-fact courtesy, a genial kindliness, quick perception of opportunities for rendering any little manly assistance, a readiness to give information to strangers,—a hospitable, thawing-out atmosphere everywhere—in shops and waiting rooms, on cars and in the streets, actually seemed to her chilled little soul to transform the commonest boor in the service of the public into one of nature's noblemen, and when the old whipped-cur feeling was taken up and analyzed she could hardly tell whether it consisted mostly of self pity for her own wounded sensibilities, or of shame for her country and mortification that her countrymen offered such an unfavorable contrast.

Some American girls, I noticed recently, in search of novelty and adventure, were taking an extended trip through our country unattended by gentleman friends; their wish was to write up for a periodical or lecture the ease and facility, the comfort and safety of American travel, even for the weak and unprotected, under our well-nigh perfect railroad systems and our gentlemanly and efficient corps of officials and public servants. I have some material I could furnish these young ladies, though possibly it might not be just on the side they wish to have illuminated. The Black Woman of the South has to do considerable travelling in this country, often unattended. She thinks she is quiet and unobtrusive in her manner, simple and inconspicuous in her dress, and can see no reason why in any chance assemblage of *ladies,* or even a promiscuous gathering of ordinarily well-bred and dignified individuals, she should be signaled out for any marked consideration. And yet she has seen these same "gentlemanly and efficient" railroad conductors, when their cars had stopped at stations having no raised platforms, making it necessary for passengers to take the long and trying leap from the car step to the ground or step on the narrow little stool placed under by the conductor, after standing at their posts and handing woman after woman from the steps to the stool, thence to the ground, or else relieving her of satchels and bags and enabling her to make the descent easily, deliberately fold their arms and turn round when the Black Woman's turn came to alight—bearing her satchel, and bearing besides another unnameable burden inside the heaving bosom and tightly compressed lips. The feeling of slighted womanhood is unlike every other emotion of the soul. Happily for the human family, it is unknown to many and indescribable to all. Its poignancy, compared with which even Juno's *spretae injuria formae* is earthly and vulgar, is holier than that of jealousy, deeper than indignation, tenderer than rage. Its first impulse of wrathful protest and proud self vindication is checked and shamed by the consciousness that self assertion would outrage still further the same delicate instinct. Were there a brutal attitude of hate or of ferocious attack, the feminine response of fear or repulsion is simple and spontaneous. But when the keen sting comes through the finer sensibilities, from a hand which, by all known traditions and ideals of propriety, should have been trained to reverence and respect them, the condemnation of man's inhumanity to woman is increased and embittered by the knowledge of personal identity with a race of beings so fallen.

I purposely forbear to mention instances of personal violence to colored women travelling in less civilized sections of our country, where women have been forcibly ejected from cars, thrown out of seats, their garments rudely torn, their person wantonly and cruelly injured. America is large and must for some time yet endure its out-of-the-way jungles of barbarism as Africa its uncultivated tracts of marsh and malaria. There are murderers and thieves and villains in both London and Paris. Humanity from the first has had its vultures and sharks, and representatives of the fraternity who prey upon mankind may be expected no less in America than elsewhere. That this virulence breaks out most readily and commonly against colored persons in this country, is due of course to the fact that they are, generally speaking, weak and can be imposed upon with impunity. Bullies are always cowards at heart and may be credited with a pretty safe instinct in scenting their prey. Besides, society, where it has not exactly said to its dogs "s-s-sik him!" has at least engaged to be looking in another direction or studying the rivers on Mars. It is not of the dogs and their doings, but of society holding the leash that I shall speak. It is those subtle exhalations of atmospheric odors for which woman is accountable, the indefinable, unplaceable aroma which seems to exude from the very pores in her finger tips like the delicate sachet so dexterously hidden and concealed in her linens; the essence of her teaching, guessed rather than read, so adroitly is the lettering and wording manipulated; it is the undertones of the picture laid finely on by woman's own practiced hand, the reflection of the lights and shadows on her own brow; it is, in a word, the reputation of our nation for general politeness and good manners and of our fellow citizens to be somewhat more than cads or snobs that shall engage our present study. There can be no true test of national courtesy without travel. Impressions and conclusions based on provincial traits and characteristics can thus be modified and generalized. Moreover, the weaker and less influential the experimenter, the more exact and scientific the deductions. Courtesy "for revenue only" is not politeness, but diplomacy. Any rough can assume civility toward those of "his set," and does not hesitate to carry it even to servility toward those in whom he recognizes a possible patron or his master in power, wealth, rank, or influence. But, as the chemist prefers distilled H_2O in testing solutions to avoid complications and unwarranted reactions, so the Black Woman holds that her femininity linked with the impossibility of popular affinity or unexpected attraction through position and influence in her case makes her a touchstone of American courtesy exceptionally pure and singularly free from extraneous modifiers. The man who is courteous to her is so, not because of anything he hopes or fears or sees, but because *he is a gentlemen.*

I would eliminate also from the discussion all uncharitable reflections upon the orderly execution of laws existing in certain states of this Union, requiring persons known to be colored to ride in one car, and persons supposed to be white in another. A good citizen may use his influence to have existing laws and statutes changed or modified, but a public servant must not be blamed for obeying orders. A railroad conductor is not asked to dictate measures, nor to make and pass laws. His bread and butter are conditioned on his managing his part of the machinery as he is told to do. If, therefore, I found myself in that compartment of a train designated by the sovereign law of the state for presumable Caucasians, and for colored persons only when traveling in the capacity of nurses and maids, should a conductor inform me, as a gentleman might, that I had made a mistake, and offer to show me the proper car for black ladies; I might wonder at the expansive arrangements of the company and of the state in providing special and separate accommodations for the transportation of the various hues of humanity, but I certainly could not take it as a want of courtesy on the conductor's part that he gave the information. It is true, public sentiment precedes and begets all laws, good or bad; and on the ground I have taken, our women are to be credited largely as teachers and moulders of public sentiment. But when a law has passed and received the sanction of the land, there is nothing for our officials to do but enforce it till repealed; and I for one, as a loyal American citizen, will give those officials cheerful support and ready sympathy in the discharge of their duty. But when a great burly six feet of masculinity with sloping shoulders and unkempt beard swaggers in, and, throwing a roll of tobacco into one corner of his jaw, growls out at me over the paper I am reading, "Here gurl," (I am past thirty) "you better git out 'n dis kyar 'f yer don't, I'll put yer out,"—my mental annotation is *Here's an American citizen who has been badly trained. He is sadly lacking in both "sweetness" and "light";* and when in the same section of our enlightened and progressive country, I see from the car window, working on private estates, convicts from the state penitentiary, among them squads of boys from fourteen to eighteen years of age in a chain-gang, their feet chained together and heavy blocks attached—not in 1850, but in 1890, '91 and '92, I make a note on the flyleaf of my memorandum, *The women in this section should organize a Society for the Prevention of Cruelty to Human Beings, and disseminate civilizing tracts, and send throughout the region apostles of anti-barbarism for the propagation of humane and enlightened ideas.* And when farther on in the same section our train stops at a dilapidated station, rendered yet more unsightly by dozens of loafers with their hands in their pockets while a productive soil and inviting climate beckon in vain to industry; and when, looking a little more closely, I see two dingy little rooms with "FOR LADIES" swinging over one and "FOR COLORED PEOPLE" over the other; while wondering under which head I come, I notice a little way off the only hotel proprietor of the place whittling a pine stick as he sits with one leg thrown across an empty goods box; and as my eye falls on a sample room next door which seems to be driving the only wide-awake and popular business of the commonwealth, I cannot help ejaculating under my breath, "What a field for the missionary woman." I know that if by any fatality I should be obliged to lie over at that station, and, driven by hunger, should be compelled to seek refreshments or the bare necessaries of life at the only public accommodation in the town, that same stick-whittler would coolly inform me, without looking up from his pine splinter, "We doan uccommodate no niggers hyur." And yet we are so scandalized at Russia's barbarity and cruelty to the Jews! We pay a man a thousand dollars a night just to make us weep, by a recital of such heathenish inhumanity as is practiced on Slavonic soil.

A recent writer on Eastern nations[3] says:

> If we take through the earth's temperate zone, a belt of country whose northern and southern edges are determined by certain limiting

---

3. Presumably Percival Lowell (1855–1916), author of *Soul of the Far East,* previously quoted on p. 74.

isotherms, not more than half the width of the zone apart, we shall find that we have included in a relatively small extent of surface almost all the nations of note in the world, past or present. Now, if we examine this belt and compare the different parts of it with one another, we shall be struck by a remarkable fact. *The peoples inhabiting it grow steadily more personal as we go west.* So unmistakable is this gradation, that one is almost tempted to ascribe it to cosmical rather than to human causes. It is as marked as the change in color of the human complexion observable along any meridian, which ranges from black at the equator to blonde toward the pole. In like manner the sense of self grows more intense as we follow in the wake of the setting sun, and fades steadily as we advance into the dawn. America, Europe, the Levant, India, Japan, each is less personal than the one before. . . . *That politeness should be one of the most marked results of impersonality* may appear surprising, yet a slight examination will show it to be a fact. Considered *a priori,* the connection is not far to seek. Impersonality by lessening the interest in one's self, induces one to take an interest in others. Looked at *a posteriori,* we find that where the one trait exists the other is most developed, while an absence of the second seems to prevent the full growth of the first. This is true both in general and in detail. *Courtesy increases as we travel eastward round the world, coincidently with a decrease in the sense of self.* Asia is more courteous than Europe, Europe than America. Particular races show the same concomitance of characteristics. France, the most impersonal nation of Europe, is at the same time the most polite.

And by inference, Americans, the most personal, are the least courteous nation on the globe.

The Black Woman had reached this same conclusion by an entirely different route; but it is gratifying to vanity, nevertheless, to find one's self sustained by both science and philosophy in a conviction, wrought in by hard experience, and yet too apparently audacious to be entertained even as a stealthy surmise. In fact the Black Woman was emboldened some time since by a well put and timely article from an Editor's Drawer on the "Mannerless Sex," to give the world the benefit of some of her experience with the *"Mannerless Race";* but since Mr. Lowell shows so conclusively that the entire Land of the West is a *mannerless continent,* I have determined to plead with our women, the mannerless sex on this mannerless continent, to institute a reform by placing immediately in our national curricula a department for teaching GOOD MANNERS.

Now, am I right in holding the American Woman responsible? Is it true that the exponents of woman's advancement, the leaders in woman's thought, the preachers and teachers of all woman's reforms, can teach this nation to be courteous, to be pitiful, having compassion one of another, not rendering evil for inoffensiveness, and railing in proportion to the improbability of being struck back; but contrariwise, being *all* of one mind, to love as brethren?

I think so.

It may require some heroic measures, and like all revolutions will call for a determined front and a courageous, unwavering, stalwart heart on the part of the leaders of the reform.

The *"all"* will inevitably stick in the throat of the Southern woman. She must be allowed, please, to except the "darkey" from the "all"; it is too bitter a pill with black people in it. You must get the Revised Version to put it, *"love all white people* as brethren." She really could not enter any society on earth, or in heaven above, or in—the waters under the earth, on such unpalatable conditions.

The Black Woman has tried to understand the Southern woman's difficulties; to put herself in her place, and to be as fair; as charitable, and as free from prejudice in judging her antipathies, as she would have others in regard to her own. She has honestly weighed the apparently sincere excuse, "But you must remember that these people were once our slaves"; and that other, "But civility towards the Negroes will bring us on *social equality* with them."

These are the two bugbears; or rather, the two humbugbears: for, though each is founded on a most glaring fallacy, one would think they were words to conjure with, so potent and irresistible is their spell as an argument at the North as well as in the South.

One of the most singular facts about the unwritten history of this country is the consummate ability with which Southern influence, Southern ideas and Southern ideals, have from the very beginning even up to the present day, dictated to and domineered over the brain and sinew of this nation. Without wealth, without education, without inventions, arts, sciences, or industries, without well-nigh every one of the progressive ideas and impulses which have made this country great, prosperous and happy, personally indolent and practically stupid, poor in everything but bluster and self-esteem, the Southerner has nevertheless with Italian finesse and exquisite skill, uniformly and invariably, so manipulated Northern sentiment as to succeed sooner or later in carrying his point and shaping the policy of this government to suit his purposes. Indeed, the Southerner is a magnificent manager of men, a born educator. For two hundred and fifty years he trained to his hand a people whom he made absolutely his own, in body, mind, and sensibility. He so insinuated differences and distinctions among them, that their personal attachment for him was stronger than for their own brethren and fellow sufferers. He made it a crime for two or three of them to be gathered together in Christ's name without a white man's supervision, and a felony for one to teach them to read even the Word of Life; and yet they would defend his interest with their life blood; his smile was their happiness, a pat on the shoulder from him their reward. The slightest difference among themselves in condition, circumstances, opportunities, became barriers of jealousy and disunion. He sowed his blood broadcast among them, then pitted mulatto against black, bond against free, house slave against plantation slave, even the slave of one clan against like slave of another clan; till, wholly oblivious of their ability for mutual succor and defense, all became centers of myriad systems of repellent forces, having but one sentiment in common, and that their entire subjection to that master hand.

And he not only managed the black man, he also hoodwinked the white man, the tourist and investigator who visited his lordly estates. The slaves were doing well, in fact couldn't be happier,—plenty to eat, plenty to drink, comfortably housed and clothed—they wouldn't be free if they could; in short, in his broad brimmed plantation hat and easy aristocratic smoking gown, he make you think him a veritable patriarch in the midst of a lazy, well fed, good natured, over-indulged tenantry.

Then, too, the South represented blood—not red blood, but blue blood. The difference is in the length of the stream and your distance from its source. If your own father was a pirate, a robber, a murderer, his hands are dyed in red blood, and you don't say very much about it. But if your great great great grandfather's grandfather stole and pillaged and slew, and you can prove it, your blood has become blue and you are at great pains to establish the relationship. So the South had neither silver nor gold, but she had blood; and she paraded it with so much gusto that the substantial little Puritan maidens of the North, who had been making bread and canning currants and not thinking of blood the least bit, began to hunt up the records of the Mayflower to see if some of the passengers thereon could not claim the honor of having been one of William the Conqueror's brigands, when he killed the last of the Saxon Kings and, red-handed, stole his crown and his lands. Thus the ideal from out the Southland brooded over the nation and we sing less lustily than of yore:

Kind hearts are more than coronets
And simple faith than Norman blood.

In politics, the two great forces, commerce and empire, which would otherwise have shaped the destiny of the country, have been made to pander and cater to Southern notions. "Cotton is King" meant the South must be allowed to dictate or there would be no fun. Every statesman from 1830 to 1860 exhausted his genius in persuasion and compromises to smooth out her ruffled temper and gratify her petulant demands. But like a sullen younger sister, the South has pouted and sulked and cried: "I won't play with you now; so there!" and the big brother at the North has coaxed and compromised and given in, and—ended by letting her have her way. Until 1860 she had as her pet an institution which it was death by the law to say anything about, except that it was divinely instituted, inaugurated by Noah, sanctioned by Abraham, approved by Paul, and just ideally perfect in every way. And when, to preserve the autonomy of the family arrangements, in [18]61, '62 and '63, it became necessary for the big brother to administer a little wholesome correction and set the obstreperous Miss vigorously down in her seat again, she assumed such an air of injured innocence, and melted away so lugubriously, the big brother has done nothing since but try to sweeten and pacify and laugh her back into a companionable frame of mind.

Father Lincoln did all he could to get her to repent of her petulance and behave herself. He even promised she might keep her pet, so disagreeable to all the neighbors and hurtful even to herself, and might manage it at home to suit herself, if she would only listen to reason and be just tolerably nice. But, no—she was going to leave and set up for herself; she didn't propose to be meddled with; and so, of course, she had to be spanked. Just a little at first—didn't mean to hurt, merely to teach her who was who. But she grew so ugly, and kicked and fought and scratched so outrageously, and seemed so determined to smash up the whole business, the head of the family got red in the face, and said: "Well, now, he couldn't have any more of that foolishness. Arabella must just behave herself or take the consequences." And after the spanking, Arabella sniffed and whimpered and pouted, and the big brother bit his lip, looked half ashamed, and said: "Well, I didn't want to hurt you. You needn't feel so awfully bad about it, I only did it for your good. You know I wouldn't do anything to displease you if I could help it; but you would insist on making the row, and so I just had to. Now, there—there—let's be friends!" and he put his great

strong arms about her and just dared anybody to refer to that little unpleas-
antness—he'd show them a thing or two. Still Arabella sulked,—till the
rest of the family decided she might just keep her pets, and manage her
own affairs and nobody should interfere.

So now, if one intimates that some clauses of the Constitution are a
dead letter at the South and that only the name and support of that pet
institution are changed while the fact and essence, minus the expense and
responsibility, remain, he is quickly told to mind his own business and
informed that he is waving the bloody shirt.

Even twenty-five years after the fourteenth and fifteenth amendments
to our Constitution, a man who has been most unequivocal in his outspoken condemnation of the wrongs regularly and systematically heaped on
the oppressed race in this country, and on all even most remotely connected
with them—a man whom we had thought our staunchest friend and most
noble champion and defender—after a two weeks' trip in Georgia and
Florida immediately gives signs of the fatal inception of the virus. Not
even the chance traveller from England or Scotland escapes. The arch-
manipulator takes him under his special watch-care and training, uses up
his stock arguments and gives object lessons with his choicest specimens of
Negro depravity and worthlessness; takes him through what, in New York,
would be called "the slums," and would predicate there nothing but the
duty of enlightened Christians to send out their light and emulate their
Master's aggressive labors of love; but in Georgia is denominated "our
terrible problem, which people of the North so little understand, yet
vouchsafe so much gratuitous advice about." With an injured air he shows
the stupendous and atrocious mistake of reasoning about these people as if
they were just ordinary human beings, and amenable to the tenets of the
Gospel; and not longer after the inoculation begins to work, you hear this
old-time friend of the oppressed delivering himself something after this
fashion: "Ah, well, the South must be left to manage the Negro. She is
most directly concerned and must understand her problem better than out-
siders. We must not meddle. We must be very careful not to widen the
breaches. The Negro is not worth a feud between brothers and sisters."

Lately a great national and international movement characteristic of
this age and country, a movement based on the inherent right of every soul
to its own highest development, I mean the movement making for Woman's full, free, and complete emancipation, has, after much courting, obtained the gracious smile of the Southern woman—I beg her pardon—the
Southern *lady*.

She represents blood, and of course could not be expected to leave that out; and firstly and foremostly she must not, in any organization she may deign to grace with her presence, be asked to associate with "these people who were once her slaves."

Now the Southern woman (I may be pardoned, being one myself) was never renowned for her reasoning powers, and it is not surprising that just a little picking will make her logic fall to pieces even here.

In the first place she imagines that because her grandfather had slaves who were black, all the blacks in the world of every shade and tint were once in the position of her slaves. This is as bad as the Irishman who was about to kill a peaceable Jew in the streets of Cork,—having just learned that Jews slew his Redeemer. The black race constitutes one-seventh the known population of the globe; and there are representatives of it here as elsewhere who were never in bondage at any time to any man,—whose blood is as blue and lineage as noble as any, even that of the white lady of the South. That her slaves were black and she despises her slaves, should no more argue antipathy to all dark people and peoples, than that Guiteau,[4] an assassin, was white, and I hate assassins, should make me hate all persons more or less white. The objection shows a want of clear discrimination.

The second fallacy in the objection grows out of the use of an ambiguous middle, as the logicians would call it, or assigning a double signification to the term *"Social equality."*

Civility to the Negro implies social equality. I am opposed to *associating* with dark persons on terms of social equality. Therefore, I abrogate civility to the Negro. This is like

> Light is opposed to darkness.
> Feathers are light.
> *Ergo,* Feathers are opposed to darkness.

The "social equality" implied by civility to the Negro is a very different thing from forced association with him socially. Indeed it seems to me that the mere application of a little cold common sense would show that uncongenial social environments could by no means be forced on any one. I do not, and cannot be made to associate with all dark persons, simply on the ground that I am dark; and I presume the Southern lady can imagine some whose faces are white, with whom she would no sooner think of

---

4. Charles Julius Guiteau (1841–1882) assassinated U.S. President James Garfield in 1881.

chatting unreservedly than, were it possible, with a veritable "darkey." Such things must and will always be left to individual election. No law, human or divine, can legislate for or against them. Like seeks like; and I am sure with the Southern lady's antipathies at their present temperature, she might enter ten thousand organizations besprinkled with colored women without being any more deflected by them than by the proximity of a stone. The social equality scare then is all humbug, conscious or unconscious, I know not which. And were it not too bitter a thought to utter here, I might add that the overtures for forced association in the past history of these two races were not made by the manacled black man, nor by *the silent and suffering black woman!*

When I seek food in a public cafe or apply for first-class accommodations on a railway train, I do so because my physical necessities are identical with those of other human beings of like constitution and temperament, and crave satisfaction. I go because I want food, or I want comfort—not because I want association with those who frequent these places; and I can see no more "social equality" in buying lunch at the same restaurant, or riding in a common car, than there is in paying for dry goods at the same counter or walking on the same street.

The social equality which means forced or unbidden association would be as much depreciated and as strenuously opposed by the circle in which I move as by the most hide-bound Southerner in the land. Indeed I have been more than once annoyed by the inquisitive white interviewer, who, with spectacles on nose and pencil and note-book in hand, comes to get some "points" about *"your people."* My "people" are just like other people—indeed, too like for their own good. They hate, they love, they attract and repel, they climb or they grovel, struggle or drift, aspire or despair, endure in hope or curse in vexation, exactly like all the rest of unregenerate humanity. Their likes and dislikes are as strong; their antipathies—and prejudices too I fear, are as pronounced as you will find anywhere; and the entrance to the inner sanctuary of their homes and hearts is as jealously guarded against profane intrusion.

What the dark man wants then is merely to live his own life, in his own world, with his own chosen companions, in whatever of comfort, luxury, or emoluments his talent or his money can in an impartial market secure. Has he wealth, he does not want to be forced into convenient or unsanitary sections of cities to buy a home and rear his family. Has he art, he does not want to be cabined and cribbed into emulation with the few who merely happen to have his complexion. His talent aspires to study without proscription the masters of all ages and to rub against the broadest and fullest movements of his own day.

Has he religion, he does not want to be made to feel that there is a white Christ and a black Christ, a white Heaven and a black Heaven, a white Gospel and a black Gospel,—but the one ideal of perfect manhood and womanhood, the one universal longing for development and growth, the one desire for being, and being better, the one great yearning, aspiring, outreaching, in all the heart-throbs of humanity in whatever race or clime.

A recent episode in the Corcoran art gallery at the American capital is to the point. A colored woman who had shown marked ability in drawing and coloring, was advised by her teacher, himself an artist of no mean rank, to apply for admission to the Corcoran school in order to study the models and to secure other advantages connected with the organization. She accordingly sent a written application accompanied by specimens of her drawings, the usual *modus operandi* in securing admission.

The drawings were examined by the best critics and pronounced excellent, and a ticket of admission was immediately issued together with a highly complimentary reference to her work.

The next day my friend, congratulating her country and herself that at least in the republic of art no caste existed, presented her ticket of admission *in propria persona*. There was a little preliminary side play in Delsarte pantomine,—aghast—incredulity—wonder; then the superintendent told her in plain unartistic English that of course he had not dreamed a colored person could do such work, and had he suspected the truth he would never have issued the ticket of admission; that, to be right frank, the ticket would have to be cancelled,—she could under no condition be admitted to the studio.

Can it be possible that even art in America is to be tainted by this shrivelling caste spirit? If so, what are we coming to? Can any one conceive a Shakespeare, a Michelangelo, or a Beethoven putting away any fact of simple merit because the thought, or the suggestion, or the creation emanated from a soul with an unpleasing exterior?

What is it that makes the great English bard pre-eminent as the photographer of the human soul? Where did he learn the universal language, so that Parthians, Medes and Elamites, and the dwellers in Mesopotamia, in Egypt and Libya, in Crete and Arabia do hear every one in our own tongue the wonderful revelations of this myriad mind? How did he learn our language? Is it not that his own soul was infinitely receptive to Nature, the dear old nurse, in all her protean forms? Did he not catch and reveal her own secret by his sympathetic listening as she "would constantly sing a more wonderful song or tell a more marvellous tale" in the souls he met around him?

"Stand off! I am better than thou!" has never yet painted a true picture, nor written a thrilling song, nor given a pulsing, a soul-burning sermon. 'Tis only sympathy, another name for love,—that one poor word which, as George Eliot says, "expresses so much of human insight"—that can interpret either man or matter.

It was Shakespeare's own all-embracing sympathy, that infinite receptivity of his, and native, all-comprehending appreciation, which proved a key to unlock and open every soul that came within his radius. And *he received as much as he gave.* His own stores were infinitely enriched thereby. For it is decreed:

> Man like the vine supported lives,
> The strength he gains is from th' embrace he gives.

It is only through clearing the eyes from bias and prejudice, and becoming one with the great all pervading soul of the universe that either art or science can

> Read what is still unread
> In the manuscripts of God.

No true artist can allow himself to be narrowed and provincialized by deliberately shutting out any class of facts or subjects through prejudice against externals. And American art, American science, American literature can never be founded in truth, the universal beauty; can never learn to speak a language intelligible in all climes and for all ages, till this paralyzing grip of caste prejudice is loosened from its vitals, and the healthy sympathetic eye is taught to look out on the great universe as holding no favorites and no black beasts, but bearing in each plainest or loveliest feature the handwriting of its God.

And this is why, as it appears to me, woman in her lately acquired vantage ground for speaking an earnest helpful word, can do this country no deeper and truer and more lasting good than by bending all her energies to thus broadening, humanizing, and civilizing her native land.

"Except ye become as little children" is not a pious precept, but an inexorable law of the universe. God's kingdoms are all sealed to the seedy, moss-grown mind of self-satisfied maturity. Only the little child in spirit, the simple, receptive, educable mind can enter. Preconceived notions, blinding prejudices, and shrivelling antipathies must be wiped out, and the cultivable soul made a *tabula rasa* for whatever lesson great Nature has to teach.

This, too, is why I conceive the subject to have been unfortunately worded which was chosen by Miss Shaw at the Woman's Council and which stands at the head of this chapter.

Miss Shaw is one of the most powerful of our leaders, and we feel her voice should give no uncertain note. Woman should not, even by inference, or for the sake of argument, seem to disparage what is weak. For woman's cause is the cause of the weak; and when all the weak shall have received their due consideration, then woman will have her "rights," and the Indian will have his rights, and the Negro will have his rights, and all the strong will have learned at last to deal justly, to love mercy, and to walk humbly; and our fair land will have been taught the secret of universal courtesy which is after all nothing but the art, the science, and the religion of regarding one's neighbor as one's self, and to do for him as we would, were conditions swapped, that he do for us.

It cannot seem less than a blunder, whenever the exponents of a great reform or the harbingers of a noble advance in thought and effort allow themselves to seem distorted by a narrow view of their own aims and principles. All prejudices, whether of race, sect or sex, class pride and caste distinctions are the belittling inheritance and badge of snobs and prigs.

The philosophic mind sees that its own "rights" are the rights of humanity. That in the universe of God nothing trivial is or mean; and the recognition it seeks is not through the robber and wild beast adjustment of the survival of the bullies but through the universal application ultimately of the Golden Rule.

Not unfrequently has it happened that the impetus of a mighty thought wave has done the execution meant by its Creator in spite of the weak and distorted perception of its human embodiment. It is not strange if reformers, who, after all, but think God's thoughts after him, have often "builded more wisely than they knew"; and while fighting consciously for only a narrow gateway for themselves have been driven forward by that irresistible "Power not ourselves which makes for righteousness" to open a high road for humanity. It was so with our sixteenth century reformers. The fathers of the Reformation had no idea that they were inciting an insurrection of the human mind against all domination. None would have been more shocked than they at our nineteenth century deductions from their six-teenth century premises. Emancipation of mind and freedom of thought would have been as appalling to them as it was distasteful to the pope. They were right, they argued, to rebel against Romish absolutism—because Romish preaching and Romish practicing were wrong. They denounced popes for hacking heretics and forthwith began themselves to roast witches. The Spanish Inquisition in the hands of Philip and Alva was an institution of the devil; wielded by the faithful, it would become quite another thing. The only "rights" they were broad enough consciously to fight for was the right to substitute the absolutism of their conceptions, their party, their *"ism"* for an authority whose teaching they conceived to be corrupt and vicious. Persecution for a belief was wrong only when the persecutors were wrong and the persecuted right. The sacred prerogative of the individual to decide on matters of belief they did not dream of maintaining. Universal tolerance and its twin, universal charity, were not conceived yet. The broad foundation stone of all human rights, the great democratic principle "A man's a man, *and his own sovereign* for a' that" they did not dare enunciate. They were incapable of drawing up a Declaration of Independence for humanity. The Reformation to the Reformers meant one bundle of au-thoritative opinions vs. another bundle of authoritative opinions. Justifica-tion by faith, vs. justification by ritual. Submission to Calvin vs. submission to the Pope. English and Germans vs. the Italians.

To our eye, viewed through a vista of three centuries, it was the death wrestle of the principle of thought enslavement in the throttling grasp for personal freedom; it was the great Emancipation Day of human belief, man's intellectual Independence Day, prefiguring and finally compelling the world-wide enfranchisement of his body and all its activities. Not Prot-estant vs. Catholic, then; not Luther vs. Leo, not Dominicans vs. Augustin-ians, nor Geneva vs. Rome;—but humanity rationally free, vs. the clamps of tradition and superstition which had manacled and muzzled it.

The cause of freedom is not the cause of a race or a sect, a party or a class,—it is the cause of human kind, the very birthright of humanity. Now unless we are greatly mistaken the Reform of our day, known as the Wom-an's Movement, is essentially such an embodiment, if its pioneers could only realize it, of the universal good. And specially important is it that there be no confusion of ideas among its leaders as to its scope and universality. All mists must be cleared from the eyes of woman if she is to be a teacher of morals and manners: the former strikes its roots in the individual and its training and pruning may be accomplished by classes; but the latter is to lubricate the joints and minimize the friction of society, and it is important and fundamental that there be no chromatic or other aberration when the teacher is settling the point, "Who is my neighbor?"

It is not the intelligent woman vs. the ignorant woman; nor the white woman vs. the black, the brown, and the red,—it is not even the cause of woman vs. man. Nay, 'tis woman's strongest vindication for speaking that *the world needs to hear her voice.* It would be subversive of every human interest that the cry of one-half the human family be stifled. Woman in stepping from the pedestal of statue-like inactivity in the domestic shrine, and daring to think and move and speak,—to undertake to help shape, mold, and direct the thought of her age, is merely completing the circle of the world's vision. Hers is every interest that has lacked an interpreter and a defender. Her cause is linked with that of every agony that has been dumb—every wrong that needs a voice.

It is no fault of man's that he has not been able to see truth from her standpoint. It does credit both to his head and heart that no greater mistakes have been committed or even wrongs perpetrated while she sat making tatting and snipping paper flowers. Man's own innate chivalry and the mutual interdependence of their interests have insured his treating her cause, in the main at least, as his own. And he is pardonably surprised and even a little chagrined, perhaps, to find his legislation not considered "perfectly lovely" in every respect. But in any case his work is only impoverished by her remaining dumb. The world has had to limp along with the wobbling gait and one-sided hesitancy of man with one eye. Suddenly the bandage is removed from the other eye and the whole body is filled with light. It sees a circle where before it saw a segment. The darkened eye restored, every member rejoices with it.

What a travesty of its case for this eye to become plaintiff in a suit, *Eye vs. Foot.* "There is that dull clod, the foot, allowed to roam at will, free and untrammelled; while I, the source and medium of light, brilliant and beautiful, am fettered in darkness and doomed to desuetude." The great burly black man, ignorant and gross and depraved, is allowed to vote; while the franchise is withheld from the intelligent and refined, the pure-minded and lofty souled white woman. Even the untamed and untamable Indian of the prairie, who can answer nothing but "ugh" to great economic and civic questions is thought by some worthy to wield the ballot which is still denied the Puritan maid and the first lady of Virginia.

Is not this hitching our wagon to something much lower than a star? Is not woman's cause broader, and deeper, and grander, than a blue stocking debate or an aristocratic pink tea? Why should woman become plaintiff in a suit versus the Indian, or the Negro or any other race or class who have been crushed under the iron heel of Anglo-Saxon power and selfishness? If the Indian has been wronged and cheated by the puissance of this American government, it is woman's mission to plead with her country to cease to do evil and to pay its honest debts. If the Negro has been deceitfully cajoled or inhumanly cuffed according to selfish expediency or capricious antipathy, let it be woman's mission to plead that he be met as a man and honestly given half the road. If woman's own happiness has been ignored or misunderstood in our country's legislating for bread winners, for rum sellers, for property holders, for the family relations, for any or all the interests that touch her vitally, let her rest her plea, not on Indian inferiority, nor on Negro depravity, but on the obligation of legislators to do for her as they would have others do for them were relations reversed. Let her try to teach her country that every interest in this world is entitled at least to a respectful hearing, that every sentiency is worthy of its own gratification, that a helpless cause should not be trampled down, nor a bruised reed broken; and when the right of the individual is made sacred, when the image of God in human form, whether in marble or in clay, whether in alabaster or in ebony, is consecrated and inviolable, when men have been taught to look beneath the rags and grime, the pomp and pageantry of mere circumstance and have regard unto the celestial kernel uncontaminated at the core,—when race, color, sex, condition, are realized to be the accidents, not the substance of life, and consequently as not obscuring or modifying the inalienable title to life, liberty, and pursuit of happiness,—then is mastered the science of politeness, the art of courteous contact, which is naught but the practical application of the principal of benevolence, the back bone and marrow of all religion; then woman's lesson is taught and woman's cause is won—not the white woman nor the black woman nor the red woman, but the cause of every man or woman who has writhed silently under a mighty wrong. The pleading of the American woman for the right and the opportunity to employ the American method of influencing the disposal to be made of herself, her property, her children in civil, economic, or domestic relations is thus seen to be based on a principle as broad as the human race and as old as human society. Her wrongs are thus indissolubly linked with all undefended woe, all helpless suffering, and the plenitude of her "rights" will mean the final triumph of all right over might, the supremacy of the moral forces of reason and justice and love in the government of the nation.

God hasten the day.

· 6 ·

The Status of Woman in America (1892)

*J*ust four hundred years ago an obscure dreamer and castle builder, prosaically poor and ridiculously insistent on he reality of his dreams, was enabled through the devotion of a noble woman to give to civilization a magnificent continent.

What the lofty purpose of Spain's pure-minded queen had brought to the birth, the untiring devotion of pioneer women nourished and developed. The dangers of wild beasts and of wilder men, the mysteries of unknown wastes and unexplored forests, the horrors of pestilence and famine, of exposure and loneliness, during all those years of discovery and settlement, were braved without a murmur by women who had been most delicately constituted and most tenderly nurtured.

And when the times of physical hardship and danger were past, when the work of clearing and opening up was over and the struggle for accumulation began, again woman's inspiration and help were needed and still was she loyally at hand. A Mary Lyon,[1] demanding and making possible equal advantages of education for women as for men, and, in the face of discouragement and incredulity, bequeathing to women the opportunities of Holyoke.

A Dorothea Dix,[2] insisting on the humane and rational treatment of the insane and bringing about a reform in the lunatic asylums of the country, making a great step forward in the tender regard for the weak by the strong throughout the world.

A Helen Hunt Jackson,[3] convicting the nation of a century of dishonor in regard to the Indian.

---

1. Mary Lyon (1797–1849): New England educator, founder of Mount Holyoke College.
2. Dorothea Dix (1802–1887): reformer and nurse who investigated conditions in asylums, prisons, and poorhouses.
3. Helen Hunt Jackson (1830–1885): campaigner for Native American rights.

A Lucretia Mott,[4] gentle Quaker spirit, with sweet insistence, preaching the abolition of slavery and the institution, in its stead, of the brotherhood of man; her life and words breathing out in tender melody the injunction

> Have love. Not love alone for one
> But man as man thy brother call;
> And scatter, like the circling sun,
> They charities *on all*.

And at the most trying time of what we have called the Accumulative Period, when internecine war, originated through man's love of gain and his determination to subordinate national interests and black men's rights alike to considerations of personal profit and loss, was drenching our country with its own best blood, who shall recount the name and fame of the women on both sides of the senseless strife,—those uncomplaining souls with a great heart ache of their own, rigid features and pallid cheek their ever effective flag of truce, on the battle field, in the camp, in the hospital, binding up wounds, recording dying whispers for absent loved ones, with tearful eyes pointing to man's last refuge, giving the last earthly hand clasp and performing the last friendly office for strangers whom a great common sorrow had made kin, while they knew that somewhere—somewhere a husband, a brother, a father, a son, was being tended by stranger hands—or mayhap those familiar eyes were even then being closed forever by just such another ministering angel of mercy and love.

But why mention names? Time would fail to tell of the noble army of women who shine like beacon lights in the otherwise sordid wilderness of this accumulative period—prison reformers and tenement cleansers, quiet unnoted workers in hospitals and homes, among imbeciles, among outcasts—the sweetening, purifying antidotes for the poisons of man's acquisitiveness,—mollifying and soothing with the tenderness of compassion and love the wounds and bruises caused by his overreaching and avarice.

The desire for quick returns and large profits tempts capital ofttimes into unsanitary, well nigh inhuman investments,—tenement tinder boxes, stifling, stunting, sickening alleys and pestiferous slums; regular rents, no waiting, large percentages,—rich coffers coined out of the life-blood of human bodies and souls. Men and women herded together like cattle,

---

4. Lucretia Mott (1793–1880): feminist and abolitionist, probably the author of the short poem "Have love . . ." quoted in this paragraph.

breathing in malaria and typhus from an atmosphere seething with moral as well as physical impurity, revelling in vice as their native habitat and then, to drown the whisperings of their higher consciousness and effectually to hush the yearnings and accusations within, flying to narcotics and opiates—rum, tobacco, opium, binding hand and foot, body and soul, till the proper image of God is transformed into a fit associate for demons,—a besotted, enervated, idiotic wreck, or else a monster of wickedness terrible and destructive.

These are some of the legitimate products of the unmitigated tendencies of the wealth-producing period. But, thank Heaven, side by side with the cold, mathematical, selfishly calculating, so-called practical and unsentimental instinct of the business man, there comes the sympathetic warmth and sunshine of good women, like the sweet and sweetening breezes of spring, cleansing, purifying, soothing, inspiring, lifting the drunkard from the gutter, the outcast from the pit. Who can estimate the influence of these "daughters of the king," these lend-a-hand forces, in counteracting the selfishness of an acquisitive age?

To-day America counts her millionaires by the thousand; questions of tariff and questions of currency are the most vital ones agitating the public mind. In this period, when material prosperity and well earned ease and luxury are assured facts from a national standpoint, woman's work and woman's influence are needed as never before; needed to bring a heart power into this money getting, dollar-worshipping civilization; needed to bring a moral force into the utilitarian motives and interests of the time; needed to stand for God and Home and Native Land *versus gain and greed and grasping selfishness.*

There can be no doubt that this fourth centenary of America's discovery which we celebrate at Chicago, strikes the keynote of another important transition in the history of this nation; and the prominence of woman in the management of its celebration is a fitting tribute to the part she is destined to play among the forces of the future. This is the first congressional recognition of woman in this country, and this Board of Lady Managers constitute the first women legally appointed by any government to act in a national capacity. This of itself marks the dawn of a new day.

Now the periods of discovery, of settlement, of developing resources and accumulating wealth have passed in rapid succession. Wealth in the nation as in the individual brings leisure, repose, reflection. The struggle with nature is over, the struggle with ideas begins. We stand then, it seems to me, in this last decade of the nineteenth century, just in the portals of a new and untried movement on a higher plain and in a grander strain than any the past has called forth. It does not require a prophet's eye to divine its trend and image its possibilities from the forces we see already at work around us; nor is it hard to guess what must be the status of woman's work under the new regime.

In the pioneer days her role was that of a camp-follower, an additional something to fight for and be burdened with, only repaying the anxiety and labor she called forth by her own incomparable gifts of sympathy and appreciative love; unable herself ordinarily to contend with the bear and the Indian, or to take active part in clearing the wilderness and constructing the home.

In the second or wealth producing period her work is abreast of man's, complementing and supplementing, counteracting excessive tendencies, and mollifying over rigorous proclivities.

In the era now about to dawn, her sentiments must strike the keynote and give the dominant tone. And this because of the nature of her contribution to the world.

Her kingdom is not over physical forces. Not by might, nor by power can she prevail. Her position must ever be inferior where strength of muscle creates leadership. If she follows the instincts of her nature, however, she must always stand for the conservation of those deeper moral forces which make for the happiness of homes and the righteousness of the country. In a reign of moral ideas she is easily queen.

There is to my mind no grander and surer prophecy of the new era and of woman's place in it, than the work already begun in the waning years of the nineteenth century by the W. C. T. U.[5] in America, an organization which has even now reached not only national but international importance, and seems destined to permeate and purify the whole civilized world. It is the living embodiment of woman's activities and woman's ideas, and its extent and strength rightly prefigure her increasing power as a moral factor.

The colored woman of to-day occupies, one may say, a unique position in this country. In a period of itself transitional and unsettled, her status seems one of the least ascertainable and definitive of all the forces which make for our civilization. She is confronted by both a woman question and a race problem, and is as yet an unknown or an unacknowledged factor in

---

5. W.C.T.U.: **Women's** Christian Temperance Union, an organization of women that crusaded against saloons and the drinking of alcohol.

both. While the women of the white race can with calm assurance enter upon the work they feel by nature appointed to do, while their men give loyal support and appreciative countenance to their efforts, recognizing in most avenues of usefulness the propriety and the need of woman's distinctive co-operation, the colored woman too often finds herself hampered and shamed by a less liberal sentiment and a more conservative attitude on the part of those for whose opinion she cares most. That this is not universally true I am glad to admit. There are to be found both intensely conservative white men and exceedingly liberal colored men. But as far as my experience goes the average man of our race is less frequently ready to admit the actual need among the sturdier forces of the world for woman's help or influence. That great social and economic questions await her interference, that she could throw any light on problems of national import, that her intermeddling could improve the management of school systems, or elevate the tone of public institutions, or humanize and sanctify the far reaching influence of prisons and reformatories and improve the treatment of lunatics and imbeciles,—that she has a word worth hearing on mooted questions in political economy, that she could contribute a suggestion on the relations of labor and capital, or offer a thought on honest money and honorable trade, I fear the majority of "Americans of the colored variety" are not yet prepared to concede. It may be that they do not yet see these questions in their right perspective, being absorbed in the immediate needs of their own political complications. A good deal depends on where we put the emphasis in this world; and our men are not perhaps to blame if they see everything colored by the light of those agitations in the midst of which they live and move and have their being. The part they have had to play in American history during the last twenty-five or thirty years has tended rather to exaggerate the importance of mere political advantage, as well as to set a fictitious valuation on those able to secure such advantage. It is the astute politician, the manager who can gain preferment for himself and his favorites, the demagogue known to stand in with the powers at the White House and consulted on the bestowal of government plums, whom we set in high places and denominate great. It is they who receive the hosannas of the multitude and are regarded as leaders of the people. The thinker and the doer, the man who solves the problem by enriching his country with an invention worth thousands or by a thought inestimable and precious is given neither bread nor a stone. He is too often left to die in obscurity and neglect even if spared in his life the bitterness of fanatical jealousies and detraction.

And yet politics, and surely American politics, is hardly a school for great minds. Sharpening rather than deepening, it develops the faculty of taking advantage of present emergencies rather than the insight to distinguish between the true and the false, the lasting and the ephemeral advantage. Highly cultivated selfishness rather than consecrated benevolence is its passport to success. Its votaries are never seers. At best they are but manipulators—often only jugglers. It is conducive neither to profound statesmanship nor to the higher type of manhood. Altruism is its *mauvais succès* and naturally enough it is indifferent to any factor which cannot be worked into its own immediate aims and purposes. As woman's influence as a political element is as yet nil in most of the commonwealths of our republic, it is not surprising that with those who place the emphasis on mere political capital she may yet seem almost a nonentity so far as it concerns the solution of great national or even racial perplexities.

There are those, however, who value the calm elevation of the thoughtful spectator who stands aloof from the heated scramble; and, above the turmoil and din of corruption and selfishness, can listen to the teachings of eternal truth and righteousness. There are even those who feel that the black man's unjust and unlawful exclusion temporarily from participation in the elective franchise in certain states is after all but a lesson "in the desert" fitted to develop in him insight and discrimination against the day of his own appointed time. One needs occasionally to stand aside from the hum and rush of human interests and passions to hear the voices of God. And it not unfrequently happens that the All-loving gives a great push to certain souls to thrust them out, as it were, from the distracting current for awhile to promote their discipline and growth, or to enrich them by communion and reflection. And similarly it may be woman's privilege from her peculiar coigne of vantage as a quiet observer, to whisper just the needed suggestion or the almost forgotten truth. The colored woman, then, should not be ignored because her bark is resting in the silent waters of the sheltered cove. She is watching the movements of the contestants none the less and is all the better qualified, perhaps, to weigh and judge and advise because not herself in the excitement of the race. Her voice, too, has always been heard in clear, unfaltering tones, ringing the changes on those deeper interests which make for permanent good. She is always sound and orthodox on questions affecting the well-being of her race. You do not find the colored woman selling her birthright for a mess of pottage. Nay, even after reason has retired from the contest, she has been known to cling blindly with the instinct of a turtle dove to those principles and policies which to her mind promise hope and safety for children yet unborn. It is notorious that ignorant black women in the South have actually left their husbands' homes and repudiated their support for what was understood by the wife to be race disloyalty, or "voting away," as she expresses it, the privileges of herself and little ones.

It is largely our women in the South to-day who keep the black men solid in the Republican party. The latter as they increase in intelligence and power of discrimination would be more apt to divide on local issues at any rate. They begin to see that the Grand Old Party regards the Negro's cause as an outgrown issue, and on Southern soil at least finds a too intimate acquaintanceship with him a somewhat unsavory recommendation. Then, too, their political wits have been sharpened to appreciate the fact that it is good policy to cultivate one's neighbors and not depend too much on a distant friend to fight one's home battles. But the black woman can never forget—however lukewarm the party may to-day appear—that it was a Republican president who struck the manacles from her own wrists and gave the possibilities of manhood to her helpless little ones; and to her mind a Democratic Negro is a traitor and a time-server. Talk as much as you like of venality and manipulation in the South, there are not many men, I can tell you, who would dare face a wife quivering in every fiber with the consciousness that her husband is a coward who could be paid to desert her deepest and dearest interests.

Not unfelt, then, if unproclaimed has been the work and influence of the colored women of America.[6] Our list of chieftains in the service, though not long, is not inferior in strength and excellence, I dare believe, to any similar list which this country can produce.

Among the pioneers, Frances Watkins Harper could sing with prophetic exaltation in the darkest days, when as yet there was not a rift in the clouds overhanging her people:

> Yes, Ethiopia shall stretch
> Her bleeding hands abroad;

---

6. In the paragraphs following, Cooper discusses the nineteenth century's most influential "colored women of America": Frances Watkins Harper (1825–1911), writer, lecturer and poet, author of the quoted "Yes, Ethiopia . . ."; Sojourner Truth (1797–1883), evangelist, abolitionist, and feminist; Amanda Smith (1837–1915), evangelist and reformer; Sarah Woodson Early (1825–1907), pioneer black feminist-nationalist; Martha Briggs (1838–1889), faculty member and public school administrator; Charlotte Forten Grimké (1837–1914), antislavery poet, educator, and minister's wife; Hallie Quinn Brown (1845–1949), educator and social reformer, a founder of the National Association of Colored Women; and Fanny Jackson Coppin (1837–1913), educator and missionary.

Her cry of agony shall reach the burning throne of God.
Redeemed from dust and freed from chains
Her sons shall lift their eyes,
From cloud-capt hills and verdant plains
Shall shouts of triumph rise.

Among preachers of righteousness, an unanswerable silencer of cavilers and objectors, was Sojourner Truth, that unique and rugged genius who seemed carved out without hand or chisel from the solid mountain mass; and in pleasing contrast, Amanda Smith, sweetest of natural singers and pleaders in dulcet tones for the things of God and of His Christ.

Sarah Woodson Early and Martha Briggs, planting and watering in the school room, and giving off from their matchless and irresistible personality an impetus and inspiration which can never die so long as there lives and breathes a remote descendant of their disciples and friends.

Charlotte Forten Grimké, the gentle spirit whose verses and life link her so beautifully with America's great Quaker poet and loving reformer.

Hallie Quinn Brown, charming reader, earnest, effective lecturer and devoted worker of unflagging zeal and unquestioned power.

Fanny Jackson Coppin, the teacher and organizer, pre-eminent among women of whatever country or race in constructive and executive force.

These women represent all shades of belief and as many departments of activity; but they have one thing in common—their sympathy with the oppressed race in America and the consecration of their several talents in whatever line to the work of its deliverance and development.

Fifty years ago woman's activity according to orthodox definitions was on a pretty clearly cut "sphere," including primarily the kitchen and the nursery, and rescued from the barrenness of prison bars by the womanly mania for adorning every discoverable bit of china or canvass with forlorn looking cranes balanced idiotically on one foot. The woman of to-day finds herself in the presence of responsibilities which ramify through the profoundest and most varied interests of her country and race. Not one of the issues of this plodding, toiling, sinning, repenting, falling, aspiring humanity can afford to shut her out, or can deny the reality of her influ-ence. No plan for renovating society, no scheme for purifying politics, no reform in church or in state, no moral, social, or economic question, no movement upward or downward in the human plane is lost on her. A man once said when told his house was afire: "Go tell my wife; I never meddle with household affairs." But no woman can possibly put herself or her sex outside any of the interests that affect humanity. All departments in the new era are to be hers, in the sense that her interests are in all and through all; and it is incumbent on her to keep intelligently and sympathetically *en rapport* with all the great movements of her time, that she may know on which side to throw the weight of her influence. She stands now at the gateway of this new era of American civilization. In her hands must be moulded the strength, the wit, the statesmanship, the morality, all the psychic force, the social and economic intercourse of that era. To be alive at such an epoch is a privilege, to be a woman then is sublime.

In this last decade of our century, changes of such moment are in progress, such new and alluring vistas are opening out before us, such original and radical suggestions for the adjustment of labor and capital, of government and the governed, of the family, the church and the state, that to be a possible factor though an infinitesimal in such a movement is pregnant with hope and weighty with responsibility. To be a woman in such an age carries with it a privilege and an opportunity never implied before. But to be a woman of the Negro race in America, and to be able to grasp the deep significance of the possibilities of the crisis, is to have a heritage, it seems to me, unique in the ages. In the first place, the race is young and full of the elasticity and hopefulness of youth. All its achievements are before it. It does not look on the masterly triumphs of nineteenth century civilization with that *blasé* world-weary look which characterized the old washed out and worn out races which have already, so to speak, seen their best days.

Said a European writer recently: "Except the Slavonic, the Negro is the only original and distinctive genius which has yet to come to growth—and the feeling is to cherish and develop it."

Everything to this race is new and strange and inspiring. There is a quickening of its pulses and a glowing of its self-consciousness. Aha, I can rival that! I can aspire to that! I can honor my name and vindicate my race! Something like this, it strikes me, is the enthusiasm which stirs the genius of young Africa in America; and the memory of past oppression and the fact of present attempted repression only serve to gather momentum for its irrepressible powers. Then again, a race in such a stage of growth is peculiarly sensitive to impressions. Not the photographer's sensitized plate is more delicately impressionable to outer influences than is this high strung people here on the threshold of a career.

What a responsibility then to have the sole management of the primal lights and shadows! Such is the colored woman's office. She must stamp weal or woe on the coming history of this people. May she see her opportunity and vindicate her high prerogative.

· II ·

Race and Culture:
A Voice from the South, Part 2

Part II: Tutti ad Libitum

A *People* is but the attempt of many
To rise to the completer life of one.
　　　★　★　★
The common *Problem*, yours, mine, every one's
Is—not to fancy what were fair in life
Provided it could be,—but, finding first
What may be, then find how to make it fair
Up to our means; a very different thing!

　　　　　　　　　　　　　—*Robert Browning*

The greatest question in the world is how to give every man a man's share in what goes on in life—we want a freeman's share, and that is to think and speak and act about what concerns us all, and see whether these fine gentlemen who undertake to govern us are doing the best they can for us.—*Felix Holt*★

★Felix Holt is the hero of George Eliot's novel *Felix Holt, the Radical* (1866).

120

Has America a Race Problem?
If So, How Can It Best Be Solved? (1892)

$\mathscr{T}$here are two kinds of peace in this world. The one produced by suppression, which is the passivity of death; the other brought about by a proper adjustment of living, acting forces. A nation or an individual may be at peace because all opponents have been killed or crushed; or, nation as well as individual may have found the secret of true harmony in the determination to live and let live.

A harmless looking man was once asked how many there were in his family.

"Ten," he replied grimly; "my wife's a one and I a zero." In that family there was harmony, to be sure, but it was the harmony of a despotism—it was the quiet of a muzzled mouth, the smoldering peace of a volcano crusted over.

Now I need not say that peace produced by suppression is neither natural nor desirable. Despotism is not one of the ideas that man has copied from nature. All through God's universe we see eternal harmony and symmetry as the unvarying result of the equilibrium of opposing forces. Fair play in an equal fight is the law written in Nature's book. And the solitary bully with his foot on the breast of his last antagonist has no warrant in any fact of God.

The beautiful curves described by planets and suns in their courses are the resultant of conflicting forces. Could the centrifugal force for one instant triumph, or should the centripetal grow weary and give up the struggle, immeasurable disaster would ensue—earth, moon, sun would go spinning off at a tangent or must fall helplessly into its master sphere. The acid counterbalances and keeps in order the alkali; the negative, the positive electrode. A proper equilibrium between a most inflammable explosive and the supporter of combustion, gives us water, the bland fluid that we cannot dispense with. Nay, the very air we breathe, which seems so calm, so peaceful, is rendered innocuous only by the constant conflict of opposing gases. Were the fiery, never-resting, all-corroding oxygen to gain the mastery we should be burnt to cinders in a trice. With the sluggish, inert nitrogen triumphant, we should die of inanition.

These facts are only a suggestion of what must be patent to every student of history. Progressive peace in a nation is the result of conflict; and conflict, such as is healthy, stimulating, and progressive, is produced through the co-existence of radically opposing or racially different elements. Bellamy's ox-like men pictured in *Looking Backward*, taking their daily modicum of provender from the grandmotherly government, with nothing to struggle for, no wrong to put down, no reform to push through, no rights to vindicate and uphold, are nice folks to read about; but they are not natural; they are not progressive. God's world is not governed that way. The child can never gain strength save by resistance, and there can be no resistance if all movement is in one direction and all opposition made forever an impossibility.

I confess I can see no deeper reason than this for the specializing of racial types in the world. Whatever our theory with reference to the origin of species and the unity of mankind, we cannot help admitting the fact that no sooner does a family of the human race take up its abode in some little nook between mountains, or on some plain walled in by their own hands, no sooner do they begin in earnest to live their own life, think their own thoughts, and trace out their own arts, than they begin also to crystallize some idea different from and generally opposed to that of other tribes or families.

Each race has its badge, its exponent, its message, branded in its forehead by the great Master's hand which is its own peculiar keynote, and its contribution to the harmony of nations.

Left entirely alone,—out of contact, that is with other races and their opposing ideas and conflicting tendencies, this cult is abnormally developed and there is unity without variety, a predominance of one tone at the expense of moderation and harmony, and finally a sameness, a monotonous dullness which means stagnation,—death.

It is this of which M. Guizot complains in Asiatic types of civilization; and in each case he mentions I note that there was but one race, one free force predominating. In Lect. II *History of Civilization* he says:

In Egypt the theocratic principle took possession of society and showed itself in its manners, its monuments and in all that has come down to us of Egyptian civilization. In India the same phenomenon occurs—a repetition of the almost exclusively prevailing influence of theocracy. In other regions the domination of a conquering caste; where such is the case the principle of force takes entire possession of society. In another place we discover society under the entire influence of the democratic principle. Such was the case in the commercial republics which covered the coasts of Asia Minor and Syria, in Ionia and Phoenicia. In a word whenever we contemplate the civilization of the ancients, we find them all impressed with *one ever prevailing character of unity*, visible in their institutions, their ideas and manners; *one sole influence seems to govern and determine all things.* . . . In one nation, as in Greece, the unity of the social principle led to a development of wonderful rapidity; no other people ever ran so brilliant a career in so short a time. But Greece had hardly become glorious before she appeared worn out. Her decline was as sudden as her rise had been rapid. It seems as if the principle which called Greek civilization into life was exhausted. No other came to invigorate it or supply its place. In India and Egypt where again only one principle of civilization prevailed [*one race predominant you see*] society became stationary. Simplicity produced monotony. Society continued to exist, but there was no progression. It remained torpid and inactive.

Now I beg you to note that in none of these systems was a RACE PROBLEM possible. The dominant race had settled that matter forever. Asiatic society was fixed in cast iron molds. Virtually there was but one race inspiring and molding the thought, the art, the literature, the government. It was against this shriveling caste prejudice and intolerance that the zealous Buddha set his face like a flint. And I do not think it was all blasphemy in Renan[1] when he said Jesus Christ was first of democrats, i.e., a believer in the royalty of the individual, a preacher of the brotherhood of man through the fatherhood of God, a teacher who proved that the lines on which worlds are said to revolve are *imaginary*, that for all the distinctions of blue blood and black blood and red blood—*a man's a man for a' that*. Buddha and the Christ, each in his own way, wrought to rend asunder the clamps and bands of caste, and to thaw out the ice of race tyranny and exclusiveness. The Brahmin,[2] who was Aryan, spurned a suggestion even, from the Sudra, who belonged to the hated and proscribed Turanian race. With a

---

1. Ernest Renan (1823–1892): French philosopher and historian.
2. Cooper here refers to the Hindu caste system in which the Brahmin is of the highest (usually priestly) caste, and the Sudra the lowest. "Aryan" and "Turanian" refer, however, to the ethnic and cultural groups of different statuses.

Pariah he could not eat or drink. They were to him outcasts and unclean. Association with them meant contamination; the hint of their social equality was blasphemous. Respectful consideration for their rights and feelings was almost a physical no less than a moral impossibility.

No more could the Helots among the Greeks have been said to contribute anything to the movement of their times. The dominant race had them effectually under its heel. It was the tyranny and exclusiveness of these nations, therefore, which brought about their immobility and resulted finally in the barrenness of their one idea. From this came the poverty and decay underlying their civilization, from this the transitory, ephemeral character of its brilliancy.

To quote Guizot again:

> Society belonged to *one exclusive* power which could bear with no other. Every principle of a different tendency was proscribed. The governing principle would nowhere suffer by its side the manifestation and influence of a rival principle. This character of unity in their civilization is equally impressed upon their literature and intellectual productions. Those monuments of Hindoo literature lately introduced into Europe seem all struck from the same die. They all seem the result of one same fact, the expression of one idea. Religious and moral treatises, historical traditions, dramatic poetry, epics, all bear the same physiognomy. The same character of unity and monotony shines out in these works of mind and fancy, as we discover in their life and institutions.

Not even Greece with all its classic treasures is made an exception from these limitations produced by exclusiveness.

But the course of empire moves one degree westward. Europe becomes the theater of the leading exponents of civilization, and here we have a *Race Problem*,—if, indeed, the confused jumble of races, the clash and conflict, the din and devastation of those stormy years can be referred to by so quiet and so dignified a term as "problem." Complex and appalling it surely was. Goths and Huns, Vandals and Danes, Angles, Saxons, Jutes— could any prophet foresee that a vestige of law and order, of civilization and refinement would remain after this clumsy horde of wild barbarians had swept over Europe?

"Where is somebody'll give me some white for all this yellow?" cries one with his hands full of the gold from one of those magnificent monuments of antiquity which he and his tribe had just pillaged and demolished. Says the historian: "Their history is like a history of kites and crows."

Tacitus writes: "To shout, to drink, to caper about, to feel their veins heated and swollen with wine, to hear and see around them the riot of the orgy, this was the first need of the barbarians. The heavy human brute gluts himself with sensations and with noise." Taine[3] describes them as follows:

> Huge white bodies, cool-blooded, with fierce blue eyes, reddish flaxen hair; ravenous stomachs, filled with meat and cheese, heated by strong drinks. Brutal drunken pirates and robbers, they dashed to sea in their two-sailed barks, landed anywhere, killed everything; and, having sacrificed in honor of their gods the tithe of all their prisoners, leaving behind the red light of their burning, went farther on to begin again.

A certain litany of the time reads: "From the fury of the Jutes, Good Lord deliver us." "Elgiva, the wife of one of their kings," says a chronicler of the time, "they hamstrung and subjected to the death she deserved"; and their heroes are frequently represented as tearing out the heart of their human victim and eating it while it still quivered with life.

A historian of the time, quoted by Taine, says it was the custom to buy men and women in all parts of England and to carry them to Ireland for sale. The buyers usually made the women pregnant and took them to market in that condition to ensure a better price. "You might have seen," continues the historian, "long files of young people of both sexes and of great beauty, bound with ropes and daily exposed for sale. They sold as slaves in this manner, their nearest relatives and even their own children."

What could civilization hope to do with such a swarm of sensuous, bloodthirsty vipers? Assimilation was horrible to contemplate. They will drag us to their level, quoth the culture of the times. Deportation was out of the question; and there was no need to talk of their emigrating. The fact is, the barbarians were in no hurry about moving. They didn't even care to colonize. They had come to stay. And Europe had to grapple with her race problem till time and God should solve it.

And how was it solved, and what kind of civilization resulted?

Once more let us go to Guizot. "Take ever so rapid a glance," says he,

> at modern Europe and it strikes you at once as diversified, confused, and stormy. All the principles of social organization are found existing together within it; powers temporal, and powers spiritual, the theocratic, monarchic, aristocratic, and democratic elements, all classes of society *in*

---

3. Hippolyte Taine (1828–1893): French critic, historian, and philosopher.

a state of continual struggle without any one having sufficient force to master the others and take sole possession of society.

Then as to the result of this conflict of forces:

> Incomparably more rich and diversified than the ancient, European civilization has within it the promise of *perpetual progress*. It has now endured more than fifteen centuries and in all that time has been in a state of progression, not so rapidly as the Greek nor yet so ephemeral. While in other civilizations the exclusive domination of a principle [*or race*] led to tyranny, in Europe the diversity of social elements [*growing out of the contact of different races*] the incapability of any one to exclude the rest, gave birth to the LIBERTY which now prevails. This inability of the various principles to exterminate one another compelled each to endure the others and made it necessary for them in order to live in common to enter into a sort of mutual understanding. Each consented to have only that part of civilization which equitably fell to its share. Thus, while everywhere else the predominance of one principle produced tyranny, the variety and warfare of the elements of European civilization gave birth to *reciprocity and liberty*.

There is no need to quote further. This is enough to show that the law holds good in sociology as in the world of matter, *that equilibrium, not repression among conflicting forces is the condition of natural harmony, of permanent progress, and of universal freedom.* That exclusiveness and selfishness in a family, in a community, or in a nation is suicidal to progress. Caste and prejudice mean immobility. One race predominance means death. The community that closes its gates against foreign talent can never hope to advance beyond a certain point. Resolve to keep out foreigners and you keep out progress. Home talent develops its one idea and then dies. Like the century plant it produces its one flower, brilliant and beautiful it may be, but it lasts only for a night. Its forces have exhausted themselves in that one effort. Nothing remains but to wither and to rot.

It was the Chinese wall that made China in 1800 A.D. the same as China in the days of Confucius. Its women have not even yet learned that they need not bandage their feet if they do not relish it. The world has rolled on, but within that wall the thoughts, the fashions, the art, the tradition, and the beliefs are those of a thousand years ago. Until very recently, the Chinese were wholly out of the current of human progress. They were like gray headed infants—a man of eighty years with the concepts and imaginings of a babe of eight months. A civilization measured by thousands of years with a development that might be comprised within as many days—arrested development due to exclusive living.

But European civilization, rich as it was compared to Asiatic types, was still not the consummation of the ideal of human possibilities. One more degree westward the hand on the dial points. In Europe there was conflict, but the elements crystallized out in isolated nodules, so to speak. Italy has her dominant principle, Spain hers, France hers, England hers, and so on. The proximity is close enough for interaction and mutual restraint, though the acting forces are at different points. To preserve the balance of power, which is nothing more than the equilibrium of warring elements, England can be trusted to keep an eye on her beloved step-relation-in-law, Russia,—and Germany no doubt can be relied on to look after France and some others. It is not, however, till the scene changes and America is made the theater of action, that the interplay of forces narrow[s] down to a single platform.

Hither came Cavalier and Roundhead, Baptist and Papist, Quaker, Ritualist, Freethinker and Mormon, the conservative Tory, the liberal Whig, and the radical Independent,—the Spaniard, the Frenchman, the Englishman, the Italian, the Chinaman, the African, Swedes, Russians, Huns, Bohemians, Gypsies, Irish, Jews. Here surely was a seething caldron of conflicting elements. Religious intolerance and political hatred, race prejudice and caste pride—

> Double, double, toil and trouble;
> Fire burn and cauldron bubble.[4]

Conflict, Conflict, Conflict.

America for Americans! This is the white man's country! The Chinese must go, shrieks the exclusionist. Exclude the Italians! Colonize the blacks in Mexico or deport them to Africa. Lynch, suppress, drive out, kill out! America for Americans!

"*Who are Americans?*" comes rolling back from ten million throats. Who are to do the packing and delivering of the goods? Who are the homefolks and who are the strangers? Who are the absolute and original tenants in fee-simple?

The red men used to be owners of the soil,—but they are about to be

---

4. Chorus of the three witches in act 4 of Shakespeare's *Macbeth*.

pushed over into the Pacific Ocean. They, perhaps, have the best right to call themselves "Americans" by law of primogeniture. They are at least the oldest inhabitants of whom we can at present identify any traces. If early settlers from abroad merely are meant and it is only a question of squatters' rights—why, the Mayflower, a pretty venerable institution, landed in the year of Grace 1620, and the first delegation from Africa just one year ahead of that,—in 1619. The first settlers seem to have been almost as much mixed as we are on this point; and it does not seem at all easy to decide just what individuals we mean when we yell "America for the Americans." At least the cleavage cannot be made by hues and noses, if we are to seek for the genuine F. F. V.'s[5] as the inhabitants best entitled to the honor of that name.

The fact is this nation was foreordained to conflict from its incipiency. Its elements were predestined from their birth to an irrepressible clash followed by the stable equilibrium of opposition. Exclusive possession belongs to none. There never was a point in history when it did. There was never a time since America became a nation when there were not more than one race, more than one party, more than one belief contending for supremacy. Hence no one is or can be supreme. All interests must be consulted, all claims conciliated. Where a hundred free forces are lustily clamoring for recognition and each wrestling mightily for the mastery, individual tyrannies must inevitably be chiselled down, individual bigotries worn smooth and malleable, individual prejudices either obliterated or concealed. America is not from choice more than of necessity republic in form and democratic in administration. The will of the majority must rule simply because no class, no family, no individual has ever been able to prove sufficient political legitimacy to impose [its] yoke on the country. All attempts at establishing oligarchy must be made by wheedling and cajoling, pretending that not supremacy but service is sought. The nearest approach to outspoken self-assertion is in the conciliatory tones of candid compromise. "I will let you enjoy that if you will not hinder me in the pursuit of this" has been the American sovereign's home policy since his first Declaration of Independence was inscribed as his policy abroad. Compromise and concession, liberality and toleration were the conditions of the nation's birth and are the *sine qua non* of its continued existence. A general amnesty and universal reciprocity are the only *modus vivendi* in a nation whose every citizen is his own king, his own priest and his own pope.

---

5. F.F.V.'s: Reference is obscure; perhaps, from the context, "First Foreign Visitors."

Tocqueville,[6] years ago, predicted that republicanism must fail in America. But if republicanism fails, America fails, and somehow I can not think this colossal stage was erected for a tragedy. I must confess to being an optimist on the subject of my country. It is true we are too busy making history, and have been for some years past, to be able to write history yet, or to understand and interpret it. Our range of vision is too short for us to focus and image our conflicts. Indeed Von Holtz, the clearest headed of calm spectators, says he doubts if the history of American conflict can be written yet even by a disinterested foreigner. The clashing of arms and the din of battle, the smoke of cannon and the heat of combat, are not yet cleared away sufficiently for us to have the judicial vision of historians. Our jottings are like newspaper reports written in the saddle, mid prancing steeds and roaring artillery.

But of one thing we may be sure: the God of battles is in the conflicts of history. The evolution of civilization is His care, eternal progress His delight. As the European was higher and grander than the Asiatic, so will American civilization be broader and deeper and closer to the purposes of the Eternal than any the world has yet seen. This the last page is to mark the climax of history, the bright consummate flower unfolding *charity toward all and malice toward none,*—the final triumph of universal reciprocity born of universal conflict with forces that cannot be exterminated. Here at last is an arena in which every agony has a voice and free speech. Not a spot where no wrong can exist, but where each feeblest interest can cry with Themistocles, *"Strike, but hear me!"* Here you will not see as in Germany women hitched to a cart with donkeys; not perhaps because men are more chivalrous here than there, but because woman can speak. Here labor will not be starved and ground to powder, because the laboring man can make himself heard. Here races that are weakest can, *if they so elect*, make themselves felt.

The supremacy of one race,—the despotism of a class or the tyranny of an individual can not ultimately prevail on a continent held in equilibrium by such conflicting forces and by so many and such strong fibred races as there are struggling on this soil. Never in America shall one man dare to say as Germany's somewhat bumptious emperor[7] is fond of proclaiming: "There is only one master in the country and I am he. I shall suffer no other beside me. Only to God and my conscience am I accountable."

---

6. Alexis de Tocqueville (1805–1859): French historian and political scientist, author of *Democracy in America* (1835).

7. Kaiser Wilhelm II (1859–1941), who abdicated at the end of World War I.

The strength of the opposition tones down and polishes off all such ugly excrescencies as that. "I am the State," will never be proclaimed above a whisper on a platform where there is within arm's length another just as strong, possibly stronger, who holds, or would like to hold that identical proposition with reference to himself. In this arena then is to be the last death struggle of political tyranny, of religious bigotry, and intellectual intolerance, of caste illiberality and class exclusiveness. And the last monster that shall be throttled forever methinks is race prejudice. Men will here learn that a race, as a family, may be true to itself without seeking to exterminate all others. That for the note of the feeblest there is room, nay a positive need, in the harmonies of God. That the principles of true democracy are founded in universal reciprocity, and that "A man's a man" was written when God first stamped His own image and superscription on His child and breathed into his nostrils the breath of life. And I confess I can pray for no nobler destiny for my country than that it may be the stage, however far distant in the future, whereon these ideas and principles shall ultimately mature; and culminating here at whatever cost of production shall go forth hence to dominate the world.

Methought I saw a mighty conflagration, plunging and heaving, surging and seething, smoking and rolling over this American continent. Strong men and wise men stand helpless in mute consternation. Empty headed babblers add the din of their bray to the crashing and crackling of the flames. But the hungry flood rolls on. The air is black with smoke and cinders. The sky is red with lurid light. Forked tongues of fiery flame dart up and lick the pale stars, and seem to laugh at men's feebleness and frenzy. As I look on I think of Schiller's[8] sublime characterization of fire: "Frightful becomes this God-power, when it snatches itself free from fetters and stalks majestically forth on its own career—the free daughter of Nature." Ingenuity is busy with newly patented snuffers all warranted to extinguish the flame. The street gamin with a hooked wire pulls out a few nuggets that chanced to be lying on the outskirts where they were cooked by the heat; and gleefully cries "What a nice fire to roast my chestnuts," and like little Jack Horner, "what a nice boy am I!"

Meantime this expedient, that expedient, the other expedient is suggested by thinkers and theorizers hoping to stifle the angry, roaring, devouring demon and allay the mad destruction.

---

8. Friedrich von Schiller (1759–1805): German historian, playwright, and poet. The three extracts of poetry in the following paragraph are probably from his work—the first almost certainly.

> Wehe wenn sie losgelassen,
>   Wachsend ohne Widerstand,
> Durch die volkbelebten Gassen
>   Walzt den ungeheuren Brand!

But the strength of the Omnipotent is in it. The hand of God is leading it on. It matters not whether you and I in mad desperation cast our quivering bodies into it as our funeral pyre; or whether, like the street urchins, we pull wires to secure the advantage of the passing moment. We can neither help it nor hinder; only

> Let thy gold be cast in the furnace,
>   Thy red gold, precious and bright.
> Do not fear the hungry fire
>   With its caverns of burning light.

If it takes the dearest idol, the pet theory or the darling "ism," the pride, the selfishness, the prejudices, the exclusiveness, the bigotry and intolerance, the conceit of self, of race, or of family superiority,—nay, if it singe from thee thy personal gratifications in thy distinction by birth, by blood, by sex—everything,—and leave thee nothing but thy naked manhood, solitary and unadorned,—let them go—let them go!

> And thy gold shall return more precious,
> Free from every spot and stain,
> For gold must be tried by fire.

And the heart of nations must be tried by pain; and their polish, their true culture must be wrought in through conflict.

Has America a Race Problem?

Yes.

What are you going to do about it?

Let it alone and mind my own business. It is God's problem and He will solve it in time. It is deeper than Gehenna. What can you or I do!

Are there then no duties and special lines of thought growing out of the present conditions of this problem?

Certainly there are. *Imprimis;* let every element of the conflict see that it represent a positive force so as to preserve a proper equipoise in the conflict. No shirking, no skulking, no masquerading in another's uniform. Stand by your guns. And be ready for the charge. The day is coming, and now is, when America must ask each citizen not "who was your grand-father and what the color of his cuticle," but "*What can you do?*" Be ready each individual element,—each race, each class, each family, each man to reply "*I engage to undertake an honest man's share.*"

God and time will work the problem. You and I are only to stand for the quantities *at their best*, which he means us to represent.

Above all, for the love of humanity stop the mouth of those learned theorizers, the expedient mongers, who come out annually with their new and improved method of getting the answer and clearing the slate: amal-gamation, deportation, colonization and all the other "ations" that were ever devised or dreamt of. If Alexander wants to be a god, let him; but don't have Alexander hawking his patent plan for universal deification. If all could or would follow Alexander's plan, just the niche in the divine cosmos meant for man would be vacant. And we think that men have a part to play in this great drama no less than gods, and so if a few are determined to be white—amen, so be it; but don't let them argue as if there were no part to be played in life by black men and black women, and as if to become white were the sole specific and panacea for all the ills that flesh is heir to—the universal solvent for all America's irritations. And again, if an American family of whatever condition or hue takes a notion to reside in Africa or in Mexico, or in the isles of the sea, it is most un-American for any power on this continent to seek to gainsay or obstruct their departure; but on the other hand, no power or element of power on this continent, least of all a self-constituted tribunal of "recent arrivals," possesses the right to begin figuring beforehand to calculate what it would require *to send* ten millions of citizens, whose ancestors have wrought here from the planting of the nation, to the same places at so much per head—at least till some one has consulted those heads.

We would not deprecate the fact, then, that America has a Race Prob-lem. It is guaranty of the perpetuity and progress of her institutions, and insures the breadth of her culture and the symmetry of her development. More than all, let us not disparage the factor which the Negro is appointed to contribute to that problem. America needs the Negro for ballast if for nothing else. His tropical warmth and spontaneous emotionalism may form no unseemly counterpart to the cold and calculating Anglo-Saxon. And then his instinct for law and order, his inborn respect for authority, his inaptitude for rioting and anarchy, his gentleness and cheerfulness as a la-borer, and his deep-rooted faith in God will prove indispensable and in-valuable elements in a nation menaced as America is by anarchy, socialism, communism, and skepticism poured in with all the jail birds from the continents of Europe and Asia. I believe with our own Dr. Crummell that "the Almighty does not preserve, rescue, and build up a lowly people merely for ignoble ends." And the historian of American civilization will yet congratulate this country that she has had a Race Problem and that descendants of the black race furnished one of its largest factors.

· 8 ·

The Negro As Presented in American Literature (1892)

$\mathcal{F}$or nations as for individuals, a product, to be worthy the term literature, must contain something characteristic and *sui generis*.

So long as America remained a mere English colony, drawing all her life and inspiration from the mother country, it may well be questioned whether there was such a thing as American literature. "Who ever reads an American book?" it was scornfully asked in the eighteenth century. Imitation is the worst of suicides; it cuts the nerve of originality and condemns to mediocrity: and 'twas not till the pen of our writers was dipped in the life blood of their own nation and pictured out its own peculiar heart throbs and agonies that the world cared to listen. The nightingale and the skylark had to give place to the mocking bird, the bobolink and the whippoorwill, the heather and the blue bells of Britain, to our own golden-rod and daisy; the insular and monarchic customs and habits of thought of old England must develop into the broader, looser, freer swing of democratic America, before her contributions to the world of thought could claim the distinction of individuality and gain an appreciative hearing.

And so our writers have succeeded in becoming national and representative in proportion as they have from year to year entered more and more fully, and more and more sympathetically, into the distinctive life of their nation, and endeavored to reflect and picture its homeliest pulsations and its elemental components. And so in all the arts, as men have gradually come to realize that

> Nothing useless is or low
> Each thing in its place is best,

and have wrought into their products, lovingly and impartially and reverently, every type, every tint, every tone that they felt or saw or heard, just to that degree have their expressions, whether by pen or brush or rhythmic cadence, adequately and simply given voice to the thought of Nature around them. No man can prophesy with another's parable. For each of us truth means merely the re-presentation of the sensations and experiences of our personal environment, colored and vivified—fused into consistency and crystallized into individuality in the crucible of our own feelings and imaginations. The mind of genius is merely the brook, picturing back its own tree and bush and bit of sky and cloud ensparkled by individual salts and sands and rippling motion. And paradoxical as it may seem, instead of making us narrow and provincial, this trueness to one's habitat, this appreciative eye and ear for the tints and voices of one's own little wood serves but to usher us into the eternal galleries and choruses of God. It is only through the unclouded perception of our tiny "part" that we can come to harmonize with the "stupendous whole," and in order to [do] this our sympathies must be finely attuned and quick to vibrate under the touch of the commonplace and vulgar no less than at the hand of the elegant and refined. Nothing natural can be wholly unworthy; and we do so at our peril, if, what God has cleansed we presume to call common or unclean. Nature's language is not writ in cipher. Her notes are always simple and sensuous, and the very meanest recesses and commonest byways are fairly deafening with her sermons and songs. It is only when we ourselves are out of tune through our pretentiousness and self-sufficiency, or are blinded and rendered insensate by reason of our foreign and unnatural "cultivation" that we miss her meanings and inadequately construe her multiform lessons.

For two hundred and fifty years there was in the American commonwealth a great *silent* factor. Though [they were] in themselves simple and unique their offices were those of the barest utility. [Though they were] imported merely to be hewers of wood and drawers of water, no artist for many a generation thought them worthy the sympathetic study of a model. No Shakespeare arose to distil from their unmatched personality and unparalleled situations the exalted poesy and crude grandeur of an immortal Caliban. Distinct in color, original in temperament, simple and unconventionalized in thought and action [, they would have furnished, in] their spiritual development and impressionability under their novel environment . . . , it might seem, as interesting a study in psychology for the poetic pen, as would the gorges of the Yosemite to the inspired pencil. [They were so] full of vitality and natural elasticity [that] the severest persecution and oppression could not kill them out or even sour their temper. With massive brawn and indefatigable endurance they wrought under burning suns and chilling blasts, in swamps and marshes,—they cleared the forests, tunneled mountains, threaded the land with railroads, planted, picked and ginned the cotton, produced the rice and the sugar of the markets of the world. Without money and without price they poured their hearts' best blood into the enriching and developing of this country. *They wrought but were silent.*

The most talked about of all the forces in this diversified civilization, they seemed the great American fact, the one objective reality, on which scholars sharpened their wits, at which orators and statesmen fired their eloquence, and from which, after so long a time, authors, with varied success and truthfulness have begun at last to draw subjects and models. Full of imagination and emotion, their sensuous pictures of the "New Jerusalem," "the golden slippers," "the long white robe," "the pearly gates," etc., etc., seem fairly to steam with tropical luxuriance and naive abandon. The paroxysms of religious fervor into which this simple-minded, childlike race were thrown by the contemplation of Heaven and rest and freedom, would have melted into sympathy and tender pity if not into love, a race less cold and unresponsive than the one with which they were thrown in closest contact. There was something truly poetic in their weird moanings, their fitful gleams of hope and trust, flickering amidst the darkness of their wailing helplessness, their strange sad songs, the half coherent ebullitions of souls in pain, which become, the more they are studied, at once the wonder and the despair of musical critics and imitators. And if one had the insight and the simplicity to gather together, to digest and assimilate these original lispings of an unsophisticated people while they were yet close—so close—to nature and to nature's God, there is material here, one might almost believe, as rich, as unhackneyed, as original and distinctive as ever inspired a Homer, or a Cædmon or other simple genius of a people's infancy and lisping childhood.

In the days of their bitterest persecution, their patient endurance and Christian manliness inspired *Uncle Tom's Cabin*, which revolutionized the thought of the world on the subject of slavery and at once placed its author in the front rank of the writers of her country and age. Here at last was a work which England could not parallel. Here was a work indigenous to American soil and characteristic of the country—a work which American forces alone could have produced. The subject was at once seen to be fresh and interesting to the world as well as national and peculiar to America; and so it has since been eagerly cultivated by later writers with widely varying degrees of fitness and success.

By a rough classification, authors may be separated into two groups: first, those in whom the artistic or poetic instinct is uppermost—those who write to please—or rather who write because *they* please; who simply paint what they see, as naturally, as instinctively, and as irresistibly as the bird sings—with no thought of an audience—singing because it loves to sing,— singing because God, nature, truth sings through it. For such writers, to be true to themselves and true to Nature is the only canon. They cannot warp a character or distort a fact in order to prove a point. They have nothing to prove. All who care to, may listen while they make the woods resound with their glad sweet carolling; and the listeners may draw their own conclusions as to the meaning of the cadences of this minor strain, or that hushed and almost awful note of rage or despair. And the myriad-minded multitude attribute their myriad-fold impressions to the myriad-minded soul by which they have severally been enchanted, each in his own way according to what he brings to the witching auditorium. But the singer sings on with his hat before his face, unmindful, it may be unconscious, of the varied strains reproduced from him in the multitudinous echoes of the crowd. Such was Shakespeare, such was George Eliot, such was Robert Browning. Such, in America, was Poe, was Bryant,[1] was Longfellow; and such, in his own degree perhaps, is Mr. Howells.[2]

In the second group belong the preachers,—whether of righteousness or unrighteousness,—all who have an idea to propagate, no matter in what form their talent enables them to clothe it, whether poem, novel, or sermon,—all those writers with a purpose or a lesson, who catch you by the buttonhole and pommel you over the shoulder till you are forced to give assent in order to escape their vociferations; or they may lure you into listening with the soft music of the siren's tongue—no matter what the expedient to catch and hold your attention, they mean to fetter you with their one idea, whatever it is, and make you, if possible, ride their hobby. In this group I would place Milton in much of his writing, Carlyle in all of his, often our own Whittier, the great reformer-poet, and Lowell; together with such novelists as E. P. Roe,[3] Bellamy, Tourgee[4] and some others.

1. William Cullen Bryant (1794–1878): American poet and journalist. And, following, Henry Wadsworth Longfellow (1807–1862): American poet and professor.
2. Almost certainly William Dean Howells (1837–1920): novelist and critic best remembered for his novel *The Rise of Silas Lapham*.
3. Edward Payson Roe (1838–1888): novelist. And Bellamy is Edward Bellamy (1850–1898): author of *Looking Backward* (1887). And above, Thomas Carlyle (1795–1881): historian of the French Revolution.
4. Albion Winegar Tourgee (1835–1905): novelist noted for depictions of the Reconstruction South. He wrote a favorable review of Cooper's *Voice from the South*.

Now in my judgment writings of the first class will be the ones to withstand the ravages of time. "Isms" have their day and pass away. New necessities arise with new conditions and the emphasis has to be shifted to suit the times. No finite mind can grasp and give out the whole circle of truth. We do well if we can illuminate just the tiny arc which we occupy and should be glad that the next generation will not need the lessons we try so assiduously to hammer into this. In the evolution of society, as the great soul of humanity builds it "more lofty chambers," the old shell and slough of didactic teaching must be left behind and forgotten. The world for instance has outgrown, I suspect, those passages of *Paradise Lost* in which Milton[5] makes the Almighty Father propound the theology of a seventeenth century Presbyterian. But a passage like the one in which Eve with guileless innocence describes her first sensations on awaking into the world is as perennial as man.

> That day I oft remember, when from sleep
> I first awaked and found myself reposed
> Under a shade on flowers, much wondering where
> And what I was, whence thither brought and how.
> Not distant far from thence a murmuring sound
> Of waters issued from a cave, and spread
> Into a liquid plain, then stood unmoved
> Pure as the expanse of Heaven;
>   I thither went
> With unexperienced thought and laid me down
> On the green bank, to look into the clear
> Smooth lake that to me seemed another sky.
> As I bent down to look, just opposite
> A shape within the watery gleam appeared,
> Bending to look on me; I started back,
> It started back; but pleased I soon returned,
> Pleased it returned as soon with answering looks
> Of sympathy and love; there I had fixed
> Mine eyes till now,—and pined with vain desire,
> Had not a voice thus warned me.
>   "What thou seest,
> What there thou seest, fair creature, is thyself;
> With thee it came and goes; but follow me,

5. John Milton (1608–1674): author of *Paradist Lost,* (1667), from which the long extract following is taken.

And I will bring thee where no shadow stays
Thy coming and thy soft embraces."
      What could I do but follow straight
Invisibly thus led?
Till I espied thee, fair indeed and tall,
Under a plantain; yet methought less fair,
Less winning soft, less amiably mild
Than that smooth watery image; back I turned
Thou following criedst aloud, "Return, fair Eve,
Whom fliest thou? whom thou fliest, of him thou art.
Part of my soul, I seek thee, and thee claim
My other half."

This will never cease to throb and thrill as long as man is man and woman is woman.

Now owing to the problematical position at present occupied by descendants of Africans in the American social polity,—growing, I presume, out of the continued indecision in the mind of the more powerful descendants of the Saxons as to whether it is expedient to apply the maxims of their religion to their civil and political relationships,—most of the writers who have hitherto attempted a portrayal of life and customs among the darker race have belonged to our class II: they have all, more or less, had a point to prove or a mission to accomplish, and thus their art has been almost uniformly perverted to serve their ends; and, to add to their disadvantage, most, if not all the writers on this line have been but partially acquainted with the life they wished to delineate and through sheer ignorance ofttimes, as well as from design occasionally, have not been able to put themselves in the darker man's place. The art of "thinking one's self imaginatively into the experiences of others" is not given to all, and it is impossible to acquire it without a background and a substratum of sympathetic knowledge. Without this power our portraits are but death's heads or caricatures and no amount of cudgeling can put into them the movement and reality of life. Not many have had Mrs. Stowe's[6] power because not many have studied with Mrs. Stowe's humility and love. They forget that underneath the black man's form and behavior there is the great bedrock of humanity, the key to which is the same that unlocks every tribe and kindred of the nations of earth. Some have taken up the subject with a view to establishing evidences of ready formulated theories and preconcep-

---

6. Harriet Beecher Stowe (1811–1896): author of *Uncle Tom's Cabin.*

tions; and, blinded by their prejudices and antipathies, have altogether ab-jured all candid and careful study. Others with flippant indifference have performed a few psychological experiments on their cooks and coachmen, and with astounding egotism, and powers of generalization positively be-wildering, forthwith aspire to enlighten the world with dissertations on racial traits of the Negro. A few with really kind intentions and a sincere desire for information have approached the subject as a clumsy microsco-pist, not quite at home with his instrument, might study a new order of beetle or bug. Not having focused closely enough to obtain a clear-cut view, they begin by telling you that all colored people look exactly alike and end by noting down every chance contortion or idiosyncrasy as a race characteristic. Some of their conclusions remind one of the enterprising German on a tour of research and self improvement through Great Britain, who recommended his favorite sauer kraut both to an Irishman, whom he found sick with fever, and to a Scotchman, who had a cold. On going that way subsequently and finding the Scotchman well and the Irishman dead, he writes: "*Mem.—Sauer kraut good for the Scotch but death to the Irish.*"

This criticism is not altered by our grateful remembrance of those who have heroically taken their pens to champion the black man's cause. But even here we may remark that a painter may be irreproachable in motive and as benevolent as an angel in intention, nevertheless we have a right to compare his copy with the original and point out in what respects it falls short or is overdrawn; and he should thank us for doing so.

It is in no captious spirit, therefore, that we note a few contributions to this phase of American literature which have been made during the present decade; we shall try to estimate their weight, their tendency, their truthfulness and their lessons, if any, for ourselves.

Foremost among the champions of the black man's cause through the medium of fiction must be mentioned Albion W. Tourgee. No man de-serves more the esteem and appreciation of the colored people of this coun-try for his brave words. For ten years he has stood almost alone as the enthusiastic advocate, not of charity and dole to the Negro, but of justice. The volumes he has written upon the subject have probably been read by from five to ten millions of the American people. Look over his list conse-crated to one phase or another of the subject: *A Fool's Errand, A Royal Gentleman, Bricks without Straw, An Appeal to Caesar, Hot Ploughshares, Pacto-lus Prime,*—over three thousand pages—enough almost for a life work, be-sides an almost interminable quantity published in periodicals.

Mr. Tourgee essays to paint life with the coloring of fiction, and yet, we must say, we do not think him a novelist primarily; that is, novel making with him seems to be a mere incident, a convenient vehicle through which to convey those burning thoughts which he is constantly trying to impress upon the people of America, whether in lecture, stump speech, newspaper column or magazine article. His power is not that already referred to of thinking himself imaginatively into the experiences of others. He does not create many men of many minds. All his offspring are little Tourgees—they preach his sermons and pray his prayers.

In *Pactolus Prime*, for example, one of his latest, his hero, a colored bootblack in a large hotel, is none other than the powerful, impassioned, convinced and convincing lecturer, Judge Tourgee himself, done over in ebony. His caustic wit, his sledge hammer logic, his incisive criticism, his righteous indignation, all reflect the irresistible arguments of the great pleader for the Negro; and all the incidents are arranged to enable this bootblack to impress on senators and judges, lawyers, and divines, his plea for justice to the Negro, along with the blacking and shine which he skillfully puts on their aristocratic toes. And so with all the types which Mr. Tourgee presents—worthy or pitiful ones always—they uniformly preach or teach, convict or convert. Artistic criticism aside, it is mainly as a contribution to polemic literature in favor of the colored man that most of Tourgee's works will be judged; and we know of no one who can more nearly put himself in the Negro's place in resenting his wrongs and pleading for his rights. In presenting truth from the colored American's standpoint Mr. Tourgee excels, we think, in fervency and frequency of utterance any living writer, white or colored.

Mr. Cable[7] is brave and just. He wishes to see justice done in the Freedman's case in equity, and we honor and revere him for his earnest manly efforts towards that end. But Mr. Cable does not forget (I see no reason why he should, of course,) that he is a white man, a Southerner and an ex-soldier in the Confederate army. To use his own words, he writes, "with an admiration and affection for the South, that for justice and sincerity yield to none; in a spirit of faithful sonship to a Southern state." Of course this but proves his sincerity, illustrates his candor, and adds weight to the axiomatic justice of a cause which demands such support from a thoroughly disinterested party, or rather a party whose interest and sympathy and affection must be all on the side he criticizes and condemns. The

---

7. Probably George Washington Cable (1844–1925): novelist noted for depictions of the Louisiana creoles.

passion of the partisan and the bias of the aggrieved can never be charged against him. Mr. Cable's is the impartiality of the judge who condemns his own son or cuts off his own arm. His attitude is judicial, convincing, irreproachable throughout.

Not only the Christian conscience of the South, but also its enlightened self-interest is unquestionably on the side of justice and manly dealing toward the black man; and one can not help feeling that a cause which thus enlists the support and advocacy of the "better self" of a nation must ultimately be invincible: and Mr. Cable, in my judgment, embodies and represents that Christian conscience and enlightened self-interest of the hitherto silent South; he vocalizes and inspires its better self. To him the dishonesty and inhumanity there practiced against the black race is a blot on the scutcheon of that fair land and [is] doomed to bring in its wake untold confusion, disaster, and disgrace. From his calm elevation he sees the impending evil, and with loving solicitude urges his countrymen to flee the wrath to come.

Mr. Tourgee, on the other hand, speaks with all the eloquence and passion of the aggrieved party himself. With his whip of fine cords he pitilessly scourges the inconsistencies, the weaknesses and pettiness of the black man's persecutors. The fire is burning within him, he cannot but speak. He has said himself that he deserves no credit for speaking and writing on this subject, for it has taken hold of him and possesses him to the exclusion of almost everything else. Necessity is laid upon him. Not more bound was Saul of Tarsus to consecrate his fiery eloquence to the cause of the persecuted Nazarene than is this white man to throw all the weight of his powerful soul into the plea for justice and Christianity in this American anomaly and huge inconsistency. Not many colored men would have attempted Tourgee's brave defense of Reconstruction and the alleged corruption of Negro supremacy, more properly termed the period of white sullenness and desertion of duty. Not many would have dared, fearlessly as he did, to arraign this country for an enormous pecuniary debt to the colored man for the two hundred and forty-seven years of unpaid labor of his ancestors. Not many could so determinedly have held up the glass of the real Christianity before these believers in a white Christ and these preachers of the gospel, "Suffer the little *white* children to come unto me." We all see the glaring inconsistency and feel the burning shame. We appreciate the incongruity and the indignity of having to stand forever hat in hand as beggars, or be shoved aside as intruders in a country whose resources have been opened up by the unrequited toil of our forefathers. We know that our bill is a true one—that the debt is as real as to any pensioners of our government. But the principles of patience and forbearance, of meekness and charity, have become so ingrained in the Negro character that there is hardly enough self-assertion left to ask as our right that part of the country's surplus wealth be *loaned* for the education of our children; even though we know that our present poverty is due to the fact that the toil of the last quarter century enriched these coffers, but left us the heirs of crippled, deformed, frost-bitten, horny-handed and empty handed mothers and fathers. Oh, the shame of it!

A coward during the war gets a few scratches and bruises—often in *fleeing from the enemy*—and his heirs are handsomely pensioned by his *grateful* country! But these poor wretches stood every man to his post for two hundred and fifty years, digging trenches, building roads, tunneling mountains, clearing away forests, cultivating the soil in the cotton fields and rice swamps till fingers dropped off, toes were frozen, knees twisted, arms stiff and useless—and when their sons and heirs, with the burdens of helpless parents to support, wish to secure enough education to enable them to make a start in life, *their* grateful country sagely deliberates as to the feasibility of sending them to another undeveloped jungle to show off their talent for unlimited pioneer work in strange climes! The Indian, during the entire occupancy of this country by white men, has stood proudly aloof from all their efforts at development, and presented an unbroken front of hostility to the introduction and spread of civilization. The Negro, though, brought into the country by force and compelled under the lash to lend his brawn and sturdy sinews to promote its material growth and prosperity, nevertheless with perfect amiability of temper and adaptability of mental structure has quietly and unhesitatingly accepted its standards and fallen in line with its creeds. He adjusts himself just as readily and as appreciatively, it would seem, to the higher and stricter requirements of freedom and citizenship; and although from beginning to end, nettled and goaded under unprecedented provocation, he has never once shown any general disposition to arise in his might and deluge this country with blood or desolate it with burning, as he might have done. It is no argument to charge weakness as the cause of his peaceful submission and to sneer at the "inferiority" of a race who would allow themselves to be made slaves—unrevenged. It *may* be nobler to perish redhanded, to kill as many as your battle axe holds out to hack and then fall with an exultant yell and savage grin of fiendish delight on the huge pile of bloody corpses,—expiring with the solace and unction of having ten thousand wounds all in front. I don't know. I sometimes think it depends on where you plant your standard and who wears the white plume which your eye inadvertently seeks. If Napoleon is the ideal of mankind, I suppose 'tis only noble to be strong; and true greatness may consist in an adamantine determination never to serve. The greatest race with which I am even partially acquainted, proudly boasts that it has never met another race save as either enemy or victim. They seem to set great store by this fact and I judge it must be immensely noble according to their ideals. But somehow it seems to me that those nations and races who choose the Nazarene for their plumed knight would find some little jarring and variance between such notions and His ideals. There could not be at all times perfect unanimity between Leader and host. A good many of his sayings, it seems to me, would have to be explained away; not a few of his injunctions quietly ignored, and I am not sure but the great bulk of his principles and precepts must after all lie like leaden lumps, an undigested and unassimilable mass on an uneasy overburdened stomach. I find it rather hard to understand these things, and somehow I feel at times as if I have taken hold of the wrong ideal. But then, I suppose, it must be because I have not enough of the spirit that comes with the blood of those grand old *sea kings* (I believe you call them) who shot out in their trusty barks speeding over unknown seas and, like a death-dealing genius, with the piercing eye and bloodthirsty heart of hawk or vulture killed and harried, burned and caroused. This is doubtless all very glorious and noble, and the seed of it must be an excellent thing to have in one's blood. But I haven't it. I frankly admit my limitations. I am hardly capable of appreciating to the full such grand intrepidity,—due of course to fact that the stock from which I am sprung did not attain that royal kink in its blood ages ago. My tribe has to own kinship with a very tame and unsanguinary individual who, a long time ago when blue blood was a distilling in the stirring fiery world outside, had no more heroic and daring a thing to do than help a pale sorrow-marked man as he was toiling up a certain hill at Jerusalem bearing his own cross whereon he was soon to be ignominiously nailed. This Cyrenian fellow was used to bearing burdens and he didn't mind giving a lift over a hard place now and then, with no idea of doing anything grand or memorable, or that even so much as his name would be known thereby. And then, too, by a rather strange coincidence this unwarlike and insignificant kinsman of ours had his home in a country (the fatherland of all the family) which had afforded kindly shelter to that same mysterious Stranger, when, a babe and persecuted by bloody power and heartless jealousy, He had to flee the land of his birth. And somehow this same country has in its day done so much fostering and sheltering of that kind—has watched and hovered over the cradles of religions and given refuge and comfort to the persecuted, the world weary, the storm tossed benefactors of mankind so often that she has come to represent nothing stronger or more imposing than the "eternal womanly" among the nations, and to accept as her mission and ideal, *loving service* to mankind.

With such antecedents then the black race in America should not be upbraided for having no taste for blood and carnage. It is the fault of their constitution that they prefer the judicial awards of peace and have an eternal patience to abide the bloodless triumph of right. It is no argument, therefore, when I point to the record of their physical supremacy—when the homes and helpless ones of this country were absolutely at the black man's mercy and not a town laid waste, not a building burned, and *not a woman insulted*—it is no argument, I say, for you to retort: *"He was a coward; he didn't dare!"* The facts simply do not show this to have been the case.

Now the tardy conscience of the nation wakes up one bright morning and is overwhelmed with blushes and stammering confusion because convicted of dishonorable and unkind treatment of *the Indian*; and there is a wonderful scurrying around among the keepers of the keys to get out more blankets and send out a few primers for the "*wards*." While the black man, a faithful son and indefeasible heir,—who can truthfully say, "Lo, these many years do I serve thee, neither transgressed I at any time thy commandment, and yet thou never gavest me a kid that I might make merry with my friends,"—is snubbed and chilled and made unwelcome at every merry-making of the family. And when appropriations for education are talked of, the section for which he has wrought and suffered most, actually defeats the needed and desired assistance for fear they may not be able to prevent his getting a fair and equitable share in the distribution.

Oh, the shame of it!

In *Pactolus Prime* Mr. Tourgee has succeeded incomparably, we think, in photographing and vocalizing the feelings of the colored American in regard to the Christian profession and the pagan practice of the dominant forces in the American government. And as an impassioned denunciation of the heartless and godless spirit of caste founded on color, as a scathing rebuke to weak-eyed Christians who cannot read the golden rule across the color line, as an unanswerable arraignment of unparalleled ingratitude and limping justice in the policy of this country towards the weaker of its two children, that served it so long and so faithfully, the book is destined to live and to furnish an invaluable contribution to this already plethoric department of American literature.

Mr. Cable and Mr. Tourgee represent possibly the most eminent as well as the most prolific among the writers on this subject belonging to the didactic or polemic class. A host of others there are—lesser lights, or of more intermittent coruscations—who have contributed on either side [of] the debate single treatises, numerous magazine articles or newspaper editorials, advocating some one theory some another on the so-called *race problem*. In this group belongs the author of "An Appeal to Pharaoh," advocating the deportation absurdity; also the writings of H. W. Grady;[8] "In Plain Black and White," "The Brother in Black," "The South Investigated," "A Defense of the Negro Race," "The Prosperity of the South Dependent on the Elevation of the Negro," "The Old South and the New," "Black and White," etc., etc., among which are included articles from the pen of colored men themselves, such as Mr. Douglass, Dr. Crummell, Dr. Arnett, Dr. Blyden, Dr. Scarborough, Dr. Price, Mr. Fortune, and others.[9] These are champions of the forces on either side. They stand ever at the forefront dealing desperate blows right and left, now fist and skull, now broad-sword and battle-axe, now with the flash and boom of artillery; while the little fellows run out ever and anon from the ranks and deliver a telling blow between the eyes of an antagonist. All are wrought up to a high tension, some are blinded with passion, others appalled with dread,—all sincerely feel the reality of their own vision and earnestly hope to compel their world to see with their eyes. Such works, full of the fever and heat of debate belong to the turmoil and turbulence of the time. A hundred years from now they may be interesting history, throwing light on a feature of these days which, let us hope, will then be hardly intelligible to an American citizen not over fifty years old.

Among our artists for art's sweet sake, Mr. Howells has recently tried his hand also at painting the Negro, attempting merely a side light in half

---

8. Henry Woodfin Grady (1850–1889): journalist, editor and co-owner of the *Atlanta Constitution* after the Civil War.

9. Cooper here is citing some of the most influencial American black men of the nineteenth century: Frederick Douglass (1817–1895), orator, journalist, reformer, and public servant, often called "the father of the civil rights movement"; Alexander Crummell, discussed in note 13, chapter 3 above; Bishop Benjamin William Arnett (1838–1906), seventeenth bishop of the African Methodist Episcopal Church, to whom Cooper inscribed *A Voice from the South;* Edward Wilmot Blyden (1832–1912), West Indian scholar, diplomat, journalist, and educator, who lived most of his life in Liberia; William Sanders Scarborough (1852–1926), educator; Joseph C. Price (1854–?), clergyman and educator; Timothy Thomas Fortune (1856–1928), journalist.

tones, on his life and manners; and I think the unanimous verdict of the subject is that, in this single department at least, Mr. Howells does not know what he is talking about. And yet I do not think we should quarrel with *An Imperative Duty* because it lacks the earnestness and bias of a special pleader. Mr. Howells merely meant to press the button and give one picture from American life involving racial complications. The kodak does no more; it cannot preach sermons or solve problems.

Besides, the portrayal of Negro characteristics was by no means the main object of the story, which was rather meant, I judge, to be a thumb nail sketch containing a psychological study of a morbidly sensitive conscience hectoring over a weak and vacillating will and fevered into increased despotism by reading into its own life and consciousness the analyses and terrible retributions of fiction,—a product of the Puritan's uncompromising sense of *"right though the heavens fall,"* irritated and kept sore by being unequally yoked with indecision and cowardice. Of such strokes Mr. Howells is undoubtedly master. It is true there is little point and no force of character about the beautiful and irresponsible young heroine; but as that is an attainment of so many of Mr. Howells' models, it is perhaps not to be considered as illustrating any racial characteristics. I cannot help sharing, however, the indignation of those who resent the picture in the colored church,—"evidently," Mr. Howells assures us, "representing *the best colored society*"; where the horrified young prig, Rhoda Aldgate, meets nothing but the frog-like countenances and cat-fish mouths, the musky exhalations and the "bres de Lawd, Honey," of an uncultivated people. It is just here that Mr. Howells fails—and fails because he gives only a half truth, and that a partisan half truth. One feels that he had no business to attempt a subject of which he knew so little, or for which he cared so little. There is one thing I would like to say to my white fellow countrymen, and especially to those who dabble in ink and affect to discuss the Negro; and yet I hesitate because I feel it is a fact which persons of the finer sensibilities and more delicate perceptions must know instinctively: namely, that it is an insult to humanity and a sin against God to publish any such sweeping generalizations of a race on such meager and superficial information. We meet it at every turn—this obtrusive and offensive vulgarity, this gratuitous sizing up of the Negro and conclusively writing down his equation, sometimes even among his ardent friends and bravest defenders. Were I not afraid of falling myself into the same error that I am condemning, I would say it seems an *Anglo Saxon characteristic* to have such overweening confidence in his own power of induction that there is no equation which he would acknowledge to be indeterminate, however many unknown quantities it may possess.

Here is an extract from Dr. Mayo,[10] a thoroughly earnest man[,] sincerely friendly, as I believe, to the colored people.

> Among these women are as many grades of native, intellectual, moral and executive force as among the white people. The plantations of the Gulf, the Atlantic coast and the Mississippi bottoms swarm with negro women who seem hardly lifted above the brutes. I know a group of young colored women, many of them accomplished teachers, who bear themselves as gently and with as varied womanly charms as any score of ladies in the land. The one abyss of perdition *to this class* is the slough of unchastity in which, *as a race* they still flounder, half conscious that it is a slough—the double inheritance of savage Africa and slavery.

Now there may be one side of a truth here, yet who but a self-confident Anglo Saxon would dare make such a broad unblushing statement about a people *as a race?* Some developments brought to light recently through the scientific Christianity and investigating curiosity of Dr. Parkhurst[11] may lead one to suspect the need of missionary teaching to "elevate" the white race; and yet I have too much respect for the autonomy of races, too much reverence for the collective view of God's handiwork to speak of any such condition, however general, as characterizing *the race.* The colored people do not object to the adequate and truthful portrayal of types of their race in whatever degree of the scale of civilization, or of social and moral development, is consonant with actual facts or possibilities. As Mr. Howells himself says, "A man can be anything along the vast range from angel to devil, and without living either the good thing or the bad thing in which his fancy dramatizes him, he can perceive it"—and I would add, can appreciate and even enjoy its delineation by the artist. The average Englishman takes no exception to the humorous caricatures of Dickens or to the satires and cynicisms of Thackeray. The Quilps and the Bernsteins are but strongly developed negatives of our universal human nature on the dark side. We recognize them as genre sketches,—and with the Agneses

---

10. Probably William Worrall Mayo (1819–1911): a Minnesota physician who was active in politics. He was the father of William James and Charles Horace Mayo, who together founded the Mayo Clinic.

11. Probably Charles Henry Parkhurst (1842–1933): clergyman and reformer, instrumental in defeating Tammany Hall.

and Esthers and Aunt Lamberts as foils and correctives, we can appreciate them accordingly: while we do not believe ourselves to be the original of the portrait, there is enough sympathy and fellow feeling for the character to prevent our human relationship from being outraged and insulted. But were Dickens to introduce an average scion of his countrymen to a whole congregation of *Quilps,* at the same time sagely informing him that these represented *the best there was* of English life and morals, I strongly suspect the charming author would be lifted out on the toe of said average Englishman's boot, in case there shouldn't happen to be a good horsewhip handy.

Our grievance then is not that we are not painted as angels of light or as goody-goody Sunday-school developments; but we do claim that a man whose acquaintanceship is so slight that he cannot even discern diversities of individuality, has no right or authority to hawk, "the only true and authentic" pictures of a race of human beings. Mr. Howells' point of view is precisely that of a white man who sees colored people at long range or only in certain capacities. His conclusions about the colored man are identical with the impressions that will be received and carried abroad by foreigners from all parts of the globe, who shall attend our Columbian Exposition[12] for instance, and who, through the impartiality and generosity of our white countrymen, will see colored persons only as bootblacks and hotel waiters, grinning from ear to ear and bowing and curtseying for the extra tips. In the same way Mr. Howells has met colored persons in hotels or on the commons promenading and sparking, or else acting as menials and lazzaroni. He has not seen, and therefore cannot be convinced that there exists a quiet, self-respecting, dignified class of easy life and manners (save only where it crosses the roughness of their white fellow countrymen's barbarity), of cultivated tastes and habits, and with no more in common with the class of his acquaintance than the accident of complexion,—beyond a sympathy with their wrongs, or a resentment at being socially and morally classified with them, according as the principle of altruism or of self love is dominant in the individual.

I respectfully submit that there is hardly a colored church in any considerable city in this country, which could be said in any sense to represent *the best colored society,* in which Rhoda Aldgate could not have seen, when she opened her eyes, persons as quietly and as becomingly dressed, as cultivated in tone and as refined in manner, as herself; persons, too, as sensitive to rough contact and as horribly alive as she could be (thought they had known it from childhood) to the galling distinctions in this country which

---

12. Columbian Exposition: the 1893 Chicago World's Fair, at which Cooper spoke.

insist on *levelling down* all individuals more or less related to the Africans. So far from the cringing deference which Mr. Howells paints as exhibited to "the young white lady," in nine cases out of ten the congregation would have supposed intuitively that she was a quadroon, so far from the unusual was her appearance and complexion. In not a few such colored churches would she have found young women of aspiration and intellectual activity with whom she could affiliate without nausea and from whom she could learn a good many lessons—and, sadly I say it, even more outside the churches whom bitterness at racial inconsistency of white Christians had soured into a silent disbelief of all religion. In either class she would have found no trouble in reaching a heart which could enter into all the agony of her own trial and bitter grief. Nor am I so sure, if she had followed her first gushing impulse to go South and "elevate" the race with whom she had discovered her relationship, that she would have found even them so ready to receive her condescending patronage.

There are numerous other inadvertent misrepresentations in the book—such as supposing that colored people voluntarily and deliberately prefer to keep to themselves in all public places and that from choice "they have their own neighborhoods, their own churches, their own amusements, their own resorts,"—the intimation that there is a "*black* voice," a black character, easy, irresponsible and fond of what is soft and pleasant, a black ideal of art and a black barbaric taste in color, a black affinity—so that in some occult and dreadful way one, only one-sixteenth related and totally foreign by education and environment, can still feel that one-sixteenth race calling her more loudly than the fifteen-sixteenths. I wish to do Mr. Howells the justice to admit, however, that one feels his blunders to be wholly unintentional and due to the fact that he has studied his subject merely from the outside. With all his matchless powers as a novelist, not even he can yet "think himself imaginatively" into the colored man's place.

To my mind the quaintest and truest little bit of portraiture from low-life that I have read in a long time is the little story that appeared last winter in the *Harpers*, of the "*Widder Johnsing and how she caught the preacher.*" It is told with naive impersonality and appreciative humor, and is quite equal, I think, both in subject and treatment to the best of Mrs. Stowe's New England dialect stories. It is idyllic in its charming simplicity and naturalness, and delightfully fresh in its sparkling wit and delicious humor. We do not resent such pictures as this of our lowly folk—such a homely and honest

> Pomegranate, which, if cut deep down the middle,
> Shows a heart within blood tinctured of a *veined humanity*,

is always sweet to the taste and dear to the heart, however plain and humble the setting.

A longer and more elaborate work, *Harold*, published anonymously, comes properly in our group second, the didactic novel. It gives the picture of a black Englishman cultured and refined, brought in painful contact with American,—or rather *un-American*, color prejudice. The point of the book seems to be to show that education for the black man is a curse, since it increases his sensitivities to the indignities he must suffer in consequence of white barbarity. The author makes Harold, after a futile struggle against American inequalities, disappear into the jungles of Africa, "there to wed a dusky savage," at the last cursing the day he had ever suspected a broader light or known a higher aspiration; a conclusion which, to my mind, is a most illogical one. If the cultivated black man cannot endure the white man's barbarity—the cure, it seems to me, would be to cultivate the white man. Civilize both, then each will know what is due from man to man, and that reduces at once to a minimum the friction of their contact.

In the same rank as *Harold* belongs that improbability of improbabilities, *Doctor Huguet*, by the arch-sensationalist, Ignatius Donelly. As its purpose is evidently good, I shall not undertake to review the book. Suffice it to say the plot hinges on the exchange of soul between the body of a black chicken-thief and that of a cultivated white gentleman, and sets forth the indignities and wrongs to which the cultured soul, with all its past of refinement and learning, has to submit in consequence of its change of cuticle. The book is an able protest against that snobbishness which elevates complexion into a touchstone of aristocracy and makes the pigment cells of a man's skin his badge of nobility regardless of the foulness or purity of the soul within; the only adverse criticism from the colored man's point of view being the selection of a chicken thief as his typical black man; but on the principle of antitheses this may have ben artistically necessary.

I shall pass next to what I consider the most significant contribution to this subject for the last ten years—a poem by Maurice Thompson[13] in the *New York Independent* for January 21, 1892, entitled "A Voodoo Prophecy." From beginning to end it is full of ghoulish imagery and fine poetic madness. Here are a few stanzas of it:

---

13. Maurice Thompson (1844–1901): poet and novelist.

I am the prophet of the dusky race,
   The poet of wild Africa. Behold,
The midnight vision brooding in my face!
       Come near me,
       And hear me,
While from my lips the words of Fate are told.

A black and terrible memory masters me,
   The shadow and the substance of deep wrong;
You know the past, hear now what is to be:
       From the midnight land,
       Over sea and sand,
From the green jungle, hear my Voodoo-song:

A tropic heat is in my bubbling veins,
   Quintessence of all savagery is mine,
The lust of ages ripens in my reins,
       And burns
       And yearns,
Like venom-sap within a noxious vine.

Was I a heathen? Ay, I was—am still
   A fetich worshipper; but I was free
To loiter or to wander at my will,
       To leap and dance,
       To hurl my lance,
And breathe the air of savage liberty.

You drew me to a higher life, you say;
   Ah, drove me, with the lash of slavery!
Am I unmindful? Every cursed day
       Of pain
       And chain
Roars like a torrent in my memory.

You make my manhood whole with "equal rights!"
   Poor empty words! Dream you I honor them?—
I who have stood on Freedom's wildest h[e]ights?
       My Africa,
       I see the day
When none dare touch thy garment's lowest hem.

You cannot make me love you with your whine
   Of fine repentance. Veil your pallid face
In presence of the shame that mantles mine;
        Stand
        At command
   Of the black prophet of the Negro race!

I hate you, and I live to nurse my hate,
   Remembering when you plied the slaver's trade
In my dear land . . . How patiently I wait
        The day,
        Not far away,
   When all your pride shall shrivel up and fade.

Yes, all your whiteness darken under me!
   Darken and be jaundiced, and your blood
Take in dread humors from my savagery,
        Until
        Your will
   Lapse into mine and seal my masterhood.

You, seed of Abel, proud of your descent,
   And arrogant, because your cheeks are fair,
Within my loins an inky curse is pent,
        To flood
        Your blood
   And stain your skin and crisp your golden hair.

As you have done by me, so will I do
   By all the generations of your race;
Your snowy limbs, your blood's patrician blue
        Shall be
        Tainted by me,
   And I will set my seal upon your face!

Yes, I will dash my blackness down your veins,
   And through your nerves my sensuousness I'll fling;
Your lips, your eyes, shall bear the musty stains
        Of Congo kisses,
        While shrieks and hisses
   Shall blend into the savage songs I sing!

Your temples will I break, your fountains fill,
 Your cities raze, your fields to deserts turn;
My heathen fires shall shine on every hill,
   And wild beasts roam,
   Where stands your home;—
Even the wind your hated dust shall spurn.

I will absorb your very life in me,
 And mold you to the shape of my desire;
Back through the cycles of all cruelty
   I will swing you,
   And wring you,
And roast you in my passions' hottest fire.

You, North and South, you, East and West,
 Shall drink the cup your fathers gave to me;
My back still burns, I bare my bleeding breast,
   I set my face,
   My limbs I brace,
To make the long, strong fight for mastery.

My serpent fetich lolls its withered lip
 And bares its shining fangs at thought of this:
I scarce can hold the monster in my grip.
   So strong is he,
   So eagerly
He leaps to meet my precious prophecies.

Hark for the coming of my countless host,
 Watch for my banner over land and sea.
The ancient power of vengeance is not lost!
   Lo! on the sky
   The fire-clouds fly,
And strangely moans the windy, weltering sea.

Now this would be poetry if it were only truthful. Simple and sensuous it surely is, but it lacks the third requisite—truth. The Negro is utterly incapable of such vindictiveness. Such concentrated venom might be distilled in the cold Saxon, writhing and chafing under oppression and repression such as the Negro in America has suffered and is suffering. But the black man is in real life only too glad to accept the olive branch of reconciliation. He merely asks to be let alone. To be allowed to pursue his destiny as a free man and an American citizen, to rear and educate his children in peace, to engage in art, science, trades or industries according to his ability,—and *to go to the wall if he fail*. He is willing, if I understand him, to let bygones be bygones. He does not even demand satisfaction for the centuries of his ancestors' unpaid labor. He asks neither pension, nor dole nor back salaries; but is willing to start from the bottom, all helpless and unprovided for as he is, with absolutely nothing as his stock in trade, with no capital, in a country developed, enriched, and made to blossom through his father's "sweat and toil,"—with none of the accumulations of ancestors' labors, with no education or moral training for the duties and responsibilities of freedom; nay, with every power, mental, moral, and physical, emasculated by a debasing slavery—he is willing, even glad to take his place in the lists alongside his oppressors, who have had every advantage, to be tried with them by their own standards, and to ask no quarter from them or high Heaven to palliate or excuse the ignominy of a defeat.

The "Voodoo Prophecy" has no interest then as a picture of the black, but merely as a revelation of the white man. Maurice Thompson in penning this portrait of the Negro, has, unconsciously it may be, laid bare his own soul—its secret dread and horrible fear. And this, it seems to me, is the key to the Southern situation, the explanation of the apparent heartlessness and cruelty of some, and the stolid indifference to atrocity on the part of others, before which so many of us have stood paralyzed in dumb dismay. The Southerner is not a cold-blooded villain. Those of us who have studied the genus in its native habitat can testify that his impulses are generous and kindly, and that while the South presents a solid phalanx of iron resistance to the Negro's advancement, still as individuals to individuals they are warm-hearted and often even tender. And just here is the difference between the Southerner and his more philosophical, less sentimental Northern brother. The latter in an abstract metaphysical way rather wants you to have all the rights that belong to you. He thinks it better for the country, better for him that justice, universal justice be done. But he doesn't care to have the blacks, in the concrete, too near him. He doesn't know them and doesn't want to know them. He really can't understand how the Southerner could have let those little cubs get so close to him as they did in the old days—nursing from the same bottle and feeding at the same breast.

To the Southerner, on the other hand, race antipathy and color-phobia *as such* does not exist. Personally, there is hardly a man of them but knows, and has known from childhood, some black fellow whom he loves as dearly as if he were white, whom he regards as indispensable to his own pleasures, and for whom he would break every commandment in the decalogue to save him from any general disaster. But our Bourbon seems utterly incapable of generalizing his few ideas. He would die for A or B, but suddenly becomes utterly impervious to every principle of logic when you ask for the simple golden rule to be applied to the class of which A or B is one. Another fact strikes me as curious. A Southern white man's regard for his black friend varies in inverse ratio to the real distance between them in education and refinement. Puck expresses it—"I can get on a great deal better with a nigger than I can with a Negro." And Mr. Douglass puts it: "Let a colored man be out at elbows and toes and half way into the gutter and there is no prejudice against him; but let him respect himself and be a man and Southern whites can't abide to ride in the same car with him."

Why this anomaly? Is it pride? Ordinarily, congeniality increases with similarity in taste and manners. Is it antipathy to color? It does not exist. The explanation is the white man's dread dimly shadowed out in this "Voodoo Prophecy" of Maurice Thompson, and fed and inspired by such books as *Minden Armais* and a few wild theorizers who have nothing better to do with their time than spend it advocating the fusion of races as a plausible and expedient policy. Now I believe there are two ideas which master the Southern white man and incense him against the black race. On this point he is a monomaniac. In the face of this feeling he would not admit he was convinced of the axioms of Geometry. The one is personal and present, the fear of Negro political domination. The other is for his posterity—the future horror of being lost as a race in this virile and vigorous black race. Relieve him of this nightmare and he becomes "as gentle as the sucking dove." With that dread delusion maddening him he would drive his sword to the hilt in the tender breast of his darling child, did he fancy that through her the curse would come.

Now argument is almost supersensible with a monomaniac. What is most needed is a sedative for the excited nerves, and then a mental tonic to stimulate the power of clear perception and truthful cerebration. The Southern patient needs to be brought to see, by the careful and cautious injection of cold facts and by the presentation of well selected object lessons that so far as concerns his first named horror of black supremacy politically, the usual safeguards of democracy are in the hands of intelligence and wealth in the South as elsewhere. The weapons of fair argument and persuasion, the precautionary bulwark of education and justice, the unimpeachable supremacy and insuperable advantage of intelligence and discipline over mere numbers—are all in his reach. It is to his interest to help make the black peasant an intelligent and self-respecting citizen. No section can thrive under the incubus of an illiterate, impoverished, cheerless and hopeless peasantry. Let the South once address herself in good faith to the improvement of the condition of her laboring classes, let her give but a tithe of the care and attention which are bestowed in the North on its mercurial and inflammable importations, let her show but the disposition in her relative poverty merely to utter the benediction, *Be ye warmed and fed and educated*, even while she herself has not the wherewithal to emulate the Pullman villages and the Carnegie munificence, let her but give him [the black peasant] a fair wage and an honest reckoning and a kindly God-speed,—and she will find herself in possession of the most tractable laborer, the most faithful and reliable henchman, the most invaluable co-operator and friendly vassal of which this or any country can boast.

So far as regards the really less sane idea that amicable relations subsisting between the races may promote their ultimate blending and loss of identity, it hardly seems necessary to refute it. Blending of races in the aggregate is simply an unthinkable thought, and the union of individuals can never fall out by accident or haphazard. There must be the deliberate wish and intention on each side; and the average black man in this country is as anxious to preserve his identity and transmit his type as is the average white man. In any case, hybridity is in no sense dependent on sectional or national amity. Oppression and outrage are not the means to chain the affections. Cupid, who knows no bolt or bars, is more wont to be stimulated with romantic sympathy towards a forbidden object unjustly persecuted. The sensible course is to remove those silly and unjust barriers which protect nothing and merely call attention to the possibilities of law-breaking, and depend instead on religion and common sense to guide, control and direct in the paths of purity and right reason.

The froth and foam, the sticks and debris at the watertop may have an uncertain movement, but as deep calleth unto deep the mighty ocean swell is always true to the tides; and whatever the fluctuations along the ragged edge between the races, the home instinct is sufficiently strong with each to hold the great mass true to its attractions. If Maurice Thompson's nightmare vision is sincere on his part, then, it has no objective reality; 'tis merely a hideous phantasm bred of his own fevered and jaundiced senses; if he does not believe in it himself, it was most unkind and uncalled for to publish abroad such inflaming and irritating fabrications.

After this cursory glance at a few contributions which have peculiarly emphasized one phase of our literature during the last decade or two, I am brought to the conclusion that an authentic portrait, at once aesthetic and true to life, presenting the black man as a free American citizen, not the humble slave of *Uncle Tom's Cabin*—but the *man*, divinely struggling and aspiring yet tragically warped and distorted by the adverse winds of circumstance, has not yet been painted. It is my opinion that the canvas awaits the brush of the colored man himself. It is a pathetic—a fearful arraignment of America's conditions of life, that instead of that enrichment from the years and days, the summers and springs under which, as Browning says, "The flowers turn double and the leaves turn flowers,"—the black man's native and original flowers have in this country been all hardened and sharpened into thorns and spurs. In literature we have no artists for art's sake. Albery A. Whitman[14] in "Twasinta's Seminoles" and "Not a Man and Yet a Man" is almost the only poet who has attempted a more sustained note than the lyrics of Mrs. Harper, and even that note is almost a wail.

The fact is, a sense of freedom in mind as well as in body is necessary to the appreciative and inspiring pursuit of the beautiful. A bird cannot warble out his fullest and most joyous notes while the wires of his cage are pricking and cramping him at every heart beat. His tones become only the shrill and poignant protest of rage and despair. And so the black man's vexations and chafing environment, even since his physical emancipation has given him speech, have goaded him into the eloquence and fire of oratory rather than the genial warmth and cheery glow of either poetry or romance. And pity 'tis, 'tis true. A race that has produced for America the only folk-lore and folk songs of native growth, a race which has grown the most original and unique assemblage of fable and myth to be found on the continent, a race which has suggested and inspired almost the only distinctive American note which could chain the attention and charm the ear of the outside world—has as yet found no mouthpiece of its own to unify and perpetuate its wondrous whisperings—no painter-poet to distil in the alembic of his own imagination the gorgeous dyes, the luxuriant juices of this rich and tropical vegetation. It was the glory of Chaucer that he justified the English language to itself—that he took the homely and hitherto despised Saxon elements and ideas, and lovingly wove them into an artistic product which even Norman conceit and uppishness might be glad to acknowledge and imitate. The only man who is doing the same for Negro

---

14. Albery Alson Whitman (1851–1902): Negro poet and clergyman.

folk-lore is one not to the manner born. Joel Chandler Harris[15] has made himself rich and famous by simply standing around among the black railroad hands and cotton pickers of the South and compiling the simple and dramatic dialogues which fall from their lips. What I hope to see before I die is a black man honestly and appreciatively portraying both the Negro as he is, and the white man, occasionally, as seen from the Negro's standpoint.

There is an old proverb "The devil is always painted *black*—by white painters." And what is needed perhaps, to reverse the picture of the lordly man slaying the lion, is for the lion to turn painter.

Then too we need the calm clear judgment of ourselves and of others born of a disenchantment similar to that of a little girl I know in the South, who was once being laboriously held up over the shoulders of a surging throng to catch her first glimpse of a real live president. "Why Nunny," she cried half reproachfully, as she strained her little neck to see—"*It's nuffin but a man!*"

When we have been sized up and written down by others, we need not feel that the last word is said and the oracles sealed. "It's nuffin but a man." And there are many gifts the giftie may gie us, far better than seeing ourselves as others see us—and one is that of Bion's[16] maxim "*Know Thyself.*" Keep true to your own ideals. Be not ashamed of what is homely and your own. Speak out and speak honestly. Be true to yourself and to the message God and Nature meant you to deliver. The young David cannot fight in Saul's unwieldy armor. Let him simply therefore gird his loins, take up his own parable and tell this would-be great American nation "*A chile's amang ye takin' notes*"; and when men act the part of cowards or wild beasts, this great silent but open-eyed constituency has a standard by which they are being tried. Know thyself, and know those around at their true weight of solid intrinsic manhood without being dazzled by the fact that littleness of soul is often gilded with wealth, power and intellect. There can be no nobility but that of soul, and no catalogue of adventitious circumstances can wipe out the stain or palliate the meanness of inflicting one ruthless, cruel wrong. 'Tis not only safer, but nobler, grander, diviner,

> To be that which we destroy
> Than, by destruction, dwell in doubtful joy.

---

15. Joel Chandler Harris (1848–1908): humorist and dialect writer, author of the Uncle Remus stories, featuring Brer Fox and Brer Rabbit.
16. Bion (3rd or 2nd century B.C.): Greek poet, author of *Lament of Adonis*.

With this platform to stand on we can with clear eye weigh what is written and estimate what is done and ourselves paint what is true with the calm spirit of those who know their cause is right and who believe there is a God who judgeth the nations.

· 9 ·

What Are We Worth? (1892)

$\mathcal{I}$ once heard Henry Ward Beecher[1] make this remark: "Were Africa and the Africans to sink to-morrow, how much poorer would the world be? A little less gold and ivory, a little less coffee, a considerable ripple, perhaps, where the Atlantic and Indian Oceans would come together—that is all; not a poem, not an invention, not a piece of art would be missed from the world."

This is not a flattering statement; but then we do not want flattery if seeing ourselves as others see us is to help us in fulfilling the higher order, "know thyself." The world is often called cold and hard. I don't know much about that; but of one thing I am sure, it is intensely practical. Waves of sentiment or prejudice may blur its old eyes for a little while but you are sure to have your bill presented first or last with the inexorable "How much owest thou?" What have you produced, what consumed? What is your real value in the world's economy? What do you give to the world over and above what you have cost? What would be missed had you never lived? What are you worth? What of actual value would go down with you if you were sunk into the ocean or buried by an earthquake to-morrow? Show up your cash account and your balance sheet. In the final reckoning do you belong on the debit or the credit side of the account? according to a fair and square, an impartial and practical reckoning. It is by this standard that society estimates individuals; and by this standard finally and inevitably the world will measure and judge nations and races.

It may not be unprofitable then for us to address ourselves to the task of casting up our account and carefully overhauling our books. It may be well to remember at the outset that the operation is purely a mathematical one and allows no room for sentiment. The good housewife's pet chicken which she took when first hatched, fed from her own hand and fondled on

---

1. Henry Ward Beecher (1813–1887): Congregationalist preacher who advocated temperance and denounced slavery. Brother of Harriet Beecher Stowe.

her bosom as lovingly as if it were a babe, is worth no more (for all the affection and care lavished on it) when sold in the shambles: and that never-to-be-forgotten black hen that stole into the parlor, flew upon the mantel looking for a nest among those handsome curios, smashed the sèvres vases and picked the buds from the lovely tea rose—so exasperatingly that the good woman could never again endure the sight of her—this ill-fated bird is worth no less. There are sections of this country in which the very name of the Negro, even in homeopathic doses, stirs up such a storm of feeling that men fairly grow wild and are unfit to discuss the simplest principles of life and conduct where the colored man is concerned; and you would think it necessary for the Ethiopian actually to change his skin before there can be any harmonious living or lucid thinking: there are a few nooks and crannies, on the other hand, in another quarter of the same country, in which that name embodies an idealized theory and a benevolent sentiment; and the black man (the blacker the better) is the petted nursling, the haloed idea, the foregone conclusion. In these Arcadias, it is as good capital as pushing selfishness and aspiring mediocrity need ask, to be advertised as one of the oppressed race and probably born a slave.

But after all sentiment, whether adverse or favorable, is ephemeral. Ever shifting and unreliable, it can never be counted in estimating values. The sentiments of youth are outgrown in age, and we like to-day what we despised or were indifferent to yesterday. Nine-tenths of the mis-called color prejudice or race prejudice in this country is mere sentiment governed by the association of ideas. It is not color prejudice at all. The color of a man's face *per se* has no more to do with his worthiness and companionableness than the color of his eyes or the shades of his hair. You admire the one or think the other more beautiful to rest the gaze upon. But every one with brains knows and must admit that he must look deeper than this for the man. Mrs. Livermore once said in my hearing: "It is not that the Negro is black; Spaniards, Portuguese, East Indians, enter our parlors, sup at our tables, and, if they have a sufficiently long bank account, they may marry our daughters: but the Negro is weak—and we don't like weakness."

Now this dislike it is useless to inveigh against and folly to rail at. We share it ourselves and often carry it to a more unjustifiable extent. For as a rule the narrower the mind and the more circumscribed the experience, the greater will be the exaggeration of accidents over substance, and of circumstance over soul. It does no good to argue with the poor sea-sick wretch who, even on land after the voyage, is nauseated by the sight of clear spring water. In vain you show the unreason of the feeling. This, you explain, is a different time, a different place, a different stage of progress in the circulation of waters. That was salt, this is fresh, and so on. You might as well be presenting syllogisms to Aetna. "Yes, my dear Fellow," he cries, "You talk admirably; but you don't know how I feel. You don't know how sick I was on that nasty ship!' And so your rhetoric cannot annihilate the association of ideas. He feels; *you know.* But he will outgrow his feeling,—and you are content to wait.

Just as impervious to reason is the man who is dominated by the sentiment of race prejudice. You can only consign him to the fatherly hand of Time; and pray that your own mental sight be not thus obscured and your judgment warped in your endeavors to be just and true.

Sentiment and cant, then, both being ruled out, let us try to study our subject as the world finally reckons it—not certain crevices and crannies of the earth, but the cool, practical, business-like world. What are we worth? not in Georgia nor in Massachusetts; not to our brothers and sisters and cousins and aunts, every one of whom would unhesitatingly declare us worth a great gold-lump; nor to the exasperated neighbor over the way who would be just as ready, perhaps, to write us down a most unmitigated nuisance. But what do we represent to the world? What is our market value. Are we a positive and additive quantity or a negative factor in the world's elements. What have we cost and what do we come to?

The calculation may be made in the same way and on the same principle that we would estimate the value of any commodity on the market. Men are not very unlike watches. We might estimate first the cost of material—is it gold or silver or alloy, solid or plated, jewelled or sham paste. Settle the relative value of your raw material, and next you want to calculate how much this value has been enhanced by labor, the delicacy and fineness, the honesty and thoroughness of the workmanship; then the utility and beauty of the product and its adaptability to the end and purpose of its manufacture; and lastly is there a demand in the market for such an article. Does it meet a want, *will it go* and *go right?* Is it durable and reliable. How often do you have to wind it before it runs down, how often repair it. Does it keep good time and require but little watching and looking after. And there is no radical difference, after all, between the world's way of estimating men and our usual way of valuing watches. In both the fundamental item is the question of material, and then the refining and enhancement of that material through labor, and so on through the list.

What then can we say for our raw material?

Again I must preface an apology for anything unpalatable in our menu.

I promised, you remember, to leave out the sentiment—you may stir it in afterwards, mixing thoroughly according to taste. We must discuss facts, candidly and bluntly, without rhetoric or cant if we would have a clear light on our problem.

Now whatever notions we may indulge on the theory of evolution and the laws of atavism or heredity, all concede that no individual character receives its raw material newly created and independent of the rock from whence it was hewn. No life is bound up within the period of its conscious existence. No personality dates its origin from its birthday. The elements that are twisted into the cord did not begin their formation when first the tiny thread became visible in the great warp and filling of humanity. When first we saw the light many of the threads undoubtedly were spun and the color and fineness of the weft determined. The materials that go to make the man, the probabilities of his character and activities, the conditions and circumstances of his growth, and his quantum of resistance and mastery are the resultant of forces which have been accumulating and gathering momentum for generations. So that, as one tersely expresses it, in order to reform a man, you must begin with his great grandmother.

A few years ago a certain social scientist was struck by a remarkable coincidence in the name of a number of convicts in the State prison of New York. There were found thirty-five or forty men, of the same name with but slight modification in the spelling, all convicted of crimes similar in character. Looking into the matter, he traced them every one back to one woman of inferior character who had come from England in one of the first colonial ships. *And that woman had been a convict and charged with pretty nearly the same crime.*

Rightly to estimate our material, then, it is necessary to go back of the twenty or thirty years during which we have been in possession, and find out the nature of the soil in which it has been forming and growing.

There is or used to be in England a system of entail by which a lot of land was fixed to a family and its posterity forever, passing always on the death of the father to his eldest son. A man may misuse or abuse, he may impoverish, mortgage, sterilize, eliminate every element of value—but he can never sell. He may cut down every tree, burn every fence and house, abstract by careless tillage, or by no tillage, every nutritive element from the soil, encumber it to two or three times its value and destroy forever its beauty and fertility—but he can never rid himself of it. That land with all its encumbrances and liabilities, its barrenness and squalidness, its poverty and its degradation is inexorably, inevitably, inalienably his; and like a shattered and debased personality it haunts him wherever he goes. An heir coming into an estate is thus often poorer than if he had no inheritance. He is chained to a life long possession of debt, toil, responsibility, often disgrace. Happier were it for him if he could begin life with nothing—an isolated but free man with no capital but his possibilities, with no past and no pedigree. And so it often is with men. These bodies of ours often come to us mortgaged to their full value by the extravagance, self-indulgence, sensuality of some ancestor. Some man, generations back, has encumbered his estate for strong drink, his descendants coming into that estate have the mortgage to pay off; principal and interest. Another cut down the fences of character by debauchery and vice,—and these have to ward off attacks of the enemy without bulwarks or embattlements. They have burnt their houses of purity and integrity, have rendered the soil poor and unproductive by extravagance and folly,—and the children have to shiver amid the storms of passion and feed on husks till they can build for themselves a shelter and fertilize their farms. Not very valuable estates, you will say. Well, no,—nothing to boast of, perhaps. But an energetic heir can often pay off some of the liabilities and leave the estate to his children less involved than when he received it. At least he can arrest the work of destruction and see to it that no further encumbrances are added through his folly and mismanagement.

In estimating the value of our material, therefore, it is plain that we must look into the deeds of our estates and ferret out their history. The task is an individual one, as likewise its application. Certainly the original timber as it came from the African forests was good enough. No race of heathen are more noted for honest and chastity than are the tribes of Africa. For one of their women to violate the laws of purity is a crime punishable with death; and so strictly honest are they, it is said, that they are wont to leave their commodities at the place of exchange and go about their business. The buyer coming up takes what he wishes to purchase and leaves its equivalent in barter or money. A returned missionary tells the story that certain European traders, when at a loss as to the safe keeping of their wares, were told by a native chief, "Oh just lay them down there. *They are perfectly safe, there are no Christians here.*"

Whatever may be said of its beauty, then, the black side of the stream with us is pretty pure, and has no cause to blush for its honesty and integrity. From the nature of the case the infusions of white blood that have come in many instances to the black race in this country are not the best that race afforded. And if anything further is needed to account for racial irregularities—the warping and shrinking, the knotting and cracking of the sturdy old timber, the two hundred and fifty years of training here are quite sufficient to explain all. I have often thought, since coming in closer contact with the Puritan element in America, what a different planing and shaping this timber might have received under their hands!

As I compare the Puritan's sound, substantial, sanctified common sense with the Feudal froth and foam of the South; the Puritan's liberal, democratic, ethical and at the same time calculating, economical, stick-to-ative and go-ahead-ative spirit,—with the free and easy lavishness, the aristocratic notions of caste and class distinctions, the pliable consciences and unbending social bars amid which I was reared;—I have wished that it might have been ordered that as my race had to serve a term of bondage it might have been under the discipline of the successors of Cromwell and Milton, rather than under the training and example of the luxurious cavaliers. There is no doubt that the past two hundred and fifty years of working up the material we now inherit, has depreciated rather than enhanced its value. We find in it the foolish ideas of aristocracy founded on anything else than a moral claim; we find the contempt for manual labor and the horror of horny palms, the love of lavish expenditure and costly display, and—alas, that we must own it—the laxness of morals and easy-going consciences inherited and imitated from the old English gentry of the reigns of Charles and Anne. But to know our faults is one step toward correcting them, and there are, I trust, no flaws in this first element of value, *material*, which may not be planed and scraped and sand-papered out by diligent and strenuous effort. One thing is certain, the flaws that are simply ingrained in the timber are not our responsibility. A man is to be praised primarily not for having inherited fine tools and faultless materials but for making the most of the stuff he has, and doing his best in spite of disadvantages and poor material. The individual is responsible, not for what he has not, but for what he has; and the vital part for us after all depends on the use we make of our material.

Many a passable article has by diligent workmanship been made even from inferior material. And this brings us to our second item of value—Labor.

This is a most important item. It would seem sometimes that it is labor that creates all value. A gold mine is worth no more than common clay till it is worked. The simple element of labor bestowed on iron, the cheapest and commonest of metals, multiplies its value four hundred thousand times, making it worth sixty-five times its weight in gold, *e.g.:*

A pound of good iron is worth about .... 4 cts.
A pound of inch screws $1.00
A pound of steel wire from .... $3.00 to $7.00
A pound of sewing needles $14.00
A pound of fish hooks from .... $20.00 to $50.00
A pound of jewel screws for watches $3,500.00
A pound of hair springs for watches $16,000.00
While a pound of fine gold in standard coin
   is worth only about $248.00

Now it is the same fundamental material in the hair springs valued at $16,000.00 which was sold in the rough at 4 cts. per pound. It is labor that has thus enhanced its value. Now let us see if there is a parallel rise of value in the material of which men are made.

No animal, the scientists tell us, is in infancy so utterly helpless, so completely destitute of the means of independent existence, so entirely worthless in itself as the world estimates values, as is man. The chick just out of the shell can pick up its own food and run away from approaching danger. Touch a snapping turtle just a moment after its birth, and it will bite at you. Cut off its head and it will still bite. Break open the egg of the young and the vivacious little creature will, even in the embryo, try to fight for its rights and maintain its independence. But the human babe can for weeks and months, do nothing but cry and feed and fear. It is a constant drain on the capital of its parents, both physically and mentally. It is to be fed, and worked for, and sheltered and protected. It cannot even defend itself against a draft of wind.

What is it worth? Unsentimentally and honestly,—it is worth just as much as a leak is worth to a ship, or what the mistletoe is worth to the oak. He is a parasite, a thief, a destroyer of values. He thrives at another's expense, and filches from that other every atom of his own existence. The infatuated mother, it is true, would not sell him, she will tell you, for his weight in gold; but that is sentiment—not business. Besides, there is no danger of her having the chance to make such a bargain. No one will ever tempt her with any such offer. The world knows too well what an outlay of time and money and labor must be made before he is worth even his weight in ashes. His present worth no one would accept even as a gift—and it is only the prospect of future development of worth that could induce any one, save that mother, to take up the burden. What an expenditure of toil and care, of heart power and brain power, what planning, what working, what feeding, what enriching, what sowing and sinking of values before one can tell whether the harvest is worth the output. Yet, how gladly does the mother pour out her strength and vitality, her energy, her life that the little bankrupt may store up capital for its own use. How anxiously does she hang over the lumpish little organism to catch the first awakening of a soul. And when the chubby little hands begin to swing consciously before the snapping eyes, and the great toe is caught and tugged towards the open mouth, when the little pink fists for the first time linger caressingly on her cheek and breast, and the wide open eyes say distinctly "I know you, I love you,"—how she strains him to her bosom as her whole soul goes out to this newly found intelligence in the impassioned cry of Carlyle:[2] "*Whence—and Oh Heavens, whither!*"

> How poor, how rich, how abject, how august,
> How complicate, how wonderful is man!

It is labor, development, training, careful, patient, painful, diligent toil that must span the gulf between this vegetating life germ (now worth nothing but toil and care and trouble, and living purely at the expense of another)—and that future consummation in which "the elements are so mixed that Nature can stand up and say to all the world, '*This is a man.*'"

It is a heavy investment, requires a large outlay of money on long time and large risk, no end of labor, skill, pains. Education is the word that covers it all—the working up of this raw material and fitting it into the world's work to supply the world's need—the manufacture of men and women for the markets of the world. But there is no other labor which so creates value. The value of the well developed man has been enhanced far more by the labor bestowed than is the iron in the watch springs. The value of the raw material was far below zero to begin with; but this "quintessence of dust" has become, *through labor,* "the beauty of the world, the paragon of animals,—noble in reason and infinite in faculty!"

What a piece of work, indeed!

Education, then, is the safest and richest investment possible to man. It pays the largest dividends and gives the grandest possible product to the world—a man. The demand is always greater than the supply—and the world pays well for what it prizes.

Now what sort of workmanship are we putting on our raw material.

---

2. Thomas Carlyle (1795–1881): Welsh historian who wrote on the French Revolution.

What are we doing for education? The man-factories among our people make, I think, a fairly good showing. Figures are encouraging things to deal with, and too they represent something tangible in casting up our accounts. There are now 25,530 colored schools in the United States with 1,353,352 pupils; the colored people hold in landed property for churches and schools $25,000,000. Twenty-five hundred thousand colored children have learned to read and most of these to write also. Twenty-two thousand nine hundred fifty-six colored men and women are teaching in these schools. There are sixty-six academies and high schools and one hundred and fifty schools for advanced education taught by colored teachers, together with seven colleges administered by colored presidents and faculties. There are now one thousand college bred Negro ministers in the country, 250 lawyers, 749 physicians; while, according to Dr. Rankin,[3] there are 247 colored students preparing themselves in the universities of Europe.

The African Methodists[4] alone, representing the unassisted effort of the colored people for self-development, have founded thirty-eight institutes and colleges, with landed property valued at $502,650, and 134 teachers supported entirely by the self denying effort of the colored people themselves.

This looks like an attempt, to say the least, to do the best we can with our material. One feels there has not been much shirking here; the workmanship may be crude sometimes, when measured by more finished standards,—but they have done what they could; in their poverty and inexperience, through self denial and perseverance, they are struggling upward toward the light.

There is another item to be taken into account in estimating the value of a product, to which we must give just a thought in passing, *i.e.*, the necessary waste of material in the making.

The Sultan of Turkey once sent to China to procure a *fac simile* of some elegant plates he had had, all of which were now broken but one and that, unfortunately, was cracked. He sent this one as a pattern and requested that the set be renewed exactly like the former ones. He was surprised on receiving the plates to note the fabulous sum charged for them,—but the Celestial explained that the cost was greatly increased by having *to put in the crack*,—so many had been lost in the making.

The anecdote is not my own, but it suggests a thought that may be

---

3. John Rankin (1793–1886): abolitionist clergyman; assisted in the escape of the slaves who were the originals for Eliza and her son in *Uncle Tom's Cabin*.

4. Presumably, the African Methodist Episcopal (AME) church.

useful to us and I borrow it for that purpose. They tell us that the waste of material is greater in making colored men and women than in the case of others—that a larger percentage of our children die under twenty-one years of age, especially in large cities, and that a larger number who reach that age and beyond, are to be classed among the world's invalids and paupers. According to the census of 1880 the average death rate throughout the country was, among the whites 14.74 per 1000; among colored 17.28 per 1000: the highest among whites being in New Mexico, 22.04, lowest in Arizona, 7.91 per 1000. Among colored, the mortality ranges from 35.25 in the District of Columbia where it is the highest, to 1.89 in Arizona, the lowest.

For 1889 the relative death-rate of the two races in the District of Columbia was: whites, 15.96 per 1000; colored, 30.48, about double. In 1888 they stood 18 + to 30 +; in 1886 and '87, about 17 to 31; in '85 and '86, 17 to 32. Especially noticeable is the difference in the mortality of children. This is simply alarming. The report for 1889 shows that out of the 5,152 deaths occurring in the District of Columbia during that year, 634 were white infants under one year old, while 834, an excess of 200, within the same limits were colored. Yet the white population of the District outnumbers the colored two to one. The Health Commissioner, in his report for that year, says:

> This material difference in mortality may be charged to a great extent to the massing of colored people in alleys and unhealthy parts of the city and to their unsanitary surroundings: while there is no doubt that a very large proportion of these children die in consequence of being fed improper and unhealthy food, especially cheap and badly prepared condensed milk, and cow's milk which has been allowed to stand to the point of acidity after having been kept in vessels badly or unskillfully cleaned.

And he adds, "if the general statistics of infant mortality seem astounding to the public, the cause can most frequently be found in the reprehensible custom of committing little impoverished waifs to hired nurses and foul feeding bottles rather than allow them the food that nature has provided."

Now all this unquestionably represents a most wanton and flagrant *waste* of valuable material. By sapping out the possibilities of a healthy and vigorous existence it is deliberately and flagitiously breeding and multiplying paupers, criminals, idiots, drunkards, imbeciles and lunatics to infest and tax the commonwealth. The number spoiled in the making necessarily adds to the cost of those who survive. It is like the Sultan's cracked dinner-plates. It is no use to go into hysterics and explode in Ciceronian philippics against life insurance companies for refusing to insure or charging a higher premium for colored policies. With them it is simply a question of dollars and cents. What are you worth? What are your chances, and what does it cost to take your risks in the aggregate? If thirty-five colored persons out of every thousand are, from any cause whatever, lost in the making, the remaining nine hundred and sixty-five will have to share the loss among them. This is an unavoidable law. No man can dissociate himself from his kind. The colored gentleman who keeps his horses, fares sumptuously, and lives in luxury is made to feel the death gasps of every squalid denizen of the alley and poor-house. It is God's own precaution to temper our self-seeking by binding our sympathies and interests indissolubly with the help-less and the wretched.

What our men of means need to do, then, is to devote their money, their enlightened interests, their careful attention to the improvement of sanitation among the poor. Let some of those who can command real estate in healthful localities build sweet and clean and wholesome tenements *on streets* and rent them at reasonable rates to the worthy poor who are at present forced into association with the vileness and foulness of alleys and filthy courts by the unfeeling discrimination of white dealers. Let some colored capitalists buy up a few of those immense estates in the South, divide them into single farms with neat, cheery, well-ventilated, health-some cottages to be rented to the colored tenants who are toiling all these weary years in the one-room log hut, like their own cheerless mules—just to fodder themselves.

In cities, low priced houses on streets are almost uniformly kept for the white poor. I know of numerous houses in Washington the rent of which is no dearer than colored people are paying in alleys—but the adver-tisement says, "not rented to colored people." If the presence of a colored tenant in a neighborhood causes property to depreciate, it may be a ques-tion of sentiment,—it must be a question of business. The former it is superfluous to inveigh against or even to take cognizance of. It is possibly subject to enlightenment, and probably a sickness not unto death. But the practical reason underlying it is directly our concern and should command our energetic consideration. It is largely a question of what are we worth—and as such, subject to our immediate responsibility and amendment. If improvement is possible, if it is in our power to render ourselves *valuable* to a community or neighborhood, it should be the work of the earnest and able men and women among us, the moral physicians and reformers, to devise and apply a remedy. Sure it is that the burden rests on all till the deliverance comes. The richest and most highly favored cannot afford to be indifferent or to rest quietly complacent.

In rural districts, the relative mortality of colored people is not so excessive, still the poverty and destitution, the apparent dearth of accumulation notwithstanding ceaseless drudging toil is something phenomenal in labor statistics. I confess I have felt little enthusiasm for the labor riots which seem epidemic at the North. Carnegie's men at Homestead, for instance, were among the best paid workmen in the country, receiving many of them $240 per month, living luxuriously, dictating their own terms as to who should work with them, how many hours, and what special labor they will perform. Their employers are forced to hire so many and such men—for these laboring despots insist on an exact division of labor, no one must be called on to work outside his specialty. Then they must share profits, but be excused from all concern in losses—a patent adjustable sliding scale for wages which slides up beautifully, but never down! If the Northern laboring man has not become a tyrant, I would like to know what tyranny is.

But I wonder how many know that there are throughout the Southland able bodied, hard working men, toiling year in and year out, from sunrise to dusk, for fifty cents per day, out of which they must feed and shelter and clothe themselves and their families! That they often have to take their wage in tickets convertible into meat, meal and molasses at the village grocery, owned by the same ubiquitous employer! That there are tenants holding leases on farms who toil sixteen hours to the day and work every chick and child in their possession, not sparing even the drudging wife—to find at the end of the harvesting season and the squaring up of accounts that their accumulations have been like gathering water in a sieve.

Do you ask the cause of their persistent poverty? It is not found in the explanation often vouchsafed by the white landlord—that the Negro is indolent, improvident and vicious. Taking them man for man and dollar for dollar, I think you will find the Negro, in ninety-nine cases out of a hundred, not a whit behind the Anglo-Saxon of equal chances. It is a fact which every candid man who rides through the rural districts in the South will admit, that in progressive aspirations and industry the Negro is ahead of the white man of his chances. Indeed it would not be hard to show that the white man *of his chances* does not exist. The "Crackers" and "poor-whites" were never slaves, were never oppressed or discriminated against. Their time, their earnings, their activities have always been at their own disposal; and pauperism in their case can be attributed to nothing but stagnation,—moral, mental, and physical immobility: while in the case of the Negro, poverty can at least be partially accounted for by the hard conditions of life and labor,—the past oppression and continued repression which form the vital air in which the Negro lives and moves and has his being.

One often hears in the North an earnest plea from some lecturer for "our working girls" (of course this means white working girls). And recently I listened to one who went into pious agonies at the thought of the future mothers of Americans having to stand all day at shop counters; and then advertised with applause a philanthropic firm who were giving their girls a trip to Europe for rest and recreation! I am always glad to hear of the establishment of reading rooms and social entertainments to brighten the lot of any women who are toiling for bread—whether they are white women or black women. But how many have ever given a thought to the pinched and down-trodden colored women bending over wash-tubs and ironing boards—with children to feed and house rent to pay, wood to buy, soap and starch to furnish—lugging home weekly great baskets of clothes for families who pay them for a month's laundrying barely enough to purchase a substantial pair of shoes!

Will you call it narrowness and selfishness, then, that I find it impossible to catch the fire of sympathy and enthusiasm for most of these labor movements at the North?

I hear these foreigners, who would boycott an employer if he hired a colored workman, complain of wrong and oppression, of low wages and long hours, clamoring for eight-hour systems and insisting on their right to have sixteen of the twenty-four hours for rest and self-culture, for recreation and social intercourse with families and friends—ah, come with me, I feel like saying, I can show you workingmen's wrong and workingmen's toil which, could it speak, would send up a wail that might be heard from the Potomac to the Rio Grande; and *should it unite and act*, would shake this country from Carolina to California.

But no man careth for their souls. The labor interests of the colored man in this country are as yet dumb and limp. The unorganized mass has found neither tongue nor nerve. In the free and liberal North, thanks to the amalgamated associations and labor unions of immigrant laborers, who cannot even speak English,—the colored man is relegated to the occupations of waiter and barber, unless he has a taste for school teaching or politics. A body of men who still need an interpreter to communicate with their employer, will threaten to cut the nerve and paralyze the progress of an industry that gives work to an American-born citizen, or one which takes measures to instruct any apprentice not supported by the labor monopoly. A skilled mechanic, a friend of mine, secured a job in one of our cities and was seen by union men at work on his house. He was immediately ordered in murderous English to take down his scaffolding and leave the town. Refusing to do so, before night he was attacked by a force that overwhelmed him and he was obliged to leave. Such crushing opposition is not alone against colored persons. These amalgamated and other unions hold and are determined to continue holding an impenetrable monopoly on the labor market, assuming supreme censorship as regards the knowledge and practice of their trade.

In the South, on the other hand, where the colored man virtually holds the labor market, he is too uncertain and unorganized to demand anything like a fair share of the products of his toil. And yet the man who thinks, must see that our labor interests lie at the foundation of our material prosperity. The growth of the colored man in this country must for a long time yet be estimated on his value and productiveness as a laborer. In adding up the account the aggregate of the great toiling mass largely overbalances the few who have acquired means and leisure. The nation judges us as workingmen, and poor indeed is that man or race of men who are compelled to toil all the weary years ministering to no higher want than that of bread. To feed is not the chief function of this material that has fallen to our care to be developed and perfected. It is an enormous waste of values to harness the whole man in the narrow furrow, plowing for bread. There are other hungerings in man besides the eternal all-subduing hungering of his despotic stomach. There is the hunger of the eye for beauty, the hunger of the ear for concords, the hungering of the mind for development and growth, of the soul for communion and love, for a higher, richer, fuller living—a more abundant life! And every man owes it to himself to *let nothing in him starve* for lack of the proper food. "What is man," says Shakespeare, "if his chief good and market of his time be but to sleep and feed!" Yet such slavery as that is the settled lot of four-fifths the laboring men of the Southland. This, I contend, is an enormous, a profligate waste of the richest possibilities and the divinest aptitudes. And we owe it to humanity, we owe it preeminently to those of our own household, to enlarge and enrich, so far as in us lies, the opportunity and grasp of every soul we can emancipate. Surely there is no greater boon we can bestow on our fellow-man in this life, none that could more truly command his deepest gratitude and love, than to disclose to his soul its possibilities and mend its opportunities,—to place its rootlets in the generous loam, turn its leaves towards the gracious dews and warm sunlight of heaven and let it grow, let it mature in foliage, flower and fruit for GOD AND THE RACE! Philanthropy will devise means—an object is not far to seek.

Closely akin to the value that may be said to have been wasted through the inclemency and barrenness of circumstance, through the sickness, sin and death that wait on poverty and squalor, a large item of worth has undoubtedly been destroyed by mistaken and unscientific manufacture— foolhardy educators rashly attempting to put in some theoretically desirable *crack*—the classical crack, or the professional crack, or the artistic-aesthetic-accomplishments crack—into material better fitted for household pottery and common every-day stone and iron ware. I want nothing I may say to be construed into an attack on classical training or on art development and culture. I believe in allowing every longing of the human soul to attain its utmost reach and grasp. But the effort must be a fizzle which seeks to hammer souls into preconstructed molds and grooves which they have never longed for and cannot be made to take comfort in. The power of appreciation is the measure of an individual's aptitudes; and if a boy hates Greek and Latin and spends all his time whittling out steamboats, it is rather foolish to try to force him into the classics. There may be a locomotive in him, but there is certainly no foreshadowing evidence of either the teacher or preacher. It is a waste of forces to strain his incompetence, and smother his proficiencies. If his hand is far more cunning and clever than his brain, see what he can best do, and give him a chance according to his fitness; try him at a trade.

Industrial training has been hitherto neglected or despised among us, due, I think, as I have said elsewhere, to two causes: first, a mistaken estimate of labor arising from its association with slavery and from its having been despised by the only class in the South thought worthy of imitation; and secondly, the fact that the Negro's ability to work had never been called in question, while his ability to learn Latin and construe Greek syntax needed to be proved to sneering critics. "Scale the heights!" was the cry. "Go to college, study Latin, preach, teach, orate, wear spectacles and a beaver!"

Stung by such imputations as that of Calhoun[5] that if a Negro could prove his ability to master the Greek subjunctive he might vindicate his title to manhood, the newly liberated race first shot forward along this line with an energy and success which astonished its most sanguine friends.

This may not have been most wise. It certainly was quite natural; and the result is we find ourselves in almost as ludicrous a plight as the African in the story, who, after a sermon from his missionary pleading for the habiliments of civilization, complacently donned a Gladstone hat leaving the rest of his body in its primitive simplicity of attire. Like him we began at the wrong end. Wealth must pave the way for learning. Intellect, whether of races or individuals, cannot soar to the consummation of those sublime products which immortalize genius, while the general mind is assaulted and burdened with "what shall we eat, what shall we drink, and wherewithal shall we be clothed." Work must first create wealth, and wealth leisure, before the untrammeled intellect of the Negro, or any other race, can truly vindicate its capabilities. Something has been done intellectually we all know. That one black man has written a Greek grammar is enough to answer Calhoun's sneer; but it is leisure, the natural outgrowth of work and wealth, which must furnish room, opportunity, possibility for the highest endeavor and most brilliant achievement. Labor must be the solid foundation stone—the *sine qua non* of our material value; and the only effective preparation for success in this, as it seems to me, lies in the establishment of industrial and technical schools for teaching our colored youth trades. This necessity is obvious for several reasons. First, a colored child, in most cases, can secure a trade in no other way. We had master mechanics while the Negro was a chattel, and the ingenuity of brain and hand served to enrich the coffers of his owner. But to-day skilled labor is steadily drifting into the hands of white workmen—mostly foreigners. Here it is cornered. The white engineer holds a tight monopoly both of the labor market and of the science of his craft. Nothing would induce him to take a colored apprentice or even to work beside a colored workman. Unless then trades are to fall among the lost arts for us as a people, they must be engrafted on those benevolent institutions for Negro training established throughout the land. The youth must be taught to use his trigonometry in surveying his own and his neighbor's farm; to employ his geology and chemistry in finding out the nature of the soil, the constituents drafted from it by each year's

---

5. Probably John C. Calhoun (1782–1850): a South Carolina politician and leader of the states' rights movement in the Senate.

crop and the best way to meet the demand by the use of suitable renewers; to apply his mechanics and physics to the construction and handling of machinery—to the intelligent management of iron works and water works and steam works and electric works. One mind in a family or in a town may show a penchant for art, for literature, for the learned professions, or more bookish lore. You will know it when it is there. No need to probe for it. It is a light that cannot be hid under a bushel—and I would try to enable that mind to go the full length of its desires. Let it follow its bent and develop its talent as far as possible: and the whole community might well be glad to contribute its labor and money for the sustenance and cultivation of this brain. Just as earth gives its raw material, its carbons, hydrogen, and oxygen, for the tree which is to elaborate them into foliage, flower and fruit, so the baser elements, bread and money furnished the true brain worker come back to us with compound interest in the rich thought, the invention, the poem, the painting, the statue. Only let us recognize our assignment and not squander our portion in over fond experiments. James Russell Lowell[6] says, "As we cannot make a silk purse out of a sow's ear, no more can we perform the opposite experiment without having a fine lot of spoiled silk on our hands."

With most of us, however, the material, such as it is, has been already delivered. The working of it up is also well under way. The gold, the silver, the wood, the hay, the stubble, whatever there was at hand has all gone in. Now can the world use it? Is there a demand for it, does it perform the function for which it was made, and is its usefulness greater than the cost of its production? Does it pay expenses and have anything over.

The world in putting these crucial questions to men and women, or to races and nations, classifies them under two heads—as consumers or producers. The man who consumes as much as he produces is simply *nil*. It is no matter to the world economically speaking whether he is in it or out of it. He is merely one more to count in taking the census. The man who consumes more than he produces is a destroyer of the world's wealth and should be estimated precisely as the housekeeper estimates moths and mice. These are the world's parasites, the shirks, the lazy lubbers who hang around rum shops and enter into mutual relationships with lamp posts to bear each the other's burdens, moralizing all the while (wondrous moralists and orators they often are!) and insisting that the world owes them a living!

---

6. James Russell Lowell (1819–1891): Massachusetts poet, essayist, and diplomat, author of "The Biglow Papers," a poem denouncing the proslavery party.

To be sure the world owes them nothing of the kind. The world would consider it a happy riddance from bad rubbish if they would pay up their debt and move over to Mars. Every day they live their unproductive bodies sink and destroy a regular portion of the world's values. At the very lowest estimate, a boy who has reached the age of twenty, has already burned up between three and four thousand dollars of the world's possessions. This is on the very closest and most economical count; I charge him nothing for fuel or lights, allowing him to have warmed by fires that would have burned for others and estimating the cost simply of what he has eaten and worn, *i.e.* the amount which he has actually sunk of the world's wealth. I put his board at the moderate sum of ten dollars per month, and charge him the phenomenally small amount of thirty dollars a year for clothing and incidentals. This in twenty years gives him a debt of three thousand dollars, which no honest man should be willing to leave the world without settling. The world does not owe them a living then—the world only waits for them to square up and change their residence. It is only they who produce more than they consume, that the world owes, or even acknowledges as having any practical value.

Now to which class do we belong? The question must in the first place be an individual one for every man of whatever race: Am I giving to the world an equivalent of what it has given and is giving me? Have I a margin on the outside of consumption for surplus production? We owe it to the world to give out at least as much as we have taken in, but if we aim to be accounted a positive value we must leave it a little richer than we found it. The boy who dies at twenty leaving three thousand dollars in bank to help another, has just paid expenses. If he lives longer it increases his debit and should be balanced by a corresponding increase on the credit side. The life that serves to develop another, the mother who toils to educate her boy, the father who invests his stored-up capital in education, giving to the world the energies and usefulness of his children trained into a well disciplined manhood and womanhood has paid his debt in the very richest coin,—a coin which is always legal tender, a priceless gift, the most precious payment we can make for what we have received. And we may be sure, if we can give no more than a symmetric life, an inspiring thought, a spark caught from a noble endeavor, its value will not be lost.

Previous to 1793 America was able to produce unlimited quantities of cotton, but unable to free the fibre from the seeds. Eli Whitney[7] came to

---

7. Eli Whitney (1765–1825): inventor of the cotton gin.

the rescue of the strangled industry and perfected a machine which did the work needed. The deliverance which he wrought was complete. The following year America's exports of cotton to England were increased from not one pound in previous years to 1,600,000 pounds. He gave dollars.

Just before the battle of Quebec Wolf[e][8] repeated and enjoyed Gray's "Elegy" saying he valued that gem more highly than the capture of the city before which he was encamped. The next day the city was taken and Wolf[e] was laid to rest. But the world is in debt to both the poet and the soldier—a boundless debt, to the one for an eternal thought-gem, to the other for immortal heroism and devoted patriotism.

Once there lived among men One whom sorrowing millions for centuries since have joyed to call friend—One whose "come unto me ye that are heavy laden" has given solace and comfort to myriads of the human race. *He gave a life.*

We must as individuals compare our cost with what we are able to give. The worth of a race or a nation can be but the aggregate worth of its men and women. While we need not indulge in offensive boasting, it may not be out of place in a land where there is some adverse criticism and not a little unreasonable prejudice, quietly to take account of stock and see if we really represent a value in this great American commonwealth. The average American is never too prejudiced, I think, to have a keen appreciation for the utilities; and he is certainly not behind the rest of the world in his clear perception of the purchasing power of a dollar. Beginning here, then, I find that, exclusive of the billions of wealth *given* by them to enrich another race prior to the passage of the Thirteenth Amendment, the colored people of America to-day hold in their own right $264,000,000 of taxable property; and this is over and above the $50,000,000 which collapsed in the Freedman's Savings Bank when that gigantic iniquity paralyzed the hope and shocked the faith of an inexperienced and unfinancial people.

One would like to be able to give reliable statistics of the agricultural and mechanical products of the colored laborer, but so far I have not been able to obtain them. It is a modest estimate, I am sure, to ascribe fully two-thirds of the 6,940,000 bales of cotton produced in 1888 to Negro cultivation. The reports give estimates only in bulk as to the products of a state or county. Our efficient and capable census enumerators never draw

---

8. James Wolfe (1727–1759): British commander of the capture of Quebec in 1759, where he was killed. "Gray's Elegy" is the "Elegy Written in a Country Churchyard" by Thomas Gray (1716–1771).

the color line on labor products. You have no trouble in turning to the page that shows exactly what percentage of colored people are illiterate, or just how many have been condemned by the courts; no use taking the trouble to specify whether it was for the larceny of a ginger cake, or for robbing a bank of a cool half million and skipping off to Canada: it's all crime of course, and crime statistics and illiteracy statistics must be accurately detailed—and colored.

Similar commendable handling meets the colored producer from the managers of our Big American Show at Chicago[9] which we are all so nervously anxious shall put the best foot foremost in bowing to the crowned heads and the gracious lords and ladies from over the waters. To allow any invention or mechanism, art or farm product to be accredited [to] a black man would be drawing the color line! And our immaculate American would never be guilty of anything so vile as drawing a color line!!!

I am unable to say accurately, then, just how many bales of cotton, pounds of tobacco, barrels of molasses and bushels of corn and wheat are given to the world through Negro industry. The same difficulty is met in securing authentic information concerning their inventions and patents. The records of the Patent Office at Washington do not show whether a patentee is white or colored. And all inventions and original suggestions made by a colored man before emancipation were necessarily accredited to some white individual, a slave not being able to take the oath administered to the applicant for a patent. Prof. Wright, however, by simply collecting through personal inquiry the number of colored patentees which could be remembered and identified by examiners and attorneys practicing before the Patent Office authorities, published upwards of fifty in the *A.M.E. Review* for April, 1886. Doubtless this number was far within the truth, and many new patents have been taken out since his count was made. Almost daily in my walk I pass an ordinary looking black man, who, I am told, is considering an offer of $30,000 for his patent rights on a corn planter, which, by the way, has been chosen as part of the Ohio exhibit for the Columbian Exposition. He has secured as many as half a dozen patents within a few years and is carrying around a "new machine" in his head every day.

Granville Wood, of Cincinnati, has given valuable returns to the world as an electrician; and there is no estimating the money in the outright gift of this people through unremunerated toil. The Negro does not always

---

9. Again, Cooper refers to the 1893 Chicago World's Fair.

show a margin over and above consumption; but this does not necessarily in his case prove that he is not a producer. During the agitations for adverse legislation against the Chinese, the charge was alleged that they spent nothing in the country. They hoarded their earnings, lived on nothing, and finally returned to China to live in luxury and to circulate the wealth amassed in this country. A similar complaint can never be lodged against the Negro. Poor fellow, he generally lives pretty well up to his income. He labors for little and spends it all. He has never yet gained the full consent of his mind to "take his gruel a little thinner" till his little pile has grown a bit. He does not like to seem short. And had he the wage of a thousand a year his big-heartedness would immediately put him under the painful necessity of having it do the entertainment of five thousand. He must eat, and is miserable if he can't dress; and seems on the whole internally fitted every way to the style and pattern of a millionaire, rather than to the plain, plodding, stingy old path of common sense and economy. This is a flaw in the *material* of the creature. The grain just naturally runs that way. If our basal question of economics were put to him: "*What do you give—are you adding something every year to the world's stored up capital?*" His ingenuous answer would be, as the ghost of a smile flits across his mobile lips—"Yea, Lord; I give back *all*. I am even now living on the prospects of next year's income. I give my labor at accommodation rates, and forthwith reconvert my wages into the general circulation. Funds, somehow, don't seem to stick to me. I have no talents, or smaller coins either, hid in a napkin." It will be well for him to learn, however, that it is not what we make but what we save that constitutes wealth. The hod-carrier who toils for $1.50 a day, spending the dollar and laying up the half, is richer than the congressman with an annual income of $5000 and annual duns of $8000. What he most urgently needs to learn is systematic saving. He works hard enough generally—but does not seem able to retrench expenses—to cut off the luxuries which people of greater income and larger foresight, seeing to be costly and unnecessary would deny themselves. He wants to set to work vigorously to widen the margin outside the expenditures. He cannot be too deeply impressed with the fact that tobacco and liquors—even leaving out their moral aspects—are too costly to be indulged in by any who are not living on the interest of capital ready in store. A man living on his earnings should eschew luxuries, if he wishes to produce wealth. But when those luxuries deteriorate manhood, they impoverish and destroy the most precious commodity we can offer the world.

For after all, the highest gifts are not measurable in dollars and cents.

Beyond and above the class who run an account with the world and merely manage honestly to pay *in kind* for what they receive, there is a noble army—the Shakespeares and Miltons, the Newtons, Galileos and Darwins,—Watts, Morse, Howe, Lincoln, Garrison, John Brown—a part of the world's roll of honor—whose price of board and keep dwindles into nothingness when compared with what the world owes them; men who have taken of the world's bread and paid for it in immortal thoughts, invaluable inventions, new facilities, heroic deeds of loving self-sacrifice; men who dignify the world for their having lived in it and to whom the world will ever bow in grateful worship as its heroes and benefactors. It may not be ours to stamp our genius in enduring characters—but we can give what we are *at its best*.

Visiting the slave market in Boston one day in 1761, Mrs. John Wheatley[10] was attracted by the modest demeanor and intelligent countenance of a delicate looking black girl just from the slave ship. She was quite nude save for a piece of coarse carpet she had tied about her loins, and the only picture she could give of her native home was that she remembered her mother in the early morning every day pouring out water before the rising sun. The benevolent Mrs. Wheatley expended some labor in polishing up this crude gem, and in 1773 the gifted Phillis gave to the world a small octavo volume of one hundred and twenty precious pages, published in London and dedicated to the Countess of Huntingdon. In 1776, for some lines she had sent him, she received from the greatest American the following tribute dated at Cambridge:

> Miss Phillis:
>   . . . I thank you most sincerely for your polite notice of me in the elegant lines you enclosed; and however undeserving I may be of such encomium and panegyric, the style and manner exhibit a striking proof of your poetical talents; in honor of which and as a tribute justly due to you, I would have published the poem had I not been apprehensive that, while I only meant to give the world this new instance of your genius, I might have incurred the imputation of vanity. This and nothing else determined me not to give it place in the public prints. If you should ever come to Cambridge or near headquarters, I shall be happy to see a person so favored by the Muses, and to whom nature has been so liberal and beneficent in her dispensations. I am, with great respect,

---

10. Mrs. John Wheatley: owner of the slave Phillis Wheatley (1753–1785), who became a well-known poet in defiance of the eighteenth-century belief that blacks were incapable of literary culture.

Your obedient humble servant,
George Washington

That girl paid her debts *in song*.

In South Carolina there are two brothers, colored men, who own and conduct one of the most extensive and successful farms in this country for floriculture. Their system of irrigating and fertilizing is the most scientific in the state, and by their original and improved methods of grafting and cultivating they have produced a new and rich variety of the rose called *Loiseaux*, from their name. Their roses are famous throughout Europe and are specially prized by the French for striking and marvelous beauty. The Loiseaux brothers send out the incense of their grateful returns to the world in the *sweet fragrance of roses*.

Some years ago a poor and lowly orphan girl stood with strange emotions before a statue of Benjamin Franklin in Boston. Her bosom heaved and her eyes filled as she whispered between her clenched teeth, "Oh, how I would like to make a stone man?" Wm. Lloyd Garrison[11] became her providence and enlarged her opportunity; *she paid for it* in giving to the world the *Madonna with the Christ and adoring Angels*, now in the collection of the Marquis of Bute. From her studio in Rome Edmonia Lewis,[12] the colored sculptress, continues to increase the debt of the world to her by her graceful thoughts in the chaste marble.

On May 27, 1863, a mixed body of troops in blue stood eagerly expectant before a rebel stronghold. On the extreme right of the line, a post of honor and of danger, were stationed the Negro troops, the first and third regiments of the Louisiana Native Guards. On going into action, says an eye witness, they were 1080 strong, and formed into four lines, Lieut.-Colonel Bassett, 1st Louisiana, forming the first line, and Lieut.-Colonel Henry Finnegas the second. Before any impression had been made upon the earth works of the enemy, and in full face of the batteries belching forth their sixty-two pounders, the order to charge was given,—and the black regiment rushed forward to encounter grape, canister, shell and musketry, having no artillery but two small howitzers—which seemed mere pop-guns to their adversaries—and with no reserve whatever. The terrible fire from the rebel guns upon the unprotected masses mowed them down like grass. Colonel Bassett being driven back, Colonel Finnegas took his place,

---

11. William Lloyd Garrison (1805–1879): a leading New England Abolitionist.
12. Mary Edmonia Lewis (Wildfire) (1843–?): sculptor of mixed African- and Native-American heritage.

and his men being similarly cut to pieces, Bassett reformed and recommenced. And thus these brave fellows went on from 7 o'clock in the morning till 3:30 p.m., under the most hideous carnage that men ever had to withstand. During this time they rallied and were ordered to make six distinct charges, losing thirty-seven killed, one hundred and fifty-five wounded, and one hundred and sixteen missing, "the majority, if not all of these," adds a correspondent of the *New York Times*, who was an eye witness of the fight, "being in all probability now lying dead on the gory field without the rights of sepulture! *for when, by flag of truce our forces in other directions were permitted to reclaim their dead, the benefit, through some neglect, was not extended to these black regiments.*"

"The deeds of heroism," he continues,

> performed by these colored men were such as the proudest white men might emulate. Their colors are torn to pieces by shot, and literally bespattered by blood and brains. The color-sergeant of the 1st La. on being mortally wounded, hugged the colors to his breast when a struggle ensued between the two color-corporals on each side of him as to who should bear the sacred standard—and during this generous contention one of the corporals was wounded. One black lieutenant mounted the enemy's works three or four times, and in one charge the assaulting party came within fifty paces of them. If only ordinarily supported by artillery and reserve, no one can convince us that they would not have opened a passage through the enemy's works. Captain Callioux, of the 1st La., a man so black that he prided himself on his blackness, died the death of a hero leading on his men in the thickest of the fight. One poor wounded fellow came along with his arm shattered by a shell, jauntily swinging it with the other, as he said to a friend of mine: "Massa, guess I can fight no more." I was with one of the captains looking after the wounded, when we met one limping along toward the front. Being asked where he was going, he said, "I been shot in de leg, cap'n, an' dey wants me to go to de hospital—but I reckon I c'n gib 'em some mo' yit."

Says Major-General Banks in the report from Headquarters of the Army of the Gulf, before Port Hudson, May 30, 1863, writing to Major-General Halleck, General-in-Chief at Washington: "The position occupied by the Negro troops was one of importance and called for the utmost steadiness and bravery in those to whom it was confided. It gives me pleasure to report that they answered every expectation. Their conduct was heroic. No troops could be more determined or more daring."

"Charge!" Trump and drum awoke,
Onward the bondmen broke;
Bayonet and sabre-stroke
Vainly opposed their rush.
Through the wild battle's crush,
With but one thought aflush,
Driving their lords like chaff,
In the guns' mouths they laugh;
Or at the slippery brands
Leaping with open hands,
Down they bear man and horse,
Down in their awful course;
Trampling with bloody heel
Over the crashing steel,
All their eyes forward bent,
Rushed the black regiment.

"Freedom!" their battle-cry—
"Freedom! or leave to die!"
Ah! and they meant the word,
Not as with us 'tis heard,
Not a mere party-shout:
They gave their spirits out.
Trusted the end to God,
And on the gory sod
Rolled in triumphant blood!

And thus they paid *their debt.* "They gave—*their spirits out!*"

In the heart of what is known as the "Black Belt" of Alabama and within easy reach of the great cotton plantations of Georgia, Mississippi, and Florida, a devoted young colored man ten years ago started a school with about thirty Negro children assembled in a comical looking shanty at Tuskegee. His devotion was contagious and his work grew; an abandoned farm of 100 acres was secured and that gradually grew to 640 acres, largely wood-land, on which a busy and prosperous school is located; and besides a supply farm was added, of heavy rich land, 800 acres, from which grain and sugar cane are main products. Since 1881, 2,947 students have been taught here, of whom 102 have graduated, while 200 more have received enough training to fit them to do good work as teachers, intelligent farmers, and mechanics. The latest enrollment shows girls, 247; boys, 264. Of the 102 graduates, 70 per cent. are teachers, ministers and farmers. They usually combine teaching and farming. Three are printers (learned the trades at school), one is a tinner, one a blacksmith, one a wheel-wright, three are merchants, three are carpenters, others in the professions or filling miscellaneous positions.

That man is paying his debt by giving to this country *living, working, consecrated men and women!*

Now each can give something. It may not be a poem, or marble bust, or fragrant flower even; it may not be ours to place our lives on the altar of country as a loving sacrifice, or even to devote our living activities so extensively as B. T. Washington[13] to supplying the world's need for strong and willing helpers. But we can at least *give ourselves*. Each can be *one* of those strong willing helpers—even though nature has denied him the talent of endlessly multiplying his force. And nothing less can honorably cancel our debt. Each is under a most sacred obligation not to squander the material committed to him, not to sap its strength in folly and vice, and to see at the least that he delivers a product worthy the labor and cost which have been expended on him. A sound manhood, a true womanhood is a fruit which the lowliest can grow. And it is a commodity of which the supply never exceeds the demand. There is no danger of the market being glutted. The world will always want *men*. The worth of one is infinite. To this value all other values are merely relative. Our money, our schools, our governments, our free institutions, our systems of religion and forms of creeds are all first and last to be judged by this standard: what sort of men and women do they grow? How are men and women being shaped and molded by this system of training, under this or that form of government, by this or that standard of moral action? You propose a new theory of education; *what sort of men does it turn out?* Does your system make boys and girls superficial and mechanical? Is it a producing of average percentages or a rounding out of manhood,—a sound, thorough, and practical development,—or a scramble for standing and marks?

We have a notion here in America that our political institutions,—the possibilities of a liberal and progressive democracy, founded on universal suffrage and in some hoped-for, providential way *compelling* universal education and devotion,—our peculiar American attainments are richly worth all they have cost in blood and anguish. But our form of government, divinely ordered as we dream it to be, must be brought to the bar to be

---

13. Booker T. Washington (1856–1915): educator, first principal of the Tuskegee Institute in Alabama.

tested by this standard. It is nothing worth of itself—independently of whether it furnishes a good atmosphere in which to cultivate men. Is it developing a self respecting freedom, a sound manliness on the part of *the individual*—or does it put into the power of the wealthy few the opportunity and the temptation to corrupt the many? If our vaunted *"rule of the people"* does not breed nobler men and women than monarchies have done—it must and will inevitably give place to something better.

I care not for the theoretical symmetry and impregnable logic of your moral code, I care not for the hoary respectability and traditional mysticisms of your theological institutions, I care not for the beauty and solemnity of your rituals and religious ceremonies, I care not even for the reasonableness and unimpeachable fairness of your social ethics,—if it does not turn out better, noble, truer men and women,—if it does not add to the world's stock of valuable souls,—if it does not give us a sounder, healthier, more reliable product from this great factory of *men*—I will have none of it. I shall not try to test your logic, but weigh your results—and that test is the *measure of the stature of the fullness of a man.* You need not formulate and establish the credibility and authenticity of Christian Evidences, when you can demonstrate and prove the present value of CHRISTIAN MEN. And this test for systems of belief, for schools of thought, and for theories of conduct, is also the ultimate and inevitable test of nations, of races and of individuals. What sort of men do you turn out? *How* are you supplying the great demands of the world's market? What is your true value? This, we may be sure, will be the final test by which the colored man in America will one day be judged in the cool, calm, unimpassioned, unprejudiced second thought of the American people.

Let us then quietly commend ourselves to this higher court—this final tribunal. Short sighted idiosyncrasies are but transient phenomena. It is futile to combat them, and unphilosophical to be depressed by them. To allow such things to overwhelm us, or even to absorb undue thought, is an admission of weakness. As sure as time *is*—*these mists will clear away.* And the world—our world, will surely and unerringly see us as we are. Our only care need be the intrinsic worth of our contributions. If we represent the ignorance and poverty, the vice and destructiveness, the vagabondism and parasitism in the world's economy, no amount of philanthropy and benevolent sentiment can win for us esteem: and if we contribute a positive value in those things the world prizes, no amount of negrophobia can ultimately prevent its recognition. And our great "problem" after all is to be solved not by brooding over it, and orating about it, but by *living into it.*

· *10* ·

The Gain from a Belief (1892)

$\mathcal{A}$ solitary figure stands in the marketplace, watching as from some lonely tower the busy throng that hurry past him. A strange contrast his cold, intellectual eye to the eager, strained, hungry faces that surge by in their never ending quest of wealth, fame, glory, bread.

Mark his pallid cheek and haggard brow, and the fitful gleam of those restless eyes like two lone camp-fires on a deserted plain.

Why does that smile, half cynical, half sad, flit across his countenance as he contemplates these mighty heart-throbs of human passions and woes, human hopes and human fears? Is it pity—is it contempt—is it hate for this struggling, working, believing humanity which curls those lips and settles upon that hitherto indifferent brow?

Who is he?

Earth's skepticism looking on at the protean antics of earth's enthusiasms. Speculative unbelief, curiously and sneeringly watching the humdrum, common-place, bread-and-butter toil of unspeculative belief. Lofty, unimpassioned agnosticism, *that thinks*—face to face with hobbling, blundering, unscientific faith, *that works.*

Dare we approach?

"Sir: I perceive you are not drawn into the whirl-pool of hurrying desires that sweep over earth's restless sons. Your philosophy, I presume, lifts you above the toils and anxieties, the ambitions and aspirations of the common herd. Pardon me, but do you not feel called to devote those superior powers of yours to the uplifting of your less favored brethren? May not you pour the oil of human kindness and love on these troubled waters? May not your wisdom shape and direct the channel of this tortuous stream, building up here, and clearing out there, till this torrent become once more a smiling river, reflecting Heaven's pure love in its silvery bosom, and again this fruitful valley blossom with righteousness and peace? Does not your soul burn within you as you look on this seething mass of struggling, starving, sinning souls? Are you not inspired to lift up despairing, sinking, grovelling man,—to wipe the grime and tears from his marred countenance, and bid him Look aloft and be strong, Repent and be saved, Trust God and live!''

Ah! the coldness of the look he turned on me! Methought 'twould freeze my soul. "Poor fool!'' it seemed to say; and yet I could not but think I discovered a trace of sadness as he replied:—

"What is man?—A curiously fashioned clock; a locomotive, capable of sensations;—a perfected brute. Man is a plant that grows and thinks; the form and place of his growth and the product of his thought are as little dependent on his will or effort as are the bark, leaves, and fruit of a tree on its choice. Food, soil, climate,—those make up the man,—the whole man, his life, his soul (if he have one). Man's so-called moral sense is a mere dance of molecules; his spiritual nature, a pious invention. Remorse is a blunder, repentance is vain, self-improvement or reformation an impossibility. The laws of matter determine the laws of intellect, and these shape man's nature and destiny and are as inevitable and uncontrollable as are the laws of gravitation and chemical affinity. You would-be reformers know not the stupendous nonsense you are talking. Man is as little responsible for vice or crime as for fever or an earthquake. Those in whom the cerebrum shows a particular formation, will make their holidays in gambling, betting, drinking, horse-racing—their more serious pursuits in stealing, ravening, murdering. They are not immoral any more than a tiger is immoral; they are simply *un*moral. They need to be restrained, probably, as pests of society, or submitted to treatment as lunatics. Their fellows in whom the white and gray matter of the brain cells are a little differently correlated, will in their merry moods sing psalms and make it their habitual activity to reach out after the Unknown in various ways, trying to satisfy the vague and restless longings of what they call their souls by punishing themselves and pampering the poor. I have neither blame nor praise. Each class simply believe and do as they must. And as for God—science finds him not. If there be a God—He is unknown and unknowable. The finite mind of man cannot conceive the Infinite and Eternal. And if such a being exists, he cannot be concerned about the miserable wretches of earth. Searching after him is vain. Man has simply projected his own personality into space and worshipped it as a God—a person—himself. My utmost knowledge is limited to a series of sensations within, aware of itself; and a possibility of sensations without, both governed by unbending laws within the limits of experience and a reasonable distance beyond.''

"And beyond that Beyond" I ask breathlessly—"beyond that Beyond?"

I am sure I detected just then a tremor as of a chill running through the fragile frame; and the eye, at first thoughtful and coldly scornful only, is now unmistakably shaded with sadness. "Beyond that Beyond?" he repeated slowly, "—beyond that Beyond, *if* there be such,—*spaces of darkness and eternal silence!* ["]Whether this prolonged throb of consciousness exists after its external possibilities have been dissolved—I cannot tell. That is to me—a horrible plunge—*in the dark!* I stand at the confluence of two eternities and three immensities. I see, with Pascal, only infinities in all directions which envelop me like an atom—like a shadow which endures for a moment and—will never return! All that I know is that I must die, but what I now the very least of is that very death—which I can not avoid! *The eternal silence* of these infinite spaces maddens me!"

Sick at heart, I turn away and ask myself what is this system which, in the words of Richter,[1] makes the universe an automaton, and man's future—a coffin! Is this the cold region to which thought, as it moves in its orbit, has brought us in the nineteenth century? Is this the germ of the "Philosophy of the future"—the exponent of our "advanced ideas," the "new light" of which our age so uproariously boasts? Nay rather is not this *monstrum horrendum* of our day but a renewal of the empiricism and skepticism of the days of Volatire? Here was undoubtedly the nucleus of the cloud no bigger than a man's hand, which went on increasing in bulk and blackness till it seemed destined to enshroud earth and heaven in the gloom of hell.

David Hume,[2] who, though seventeen years younger than Voltaire, died in 1776 just two years before the great French skeptic, taught skepticism in England on purely metaphysical grounds. Hume knew little or nothing about natural science; but held that what we call mind consists merely of successive perceptions, and that we can have no knowledge of anything but phenomena.

His system afterwards passes through France, is borrowed and filtered through the brain of a half crazy French schoolmaster, Auguste Comte,[3]

---

1. Possibly the German novelist Jean Paul Richter (1763–1825), who portrayed life in simple country villages.
2. David Hume (1711–1776): Scottish philosopher and historian who extended the empiricist legacy of John Locke. And, Voltaire (1694–1778), pseudonym of Francois Makel Aranet: French Enlightenment writer and the skeptic to whom Cooper refers.
3. Auguste Comte (1798–1857): French philosopher and sociologist, founder of positivism.

who thus becomes the founder of the Comtist school of Positivism or Nescience or Agnosticism as it is variously called. The adherents of his school admit neither revelation, nor a God, nor the immortality of the soul. Comte held, among other things, that two hours a day should be spent in the worship of Collective Humanity to be symbolized by some of the *sexe aimant*. On general principles it is not quite clear which is the *sexe aimant*. But as Comte proceeds to mention one's wife, mother, and daughter as fitting objects of religious adoration because they represent the present, past and future of Humanity—one is left to infer that he considered the female the *loving sex* and the ones to be worshipped; though he does not set forth who were to be objects of woman's own adoring worship. In this ecclesiastical system which Prof. Huxley[4] wittily denominates *Romanism minus Christianity*, Comte made himself High Pontiff, and his inamorata, the widow of a galley slave, was chief saint. This man was founder of the system which the agnostic prefers to the teachings of Jesus!

However, had this been all, the positivist would have been as harmless as any other lunatic. But he goes a step farther and sets up his system as the philosophy of *natural science*, originating in and proved by pure observation and investigation of physical phenomena; and scoffs at as presumptuous and unwarrantable all facts that cannot be discerned through the senses. In this last position he is followed by John Stuart Mill,[5] Herbert Spencer,[6] G. H. Lewes,[7] and a noble army of physicists, naturalists, physiologists, and geologists. Says one: "We have no knowledge of anything but phenomena, and the essential nature of phenomena and their ultimate causes are unknown and inscrutable to us." Says another: "All phenomena without exception are governed by invariable laws with which no volitions natural or supernatural interfere." And another: "Final causes are unknown to us and the search after them is fruitless, a mere chase of a favorite will-o'-the-wisp. We know nothing about any supposed purposes for which organs 'were made.' Birds fly because they have wings, a true naturalist will never say—he can never know they have wings *in order that* they may fly."

And Mr. Ingersoll,[8] the American exponent of positivism, in his "Why

---

4. Thomas Henry Huxley (1825–1895): English biologist. A proponent of Darwinism, he also wrote theology.

5. John Stuart Mill (1806–1873): English empiricist philosopher and social reformer.

6. Herbert Spencer (1820–1903): English evolutionary philosopher, a leading advocate of social Darwinism.

7. George Henry Lewes (1817–1878): English writer, lover of novelist George Eliot (Mary Ann Evans).

8. Robert Green Ingersoll (1833–1899): lawyer and lecturer, known as the "Great Agnostic" for his freethinking views.

I Am an Agnostic," winds up a glittering succession of epigrammatic inconsistencies with these words:

> "Let us be honest with ourselves. In the presence of countless mysteries, standing beneath the boundless heaven sown thick with constellations, knowing that each grain of sand, each leaf, each blade of grass, asks of every mind the answerless question; knowing that the simplest thing defies solution; feeling that we deal with the superficial and the relative and that we are forever eluded by the real, the absolute,—let us admit the limitations of our minds, and let us have the courage and the candor to say: we do not know.

It is no part of my purpose to enter into argument against the agnostics. Had I the wish, I lack the ability. It is enough for me to know that they have been met by foemen worthy their steel and that they are by no means invincible.

"The average man," says Mr. Ingersoll, "does not reason—he feels." And surely 'twere presumption for an average woman to attempt more. For my part I am content to "feel." The brave Switzer who sees the awful avalanche stealing down the mountain side threatening death and destruction to all he holds dear, hardly needs any very correct ratiocination on the mechanical and chemical properties of ice. He *feels* there is danger nigh and there is just time for him to sound the tocsin of alarm and shout to his dear ones "fly!"

For me it is enough to know that by this system God and Love are shut out; prayer becomes a mummery; the human will but fixed evolutions of law; the precepts and sanctions of morality a lie; the sense of responsibility a disease. The desire for reformation and for propagating conviction is thus a fire consuming its tender. Agnosticism has nothing to impart. Its sermons are the exhortations of one who convinces you he stands on nothing and urges you to stand there too. If your creed is that nothing is sure, there is certainly no spur to proselytize. As in an icicle the agnostic abides alone. The vital principle is taken out of all endeavor for improving himself or bettering his fellows. All hope in the grand possibilities of life are blasted. The inspiration of beginning now a growth which is to mature in endless development through eternity is removed from our efforts at self culture. The sublime conception of life as the seed-time of character for the growing of a congenial inner-self to be forever a constant conscious presence is changed into the base alternative conclusion, *Let us eat and drink for to-morrow we die.*

To my mind the essence of the poison is just here. As far as the meta-physical grounds for skepticism are concerned, they are as harmless to the masses as if they were entombed in Greek or Hebrew. Many of the terms, it is true, are often committed to memory and paraded pretty much in the spirit of the college sophomore who affects gold-bowed spectacles and stooping shoulders—it is scholarly, you know. But the real reasons for and against agnosticism rest on psychological and scientific facts too abstruse for the laity to appreciate. There is much subtle sophistry in the oracular utter-ances of a popular speaker like Mr. Ingersoll, which catch the fancy and charm the imagination of the many. His brilliant blasphemies like the winged seed of the thistle are borne on the slightest breath of wind and find lodgment in the shallowest of soils; while the refutation of them, un-dertaken in a serious and logical vein is often too conclusive to convince: that is, it is too different in kind to reach the same class of minds that have been inoculated with the poison germs.

My own object, however, is neither to argue nor to refute argument here. I want to utter just this one truth:—The great, the fundamental need of any nation, any race, is for heroism, devotion, sacrifice; and there cannot be heroism, devotion, or sacrifice in a primarily skeptical spirit. A great man said of France, when she was being lacerated with the frantic stripes of her hysterical children,—*France needs a religion!* And the need of France during her trying Revolution is the need of every crisis and conflict in the evolution of nations and races. At such times most of all, do men need to be anchored to what they *feel* to be eternal verities. And nothing else at any time can propel men into those sublime efforts of altruism which constitute the moral heroes of humanity. The demand for heroism, devotion and sacrifice founded on such a faith is particularly urgent in a race at almost the embryonic stage of character-building. The Hour is *now;*—where is the man? He must *believe* in the infinite possibilities of devoted self-sacrifice and in the eternal grandeur of a human idea heroically espoused. It is the enthusiasms, the faiths of the world that have heated the crucibles in which were formed its reformations and its impulses toward a higher growth. And I do not mean by faith the holding of correct views and unimpeachable opinions on mooted questions, merely; nor do I understand it to be the ability to forge cast-iron formulas and dub them TRUTH. For while I do not deny that absolute and eternal truth *is*,—still truth must be infinite, and as incapable as infinite space, of being encompassed and confined by one age or nation, sect or country—much less by one little creature's finite brain.

To me, faith means *treating the truth as true.* Jesus *believed* in the infinite possibilities of an individual soul. His faith was a triumphant realization of the eternal development of *the best* in man—an optimistic vision of the human aptitude for endless expansion and perfectibility. This truth to him placed a sublime valuation on each individual sentiency—a value magnified infinitely by reason of its immortal destiny. He could not lay hold of this truth and let pass an opportunity to lift men into nobler living and firmer building. He could not lay hold of this truth and allow his own benevolence to be narrowed and distorted by the trickeries of circumstance or the colorings of prejudice.

Life must be something more than dilettante speculation. And religion (ought to be if it isn't) a great deal more than mere gratification of the instinct for worship linked with the straight-teaching of irreproachable credos. Religion must be *life made true;* and life is action, growth, development—begun now and ending never. And a life made true cannot confine itself—it must reach out and twine around every pulsing interest within reach of its uplifting tendrils. If then you *believe* that intemperance is a growing vice among a people within touch of your sympathies; if you see that, whereas the "Lord had shut them in," so that from inheritance there are but few cases of alcoholized blood,—yet that there is danger of their becoming under their changed circumstances a generation of inebriates—if you believe this, then this is your truth. Take up your parable and in earnestness and faith *give it out* by precept and by example.

Do you *believe* that the God of history often chooses the weak things of earth to confound the mighty, and that the Negro race in America has a veritable destiny in His eternal purposes,—then don't spend your time discussing the "Negro Problem" amid the clouds of your fine havana, ensconced in your friend's well-cushioned arm-chair and with your patent leather boot-tips elevated to the opposite mantel. Do those poor "cowards in the South" need a leader—then get up and lead them! Let go your purse-strings and begin to *live* your creed. Or is it your modicum of truth that God hath made of one blood all nations of the earth; and that all interests which specialize and contract the broad, liberal, cosmopolitan idea of universal brotherhood and equality are narrow and pernicious, then treat that truth as true. Don't inveigh against lines of longitude drawn by others when at the same time you are applying your genius to devising lines of latitude which are neither race lines, nor character lines, nor intelligence lines—but certain social-appearance circlets assorting your "universal brotherhood" by shapes of noses and texture of hair. If you object to imaginary lines—don't draw them! Leave only the real lines of nature and character. And so whatever the vision, the revelation, the idea, vouchsafed *you,*

> Think it truly and thy thoughts shall the soul's famine feed.
> *Speak* it truly and each word of thine shall be a fruitful seed;
> *Live* it truly and thy life shall be a grand and holy creed!

Macaulay has left us in his masterly description of Ignatius Loyola a vivid picture of the power of a belief and its independence of material surroundings.

> On the road from the Theatine convent in Venice might have been seen once a poor crippled Spaniard, wearily but as fast as his injured limbs can carry him making his way toward Rome. His face is pinched, his body shrunken, from long fast and vigil. He enters the City of the Caesars without money, without patrons, without influence! but there burns a light in his eye that reeks not of despair. In a frequented portion of a busy street he stops and mounts a stone, and from this rude rostrum begins to address the passers by in barbarous Latin. Lo, there is contagion in the man! He has actually imparted of his spirit to that mottled audience! And now the same fire burns in a hundred eyes, that shone erewhile from his. Men become his willing slaves to do his bidding even unto the ends of the earth. With what courage, what zeal, what utter self-abnegation, with what blind devotion to their ends regardless of means do they preach, teach, write, act! Behind the thrones of kings, at the bedside of paupers, under every disguise in every land, mid pestilence and famine, in prisons oft, in perils by land and perils by sea, the Jesuit, undaunted, pursues his way.

Do you seek to know the secret charm of Ignatius Loyola, the hidden spring of the Jesuit's courage and unfaltering purpose? It is these magic words, "*I believe.*" That is power That is the stamping attribute in every impressive personality, that is the fire to the engine and the motor force in every battery. That is the live coal from the altar which at once unseals the lips of the dumb—and that alone which makes a man a positive and not a negative quantity in the world's arithmetic. With this potent talisman man no longer "abideth alone." He cannot stand apart, a cold spectator of earth's pulsing struggles. The flame must burst forth. The idea, the doctrine, the device for betterment must be imparted. "*I believe,*" [these words were] strength and power to Paul, to Mohammed, to the Saxon Monk and the Spanish Zealot,—and they must be our strength if our lives are to be worth the living. They mean as much to-day as they did in the breast of Luther or of Loyola. Who cheats me of [them] robs me of both shield and spear. Without them I have no inspiration to better myself, no inclination to help another.

It is small service to humanity, it seems to me, to open men's eyes to the fact that the world rests on nothing. Better the turtle of the myths, than a *perhaps*. If "fooled they must be, though wisest of the wise," let us help to make them the fools of virtue. You may have learned that the pole star is twelve degrees from the pole and forebear to direct your course by it—preferring your needle taken from earth and fashioned by man's device. The slave brother, however, from the land of oppression once saw the celestial beacon and dreamed not that it ever deviated from due North. He *believed* that *somewhere* under its beckoning light, lay a far away country where a man's a man. He sets out with his heavenly guide before his face— would you tell him he is pursuing a wandering light? Is he the poorer for his ignorant hope? Are you the richer for your enlightened suspicion?

Yes, I believe there is existence beyond our present experience; that that existence is conscious and culturable; and that there is a noble work here and now in helping men to live *into* it.

> Not in Utopia,—subterraneous fields,—
> Or some secreted island, Heaven knows where!
> But in this very world, which is the world
> Of all of us—the place where in the end
> We find our happiness, or not at all!

There are nations still in darkness to whom we owe a light. The world is to be moved one generation forward—whether by us, by blind force, by fate, or by God! If thou believest, all things are possible; and *as* thou believest, so be it unto thee.

· III ·

The Range of Cooper's Voice: Feminism, Social Service, Education, and Race Politics

Though A Voice from the South *is, today, Anna Julia Cooper's most famous writing, it was far from being her only important work. She wrote an astonishing number and kind of books, articles, letters, and poems over at least sixty-five years. Cooper's first known public writing, the lead chapter in* A Voice from the South, *was written in 1886 when she was not yet thirty. She continued to write, and publish, through the years. Her last major work was a book in tribute to her closest and oldest Washington friends, the Grimké family.* Personal Recollections of the Grimké Family and the Life and Writings of Charlotte Forten Grimké *(excerpted in chapter 26) was published in 1951 when Cooper was well into her tenth decade of life.*

As extraordinary as is the length of Cooper's public life and work the variety of topics upon which she wrote is just as impressive. The chapters of A Voice from the South *already suggest the remarkable breadth and depth of Cooper's interests and competencies. But the essays and other papers collected in this part more completely illustrate the full extent of Cooper's accomplishments. They are arranged so as to represent Cooper's thinking across the years, with at least one selection from each of five decades of her most productive years. Included in this part are previously unpublished and hard-to-find writings from the 1890s to the 1940s, that is, from just after* A Voice from the South *in 1892 to the years before her* Personal Recollections of the Grimké Family *in 1951. This part, thereby, allows the reader to appreciate the range of Cooper's voice as it was broadcast across the decades and over her several different fields of intellectual and scholarly competence. As brilliant as she was as an essayist and public speaker, Cooper was also a superbly qualified, and professionally recognized, historian and linguist.*

Any reader who seeks fully to assess the quality, as well as contents, of Cooper's Voice from the South *must consider the work that unfolded in the years that followed. Whatever one thinks of the earliest work, there is plenty of room for reconsideration in the subsequent writings that, we would argue, demonstrate the full blossom of the many seeds to be found in* A Voice from the South. *The chapters that follow thus allow for argument against several of the most salient criticisms of Cooper's early thinking.*

Those, for example, who suspect Cooper of succumbing to the benign values of true womanhood must consider her unqualified identification with the most oppressed of black women in ''The Intellectual Progress of the Colored Women in the United States since the Emancipation Proclamation'' (chapter 11), no less than her sensible reflections on the nature and necessity of work among the urban and rural poor in ''The Social Settlement'' (chapter 13) and ''Sketches from a Teacher's Notebook'' (chapter 14). Those, also, who are troubled by Cooper's grounding of her political

and social concerns in religious values ought consult the rhetorically sharp and histori-
cally acute application of those values in her *"Ethics of the Negro Question"* (chapter
12). Those, as well, who interpret Cooper's voice theme in her first book as, perhaps, just a little too short on real political involvement might reconsider upon reading
the practical politics in her philosophies of education (chapters 16, 19, 20) or the
fine political distinctions in her comment on the difference between Stalin and Hitler
in *"Hitler and the Negro"* (chapter 21).

Finally, and perhaps most especially, anyone who might disparage Cooper as
little more than an interesting schoolteacher who wrote essays in her spare time should
consult the serious scholarly work, professional and applied, represented in this part
and the one following. Cooper's finest scholarly accomplishment is, without doubt,
her 1925 doctoral thesis, *"L'Attitude de la France à l'égard de l'esclavage pendant
la Revolution."* Selections from the thesis and Cooper's defense of it are found in
part 4. There one can see that, unlike most doctoral students, Cooper refused to
abandon her lifelong commitment to clear and direct writing. Though, as she admits
(chapter 27), Cooper was, like most students, nervous on the occasion of her oral
defense at the Sorbonne, she did not shrink from staking out a distinctive method-
ological position in opposition to the views of her examiners. It is possible to see in
Cooper's great work of historical research the faint outlines of a theoretical position
not that different from what is known today as world-system theory (about which
more in the introduction to the next part). Apart from the scholarly virtues of the
thesis, the reader should be reminded that it was a thesis presented at the University
of Paris. It was, thus, both written and orally defended in the French language.
Undergirding Cooper's historical scholarship was her many years training as a linguist.

In the same year in which she completed her doctoral work, Cooper also published her translation of a key text of medieval French literature, Le Pèlerinage de
Charlemagne *(the preface of which appears in translation as chapter 15). Cooper
had begun this work in partial qualification for the doctorate at Columbia University.
She was forced, however, to abandon the Columbia program because of its requirement of one full year of residency in New York City, which was impossible given
her child care and teaching responsibilities. Hence, in effect, she transferred (as we
would say today) to the Sorbonne, which had no such requirement. The work in
Paris was done in 1924 and 1925, a full decade after she had begun graduate work
in the Department of Romance Languages at Columbia (see chapter 27 for her
recollections). Cooper had taken her formal course work at Columbia in the summers
of 1914 through 1917 and, after World War I, turned to the translation of Le
Pèlerinage as "homework" (as she put it) approved by her Columbia advisor. The
translation from medieval to modern French was published in 1925 in Paris. Por-

tions of her work were subsequently translated into English for inclusion in a standard text of readings in medieval literature. The brief preface we include as chapter 15 illustrates Cooper's approach to the work and her view of its importance.

A more direct and striking illustration of her competence as an applied linguist is found in "The Negro's Dialect" (chapter 18). Why this text was never published we cannot say. We would guess that it was written in the 1930s after she had assumed the presidency of Frelinghuysen University (when she was well past the usual age of retirement). Perhaps there were just too many duties, even then, for her to find time to complete and publish the work. Whatever may have been, that "The Negro's Dialect" has not been hitherto widely available to readers of Cooper may well account for the occasional underestimation of the range of her abilities and convictions. The essay today would be considered an instance of public intellectual work at its best. Cooper politely demolishes white cynicism about the Amos 'n Andy brand of Negro dialect by deploying her mastery of linguistics. This essay and "Sketches from a Teacher's Notebook" are two of the most important underdiscovered gems of Cooper's brilliance, too long unknown to the general reader.

To read the works in this part is to begin to understand the prodigious accomplishments of Cooper's lifework. But, in reading them, one should keep in mind that all this work was done while Cooper taught high school classes full-time, raised seven children, managed a public life as a leader of the social settlement movement, and made her views known on the political and cultural issues of the day. All this without the assistance of a spouse and against the abiding hostility of her school administrators, who took every opportunity to punish her precisely for her unruly readiness to work above and beyond the call of classroom duty.

The Intellectual Progress of the Colored Women in the United States since the Emancipation Proclamation: A Response to Fannie Barrier Williams (1893)

This short speech was a prominent response to what may have been the most prominent speech (of more than two hundred) delivered at the 1892 Congress of Representative Women at the Columbian (or Chicago) World's Fair. The Chicago World's Fair was meant to commemorate the four hundredth anniversary of the discovery of American. It had itself become the subject of controversy as white feminists demanded (and won) inclusion in its planning and program. Once built, the fair complex was widely known as "White City" because all of its buildings were done in white exterior. Black Americans understood this nickname in its poignantly secondary, and racial, sense. Black women protested their exclusion from the fair's program.

The address to which Cooper responded was delivered by Fannie Barrier Williams (1855–1944), who had been selected (in response to the protest) as the black women's representative to the planning committee for the women's building at the Chicago World's Fair. Williams may have been selected because she was northern, light skinned, and of the affluent classes. In any case, her speech, though temperate, was notorious for its strong insistence on the unique moral and intellectual importance of black women in American life. Cooper's short response contains many of the black feminist themes of her Voice from the South, *published the year before the fair, in 1892. It is striking, however, because of the opening lines referring to "the darkest period of the colored women's oppression in this country." Here Cooper leaves no room for doubt as to the primacy she grants to the poorest, most oppressed women.*

$\mathscr{T}$he higher fruits of civilization can not be extemporized, neither can they be developed normally, in the brief space of thirty years. It requires

---

This 1893 speech was previously published in the proceedings of the Congress of Representative Women (1893).

the long and painful growth of generations. Yet all through the darkest period of the colored women's oppression in this country her yet unwritten history is full of heroic struggle, a struggle against fearful and overwhelming odds, that often ended in a horrible death, to maintain and protect that which woman holds dearer than life. The painful, patient, and silent toil of mothers to gain a fee simple title to the bodies of their daughters, the despairing fight, as of an entrapped tigress, to keep hallowed their own persons, would furnish material for epics. That more went down under the flood than stemmed the current is not extraordinary. The majority of our women are not heroines—but I do not know that a majority of any race of women are heroines. It is enough for me to know that while in the eyes of the highest tribunal in America she was deemed no more than a chattel, an irresponsible thing, a dull block, to be drawn hither or thither at the volition of an owner, the Afro-American woman maintained ideals of womanhood unshamed by any ever conceived. Resting or fermenting in untutored minds, such ideas could not claim a hearing at the bar of the nation. The white woman could at least plead for her own emancipation; the black woman, doubly enslaved, could but suffer and struggle and be silent.

I speak for the colored women of the South, because it is there that the millions of blacks in this country have watered the soil with blood and tears, and it is there too that the colored woman of America has made her characteristic history, and there her destiny is evolving. Since emancipation the movement has been at times confused and stormy, so that we could not always tell whether we were going forward or groping in a circle. We hardly knew what we ought to emphasize, whether education or wealth, or civil freedom and recognition. We were utterly destitute. Possessing no homes nor the knowledge of how to make them, no money nor the habit of acquiring it, no education, no political status, no influence, what could we do? But as Frederick Douglass[1] had said in darker days than those, "One with God is a majority," and our ignorance had hedged us in from the fine-spun theories of agnostics. We had remaining at least a simple faith that a just God is on the throne of the universe, and that somehow—we could not see, nor did we bother our heads to try to tell how—he would in his own good time make all right that seemed most wrong.

---

1. Here the reference to Frederick Douglass (1817–1895), one of the nineteenth century's greatest race-men, is particularly poignant, recalling subtly Douglass's own (never quite successful) attempts to forge an alliance between feminists and those struggling for racial justice.

Schools were established, not merely public day-schools, but home training and industrial schools,[2] at Hampton, at Fisk, Atlanta, Raleigh, and other central stations, and later, through the energy of the colored people themselves, such schools as the Wilberforce, the Livingstone, the Allen, and the Paul Quinn were opened. These schools were almost without exception co-educational. Funds were too limited to be divided on sex lines, even had it been ideally desirable; but our girls as well as our boys flocked in and battled for an education. Not even then was that patient, untrumpeted heroine, the slave-mother, released from self-sacrifice, and many an unbuttered crust was eaten in silent content that she might eke out enough from her poverty to send her young folks off to school. She "never had the chance," she would tell you, with tears on her withered cheek, so she wanted them to get all they could. The work in these schools, and in such as these, has been like the little leaven hid in the measure of meal, permeating life throughout the length and breadth of the Southland, lifting up ideals of home and of womanhood; diffusing a contagious longing for higher living and purer thinking, inspiring woman herself with a new sense of her dignity in the eternal purposes of nature.

To-day there are twenty-five thousand five hundred and thirty colored schools in the United States with one million three hundred and fifty-three thousand three hundred and fifty-two pupils of both sexes. This is not quite the thirtieth year since their emancipation, and the colored people hold in landed property for churches and schools twenty-five million dollars. Two and one-half million colored children have learned to read and write, and twenty-two thousand nine hundred and fifty-six colored men and women (mostly women) are teaching in these schools. According to Doctor Rankin, President of Howard University, there are two hundred and forty-seven colored students (a large percentage of whom are women) now preparing themselves in the universities of Europe. Of other colleges which give the B.A. course to women, and are broad enough not to erect barriers against colored applicants, Oberlin, the first to open its doors to both woman and the negro, has given classical degrees to six colored women, one of whom, the first and most eminent, Fanny Jackson Coppin,[3] we shall

---

2. In the following Cooper refers, of course, to traditionally black schools, the full current names of which are: the Hampton Institute in Hampton, Virginia; Fisk University in Nashville, Tennessee; Atlanta University; St. Augustine's College in Raleigh, North Carolina; Wilberforce University in Ohio; Livingstone College in New Jersey; Allen University in Columbia, South Carolina; and Paul Quinn College, now in Dallas, Texas.

3. Fanny Jackson Coppin (1837–1913): founder and principal of the Philadelphia Institute for Colored Youth and a leader in the missionary work of the African Methodist Episco-

listen to to-night. Ann Arbor and Wellesley have each graduated three of our women; Cornell University one, who is now professor of sciences in a Washington high school. A former pupil of my own from the Washington [M Street] high school, who was snubbed by Vassar, has since carried off honors in a competitive examination in Chicago University. The medical and law colleges of the country are likewise bombarded by colored women, and every year some sister of the darker race claims [her] professional award of "well done." Eminent in their profession are Doctor Dillon and Doctor Jones,[4] and there sailed to Africa last month a demure little brown woman who had just outstripped a whole class of men in a medical college in Tennessee.

In organized efforts for self-help and benevolence also our women have been active. The Colored Women's League, of which I am at present corresponding secretary, has active, energetic branches in the South and West. The branch in Kansas City, with a membership of upward of one hundred and fifty, already has begun under their vigorous president, Mrs. Yates,[5] the erection of a building for friendless girls. Mrs. Coppin will, I hope, herself tell you something of her own magnificent creation of an industrial society in Philadelphia. The women of the Washington branch of the league have subscribed to a fund of about five thousand dollars to erect a woman's building for educational and industrial work, which is also to serve as headquarters for gathering and disseminating general information relation to the efforts of our women. This is just a glimpse of what we are doing.

Now, I think if I could crystallize the sentiment of my constituency, and deliver it as a message to this congress of women, it would be something like this: Let woman's claim be as broad in the concrete as in the abstract. We take our stand on the solidarity of humanity, the oneness of life, and the unnaturalness and injustice of all special favoritisms, whether of sex, race, country, or condition. If one link of the chain be broken, the chain is broken. A bridge is no stronger than its weakest part, and a cause is not worthier than its weakest element. Least of all can woman's cause afford to decry the weak. We want, then, as toilers for the universal tri-

---

pal Church. Coppin spoke immediately after Cooper and was the only other response to Fannie Barrier Williams.

4. Cooper probably is referring to the distinguished black physicians: Halle Tanner Dillon Johnson (1864–1901) and Vernin Morton Harris Jones (1865–1943)—the first women licensed to practice medicine in Alabama and Mississippi, respectively.

5. Josephine Silone Yates (1859–1912): Second president of the National Association of Colored Women (1901–1906). Like Cooper, she was active in women's club work.

umph of justice and human rights, to go to our homes from this Congress, demanding an entrance not through a gateway for ourselves, our race, our sex, or our sect, but [through] a grand highway for humanity. The colored woman feels that woman's cause is one and universal; and that not till the image of God, whether in parian or ebony, is sacred and inviolable; not till race, color, sex, and condition are seen as the accidents, and not the substance of life; not till the universal title of humanity to life, liberty, and the pursuit of happiness is conceded to be inalienable to all; not till then is woman's lesson taught and woman's cause won—not the white woman's, nor the black woman's, nor the red woman's, but the cause of every man and of every woman who has writhed silently under a mighty wrong. Woman's wrongs are thus indissolubly linked with all undefended woe, and the acquirement of her "rights" will mean the final triumph of all right over might, the supremacy of the moral forces of reason, and justice, and love in the government of the nations of earth.

· *12* ·

The Ethics of the Negro Question (1902)

Cooper delivered this address on 5 September 1902 to the General Conference of the Society of Friends at Asbury Park, New Jersey.

The text, previously unpublished, has been edited to eliminate the repetitions and occasional obscure references that naturally appear in what must have been an hour-long speech. A few time-bound allusions to historical or current events have also been deleted. The original manuscript is itself marked in Cooper's hand with her own corrections and points of rhetorical emphasis.

> Where there is no vision, the people perish.
>
> *Proverbs 29:18.*

$\mathcal{A}$ nation's greatness is not dependent upon the things it makes and uses. Things without thoughts are mere vulgarities. America can boast her expanse of territory, her gilded domes, her paving stones of silver dollars; but the question of deepest moment in this nation today is its span of the circle of brotherhood, the moral stature of its men and its women, the elevation at which it receives its "vision" into the firmament of eternal truth. . . .

It is no fault of the Negro that he stands in the United States of America today as the passive and silent rebuke to the Nation's Christianity, the great gulf between its professions and its practices, furnishing the chief ethical element in its politics, constantly pointing with dumb but inexorable fingers to those ideals of our civilization which embody the Nation's highest, truest, and best thought, its noblest and grandest purposes and aspirations. . . .

Uprooted from the sunny land of his forefathers by the white man's

Reprinted by permission of Moorland-Spingarn Research Center, Howard University. Archive locator: Box 23.4/Folder 32.

cupidity and selfishness, ruthlessly torn from all the ties of clan and tribe, dragged against his will over thousands of miles of unknown waters to a strange land among strange peoples, the Negro was transplanted to this continent in order to produce chattels and beasts of burden for a nation "conceived in liberty and dedicated to the proposition that all men are created equal"[—]a nation worshiping as God one who came not to be ministered unto, but to minister; a nation believing in a Savior meek and lowly of heart who, having nowhere to lay His head, was eyes to the blind, hearing to the deaf, a gospel of hope and joy to the poor and outcast, a friend to all who travail and are heavy laden.

The whites of America revolted against the mother country for a trifling tax on tea, because they were not represented in the body that laid the tax. They drew up their Declaration of Independence, a Magna Carta of human rights, embodying principles of universal justice and equality.

Professing a religion of sublime altruism, a political faith in the inalienable rights of man as man, these jugglers with reason and conscience were at the same moment stealing heathen from their far away homes, forcing them with lash and gun to unrequited toil, making it a penal offense to teach them to read the Word of God,—nay, more, were even begetting and breeding mongrels of their own flesh among these helpless creatures and pocketing the guilty increase, the price of their own blood in unholy dollars and cents. Accursed hunger for gold!

To what dost thou not drive mortal breasts! But God did not ordain this nation to reenact the tragedy of Midas and transmute its very heart's core into yellow gold. America has a conscience as well as a pocket-book, and it comes like a pledge of perpetuity to the nation that she has never yet lost the seed of the prophets, men of inner light and unfaltering courage, who would cry aloud and spare not, against the sin of the nation. The best brain and heart of this country have always rung true and it is our hope today that the petrifying spirit of commercialism, which grows so impatient at the Negro question or any other question calculated to weaken the money getting nerve by pulling at the heart and the conscience, may still find a worthy protagonist in the reawakened ethical sense of the nation, which can take no step backward and which must eventually settle, and settle right, this and every question involving the nation's honor and integrity. . . .

The colored people of America find themselves today in the most trying period of all their trying history in this land of their trial and bondage. As the trials and responsibilities of the man weigh more heavily than do those of the infant, so the Negro under free labor and cut throat competition today has to vindicate his fitness to survive in face of a colorphobia that heeds neither reason nor religion and a prejudice that shows no quarter and allows no mitigating circumstances.

In the darkest days of slavery, there were always at the North friends of the oppressed and devoted champions of freedom who would go [to] all lengths to wipe out the accursed stain of human slavery from their country's scutcheon; while in the South the slave's close contact with the master class, mothering them in infancy, caring for them in sickness, sorrow and death, resulted as pulsing touch of humanity must ever result, in many warm sympathies and a total destruction of that repulsion to mere color which betokens narrow and exclusive intercourse among provincials.

Today all this is changed. White and black meet as strangers with cold, distant or avowed hostility. The colored domestic who is no longer specially trained for her job or taught to look on it with dignity and appreciation, is barely tolerated in the home till she can do up the supper dishes and get away—when she can go—to the devil if he will have her. The mistress who bemoans her shiftlessness and untidiness does not think of offering her a comfortable room, providing for her social needs and teaching her in the long evenings at home the simple household arts and virtues which our grandmothers found time for. Her vices are set down to the debit account of her freedom, especially if she has attended a public school and learned enough to spell her way thro a street ballad. So generally is this the case that if a reform were attempted suddenly, the girl herself of the average type would misunderstand and probably resent it.

The condition of the male laborer is even more hopeless. Receiving 50 cents a day or less for unskilled but laborious toil from which wage he boards himself and is expected to keep a family in something better than a "one room cabin," the Negro workman receives neither sympathy nor recognition from his white fellow laborers. Scandinavians, Poles and Hungarians can tie up the entire country by a strike paralysing not only industry but existence itself, when they are already getting a wage that sounds like affluence to the hungry black man. The union means war to the death against him and the worst of it is he can never be lost in the crowd and have his opprobrium forgotten. A foreigner can learn the language and out-American the American on his own soil. A white man can apply burnt cork and impute his meanness to the colored race as his appointed scape goat. But the Ethiopian cannot change his skin. On him is laid the iniquity of his whole race and his character is prejudged by formula. Even charity does not study his needs as an individual person but the good that love has planned for him must be labeled and basketed "special" for the Negro. Special kinds of education, special forms of industry, special churches and special places of amusement, special sections of our cities during life and special burying grounds in death. White America has created a *terra incognita* in its midst, a strange dark unexplored waste of human souls from which if one essay to speak out an intelligible utterance, so well known is the place of preferment accorded the mirroring of preconceived notions, that instead of being the revelation of a personality and the voice of a truth, the speaker becomes a phonograph and merely talks back what is talked into him. It is no popular task today to voice the black man's woe. It is far easier and safer to say that the wrong is all in him.

The American conscience would like a rest from the black man's ghost. It was always an unpalatable subject but preeminently now is the era of good feeling, and self complacency, of commercial omnipotence and military glorification. It seems an impertinence as did the boldness of Nathan when he caught the conscience of the great king at the pinnacle of victorious prosperity with the inglorious seizure of the ewe lamb from a man of no importance. Has not the nation done and suffered enough for the Negro? Is he worth the blood and treasure that have been spilled on his account, the heart ache and bitterness that have racked the country in easing him off its shoulders and out of its conscience? Let us have no more of it. If he is a man let him stand up and prove it. Above all let us have peace. Northern capital is newly wed to Southern industry and the honeymoon must not be disturbed. If southern conventions are ingenious enough to invent a device for disfranchising these unwelcome children of the soil, if it will work, what of it? . . .

A professor in a Southern school who in a magazine article condemned the saturnalia of blood and savagery known as lynching arguing that the Negro while inferior, was yet a man and should be accorded the fundamental rights of a man, lost his position for his frankness and fairness. The Negro is being ground to powder between the upper and the nether-millstones. The South, intolerant of interference from either outside or inside, the North too polite or too busy or too gleeful over the promised handshaking to manifest the most distant concern.

But God is not dead, neither doth the ruler of the universe slumber and sleep. As a Nation sows so shall it reap. Men do not gather grapes from thorns or figs from thistles. To sow the wind is to reap the whirlwind.

A little over two years ago while the gentlest and kindest of presidents[1] was making a tour of the South bent only on good will to men with a better understanding and the healing of all sectional rancor and ill feeling, there occurred in almost a stone's throw of where he was for the time being domiciled an outburst of diabolism that would shame a tribe of naked savages. A black wretch was to be burned alive. Without court or jury his unshrived soul was to be ushered into eternity and the prospect furnished a holiday festival for the country side.

Excursion trains with banners flying were run into the place and eager children were heard to exclaim: We have seen a hanging, we are now going to see a burning!

Human creatures with the behavior of hyenas contended with one another for choice bones of their victim as souvenirs of the occasion. So wanton was the cannibalistic thirst for blood that the Negro preacher who offered the last solace of the Christian to the doomed man was caught in the same mad frenzy and made to share his fate. A shiver ran thro the nation at such demoniacal lawlessness. But a cool analysis of the situation elicited from the Attorney General of the United States the legal opinion that the case "probably had no Federal aspects!" . . .

I will not here undertake an apology for the short comings of the American Negro. It goes without saying that the black is centuries behind the white race in material, mental and moral development. The American Negro is today but 37 years removed from chatteldom, not long enough surely to ripen the century plant of a civilization. After 250 years of a most debasing slavery, inured to toil but not to thrift, without home, without family ties, without those habits of self reliant industry by which peoples maintain their struggle for existence, poor, naked, weak, ignorant, degraded even below his pristine state as a savage, the American Negro was at the close of the War of the Rebellion "cut loose" as the slang of the day expressed it, and left to fend for himself. The master class, full of resentment and rage at the humiliations and losses of a grinding war, suffered their old time interest to turn into bitterness or cold indifference, and Ku Klux beatings with re-enslaving black codes became the sorry substitute for the overseer's lash and the auction block.

At this juncture the conscience of the Nation asserted itself and the federal constitution was so amended as to bring under the aegis of national

---

1. Probably William McKinley (1843–1901), president of the United States from 1897 to 1901.

protection these helpless babes whom the exigences of war had suddenly thrown into the maelstrom of remorseless life.

That they are learning to stem the current is ground for hope; that they have already made encouraging headway even enemies cannot deny. The Negro's productivity as a free laborer is conceded to be greater than formerly as a slave, and the general productivity of the South where he constitutes the chief labor element, has since his emancipation more than doubled. Not having inherited the "business bump" his acquisitive principles have received some shocks and many times have been paralyzed and stunted by the insecurity of his property and the disregard of his rights shown by his powerful white neighbors. Such was the case in the collapse of the Freedman's Savings Bank and the recent Wilmington massacre when the accumulations of a lifetime were wantonly swept away and home loving, lawabiding citizens were forced into exile, their homes and little savings appropriated by others. In spite of this, however, some headway is [being made] in material wealth and the tax lists in former slave states show a credit of several millions to the descendants of the enslaved. . . .

Is it credible that this race which has under freedom caught so eagerly on the rungs of progress in other respects has so shockingly deteriorated . . . as to reverse all claims to humane consideration which they had won by patient service during long years of slavery?

Have a race of men to whom masters not over kind were not afraid to entrust their helpless women and children while faring forth to rivet the fetters more firmly on their dumb driven bodies and who without one single exception demonstrated remarkable fidelity, trustworthiness, reverence for women and kindness toward children, suddenly becomes such monsters of lust and vindictiveness that a woman is not safe on the same highway with them?

A noble army of christian workers and helpers have gone to the South ever since the War, have lived with these people on terms of Christian sympathy and perfect social equality. Have you ever heard of one of these pure minded missionaries who was insulted or outraged and her delicate sensibilities shocked by the unconquerable instincts and baser passions of the men they came to help?

You ask what is the need of today.

How can the Negro be best helped?

What can be done by the man who loves his fellowmen and needs not to be convinced of duties but only to be assured of methods? What is the best means of the Negro's uplift and amelioration?

In a word I answer: Christian Education. This is nothing new you say. That experiment has been tried and tried and there are even those whose faith in the efficacy of this expedient is beginning to wane and we are looking around to see if there be not some other, some quicker and surer way of doing the job. Is it not a mistake to suppose that the same old human laws apply to these people? Is there not after all something within that dark skin not yet dreamt of in our philosophy? Can we seriously take the Negro as a man "endowed by [his] Creator with certain unalienable rights" such as "Life, Liberty, pursuit of Happiness" and the right to grow up, to develop, to reason and to live his life? In short can we hope to apply the key that unlocks all other hearts and by a little human sympathy and putting ourselves in his place learn to understand him and let him understand us? Assuredly, yes!

The black man is not a saint, neither can he be reduced to an algebraic formula. His thirty or forty checkered years of freedom have not transfigured *en masse* ten million slaves into experienced, thrifty, provident, law abiding members of society. There are some criminal, some shiftless, some provokingly intractable and seemingly uneducable classes and individuals among blacks as there are still unless I am misinformed, also among whites. But our philosophy does not balk at this nor do we lose our belief in the efficacy of Christian teaching and preaching. Turn on the light! Light, more light! There will always be some who do not live up to the light they have. But the Master has left us no alternative. Ye are the light of the world.

We cannot draw lines where He recognized none. We cannot falter so long as there is a human soul in need of the light. We owe it, and owe it independently of the worthiness or unworthiness of that soul. Does any one question that Jesus' vision would have pierced to the heart and marrow of our national problem? And what would be His teaching in America today as to *who is my* neighbor?

For after all the Negro Question in America today is the white man's problem—Nay it is humanity's problem. The past, in which the Negro was mostly passive, the white man active, has ordained that they shall be neighbors, permanently and unavoidably. To colonize or repatriate the blacks on African soil or in any other continent is physically impossible even if it were generally desired, and no sane man talks of deportation now except as an exploded chimera. For weal or for woe the lots of these two are united, indissolubly, eternally and thinking people on both sides are convinced that each race needs the other. The Negro is the most stable and reliable factor today in American industry. Patient and docile as a laborer, conservative, law abiding, totally ignorant of the anarchistic, socialistic radicalism and nihilism of other lands, the American Negro is capable of contributing not only of his brawn and sinew but also from brain and character a much needed element in American civilization, and here is his home. The only home he has ever known. His blood has mingled with the bluest and the truest on every battle field that checkers his country's history. His sweat and his toil have, more than any others, felled its forests, drained its swamps, plowed its fields and opened up its highways and waterways.

From the beginning was he here, a strong, staunch and not unwilling worker and helper. His traditions, his joys, his sorrows are all here. He has imbibed the genius and spirit of [his country's] institutions, growing with their growth, gathering hope and strength with their strength and depth. Alien neither in language, religion nor customs, the educated colored American is today the most characteristic growth of the American soil, its only genuinely indigenous development. He is the most American of Americans for he alone has no other civilization than what America has to offer. Its foibles are his foibles. Its youthful weakness and pompous self-confidence are all found here imitated or originating, as between sitter and portrait. Here in the warp and woof of his character are photographed and writ large even the grotesque caricatures, the superficial absurdities and social excrescencies of "Get-rich-quick" and "Pike's Peak-or-bust" America. Nor is it too much to hope that America's finer possibilities and promise also prefigure his ultimate struggle and achievement in evolving his civilization. As the character of Uncle Tom is rated the most unique in American literature, so the plantation melodies and corn songs form the most original contribution to [American] music. Homogeneous or not, the national web is incomplete without the African thread that glints and ripples thro it from the beginning. . . .

Mr. Bryce[2] in his study of the American Commonwealth says: "The South is confronted by a peculiar and menacing problem in the presence of a mass of Negroes larger than was the whole population of the union in 1800, persons who tho they are legally and industrially members of the nation are still virtually an alien element, unabsorbed and unabsorbable." . . .

While these are times that try men's souls, while a weak and despised people are called upon to vindicate their right to exist in the face of a race of hard, jealous, intolerant, all-subduing instincts, while the iron of [the

---

2. James Bryce (1838–1922): English author and diplomat who was ambassador to the United States from 1907 to 1913. His *American Commonwealth* appeared in 1888.

white race's] wrath and bitter prejudice cuts into the very bones and marrow of my people, I have faith to believe that God has not made us for naught and He has not ordained to wipe us out from the face of the earth. I believe, moreover, that America is the land of destiny for the descendants of the enslaved race, that here in the house of their bondage are the seeds of promise for their ultimate enfranchisement and development. This I maintain in full knowledge of what at any time may be wrought by a sudden paroxysm of rage caused by the meaningless war whoop of some obscure politicians such as the rally word of "Negro domination" which at times deafens and bemuddles all ears.

Negro domination! Think of it! The great American eagle, soaring majestically sunward, eyes ablaze with conscious power, suddenly screaming and shivering in fear of a little mouse colored starling, which he may crush with the smallest finger of his great claw. Yet this mad shriek is allowed to unbridle the worst passions of wicked men, to stifle and seal up the holiest instincts of good men. In dread of domination by a race whom they outnumber five to one, with every advantage in civilization, wealth, culture, with absolute control of every civil and military nerve center, Anglo Saxon America is in danger of forgetting how to deal justly, to love mercy, to walk humbly with its God.

In the old days, I am told that two or three Negroes gathered together in supplication and prayer, were not allowed to present their petition at the throne of Grace without having it looked over and revised by a white man for fear probably that white supremacy and its "peculiar" system might be endangered at the Court of the Almighty by these faltering lips and uncultured tongues! The same fear cowers the white man's heart today. He dare not face his God with a lie on his lips.

These "silent sullen peoples" (so called because sympathetically unknown and unloved) are the touchstone of his conscience. America with all her wealth and power, with her pride of inventions and mastery of the forces of nature, with all her breadth of principles and height of ideals, will never be at peace with herself till this question is settled and settled right. It is the conscience in her throat that is "unabsorbed and Unabsorbable!"

. . .

As for the Negro there can be no doubt that these trials are God's plan for refinement of the good gold to be found in him. The dross must be purged out. There is no other way than by fire. If the great Refiner sees that a stronger truer, purer racial character can be evolved from His crucible by heating the furnace seven times, He can mean only good.

With hearty earnestness the million and [a] half colored boys and girls in the public schools in the South repeat on June 14 the salute to their country's flag: "I pledge allegiance to my flag and to the country for which it stands." I commend these boys and girls to you for as staunch and loyal a yeomanry as any country can boast. They are Americans, true and bona fide citizens—not by adoption or naturalization but by birth and blood incontestable.

Whatever may be problematical about us, our citizenship is beyond question. We have owed no other allegiance, have bowed before no other sovereign. Never has [a] hand of ours been raised either in open rebellion or secret treachery against the Fatherland.

Our proudest aspiration has been but to serve her, the crown of our glory to die for her. We were born here thro no choice of our own or of our ancestors; we cannot expatriate ourselves, even if we would. When the wild forces of hate and unholy passion are unleashed to run riot against us our hearts recoil not more in dread of such a catastrophe for ourselves than in grief and shame at the possibility of such a fall and such a failure for our country's high destiny. It is unconceivable that we should not feel the unnatural prejudice environing us and our children. It is like stones between our teeth and like iron in the marrow of our bones. If at such times we cannot sing America it is not because of any treason lurking in our hearts. Our harps are hung on the willows and in the Babylon of our sorrow we needs must sit down and weep. But no dynamite plots are hatching amongst us. No vengeful uprising brewing. We are a song loving people and that song of all songs we would love to sing, and we challenge the lustiest singer to sing it more lustily and more eloquently than we. But when the wound is festering and the heart is so sore we can only suffer and be silent, praying God to change the hearts of our misguided countrymen and help them to see the things that make for righteousness. . . .

· *13* ·

The Social Settlement: What It Is, and What It Does (1913)

Originally published in the Oberlin College alumni journal, this short history of the Colored Settlement House in Washington, D.C., was clearly intended to explain and justify the settlement house movement to those not directly familiar with its purpose and programs.

Cooper was a longtime member of the trustees of the Colored Settlement House, as were Francis Grimké and Mary Church Terrell. But Cooper also gave of her time as a regular supervisor of the settlement house's programs, a relationship she began in the summer of 1906, just after she had been fired from the principalship of M Street High School. After a four-year exile teaching at Lincoln University in Missouri, Cooper was rehired at M Street High School in 1910. Upon returning to Washington, she continued her work with the Colored Settlement House for many years, even attending to the final distribution of the House's assets after its dissolution. In the meantime, she had taken over the presidency of Frelinghuysen University, a training school for the poor. She had also been long involved, beginning in 1905, in the founding and development of the Colored Young Women's Christian Association in Washington. Thus, throughout cooper's life in Washington, she worked without interruption with and for the poor.

*T*he Social Settlement idea is as old as the fact that "The Word was made flesh and dwelt among us." It is an attempt to carry into the city slums the incarnate Word, the idea of better living, the ideal of higher thinking, embodied or energized in earnest and resourceful men and women who LIVE THERE. It is the heart of sympathy, the hand of brotherly grip, the brain of understanding insight, of efficient and masterful good will indwelling in the midst of down-and-out humanity. It is the gospel of the good

---

Though this essay could have been written as early as 1906, it is more likely to date from after Cooper's return to Washington in 1910. In 1913, Cooper had "The Social Settlement" privately reprinted at the Murray Brothers Press, which, so far as we could learn, no longer exists. The present text is from the 1913 printing.

neighbor, the evangel of helpful sociability. It is a democracy that "levels up" by throwing into the breach its best and its holiest, it is a creed that believes in the Christianity that can save society, a religion that interprets its commission "into all the world and to every creature" to include also our own back alleys and the drunkard whom our laws and customs have helped to undo. It is set on fire with the conviction that all men are created with the divine right to a chance, and sets about hammering down some of those hideous handicaps which hamper whole sections of a community through the inequalities of environment, or the greed of the great. It sees in a little child the most precious possibilities and at the same time the most awful peril of the universe; and it endeavors to promote, for his sake, a home, as seedling soil that cultures the best, with guiding lines and props and God's own sunlight and the God-ordained chance to grow up right.

In point of time the Social Settlement movement in England antedates the attempt to form such centers in America by twenty-five or thirty years. In the early [18]60's the universities of Cambridge and Oxford were manifesting a social conscience under the influence of such men as Ruskin, Toynbee, Chas. Kingsley, Prof. Seeley and Green, the historian. The Workingmen's College in London was founded by F. D. Maurice in 1860. In 1867 Edward Denison, an Oxford man of means, went to Stepney, London, making his home among the people, seeking to understand their needs and to help them.

Toynbee Hall, in the White Chapel district, East London, is possibly the earliest full embodiment of the modern social settlement. Arnold Toynbee,[1] a brilliant young Oxonian, gave his life in devotion to this cause, and after his premature death friends who had caught the fire of his enthusiasm took up the work as a memorial. The oldest Social Settlement in the United States is "Neighborhood Guild," now known as University Settlement, in New York City. It was founded by Dr. Coit,[2] in 1887, and has had remarkable influence in municipal reform, sanitary housing, extension of parks into crowded neighborhoods, and improvement of conditions among working girls.

---

1. Arnold Toynbee (1852–1883): English reformer and historian who is said to have coined the phrase "the industrial revolution." Not to be confused with his nephew, Arnold J. Toynbee (1889–1975), also an English historian and Oxford graduate, who lived a long life and wrote a very long book, *History of the World*. Arnold, the uncle, was the leader of the English settlement house movement.

2. Stanton Coit: English clergyman and founder of the South Place Ethical Society in England in 1888, about two years after having founded the Neighborhood Guild on New York City's Lower East Side.

Hull House, in Chicago, probably the most widely known Settlement in America, was established in 1889 by Miss Jane Addams,[3] and Miss Ellen Starr. A characteristic remark of Miss Addams may be quoted as almost a warning in general how not to succeed: "SETTLEMENTS SUCCEED THRU THE CHARACTER, FORCE AND INSIGHT OF SANE AND INFORMED RESIDENTS. WORKING PEOPLE ARE QUICK TO DETECT SHAMS; AND MERELY LODGING IN A TENEMENT DISTRICT WILL NOT MAKE ONE USEFUL."

The educational work is carried on at Hull House by college men and women and by lectures under the extension work of the University of Chicago. All service, even of resident workers, is gratuitous, and it is counted an honor to have a share in the admirable work.

A few typical examples taken from activities in the Settlements in Philadelphia, New York or Chicago will illustrate what many do and what all aim to do. A library and reading room, generally a branch of the public library, is maintained for the benefit of the neighborhood, where recreation clubs and study classes enjoy social advantages under ideal circumstances. The kitchen or coffee house wages a bloodless warfare against the groggery by furnishing at low cost wholesome drinks and nutritious foods with clean, cheerful and comfortable surroundings. There are art exhibitions to cultivate the esthetic sense, and often a circulating picture library sends out mounted photographs of great pictures into the homes of the people, a printed slip giving a sketch of the artist and a description of the subject being pasted on the back.

Sometimes a co-operative coal club is formed, saving to its members several dollars per ton on coal which was formerly purchased by the bucket. This sort of lesson in economy and thrift is among the most useful means of promoting social efficiency. It is notorious that the poor pay the highest prices for necessities, and they are gilt-edge customers for the "on-time" salesman. And so the stamp system of collecting savings by the friendly visitor from the settlement inculcates the habit of saving the pennies with the result of larger returns from provident expenditures.

Lectures on economic, social and hygienic subjects attended by workers in various charitable and philanthropic institutions furnish a means of training specialists for other fields. The college settlement in a certain city

---

3. Jane Addams (1860–1935): feminist, sociologist, and founder, with Ellen Gates Starr (1859–1940), of Hull House in Chicago in 1889. Like Stanton Coit, Addams had been influenced by the pioneering work at the first settlement house, Toynbee Hall in London, established in 1884.

found in their neighborhood a space covered by old tenements unfit for human habitation. The workers went before mayor and aldermen with a request to have the property purchased by the city and made open space for fresh air, health-giving sunshine, room for play and chance for beauty. Persistent effort was crowned with success.

In a Jewish quarter in New York City flourishes the "Gospel" settlement established by a Christian woman of whom the *Outlook* says: Mrs. Bird has not endeavored to induce Jews to accept a Christian creed, nor has she desired to do so. Her object is not to teach theology, but to impart life. Her home is open from early morning to late at night; and in it are classes and clubs to which boys and girls, men and women of every faith, or none at all, receive equal welcome.

Paradoxically enough, the very period of the world that witnesses the most widespread activity in uplift movements and intensest devotion to social service finds in America the hard wall of race prejudice against Negroes most emphatically bolted and barred. This is perhaps because the transfer in narrow minds from individual selfishness to group selfishness covers with the glamor of religious consecration the sordid meanness of one race toward another. Let a man convince himself that natural selection and survival of the fittest in some way involve responsibility for the uplift of his entire group, and if he is mean anyhow, it will not be hard for him to conclude that he is doing God's service by excluding hated groups or races from all enjoyments and advantages sought for his own. A white woman said to me: "I cannot hold mothers' meetings in connection with my school, or in any way touch the social life of its people." This woman is, and has been for years, principal of a colored school in the south. Yet she confesses that she has not at all touched the social life of the people who need that touch far more than they need either books or trades.

In 1901 there came to Washington a white man, Chas. F. Weller, as executive officer of the Associated Charities of the District of Columbia. His method was to learn how best to minister to the needs of the poor by being a "good neighbor" in neglected neighborhoods; his religion, that every message to man must come expressed in the life of brother-man. He was not conscious of a color line, or, if he was, he did not believe it should fetter the soul of Service. In fact, he seemed to deepen his sense of responsibility with the knowledge of the deeper need and long neglect of colored Americans; and to feel that the social body could not be two-thirds well and one-third sick, two-thirds clean and one-third unwashed, or two-thirds virtuous and one-third impure. He rented a room in an alley given over to colored people of the poorest class, and with the aid of his trusty camera began to study conditions. In his book, *Neglected Neighbors in the National Capital,* he pays this tribute to a colored family with whom he thus sojourned: "Out of such a hole as this, Charley, Mrs. Malcom's oldest son, has come—clean, honest and ambitious." For this is the hope, beneath all social horrors, that even

> In the mud and scum of things
> There alway, alway, something sings.

But Mr. Weller was not allowed to work out this hope in his own way. The compulsion of public opinion, that psychic force which controls society, willed that no white man shall play the part of the Good Samaritan if he answers the question, "Who is my neighbor?" broadly enough to include the neediest class of the social body.

> Prone in the road he lay,
>   Wounded and sore bested;
> Priests, Levites passed that way
>   And turned aside the head.
> They were not hardened men
>   In human service slack;
> His need was great; but then,
>   His face, you see, WAS BLACK.

And the pity of it all is its obviousness to the American mind—its finality and undebatable inexorable fatefulness. It is as if you said: "Why, of course the Christ could not have meant YOU. No conception of universal brotherhood could ever be made to include YOUR race variety! That were preposterous to imagine!"

And so Mr. Weller had to modify his plan of personal work in a colored settlement, but he formed a conference class of willing workers among the colored people themselves, who met in the office of the Charities building and organized the first colored social settlement in Washington, and perhaps the first distinctive settlement of its kind in the world. A sympathetic young white woman—a woman not rich in this world's goods, only a salaried clerk in government employ—donated rent-free a small six-room house on M street southwest, in a section that had borne the ill-omened name of Bloodfield. Here clubs and classes were conducted, and, after a resident was secured, a day nursery, a kindergarten, penny saving through the stamp system and friendly visiting were added. The influence of the settlement on the neighborhood has been marvelous, and its workers have proven helpful agencies in promoting civic improvement and supporting law and order. The growth of the work has called for a larger building, which was erected three years ago, on L street southwest, about a block away from its first home and in the neighborhood of the same general need.

A milk station supplied by a philanthropic citizen has furnished wholesome nourishment to about sixty babies each day; a nurse and doctor, under the same generous provision, have given instruction in "What to Do and How to Do It" to numbers of little mothers whose slender shoulders have burdens beyond their years. Thrift and provident saving are inculcated through the friendly visitor and the penny stamps. A good library is maintained as a branch of the public library, and useful arts and crafts are taught by competent teachers. The response of the neighborhood in support of the work has been admirable. The colored people have realized that without their loyal support the work must fail, and never have people shown greater willingness. The Settlement music department contains interesting possibilities and already numbers many anxious applicants. A swimming pool is one of our dearest ideals, not yet in sight, and it is hoped that some Abou Ben Adhem,[4] who has realized the saving grace of plentiful water, may make public baths as accessible to all the people as Andrew Carnegie has made libraries and learning. A wealthy citizen of Baltimore has established public laundries among the work people of that city where a poor washer-woman may, at reasonable cost for soap and starch, wash and iron under perfectly sanitary conditions and with the best approved appliances—a philanthropy, it seems to me, more directly blessing the class who give than these who receive, if we reflect on the terrible consequences that may result from ignorant laundering under squalid conditions. It is one of the stultifying humiliations of American manners that the group pariahed as the great Unwashed are not only not encouraged to be clean, but are actually barred out from water. Personally, I would struggle to get water if I had to purchase it by the pint. If I went to hunt big game in jungle I would wash—I think. But after living through some hours of American railway service (not the best to be had for the money I paid, but the best I could get at any price), on going for refreshment and accommodation to a

---

4. "Abou Ben Adhem": a poem by the English romantic poet, writer, and activist Leigh Hunt (1784–1859). Abou is a figure of intense love for one's fellow humans.

waiting room provided for the purpose, my preference generally is to endure the dirt and stains I have rather than fly to that so palpably pestiferous.

If only a millionaire would care for my advice. Baths! Baths! Baths! for the plain people, for poor people, for colored people! Endow swimming pools, establish showers, finance laundries! Give us water, oh land of mighty rivers, give water of thy gushing fountains and mighty cataracts! Give water, oh, fatherland, to thy children of sweat and toil; water to wash in, water to play in, water to love and trust and know on terms of intimate familiarity!

In my walk to the Settlement Home I pass a saloon at every corner. The door is of easy swing, the display of obtrusive sociability and alluring hospitality. There are some churches in the neighborhood, too, but closed and dark nine-tenths of the time. At one recently, even on a Sunday, I had to stand outside a bolted door fifteen minutes because I had chanced to come one minute late. The one man, the one door that gives a comforting welcome to a colored man at all hours of the day and night, the one entertainment where his money is as good as any other, is that of the saloon and its unctuous keeper. Not a lecture hall, theater or cafe, not a musical or pictorial exhibition, not a place to catch an ideal or inspire a purpose but deliberately, relentlessly, RELIGIOUSLY, slams the door in the black man's face. One of my neighborhood friends works eight hours a day underground in the sewers of this great city. I find him sometimes in the evening fixing up a tiny flower bed in front of his little home, while his wife sings in preparation of the family meal inside. It is easy to believe that if I had to breathe the gases of the city's sewerage for my eight-hour working day, year in and year out, the good temperance people would have to offer something better than a "don't" to keep me from taking the beaten track to the dazzling hospitality that promises a forgetting.

Washington has the largest colored population of any city in the world. Whatever obtains here will stand as a model of the best or a symptom of the worst in American life. It is to the interest of this entire nation that no plague spots of hidden or segregated depravity be overlooked and ignored as outside the nation's current of life. It is to the interest of every man, woman and child in Washington that each child here, the least important in our reckoning as well as the most important, shall have the chance to develop into serviceable citizenship.

The Social Settlement, with its home life, its neighborhood visiting, its clubs, classes and personal service, is endeavoring to bring higher ideals of life and character to many who are largely cut off from good influences and opportunities; to stimulate ambition, raise moral standards, strengthen character and develop capacity for self-help.

We hear a great deal these days about a fitting memorial to the immortal Lincoln, whose name will stand through all the ages as the great Emancipator of a much-exploited people. In what truer way can we endorse and perpetuate the elemental human good for which the martyr President died and to which the great founder of Hampton devoted his life than to build and maintain at our nation's Capital a working bureau of ideals and opportunities—a "level bridge" reaching sheer to the shores of complete emancipation, the land of honest toil and self-respect, of self-control and social efficiency.

· *14* ·

Sketches from a Teacher's Notebook:
Loss of Speech through Isolation (1923?)

This previously unpublished essay is set against the tragic story of an impoverished rural family, broken by the lynching of the husband and father, yet still struggling with the effects of social isolation—from the surrounding community, which holds back in guilt for its complicity in the atrocity and from the wider society, which is ignorant and indifferent. The story recalls W. E. B. Du Bois's account in "On the Meaning of Progress," in The Souls of Black Folk *(1903), of his sojourn with Josie and her family. Cooper's essay, every bit as moving as Du Bois's, shows her to be a storyteller of the first rank.*

"Sketches" was written, obviously, after World War I, when, as she notes in the opening line, Cooper served as a director of community service programs. There is, however, some uncertainty as to her reference to supervising a War Camp playground in West Virginia. A copy of her 21 December 1921 administrative report on her teaching experience to date, completed in Cooper's unmistakable handwriting, listed the War Camp service in West Virginia as the summer of 1919, but the playground service as the summer 1920 in Indianapolis. It is possible that, even a year after the latter experience, she confused the two or the dates, especially since any report she made to the District of Columbia school administrators had to have been stressful given the manner in which she had been treated over the years. In 1926, for example, she was denied promotion on the basis of examinations that utterly ignored Cooper's teaching experience (see letter to Wilkinson in chapter 28). This was just one of the endless insults going back to the 1906 dismissal. It is possible, also, that the form she used for the administrative report, with the date "December 21, 1921" printed on the form itself, was out of date and that she was recalling some years after. The opening reference to "one summer during the World War" suggests the essay itself may have been written even later, when precise memory of the summers had begun to fade as a matter of course in the life of a busy person. The latter explanation is supported by the indication that Cooper seems to have also misremembered the year when World War I ended (1918). The Versailles peace treaty was, however, not concluded until 1919, which might allow for the references to the West Virginia experience in 1919 as "during the World War."

Reprinted with permission of the Moorland-Spingarn Research Center, Howard University. Cooper archive locator: Box 23.4/Folder 36.

224

The manuscript for "Sketches" is headed by the general title "A Problem in American Education." Before "Loss of Speech through Isolation," it includes the notation "No. 1" (scratched out, presumably by Cooper herself). Perhaps this essay was intended as the first chapter of a longer book, of which the subtitle was "Sketches from a Teacher's Notebook." This would likely put the manuscript early in the 1920s, around 1922 or early 1923—well before Cooper's retirement from high school teaching in 1930, and also before late 1923 when she became ill, using the necessary sick leave from teaching for travel to Paris in 1924 to begin work in earnest on her doctoral thesis at the Sorbonne. It would seem that, sometime before December 1923, she set aside the plan to write about her career in high school teaching in favor of more formal scholarly work. It is possible (but only possible) that a later essay, "On Education" (chapter 19), is also a fragment from that abandoned book project. The case for "Sketches" as the first, brilliant chapter in that unwritten book is stronger.

To set the date for this manuscript at 1923 is at best an informed guess based on the vigor of the writing and the vivid recollection of the experience with the Berry family, if not of the precise dates. Why she might have misremembered the dates of the summer experience is hard to say. Her mental powers were considerable well into her nineties (see chapter 26). Perhaps, in the end, she was merely human.

One summer during the World War as director of War Camp Community Service I had charge of a playground in West Virginia.

Standing out conspicuously in my impressions of that summer's experiences is a family whom I shall call Berry—chiefly because that is not their name. The two lads, about ten and twelve, who first presented themselves to my acquaintanceship were perfect little Ishmaelites—their hand against everybody and every man's hand against them. Teachers of the neighborhood said that their school record was simply an annual repetition of suspensions and expulsions. They would present themselves regularly in September all spic and span with clean shirts, clean, if patched trousers, and clean eager faces for the year's start; but something always happened before the first lap of the course was run, and everybody thought the Berry boys lucky if October found them still on "praying ground where e'en the vilest sinner may return."

They were rather shy of the playground, especially when other children were there having a good time. Decidedly anti-social, they would slip in after the gates were shut and the swings locked, pick or break the locks to enjoy criminally what they might have had freely by simply being in the current with other people. They were never openly and bravely bad—they were only bad as rats are bad—with a passion and a genius for getting around all constituted authority. They would delight in climbing a hill overlooking the playground whence they would roll down boulders and huge stones that came crashing to a full stop just outside the limits of my jurisdiction. I noticed that their bedevilment was peculiarly voiceless. Most urchins of that type would be ready to sing out in fiendish glee when they thought they had you wrought up to a charming pitch of impotent rage. Not so the Berry boys. In fact they resembled nothing more than the silent little old men of the mountains that Rip saw amusing themselves at nine-pins; and if you uttered the word "police!" the whole panorama would disappear so quickly, vanishing so completely you would imagine it had all been a horrid nightmare, and there wasn't any such thing as Berry boys after all.—You had been dreaming!

One day when I was almost alone on the playground in consequence of a steady drizzle all forenoon, I noticed a forlorn little figure with a pair of big round mellow eyes, peeping at me through chinks in the palings. As I started down to speak to her, the frightened little creature, a child of five or six made a dash as tho she would run away. I coaxed her in and putting her in one of the little folks' swings, stood by giving her a gentle push now and then, an excitement that she enjoyed very much. Tho she said nothing, one could read her gratitude in those lustrous round eyes—her joy was too deep for utterance. Alas, short lived joy! A tall soldier lad in khaki, puttees and an over-seas cap, came stalking up the walk. Without recognizing me or uttering a word he took up a position at he rear where he caught the eye of the little mite in the swing. The effect was electrical. The child fell out of the swing as if she had been shot! and pit-a-pat, pit-a-pat, as fast as her little legs could carry her she flew, neither looking back nor waving goodbye. Startled out of my Olympian calm, I turned on the stranger and demanded to know what was the matter.

"Meh wants her home," he replied sententiously.

"Yes? but why didn't you say your mother and father sent for her? You haven't said a word!"

"She know what I mean."

"Perhaps! But it isn't right for you to deal in dumb signs in conveying what you mean. You owe that child the English language. You are grown and have travelled. You can express yourself and interest her in the wonderful world outside that you have had glimpses of. She will never be anything but a dumb, shut-in creature unless you make opportunities for her to cultivate human speech!" More of the same sort I poured forth out of a full heart from my accustomed store. What struck me all the time I was talking was the unbroken stolidity with which my bursts of eloquence were re-ceived. He showed neither resentment at the lambasting I gave him nor a gleam of appreciation that it was fairly well done for a woman. He was chewing a bit of wheat straw pulled in the field and regarded me with the patient, passionless eyes of a yoke of oxen at the end of a furrow when the day is done. Finally in sheer desperation at getting no response, I turned on my heel and left him. Reaching down he pulled another bit of straw which he caught in his teeth and stalked out as he had stalked in. My notebook records this day: "Encounter with the oldest and youngest of the Berry family."

Act II, Scene 1, discovers me in the midst of my basket weavers, reed and raffia all around and busy little fingers holding up mats and baskets in various stages of imperfection—all clamoring to be set right and shown how at the same instant. Walter Berry, the younger of the two tormentors I had known from the first on the playground, now becoming less shy and perhaps, too, a little less savage, was hovering near the background, evi-dently struggling with something he wanted to say but having a hard time getting it out. At last he sidled up, and speaking over my shoulder from behind me managed to blurt out desperately:

"Mith Coo' show—*I make bick too!*"

"Why certainly, Walter," I said with ready comprehension. "I'll be glad to show you how to make a bas-ket," speaking very distinctly and letting him observe the motion of my lips in pronouncing "bas-ket." "You must try to come every day and you have to take lots of pains, you know. But it will be real nice to make a basket for your mother.—Don't you think so?"

Well, from that day till the end of my stay I was taming Walter and incidentally getting a basket ready to present to his mother. Not infre-quently I had to take out at night what Walter had put in by day so as to have him start right the next day, but on the whole the basket, between us, got on amazingly well and I determined to use it as a card of introduction to Mrs. Berry the "Meh" of whom I had heard much but never seen. Accordingly, armed with my playground products I fared forth to break the ice and force a passage into some homes I had never succeeded in luring out to any of our many tempting "occasions" at the playground.

Mrs. Berry's was my first *coup de main*. The house was at the top of a high hill with more steps to climb to reach the porch which spanned a plain but scrupulously neat living room. The floor was freshly scrubbed with white sand, there was a deal table also scrubbed to snowy whiteness and a few splint bottomed chairs scrubbed likewise. All this I noted standing on the threshold of the front door which stood wide open from habit, one could see, rather than with any notion of inviting wayfarers to enter. I knocked on the floor with the point of my umbrella and after some minutes a comely little black woman appeared in the doorway just opposite and stood with hands crossed in front of her waiting to learn the cause of the intrusion.

"Oh," I said with an ingratiating smile; "This is Mrs. Berry, is it not? I am Mrs. Cooper, Walter's teacher on the playground. I came to bring you a little basket that Walter made for you—I taught him how," I added truthfully. "Rather pretty don't you think?" Appealingly now—for I was becoming a wee bit fazed at whipping my own top. For the lady held her pose of dignified aloofness in queenly silence. She might have been an artist's conception of Juno just after that goaterd Paris had pinned the blue ribbon on his amorous little charmer. She did not frown, neither did she beam a smile. She did not ask me in nor say that she was glad I brought the basket. She did not make a pretence of thanking me for any interest I had taken in Walter nor did she try to act out the lie that she was glad to meet me, and yet with it all her manner was singularly free from active repulsion. Bryon's line comes to mind: *"I seek to shun, not hate mankind,"* and yet Bryon's misanthropy was a pose put on to write about it, and the curl of his patrician lip, the *négligé* of his open collar and the somber lilt of his dreamy eyes were sedulously cultivated before the mirror by all the dudes and dandies in New York and London. But here in this solitary little woman was something that was no pose, something commanding respect, almost akin to awe and reverence, something, I felt instinctively, too sacred for prying eyes and inquisitive "investigators." She stood and appraised me with that same unfrowning eye I had noticed in her first born that made you think of uncomplaining oxen, too strong to weep, too weighted down to smile.

After a while she parted her lips—and this is what she said: "I keep to myself; I don' want nothin' to do wit nobody." Her tone was even and clear without the slightest suspicion of hysteria or overwrought emotion. The words might have been borne in from a disembodied spirit, so passionless were they, so sublimated, so purified of the tenseness and dross of the physical and earthy.

"But Mrs. Berry," I persisted, "You can't *live* that way! You can't be in the world without having something to do with other people!"

"I been livin' that way longer'n you been livin' yo' way," she rejoined, "I'm older'n you." (She wasn't at all; but a comparatively young woman.) I accepted the compliment without debate, however, and tried by the most beguiling arts I knew to entice her out of her solitude. After using all the illustrations and arguments I could think of to suggest the interdependence of man on man I was rewarded by seeing the merest ghost of a smile flit across her countenance, more like the quivering gleam of faraway lightning than the steady radiance of sunlight and dawn. We were still standing where I could look out from the threshold of the porch on the muddy water of the Ohio River. "There's nothing you could get to eat," I continued, "without calling in someone to help you out. You can go to the river and fish—"

"And then I'd have to have lard to cook 'em wit," she put in brightly.

Good! I knew I had struck fire and we were friends at last.

As I came down the steps she called out almost shamefastly, "When you come to W—— again, come to see me!"

"Oh, no," I bantered—"you don't want to see anybody!"

"Well, if all was like you," she answered dismally.

It was not till I had left W—— that I understood the tragedy of Mrs. Berry's grim struggle with life. Her husband, an innocent man, had been torn from her arms by an infuriated mob and brutally murdered—lynched. The town realized its mistake afterwards when the true culprit confessed but it was too late to bind up that broken family, and the humble drama of that obscure black woman like a wounded animal with her cubs literally digging herself in and then at bay dumbly turning to face—*America*—her "head bloody but unbowed"—I swear the pathos and inexorable fatefulness of that titanic struggle—an inescapable one in the clash of American forces, is worthy an Epic for its heroic grandeur and unconquerable grit!

And I wondered what our brand of education, what our smug injunction that the home "is expected" to cooperate with the school will find or create for the help and guidance of such a home, a type as truly evolved from American environmental conditions as are the blind fish in the Mammoth Cave or the broncos of the western plains.

A Problem—Will isolation solve it?

· *15* ·

Foreword to *Le Pèlerinage de Charlemagne*

If I dare to offer the public this new edition of *Pilgrimage of Charlemagne*—one of the oldest works of the French, and probably the Parisian, mind—It is certainly not because I have the slightest pretension to erudition or to . . . adding anything of my own to the learned works of which the ancient poem has been the object. My more modest design has only the two following goals: to offer this publication in homage to and in recognition of the College and . . . the mentors to whom I am greatly obliged; to do a favor to American students by facilitating the study of an important and rather rare text.

The oldest manuscript in existence of the *Pilgrimage of Charlemagne* was located in the British Museum, under the code 16 E VIII. "We have lost all trace of it since June 1879," the librarian of this great institution wrote me, "and we presume that it was stolen at that time."

It was published for the first time, in London, in 1836, not without several transcription errors, by Francisque Michel, under the title of "*Charlemagne,* an Anglo-Norman poem of the twelfth century, now first published with an introduction and a glossarial index with a fac-simile."[1]

The German philologist Eduard Koschwitz edited it once again in Hellbronn under the title of *Karls des Grossen Reise nach Jerusalem und Constantinopel*[2] with more and more learned notes, dissertations, and commentaries in 1879, 1883, 1895, and 1910, Gustav Thurau published a fifth edition in 1907 and a sixth in 1913. The first edition only offered a reconstituted critical text; the later ones reproduced the primitive text of the British Museum which had disappeared, and we reproduce it here also, based upon them, very scrupulously.

The most recent work of German scholarship on the *Pilgrimage of Charlemagne* is the commentary on it which Dr. Karl Voretzsch wrote in

---

1. In English in the original. *AJC.*
2. "Charlemagne's Voyage to Jerusalem and Constantinople." *AJC.*

his *Einführung in das Studium der Altfranzösischen Sprache*.[3] This commentary only relates to verses 1 through 268 and 802 through 870, however.

The study of such a poem commanded the attention of learned Frenchmen. They have not remained indifferent to it. Paulin Paris wrote, beginning in 1859, a "Review of the Chanson de Geste entitled *The Voyage of Charlemagne to Jerusalem.*" Léon Gautier writes of it at great length in his *French Epics* (III²). Gaston Paris and Joseph Bédier, the most eminent experts of the French literature of the Middle Ages, consecrated two excellent studies to it: the former, in his *Poetic History of Charlemagne* and in *Poetry in the Middle Ages:* the latter in Volume IV of his *Epic Legends*. Finally, Mr. Jules Coulet, Adjunct Professor at the University of Montpellier, published on the same subject, in 1907, a volume of 466 pages, which he entitled *Studies on the Old French Poem of the Voyage of Charlemagne in the East.*[4]

Whatever little importance my work has next to these great works, I wish to thank those who encouraged and helped me to undertake it: In the United States, Doctor Koenig of the Library of Congress in Washington, who gave me such good advice, and the eminent Professors of Columbia University of New York, Doctor Alexander, Doctor Gerig, Professor H. F. Muller, who taught me to love and appreciate old texts; in France the anonymous and too discreet learned person who was kind enough to make a modern French translation which was clear but delicately impregnated with medieval naiveté, and finally, *the last [but] not the least,*[5] Abbé Fèlix Klein, Professor Emeritus at the Catholic Institute of Paris, the faithful friend of Americans, without whose encouragement and support, I can say with all sincerity, this volume would not have seen the light of day.

Our edition will first present the text of the manuscript with the translation in modern French on the facing pages; then the readings of the manuscript which were not accepted by Koschwitz, but which he published as notes; thirdly, the critical text reconstituted by Koschwitz: and finally our English glossary, laid down along the lines of his German glossary.

---

3. "Introduction to the Study of the Old French Language" (Halle, 1918, in 8★). *AJC.*
4. (Montpellier, Coulet et Fils, editors, 1 vol. in 8★). *AJC.*
5. In English in the original.

· *16* ·

The Humor of Teaching (1930)

When first published in the November 1930 number of Crisis, *the NAACP magazine founded and edited (until 1934) by W. E. B. Du Bois, this short article was introduced by an editorial comment: "Dr. Cooper has long been a teacher in the public schools of Washington, D.C. and was one principal of the high school. She received her doctorate at the Sorbonne, Paris. This article is a continuation of the discussion begun in the August* Crisis *by Arthur P. Davis and continued in the September* Crisis *by several other writers." Assuming that Du Bois himself wrote, or approved, the comment, this represents one of the few times he openly acknowledged Cooper's work. Though he published several of her articles (see, e.g., chapter 20), Du Bois is known to have rejected other of her writings and to have quoted her ideas without crediting her by name.*

But, in this short essay, Cooper is in her element, and Du Bois acknowledges her unique qualification to comment on the subject at hand. Her status as a lifelong teacher at one of the most prestigious Negro high schools in the country and as the possessor of a Ph.D., lent special weight to her reply to earlier essays on the Negro colleges. Crisis, *in its day, was the most widely read national publication among American blacks. No doubt, therefore, the debate was part of a wider controversy about the quality of the segregated Negro colleges. Remember that 1930 is well into the Depression years.*

In spite of its title, "The Humor of Teaching" is anything but funny. Cooper speaks from long experience as a teacher, in colleges as well as high school, and does not shrink from speaking plainly both about the frustrations of the work against poor conditions and about the temptations for the teacher to take herself all too seriously—hence, the call for a sense of humor.

I have read with interest the strictures of Professor Davis on the Negro College Student and likewise the three or four answers from students in a subsequent issue of the *Crisis*. I am impressed particularly with the true teacher-spirit of Mr. Davis' faultfinding and the high detachment of his aim

---

Though the essay is out of copyright, we thank the NAACP for the courtesy of using it here.

and purpose in writing. His criticism while severe is not carping or slander-ous, neither is it the flippant sort that seizes an opportunity to rush to print for the vain glory of making talk through the newspapers; rather is it the honest findings and chastening of an intelligent father who wishes to cor-rect an imperfect son,—constructive, as all criticism should be, with an eye single to the ideal, not a relative, standard.

The answers, too, so far are not the tiresome attack and counter-attack that get us nowhere beyond the over brilliant sparring exhibition of hit and thrust: they suggest causes and further criticisms—one, the need of ripe scholarship among teachers themselves, specifically the frivolous fledglings just out of college and serving an indeterminate sentence to teach on their way to something hoped for; a second, the dry-as-dust abstractions and mental gymnastics embalmed in an outworn college curriculum that have no discoverable connection with the practical life interests of the student and [are] never made to grip his attention and disclose where he, the indi-vidual John Jones, can catch on, etc.

If you will allow, I should like to add one other point of view in the same spirit of meeting our collective difficulties by unearthing a possible contributing factor not yet mentioned. In the first place, I believe we must admit that by [and] large our group have not the jack-be-nimble, jack-be-quick mental processes that discover short cuts and invent speed tilts into the goal. A fellow may give you the cold stare that shows he is not yet on the road, not because he is too lazy to travel (that is, if laziness has to do with will) but because he is still groping for the way out and has not yet caught on to the meaning of the word Go! Such students usually get short shrift at the hands of ambitious young professors who are thinking loftily of the cloistered walks of Oxford and Cambridge or the sacred inspirations of Heidelberg and Berlin. Many fellows come hungering and thirsting to college as to an interpreter and unfolder of life, a warm touch of an under-standing friend—but too often in place of the Bread of Life they get a stone.

In the second place, I believe that few teachers realize that segregation in education puts an undreamed of handicap on the student in the colored college from the all-unsuspecting teacher himself. I do not mean the exclu-sion from the very atmosphere of current life and thought, from lectures, plays, symphonies, oratorios, from airplanes, hotels and even in some sections from public libraries and parks,—all this is well-known and be-wailed from every pulpit and platform. I speak of a handicap unknown and unsuspected in the teaching body itself, the most cultured, painstaking, conscientious devotees of the higher learning, and just in proportion to their excellence of preparation and their devotion to their ideals.

I say that the handicap is unrecognized because it proceeds from these very qualities, which all must admire and want to emulate, a handicap of which the authors themselves are wholly unconscious and of which it would be most ungracious to speak save with the deepest appreciation and solely for the purpose of suggesting a let down of tension and an order from headquarters: *In place, Rest! Amusez-Vous!*

Segregated teachers are largely book-fed. What is worse, they believe what is in the books. They race to summer schools and institutes, to lecture courses and evening classes to "keep up" with their work and perhaps earn a much needed promotion. All of which is most commendable and highly necessary. But—the lectures and summer courses are unavoidably sketchy and packed in under pressure. They read, mark, learn, but there is no time to "inwardly digest." Besides, a white man doesn't always mean all he says in a book, and hardly ever does all he suggests in a speech. A lecturer must sell his books, that is his bread and butter. He must get out a new edition of an old thought and so he says one thing today, another tomorrow. You must "keep up"—That's the thing! He naively admits the whole subject is in flux and never supposes any rational creature would try to do all he says and keep on doing it just as he says it. By and by another "authority" comes along with another brand new wrinkle; ridicules all you've been told as fads and fancies and proceeds to give you the latest, the only true and accepted . . . precious words of gold in setting of silver which may have to be modified, adapted, even discarded altogether before the next hegira. And just here is where the conscientious teacher, sensitive over her "standards" (it is usually "she") becomes unwittingly and innocently a handicap and a hindrance to the equally conscientious student. She insists that the "Standard" (meaning the book) must be reached. She is sensitive about her "material" (meaning the colored folk she has to carry along) sensitive about the quality of her work and the mark she is to get on it, and deep down sore about her color and the suffering that entails. She is determined there shall be no flies on her teaching—and there aren't, except that she gives herself no joy in the act and loses entirely all sense of humor in the process.

If she were on the other side [of] the color line she would laugh over the mistakes she now spends sleepless nights bluepencilling and would taste a literary tang in the idiosyncrasies that she now turns from in horror and disgust because she dreads and fears any out-cropping of what may be considered "Southern" and to the manor born, that is to say, racial. The result is that the classroom platform, so long ago banished from white schools, is still an elevation to stand on, in thought at least, for most colored schools and the teacher speaks "from the chair" with authority, with dignity, and with finality. Naturalness on the part of students, initiative and an easy give and take in discussing a thought or its application to life with a chance to focus it down to "cases" is a thing too daring to be tolerated and must be summarily squelched as impudent and not duly respectful to teacher's opinions and decisions. *Thus saith the book*—and that puts the inviolable cloture on all further debate.

Not long ago a student neighbor came in to ask the use of my reference library for some task that had been set him. Busy with my own work, I left him to browse at will among the books which he seemed to do in rather a pointless haphazard way that finally began to get on my nerves clear across the room. "Don't you find what you want?" I asked. "I had to look up Antoninus," he answered gloomily. "Here are six!"

We have been so ridden with tests and measurements, so leashed and spurred for percentages and retardations that the machinery has run away with the mass production and quite a way back bumped off the driver. I wonder that a robot has not been invented to make the assignments, give the objective tests, mark the scores and—chloroform all teachers who dared bring original thought to the specific problems and needs of their pupils.

But Ideas are as potent today as they were 2,000 years ago when poor but aspiring men of Rome sent their sons all the way to Rhodes to get the touch of Appollonius. An instructor who is himself keen about the enigma of the Universe, or even about the enigma of Mississippi and Texas, will find his flaming torch as "catching" from a chair in Greek and Latin as he would with a stereotyped or borrowed syllabus in Civics or a book "plan" on the Reconstruction period.

The trouble I suspect is that those who furnish the coin and "suggest" the promotions in Negro Education are not themselves a-wearying and a-worrying to see any Renaissance or primal naissance of real thinking in Negro Schools, and yet God knows they need it.

· *17* ·

My Racial Philosophy (1930)

Cooper wrote this philosophical fragment as part of her reply to Charles S. Johnson's 1930 survey of Negro college graduates. The full question (#65 on the questionnaire) reads: "Have you a 'racial philosophy' that can be briefly stated?" Cooper's previously unpublished reply, written in her letter-perfect teacherly penmanship, is not exactly brief, but it is spontaneous— sure evidence of the depth of her convictions and of the ease of her writing style. (Elsewhere, this survey was, by the way, the occasion for Cooper's declaration of her life's work as "the education of neglected people.") Charles S. Johnson (1893–1956), sociologist and president of Fisk University, was (in the 1920s) director of research for the National Urban League and (at the time he invited Cooper to participate in his survey) a member of the Department of Sociology at Fisk.

My "racial philosophy" is not far removed from my general philosophy of life: that the greatest happiness comes from altruistic service and this is in reach of all of whatever race and condition. The "Service" here meant is not a pious idea of being used; any sort of exploitation whether active or passive is to my mind hateful. Nor is the "Happiness" a mere bit of Polly-anna stuff. I am as sensitive to handicaps as those who are always whining about them; and the whips and stings of prejudice, whether of color or sex, find me neither too calloused to suffer, nor too ignorant to know what is due me. Our own men as a group have not inherited traditions of chivalry (one sided as it may be among white men) and we women are generally left to do our race battling alone except for empty compliments now and then. Even so, one may make the mistake of looking at race handicaps through the wrong end of the telescope and imagining that oppression goes only with color. When I encounter brutality I need not always charge it to my race. It may be—and generally is—chargeable to the imperfections in

---

Reprinted with permission of the Moorland-Spingarn Research Center, Howard University. Archive locator: Box 23.1/Folder 1.

236

the civilization environing me for which as a teacher and trained thinker I take my share of responsibility.

The extent, then, of the optimism in my philosophy is that (Statisticians and Social Science Research compilers to the contrary notwithstanding) the solutions of our problem will be individual and not *en masse;* and the habit of generalization and deductive logic has done its worst.

For, after all, Social Justice, the desired goal, is not to be reached through any panacea by mass production—whether Du Bois's[1] preachment of the ballot box and intermarriage or Kelly Miller's[2] one time suggestion of self effacement, or even Booker Washington's[3] proposal of the solid hand and separate fingers. For human selfishness will always arise as the domineering *thumb* to over ride and keep down every finger weak enough to give up the struggle. The ballot operates just so far as dominant forces agree to respect it. Which again is reasoning in a circle to insure justice by having men become just, and the spectacle of gangster dominance among ballot holding Americans invites little hope for solution when the element of race is added to the problem. As I see it then, the patient persistence of the individual, working as Browning has it, "mouth wise and pen-wise" in whatever station and with whatever talent God has given, in truth and loyalty to serve the whole, will come as near as any other to proving worthwhile.

To me Life has meant a big opportunity and I am thankful that my work has always been the sort that beckoned me on, leaving no room for *blasé* philosophizing and rebellion's resentment and with just enough opposition to give zest to the struggle, just enough hope of scoring somewhere among the winners to keep my head "unbowed though bloody."

---

1. In 1930, W. E. B. Du Bois (1868–1963) was still editor of *Crisis,* the widely read magazine of the NAACP. Du Bois founded *Crisis* and was a cofounder of the NAACP, which in its early years was led by whites as well as blacks. As editor, Du Bois had urged African-Americans to vote racial interests (as he understood them) in national elections.

2. Kelly Miller (1863–1939): civil rights leader, educator, writer, lawyer, and editor. Miller taught at Howard University and assisted Du Bois in editing *Crisis.* He was known for his moderate views in racial matters.

3. Booker T. Washington (1856–1915): founding principal of Tuskegee Institute, Alabama, from which he promoted the strategy of industrial education in matters of racial uplift. The hand-and-fingers reference is an allusion to Washington's famous 1895 Atlanta Compromise address urging cooperative but separate relations between whites and blacks.

· *18* ·

The Negro's Dialect (1930s?)

The references to Amos 'n Andy *and Paul Robeson suggest that this essay dates to the mid-1930s after Cooper's retirement from public school teaching. The* Amos 'n Andy *radio broadcasts were highly popular in the 1930s in the early days of network radio. The unqualified references to Robeson suggest a date before the late 1930s, when he began to run afoul of public opinion for political reasons that led to his leaving the United States in 1940.*

In this previously unpublished essay, Cooper manages to comment on every important instance when the white culture of the day played upon often ridiculous misrepresentations of Negro language and culture. These distortions appear in works central to the history of American stage, radio, and music: Porgy and Bess, Green Pastures, *and* Amos 'n Andy, *among others. In addition to being a brilliant work of practical linguistics, the essay is also very good, if somewhat underdeveloped, cultural criticism.*

The story has gone the rounds of the press that Paul Robeson,[1] who himself tells us that he has toiled and spent to attain the accent not offensive to Mayfair, sometimes slips into the "soft slur of the Southern Negro" and even at the tragic moment of Othello's sublime fury demands: "Where am dat handkerchief, Desdemona?"

Reporters and critics must sell their stuff and one should not grudge them their little joke. Nothing helps like a bit of local color to heighten tone effects. This story listens well for heart interest on this side the Atlantic, where a black man is not true black unless he says "am dat." Mr.

Reprinted with permission of the Moorland-Spingarn Research Center, Howard University. Archive locator: Box 23.4/Folder 35.

1. Paul Robeson (1898–1976): athlete, actor, and singer whose radical politics led him into exile in London and Russia from 1940 to 1963. Drawing upon her expertise as a linguist, Cooper refutes critical reviews of Robeson's supposed southern Negro accent in his famous stage performance of *Othello*. She shows that the accent, which commentators often joked about, was a linguistic impossibility. Robeson was born in Princeton, New Jersey, and was both Phi Beta Kappa and valedictorian at Rutgers University (in addition to being all-American in football).

Robeson in his impersonation of the noble blackamoor may on his own part deliberately allow himself the racial touch, not at all inconsistent to my mind with a highly artistic effect. If he did so, be sure it was not a slip; he had been instructed and believed that such a departure would give just the original flavor he was expected to create. But speaking *ex cathedra* I claim, as one who ought to know, that no artist who has intelligently analyzed the Negro folk-speech, whether he be poet, novelist, or impersonator, can ever accept "am dat" as a possibility in Negro or southern vocalization.

It is universally conceded that racial groups attacking a foreign language with which they are forced to serve themselves, will invariably take the line of least resistance. Thus Franks, Burgundians, Goths and Visigoths uniformly clipped off the troublesome Roman terminations for declension and conjugation, points too fine to bother their matter-of-fact brains, and *homo-hominis-homini-hominem* lost everything but the essential tonic syllable or sound, which becomes for the Frenchman, *homme,* for the Spaniard *hombre,* the Portuguese *homem* and to the Italian *uomo*—a new tongue slowly evolved by characteristic differentiation thro adjacent families or groups as the real expression of racial distinctions and peculiarities of vocalization that go to make a language. Later on comes that change within the family itself that we call provincialisms or dialects, either a natural growth from age to age or resultants from movement, differences in locality and climatic conditions, differences in occupation, habits, way of living, contacts with nature, contacts with other men.

Says Bourciez, *Linguistique Romane*[2]:

> The stability of a language is wholly a relative matter. If a given language is spoken almost identically by men of the same generation and belonging to the same social group, one must see a priori that his language will necessarily undergo certain modifications on being transmitted from one generation to another, and that *the sounds* of which the words are composed may be altered as well as the sense attributed to these words. This "evolution" is not only possible, but in some sort inevitable. It is however more or less rapid according to historic conditions in the midst of which the people speaking a given language find themselves. It is slow at certain epochs when a type of literary language taught in the schools

---

2. We have been unable to identify the author of the passage Cooper quotes. Her type-written note after the quote is: "Bourciez, Elements de Linguistique Romane. Tr." The "Tr." refers, no doubt, to her own translation of the passage from what must have been, in her graduate student days (1914–1925), a standard linguistics textbook specializing in early French.

predominates, there are other periods when change is accelerated, and when with the dissolution of the ancient social ties, there appears a corresponding disorganization, even more prompt, of common idiomatic speech. One conceives equally that if a people having formed at the beginning a vast empire, speaking a language almost identical, happen to separate and to live a distinct political life, these people, no longer communicating with one another, experience each in their language particular alterations. It will be found then that at the end of a certain number of generations languages primitively identical, will be so no longer at the different points where it continues to be spoken, and the differentiation may have been so considerable, that one finds himself in the presence of several distinct dialects.

This is precisely what happened to the language of Shakespeare and Milton on American soil, and what, before automobiles and airplanes achieved their amazing annihilation of time and space, differentiated the strong burr of the West, the soft slur of the South, and the choppy staccato of the Northern United States, all of which differ from Mayfair English, not only in vocabulary and use of words, but even more in the *placing* of vocables, the muscular and I may say mechanical formation of sounds. Into the melting pot in due course was poured a witches' mixture of races,—Scotch, Irish, French, Italian, German, Swede, Negro, Pole, Slovak and what not,—all bound to make their wants known in this language of Shakespeare and Milton—the weaker less energetically than the strong, and some "with no language but a cry," but all murdering the King's English, each in his own way, modifications pivoting many times on slight differences in structure of vocal organs, or on environment, social contacts, etc.

Doctor Frissell, General Armstrong's friend and successor at Hampton,[3] used to remark: "Our boys," as he affectionately called them, "are rather venturesome with their English." Now undoubtedly to this racial or temperamental "venturesomeness" Negro folk have added their own characteristic physical equipment and endowments of organic structure such as breadth of nostril, length of vocal chords and perhaps a certain peculiar resonance of chest tones that vary all the way from the rich *basso*

---

3. Hampton Institute at Hampton, Virginia. Founded in 1886 by General Samuel Chapman Armstrong (1839–1893), who had commanded a Negro regiment in the Civil War. Hampton served Negro freedmen, and like the Tuskagee Institute (founded in 1881 by Booker T. Washington), emphasized industrial education. Dr. Frissell, as Cooper says, was Armstrong's successor as head of what was then known as the Hampton Normal and Industrial Institute.

profundo vibrations of "Andy" to the anaemic narrow chested head tones so well simulated by "Amos." But the dialect, like all attempts of *beiwohners* to serve themselves with a speech acquired exclusively by ear, never having started with the ABC at mother's knee, develops naturally by a process nothing different from the experiments of European Barbarians, who centuries ago attacked the Latin.

"Andy's" "sitchation" runs true to phonetic form, preserving the tonic syllable and all of the sound that is essential to carrying the sense (as any winged word should); the "u" never having been seen or consciously stressed is of course entirely negligible. The same analysis applies to "regusted" which has nothing whatever in common with the Irish "rr" in its first syllable, being hardly more than the movable "nu" in Greek or the "eh-r-eh" so often heard in hesitating for a word—"eh-r-eh" *gusted,* that's the thing! the tonic syllable every time. "Propolition" is, if possible, even more characteristically fashioned according to racial instinct, since it directly seeks euphony in the exchange of the harsh sibilant "s" for the smooth liquid "l"; "propolition" is as accommodating and ready to please, or rather to avoid offense, as the head waiter at a summer hotel. By the same reasoning *"am dat",* ascribed to Paul Robeson by the press and vouched for by Mr. Hannen Swaffer, must go. It is as artistically impossible to Robeson as it is untrue to nature in the primitive Negro who has never seen a book or been near a school house (or a stage prompter)—the simple reason being that the combination of alabial mute followed by a dental ("m" "d") requiring that the lips close on "m" then open again to send tip of tongue behind upper teeth for "d," is too difficult for his easy going lips to negotiate. His genius leans to flowing sounds, easy liaisons, more French than German, a prevalence of vowels, semi vowels, and liquids. He might say: "whea dat" or "wheah's dat," or even "whah dat hankycher"—but never, never, I pledge you my word, will you hear a Negro, not drilled into it for stage effect, utter of his own accord: "Where am dat kandkerchief." It is simply impossible.

Much of the literary dialect such as "dis am," "he am," "him am," "ob dis" and "am dat" which our industrious press turns out by the scoop in its willingness to pander to popular taste for unsophisticated and "colorful" native speech, would fall flat if held up thus to Nature's mirror to be tried by the rules of organic growth. It is a principle of grammar, recognized in children as well as in adult beginners, that irregularities are accepted last and that in verbs the third singular is made to serve for irregular first and second. The child speaks of "both *foots,"* says "I *drinked"* "he *hitted* me," "mine is *goodest*," learning rules before exceptions, and *"I is"* (when corrected often gets it "I are") never *"he am."* In fact I think you will find the form "am" rather late coming into play, having to be stressed and directed quite a bit before it stands without hitching, with its own proper subject. No child says "It is I," right off the bat. He seems to shy at "I am" with persisting disapproval meeting your well meant attempts with cunningly devised substitutes such as "Johnny is" and "me is" till sometimes his wrath gets the better of his pretty manners and he downs his tormentor with "AW—Me said Ahee!!" "I's gwine," for instance is folk made [as is] "dat's" for "dat is"; but "dat am" does not bear the hallmark.

The difficult "th" sound in "this" and "that," the Negro, like the Frenchman, systematically reduces to "d": "dis" and "dat" are his own peculiar contribution. But not all Southern deviations from standard English can be set down as Negro in origin. "Ole Virginny" for instance is heard just as frequently among untraveled whites of that locality as among uneducated blacks. The Negro simply speaks the language of his locals, gives back his version of what he hears.

I once had a domestic who was absolutely illiterate, could not write her own name or recognize it when she saw it, and yet her language was beautifully English—not Yankee but English. Aunt Charlotte came to us quite causally through an employment agency, but I found her such an interesting character, so original, so genteel and withal so lovable, that I kept her long after she was too old to serve my household needs. She used to say: "*My* white folks wouldn't allow their servants (she never said slaves) to 'sociate wit de poorer clahses. Said hit would teach bad habits." Pronounced "gyerl" and "gyahd 'n" with that peculiar soft purling sound that only those to the manor born can hope ever to approximate even after patient painstaking practice. An implacable aristocrat, Aunt Charlotte would let you know when she had finished berating some "low down human" as "the scum o' de yearth" that "fum de time she was six years ole clean twell she growed up" she slept on a cot in the room with her young mistress of the same age and was always taught "to carry myself 'cordin to who I am and who I be."

Much of the Negro talk that has burst into the picture since the apotheosis of the "Type" in post War literature is machine made and crassly overdone under the usual pressure of mass production. For the fact is there is no such thing as Negro dialect *per se* just as there was never such a thing as a unique Negro or African language, understood and spoken *ab origine* by all dwellers on the continent of Africa whose descendants were kidnapped for slavery. Says Du Bois:[4] "The slave raiding drew upon every part of Africa—upon the West Coast, the Western and Egyptian Sudan, the valley of the Congo, Abyssinia, the Lake regions, the East Coast and Madagascar—Bantus, Mandingoes, Songhays, the Nubian and Nile Negroes, the Fula and even the Asiatic Malay were represented in the raids." A tribal group then, even if they could chance to preserve their identity thro the decimating welter of the Middle Passage has no possibility whatever of solidarity amid the winnowing vicissitudes of the auction block; hence one might even more properly seek for a "European" than for an African "dialect." The Gullah talk of those slaves segregated on the Sea Islands off the coast of South Carolina was as unintelligible to the aristocratic colored servants of French Huguenots in Charleston as to their equally aristocratic owners, while in comparing Virginia and Texas with reference to those who really have nothing in common but their color, the differences in tone, idioms, and fundamental root words are so radical and conspicuous as to suggest that they are not racial at all, but traceable possibly to climate, environment and general habitat. It is more correct to speak of an Ohio brogue, or a Georgia drawl than of a "Negro" dialect and yet it may be conceded that the lip laziness ascribed by phoneticians to Americans in general is naturally and temperamentally exaggerated perhaps among persons of heavier maxillae and weak orbicularis oris, until developed by the gymnastics of energetic exercise, such as the French give in *tantôt le rat tata le riz* etc.

Again, it may be that the circumstances and conditions that gave rise to the bon mot: "Keep a stiff upper lip" and "Don't let on" can be held accountable in part at least for a complex that has resulted in greater immobility of those muscles that control speech organs, so noticeable here in comparison with natives of France and England. For after all the English, or attempt at English, of the American Negro is purely an American product and may be traced in each elemental characteristic to its roots in American life. Many of its syncopes and elisions are as old as Chaucer or the King James Version of the Bible, e.g. "afeard" for afraid; "holpen" or "holp" for helped (pronounced without the "l"); "hit" for it, "til" for to: "Is lykned til a fish that is waterless" (Chaucer). "Moot" for must or might: "Men moot yeve silver to the povre freres" (Chaucer); "Hit mought and den

---

4. The quote is likely from W. E. B. Du Bois's Harvard doctoral thesis on the suppression of the slave trade to North America in the nineteenth century. Though she does not specifically cite him in her Sorbonne doctoral thesis on French attitudes toward slavery in the Americas, it is reasonable to assume that Cooper was familiar with Du Bois's thesis.

agin hit moughtn't" (Negro). The common demonstrative "dis here" has its prototype as far back as the classic Latin, *hic-haec-hoc,* formed of the blending of an older demonstrative with "ce," adverb of place, written as late as Cicero enclitic on certain case forms like *hosce, hisce, huiusce,* the "ce" meaning "here." The accusative *humce* and *hamce* of course could not be pronounced. Accordingly we have *hunc* and *hanc,* but the union is evidently "this / here" as "this here man." Again, "swich or sich" for such; also "for to": "For to delen with no swich poraille" (Chaucer); "What went ye out for to see?" (Bible); "Comin' for to carry me home" (Folk Hymn).

On the other hand the conscious eye-minded "improvements" made in folk speech to render it up to date and grammatical are as undeniably racial as any dialect so labeled. The change made by present day *culture* in the beautiful spiritual

> Were you there when they crucified my Lord?
> Sometimes *it causes me* to tremble, tremble

is grammatical, but not nearly so close to the heart of the people as the folk version:

> Oh–h–h Sometimes hit *makes–eh–me* tremble, tremble
> Were you there when they nailed Him to the Cross?

I heard Paul Robeson sing "Water Boy" and I have not yet made up my mind whether it was the real Robeson I heard or the actor impersonating a shuffling, sprawling, crap shooting, chain gang Negro. True, the perfection of art is to conceal art and if Mr. Robeson, the impersonator, does perfectly the type he chooses to present, the only criticism that can attach to him is for choosing one type and not another. One feels differently about Roland Hayes;[5] when he sings Negro words he seems to interpret, not a race, but music, and that speaks a universal language—a human language that all souls understand. *Green Pastures*[6] in the opinion of the writer falls

---

5. Roland Hayes (1887–1977): tenor, noted for his performances of Negro spirituals as well as classical vocal arrangements.

6. *Green Pastures:* 1930 play, adapted by the playwright Marcus C. Connelly (1890–1980) from a then popular book by Roark Bradford (1896–1948) portraying Negro folk tales. *Green Pastures* won a Pulitzer Prize; again, white people making jokes, and money, on Negro culture. It is not surprising that Cooper, always dignified, is indignant at the play's abuses. Richard B. Harrison was, evidently, an actor in the stage performance of the play.

just short of being great for this very reason of over-specialization. As a portraiture of naive and elemental folk-reaction to a group of Bible stories reflected thro the prism of the untutored imaginations of a primitive and essentially religious people, it had the chance of being an immortal epic scintillating with all the hues of their rich and vivid temperament. But, not withstanding all the stage accessories and wealth procurable thro the modern theater this elaborate study would peter out as a cheap and rather bizarre melodrama were it not saved by the sincere artistry of Richard B. Harrison and the really good and true singing of their undying spirituals by a chorus that knows, feels and loves them. The author with his fish fry and bone in cherubic throats has labored to bring forth a *pour rire* for an audience already committed to the judgment that whatever is done by Negroes must be ludicrous, sincere self expression being out of the question. Such a judgment is the result of a myopic habit of studying behavior only, and concluding egocentrically that all behavior is "put on" for effect on the observer. I have no quarrel with the author's empyrean menu—fried fish or even pigs' feet would suit me quite as well as milk and honey—but it is lugged in adventitiously, with malice prepense, and does not at all grow from the roots of this people, having no place whatever in the racial or human imagination.

Mr. Harrison present artistically the kindly indulgent patriarch that adequately embodies the anthropomorphism of his people. All races gifted with any imagination at all represent their deities in terms of their own qualities actual or hoped for. Michelangelo's "God the Father" done in pigments for the *Last Judgment* in the Sistine Chapel is no more ethereal or spiritually satisfying than Harrison's done in the personality and tones of a living man; and the heart weary cry with which he utters: "I'm *tired of this people's disobedience and crooked doings*" comes as close to shaming us wayward moderns into the conviction of a guilty conscience as the literal translation in Genesis of the Hebrew: "and the Lord God *repented* that he had made man."

The author achieves a touch of genuine Negro humor when he makes the bibulous Noah plead with the Almighty to grant "jes one mo Kag o' likker" for the forty days cantonment in the ark; he is not so happy on the other hand when he puts undignified words in the mouth of "the Lord," however common such words may be in the supposed Negro lingo. "Doggone it" strikes home with ease in the character of "Amos," but no Negro would ever imagine the Lord using that expression. For the folk mind of the Negro is essentially reverent even when it seems grotesque to the understanding mind of a foreign or unsympathetic genius. He takes his religion seriously and never spontaneously creates a burlesque on things and thoughts that he holds sacred.

Turning to the *Amos n' Andy* creations, one is puzzled to find the secret of their tremendous vogue and irresistible appeal for all classes and all ages. Opinions differ. Some ascribe their popularity to the consummate skill with which the actors put over the Negro's dialect. Some claim it is their clever imitation of the tones, so characteristically racial. Some hurriedly turn off the radio and resent the skit *in toto* as injurious to the taxicab industry. Apprehension is expressed by others that for American youth the "well of English" is no longer undefiled and the sheer popularity of these consummate impersonators of Negro humor actually threatens the language of Shakespeare and Milton.

As a matter of course we appreciate an artist and esteem him great just so far as he succeeds in holding a glass to Nature to interpret for the less gifted thro the medium mastered by his own skill, her myriad moods, her cryptic meanings, her "various language." He becomes eyes to the blind, ears for the deaf, and sympathetic insight for those calloused with prejudice. Messrs. Gosden and Correll[7] have the gift or have caught the trick of human insight, of seeing and painting rock bottom essentials, so that in spite of superficial differences, the picture remains human, acts, speaks and reacts with that touch of Nature that makes all kin. The worries and anxieties of little "Amos" (you image him both little and threadbare) over his "hundud an 'twenty fi' dollahs'" interest and amuse a nation of millionaires just as Gulliver's Lilliputians perennially interest and amuse men of normal stature because they see that the little fellows after all are human. It is like looking at your reflection in the concave side of the mirror—you see your own foibles and follies, but on a scale so unheard of, so unsuspected and withal so amusing that you get a thrill from the very freshness and novelty of your own face. In sympathetic good humor you laugh at the good natured caricature. "This Amos is a likeable guy after all—and what a conceited ass is Andy! Oh well-a-day—Shouldn't wonder if there's a bit of the same thing in all of us!"

The miracle is that you have had revealed thro "the soft slur of the Southern Negro" and those resonant tones the Soul of a Folk you have never seen before at closer focus than the outer rim of some epidermic

---

7. Gosden and Correll were, presumably, the radio comics who gave voice to *Amos 'n Andy*.

cells—the same miracle that the creative artist must unfailingly bring to pass, whatever his tools and whoever his public. Whether he works with pigments or chisel, with tone picures or muscular action, he must reveal to you, whoever you are, a human kinship, the great human fact, whatever his race and whatever his theme. DuBose Heywood[8] can thus paint Porgy of Catfish Row and Mamba's Daughters, not because of any personal photography from experience with "Types" in those environs, still less because of any sermon or theorem he has to promulgate, but because he has the genius to look into that human ant hill down deep enough and sincerely enough to find that "Fate under the hood of environing conditions is the inexorable protagonist of Man in Life's Drama, whether the hero be Oedipus or Jean Valjean, Porgy or Othello. In the last analysis: "The Play's the thing"—not the Dialect and not the race of the Players.

---

8. Edwin DuBose Heywood (1939–1915): author of the novel *Porgy* (1925), which George Gershwin adapted for his 1935 musical *Porgy and Bess*. Heywood was white, but sensitive to the culture and language of African-Americans in his native South Carolina.

· *19* ·

On Education (1930s?)

"On Education" is one of a very few of Cooper's manuscripts that leaves almost no reliable clue as to its origin. It is reasonable, however, to suppose that this was a talk given during Cooper's tenure as president of Frelinghuysen University, probably in the mid-1930s. The previously unpublished manuscript reads like a public speech, sprinkled as it is with the "we" pronoun as if to embrace an audience or readership that would normally include Cooper as one of its own. (Note, by contrast, that her speeches to audiences not likely to be in agreement with her—for example, her early talk to the Episcopal clergy in chapter 3—do not use this "we.")

It is also possible, as suggested in the introductory note to chapter 14, that this may have been a later contribution to a projected, but unfulfilled, book on education. The manuscript begins with pages "a" and "b," which are identified as "Foreword," while the main body of the text is labeled "Educational Programs." What is unclear is, A foreword to what? To the present paper? Or to some larger project? This we may never know. And, of course, it is possible for the draft of a book chapter to serve as the reading text for a speech, or vice-versa—as with several or most of the chapters in A Voice *from the South.*

The general theme of the essay is one to which Cooper regularly devoted herself: the role of education in the cultural and moral uplift of the Negro. But there is also a secondary and somewhat controversial theme—that of providing education to professionalize the domestic worker. The two themes are meant to be one, ultimately. Cooper believed that education ought to be as much good for the soul as for the mind of the student, and she states clearly that "the trained domestic, like the trained nurse, will demand the pay, and will deserve the treatment that are accorded intelligent and efficient services rendered professionally in whatever calling of life" (p. 255). Education leads to self-respect and dignity, which lead to practical results in life. Today this may seem a servile attitude, an acceptance of the system's economic injustices. But the 1930s were economically depressed. This was a period when, as the sociologist Doris Wilkinson has demonstrated, work for black women in agriculture had declined precipitously while domestic opportunities rose apace, and were often the only jobs available. What is distinctive about Cooper's argument is that she seeks here to unite the goals of education in the higher culture with those of industrial education, an intention indicated by

Printed with the permission of the Moorland–Spingarn Research Center, Howard University. Archive locator: Box 23.4/Folder 33.

her references, early in the paper, to the separate but equally important values of Fisk and Atlanta University, on the one hand, and Hampton and Tuskegee, on the other.

It would not, therefore, be improbable that, in making her proposal for educational programs to professionalize those in the most modest jobs, Cooper was speaking out of her experience as president of Frelinghuysen. One of her most cherished projects while in this position was the founding of the Hannah Stanley Opportunity School, named in memory of her mother and meant precisely to educate those of the most limited economic opportunities. She met considerable resistance from Frelinghuysen's trustees (largely because, having lent the use of her home to the Stanley Opportunity School, Cooper also sought to assure that the school would endure as a separate entity should Frelinghuysen fail). This may be why the portion of the text dealing with her proposal for training domestics has somewhat a more aggressive tone than, say, the brief foreword. The text reads as though Cooper had been recently defending her proposal but does not read as though the argument were that between Du Bois and Washington. She seems to assume that that old debate from the earliest years of the century is long over and that she is going on to something new.

We would locate the text in the 1930s for these reasons and (though even more hesitantly) because the manuscript seems to have been typed on a machine unlike any Cooper had used before—one well broken down at that. Perhaps one of her students in the Hannah Stanley Opportunity School had been given the assignment of typing up the president's paper.

Foreword

. . . Education has been well defined as the building up of a man, the whole man; which, I take it, implies putting your crude material through whatever processes insure the highest return of the entire product at its best.

Manifestly nothing can more profitably engage the time and thought of statesmen and sages than the perfecting of these processes and the improvement of this product. The interest of the commonwealth in the result is transcendent. The smallest element is as vital to the state as heart's blood. No expenditure is extravagant that enhances the value of the output: no experiment but is suicidal if it results in the waste of any precious material. Indeed, so busy and so efficient are the forces of evil in working up the refuse into engines of deadly execution, it may with truth be said that from the standpoint of the state the most valuable part of all material, reckoned both in direction of what it may become and of what it may be saved from being, the item most momentous in potentiality is the refuse—the outcast. "And so our uncomely parts have put on more abundant comeliness," that there be no schism in the body politic. The high cannot say to the low, "I have no need of thee"; nor the well-conditioned to the lazzarone: "I have no need of thee." So long as the wretchedest hovel may culture germs of disease and misery against which the proudest palace is not immune, the submerged tenth take on a terrible significance in the building up of men, and the only salvation lies in leaving the ninety and nine in the wilderness and going after that which is lost.

The only sane education, therefore, is that which conserves the very lowest stratum, the best and most economical is that which gives to each individual, according to his capacity, that training of "head, hand, and heart," or, more literally, of mind, body and spirit which converts him into a beneficent force in the service of the world. This is the business of schools and this the true cause of the deep and vital interest of all the people in Educational Programs.

Educational Programs

As interested in the education of a neglected people, and as educators in a circumscribed field of work, we are confronted by a peculiar danger at the same time that we are buoyed up and helped by a peculiar inspiration and stimulus to devotion. Whether from force of circumstances or from choice and loving consecration, we are ministers of the Gospel of intelligence, of moral and material uplift to a people whose need is greater than the average need around us by reason of past neglect,—a people who are habitually reasoned about *en masse* as separate, distinct, and peculiar; a people who must be fitted to make headway in the face of prejudice and proscription the most bitter, the most intense, the most unrelenting the world has ever seen. Every journeyman tinker thinks he can tell you what to do with the Negro; what sort of clothes he should wear, what sort of meat he should eat, what sort of books he should and should not study: in short, just what sort of education is sane, sensible and "practical" for one of his texture of hair and hide.

In the presence of this multitude of counsellors the danger is that we lose sight altogether of basic principles as such, and remember that we are educating Negroes before we have yet realized that we are educating men. It cannot be denied that the wisest plan of education for any people should take cognizance of past and present environment, should note the forces against which they must contend, or in unison with which they must labor in the civilization of which they form a part. It should not be ignored, further, that the colored man in America, because of his marked appearance and his unique history, will for a long time need peculiar equipment for the intense, the unrelenting struggle for survival amid which he finds himself in the America of today. The weakest of the races here represented, at the same time the most conspicuous and undisguisable, the black race, has need truly of wise teachers and far-seeing leaders, to help them up the thorny road of life. When studying or planning a program of Negro education we shall need the clearest thought, the wisest counsels, the broadest charity. There is no place for jealousies or for hobbies. . . .

It is well known that the power to think, the power to appreciate, and the power to will the right and make it prevail, is the sum total of the faculties of the human soul. Education which is truly "educative" must strengthen, develop, "lead out" these faculties in preparation for those special activities which may be called "occupative," because they give the one line of training necessary for the occupation or trade of the individual. No one will deny that thought-power, will-power, and the power to discern and appreciate proportion and right relation are fundamental needs of the people for whom we toil, as of others. Indeed when we speak of their peculiar weaknesses and special lack to be overcome by education, I think if we analyse our criticism carefully, we shall find the fault resolve itself into one or all of these three faculties still latent or underdeveloped and in need of training.

The Negro has had manual education throughout his experience as a slave. For 250 years he was practically the only laborer in the American market. His training was whatever his teachers decreed it should be. His skill represented the best teaching of the section in which he found himself. If he did not reckon a knowledge of machinery among his accomplishments it must be admitted that machinery was very tardily introduced into the Southland. But his methods as a farmer, as a mechanic, as nurse, as domestic, were the result of the best teaching the peculiar institution afforded. What was the lack? What is the need today? Is it not just the power to think, the power to will, the power to appreciate true relation, which have been enumerated as the universal aim of education? The old education made him a "hand," solely and simply. It deliberately sought to suppress or ignore the soul. We must, whatever else we do, insist on those studies which by the consensus of educators are calculated to train our people to think, which will give them the power of appreciation and make them righteous. In a word we are building men, not chemists or farmers, or cooks, or soldiers, but men ready to serve the body politic in whatever avocation their talent is needed. This is fundamental. No sort of superstructure can endure on any different foundation. This first for all men—whether for white men, red men, yellow men, or black men, whether for rich men or poor men, high or low, the aim of education for the human soul is to train aright, to give power and right direction to the intellect, the sensibilities, and the will. Certain studies, certain courses, certain exercises have been tested, tried, accepted by the experience of centuries in the steady progress of humanity.

Teachers from Aristotle to the present have sifted and analysed the various branches of learning to get at their relative worth as educative factors. The results of their experiments and analyses are not hidden in dark places. They are universally accepted by teachers and thinkers as a reasonable and proper basis for the education of mankind. The only way to meet those skeptics who still ask with a half sneer "What is the use of this or that study for Negroes?" is with the query "is it good for *men?*" Has it been selected for curricula universally and has it stood the test for the discipline it gives in the direction of thought-power, power of appreciation, power of willing the right? These are the things we need. If these studies are means to those ends there can be nothing incongruous or unreasonable in trying them on our pupils in all faith as to the divine possibilities in all human development.

As to the second or "occupative" aim of our work, it cannot be denied that there has been some loss in the past through a certain lack of definiteness on our part. There has been a shifting or wavering of programs coupled with an acrimony in criticizing the other man's program which promises little in the way of progress or of mutual esteem. This has been partly our fault, partly our misfortune. It has been a misfortune that too often our program has been handed down from above, along with the cash which was to constitute our sinews of war. The Negro, being an "interesting case," all the good old ladies in the country have had a hand in prescribing his medicine, and they mean to see that he takes it. No fumbling with the bedclothes and trying to spit behind the bed! Down it must go. As head nurses we have had little opportunity to interpose. Those who had the hardihood to object, did so at their peril. The time has come, however, when the educators of Negroes must see that one narrow pattern cannot meet the demands of this people whose life is as varied and whose need is as various as the life and needs of the American people. The time has come for a rational discussion of these needs on the part of those who are interested in the shaping of educational programs, for a frank admission of individual limitations (one man can't do it all—or know it all), and lastly for an intelligent and economic division of labor on the principle of each undertaking that which he does best and standing squarely for that specialty for which his plant, his general equipment and his endowment promise the best result.

There can be no doubt that the colored families are producing children enough to keep all the schools going, from the kindergarten to the universities; the high schools, trade schools, colleges, normal schools, professional schools,—all are needed to minister to the ever broadening demand of this people. Let Fisk, Atlanta, and similar schools have the support and encouragement they need as institutions of higher learning; let Hampton, Tuskegee and similar schools wear their well earned laurels as he correspondingly great trade universities; but let not Atlanta think she must extemporize a tin shop, nor Tuskegee make shift for a chair of oratory under the apprehension that each must aim at what the other is doing well.

I feel that I can afford to speak for an occupation concerning which there has been much backwardness in schools for occupations because, perhaps, of certain suppressed odium that may attend the frank avowal of such purpose. I refer to the occupation of domestic servants. There seems a delicacy about deliberately and avowedly setting about the training for domestic service or the frank admission that the training adopted leads to such an end. On this point I can speak more freely than I would probably do if I represented a school of thought that looks towards the occupations but is hampered by this shy sensitiveness and the secret hope that somehow its young people will take a turn in this direction and do credit to their training without ever having planned a course with such a purpose in view.

We hear a great deal about Negroes leaving the rural districts and congregating in cities. Now the great cry of the cities is for *trained* domestic help. In the Northern cities especially the demand would give an almost fictitious valuation to supply measuring up in every way to the requirement. Just here, it seems to me, some one good school—not all by any means—but some school fitted for that business might undertake to supply the training for this branch of industry—frankly, and with careful planning of program. You and I know what an agonizing wail there is throughout the country on the degeneration of the Negro servant. In fact I believe that most of the sentiment existing today adverse to the race is due to the bad record *left by our missionaries—the servants!* Most people don't stop to think, and our average American public is just like "most people" in this respect. They tell you that the Negro is more degenerate under freedom than he was under slavery; they extol the virtues, the amiability and reliability of the old time servant class, whom they tell you they loved by reason of their excellencies of character as well as their faithfulness of service,—"but now",—and then the howl of despair as the shiftlessness of the up-to-date "girl" is detailed, her untrained, unkempt disorderliness, her unmitigated emptiness of all the qualities that rendered her supposed ancestors loved and respected. And then the conclusion inevitable that the whole race is immeasurably worse conditioned than "before the war"; that some such system as slavery was needed to keep us all from going to the dogs.

Let us look at the facts. Under slavery there was the most vigilant, the most intelligent, the most successful natural selection known to civilized man to form this class of house servants who were to be in immediate and constant contact of the most intimate sort with the master class. There was absolutely nothing to mar this selection or thwart the most perfect adjustment of it to the needs of the system. The house servants were the cream by natural endowment first, and by most careful training and contact afterwards. Have these same people, and their children, degenerated since or have they *gone up higher?* I think the latter. Today they represent the thrift, the mechanical industry, the business intelligence, the professional skill, the well ordered homes, and the carefully nurtured families that are to be found in every town and hamlet where the colored man is known. The whole bed-rock has been lifted up by emancipation, stratum upon stratum, so that they who know the Negro only in their kitchens are too often brought in contact with a level which they never met under the old regime. And yet it is important for our cause, no less than for the employer class, that the quality of domestic service be improved through training and through intelligent comprehension of its circumstances and opportunities. In the first place, the association of the domestic in the home of her employer is by necessity most intimate and responsible. "The help" can by her silent, self-respecting dependableness preach unanswerable sermons before audiences that you and I can never reach. She can refute pre-judgments, allay opposition, and mold favorable sentiment without ever opening her lips on the Negro problem; she can in her own person and by her own character offer a solution of that problem which will gainsay all cavil and all criticism. Is it not worth while for some school to undertake the work seriously, candidly, devotedly, of sending out a stream into these channels of usefulness so full of promise, so rich in opportunities for the race? The character of the service is important and the service itself when properly appreciated and performed has the same elements of dignity as other services. Browning has stated a universal truth in "Pippa Passes" when he says:

> All service ranks the same with God—
> With God, whose puppets, best and worst,
> Are we; there is no last nor first.

Something must be done on both sides, I grant you. Our young girls must be protected from libertines and villains who lie in wait in gorgeous palaces to entrap the innocent. Not only must the girl be trained for the home but the home, too, must be selected and prepared for the new servant—a servant whose treatment shall be worthy [of] her training, a servant whose dignity and whose serviceableness shall justify the expenditure for such a course in our educational program. We may not stem the tide rushing into our large cities. Certainly speech-making has very little to do with such things. But we may direct, guide, and help some in the cities, and, it seems to me, that the consideration of such a program is not unworthy [of] the serious attention of thoughtful educators.

I have dwelt thus at length on the occupation of domestic service for two reasons: first, I hoped to make it clear that I have no word or thought adverse to this or any honest toil. Second, I expect to make it just as plain before I am through that neither domestic service nor any other service will ever be considered anything else than menial until it is put on a professional basis by having behind it a *thorough course of general education*. The conclusion is a corollary to this that the trained domestic, like the trained nurse, will demand the pay, and will deserve the treatment that are accorded intelligent and efficient services professionally rendered in whatever calling of life, and that it is not by persuasive essays on the dignity of labor, but by broadening and dignifying the laborer, that we can secure any respectable number of recruits for this most important field of occupation. Any act performed by an ignorant slattern is menial, while no amount of indignity can really degrade a soul truly in possession of itself through scientific development of its faculties.

And just here is the battleground. The fatal American faculty of cutting corners has taught us to call that program of education "practical" which makes the shortest cut to the nearest dollar in sight. Before childhood has had time to grow, it is harassed with the feverish, mercantile question "what can you do?" Bears sometimes eat their cubs and humans not seldom fatten on child labor, but the crime becomes monstrous when whole communities systematize the stunting and warping of all normal child-development by premature specialization. The Germans understand this better than we. They realize as we do not that the total output of all industry is enhanced by the broader growth of the laborer. In her fierce competition with her foreign foes Germany set herself to building up the man,—a man useful to and to be used by the Fatherland in whatever capacity his services might be needed. To this end primary and secondary education are made the broad basis for technical or industrial training. In other words, technical schools are where colleges are with us and specialization (specializing) does not begin until the child has completed what answers to the high school course.

This places the educative before the occupative—the cultural before the special, the development before the industrial. This is the natural order of any educational program based upon scientific principles of human development.

Training of the eye to accuracy and the muscles of the hand and arm as in writing and drawing have an early place in any program of general education which, according to all enlightened planning, comprehends the culture of the physical as well as the mental and moral man. But it is well known that with the growing child a too early concentration of effort in the operation of special muscles is sure to result in partial or total atrophy of others. As a matter of course subsistence is the first problem with man as with every other animal and, if it is not at hand, the child must make shift as he can to get it or perish. But he does not grow in order to subsist; he subsists in order to grow, and if his growth be used up in the means of subsistence, the inevitable result is dwarfage. The natural father stores up this subsistence for the child during the growing or formative period in order that his development may proceed along normal and self-preservative lines. My plea is for the sacredness and inviolability of the growing period of the child. Guard it, nurture it, foster it. Give it the one thing needful,—time. If it costs sacrifice, it is richly worth it.

The state has provided in all advanced American communities free instruction for this period covering altogether about twelve years and roughly divisible into primary and secondary schools, or more accurately into kindergarten and primary, intermediate and secondary which constitute the common school course or what we are proud to call general public education. Superadded to this common course for all should come the special courses or training for a vocation: a Normal course to train for teaching and a technical course to train for certain trades. The latter are the true "higher" schools and are equal in rank as fitting [sic] for earning a living. They ought to rank with professional schools, but American communities have not yet put all the professions on a public education basis, although without doubt the way should be provided somehow and somewhere to enable a poor boy of special aptitude to make his way to whatever equipment his talents can best employ in the service of the state. Such common school equipment is and of right ought to be the birthright of every American born child. The Japanese can claim it under treaty obligation. . . .

"We learn by doing" is an educational axiom, but true as it is, it does not mean as it is often attempted to prove that sense travels only from hand to brain. The normal direction of the current would seem logically to go just the other way. Brain power insures hand power, and thought training produces industrial efficiency. We learn by doing when we dissect a crayfish or build a Latin sentence in the secondary school, when we perform a chemical reaction in the laboratory or express a thought in French, German, or Spanish, as when we read, write, or draw in the primary grades. Enlightened industrialism does not mean that the body who plows cotton must study nothing but cotton and that he who would drive a mule successfully should have contact only with mules. Indeed it has been well said "if I knew my son would drive a mule all his days, I should still give him the groundwork of a general education in his youth that would place the greatest possible distance between him and the mule." Prof. Huxley[1] who was one of the most distinguished and enthusiastic exponents of the progressive tendencies of modern education said as early as 1877 before the Working Men's Club and Institute Union in speaking on the subject of technical education:

> In my judgment, the preparatory education of the handicraftsman ought to have nothing of what is ordinarily understood by "technical" about it. The workshop is the only real school for a handicraft. The education which precedes that of the workshop should be entirely devoted to the strengthening of the body, the elevation of the moral faculties, and the cultivation of intelligence; and, especially, to the imbuing [of] the mind with a broad and clear view of the laws of the natural world with the components of which the handicraftsman will have to deal. And the earlier the period of life at which the handicraftsman has to enter into actual practice of his craft, the more important is it that he should devote the precious hours of preliminary education to things of the mind, which

---

1. Thomas Henry Huxley (1825–1895): educator as well as biologist.

have no direct and immediate bearing on his branch of industry, though they lie at the foundation of all realities.

In many a hard-fought field the foe has been routed, not by a blunder-buss, but by an epithet. Advocates of the shortcut have made good use of this ruse. In the first place, the modern designation of secondary grade schools as "high schools" has favored the confusion with "higher educa-tion" which has already fallen under the disrepute of being "mere culture" or professional or "gentlemanly" training. In any exact thinking, *culture* is the term for those studies which disclose the child to himself and put him into possession of his dormant faculties. The physician puts the germ of diphtheria or tuberculosis into a "culture" of gelatin or some substance in which the hidden spark is nurtured into life and enabled to grow. The gardener calls the little pots of nursery plants "cultures." But the poor man is almost ashamed to harbor the thought of culturing his offspring and high schools are derided as giving impractical and useless accomplishments for the few who do not have to work and as making "scholars" and high-sounding wind-bags. "You can't make," says one conclusively, "beet-root sugar out of fine phrases." This is true. But neither can you make beet-root sugar out of foolish phrases. When you come to think of it the beet-root industry has never been known to be affected by any kind of phrases. But the industries and ideals of a nation cannot but be enriched by the sound of intelligence of all the people derived from thorough general edu-cation in its schools.

Any scheme of education should have regard to the whole man—not a special class or race of men, but man as the paragon of creation, possessing in childhood and in youth almost infinite possibilities for physical, moral and mental development. If a child seem poor in inheritance, poor in envi-ronment, poor in personal endowment, by so much the more must orga-nized society bring to that child the good tidings of social salvation through the schools. . . .

· 20 ·

Angry Saxons and Negro Education (1938)

This article in the May 1938 Crisis *was probably written when Cooper was eighty years old, long retired from public school teaching. Obviously, she had lost none of her capacity for outrage at racial injustice. After dismissing the white United States senator in the opening paragraph, she directs her wrath at Booker T. Washington ("a colored leader of white American thought"). The title, and the article itself, is one of the rare instances where Cooper resorts to undisguised sarcasm.*

$\mathcal{A}$ confession of faith, clear and unequivocal, from a U. S. Senator contains these words: "No statutory law, no organic law, no military law supersedes the law of racial necessity and social identity. We have no intention of ever admitting the colored man as our social equal and we can keep him in his place, his inferior social station, by keeping away from him."

And that's that.

A colored leader[1] of white American thought, at once statesman and politician, has enunciated a policy enthusiastically hailed as workable: "The two races can be as separate as fingers and as solidly strong as the hand."

That, also, is that.

Now when the champions of either side shake hands before crossing swords in the ring, the one mutters: "We agree," eyeing the other grimly, "equal as fingers" (crossed at the time) "but *separate*." And his prescient mind vitalizes the efficient thumb, firm and unyielding over mailed fists.

"We agree," the dark brother replies, "separate, but *equal!*" and he looks expectantly on the wriggling little fingers all set to pop over one by one, now with a knockout in the prize ring, now with a hundred meter

---

Reprinted with permission of the NAACP.
1. The reference is again to Booker T. Washington's notorious 1895 Atlanta Compromise.

dash in the Olympics.[2] *"An American Negro youth ventures on to the stage occupied prominently by a Nazi dictator and steals the spot light from him for a little while"* says the *Cleveland Plain Dealer.*

A sweet singer, a wonder working chemist, a sacrificial hero emerging from the ghetto to charm and bless—"separate," but potentially identical, the same elemental human, educable like the rest and capable of patriotic cooperation with any and all forces that make for righteousness in a democratic civilization. But here ensues a titanic struggle between the American conscience and expert efficiency, both represented by the dominant thumb among very unequal fingers and virtually conceding equality while demanding separation. *A race must have its leaders provided with a liberal education.* Hence a national Negro university is visioned in equipment and appurtenances equal to the best. Efficiency experts contrive attractive sinecures in officialdom, toothsome sops for Cerberus,[3] guaranteed to keep that beast off at the approved distance from all movements in the life stream. Due honor and high praise are loudly acclaimed for Negro spirituals, Negro literature, Negro history, Negro "attempts" at art. But don't try to crash the gates on a play of Shakespeare or to listen in on a Wagnerian opera, or to study the marbles of Phidias and Praxiteles. Education *must* be separate, that is sure. The law of the Medes and Persians changeth not. Jim Crow in hotels and common carriers amounts to nothing unless you can segregate cultures. "The mind is its own place" and Education is its Maker.

The finale in this trilogy of the American saga is the offering made by Lord Bryce, by common consent the greatest analyst and commentator on our Commonwealth and a mighty wise counselor after all may be the guiding thread out of this labyrinth of purposes. He says:

> It needs something more than the virtue of a philosopher, it needs the tenderness of a saint to preserve the same courtesy and respect towards members of a backward race as are extended naturally to equals. . . . As regards political rights, race and blood should not be made the ground of discrimination. Where the bulk of the colored race are obviously unfit for political power a qualification based on property and education might be established which should permit the upper section to enjoy the suf-

---

2. The references are, obviously, to Joe Louis (1914–1981), who the year before (in 1937) had won the world heavyweight boxing championship, and to Jesse Owens (1913–1980), who in 1936 had shamed Hitler by winning four Olympic Gold Medals in Berlin.

3. Cerberus is a menacing watchdog of Roman mythology who is said to have been lulled by Orpheus and wrestled by Hercules; hence, the common expression "give a sop to Cerberus."

frage. Such qualifications would doubtless exclude some of the poorest and most ignorant whites, but it is better to face this difficulty than to wound and alienate the whole of the colored race by placing them without the pale of civic functions and duties. As regards social relations, law can do but little save in the way of expressing the view the state takes of how its members should behave to one another. Good feeling and good manners cannot be imposed by statute. When the educated sections of the dominant race realize how essential it is to the future of their country that the backward be helped forward and rendered friendly, their influence will by degrees filter down through the masses and efface the scorn they feel for the weaker.

A philosopher may say "let who will make the laws if I make the manners"; for where manners are wholesome the laws will be just and justly administered. Manners depend on sentiment and sentiment changes slowly. Still it changes. It has changed as regards torture. It has changed as regards slavery. The sentiment of race pride, the keenness of race rivalry has been intensified, but the sense of a common humanity has grown stronger. When we think of the problems which are now being raised by the contact of races, clouds seem to hang heavy on the horizon of the future; but light streams in when we remember that the spirit in which civilized states are preparing to meet those problems is higher and purer than it was when centuries ago the great outward movement of the European peoples began.

And that, undoubtedly, is that.

God give us leaders and teachers on both sides who, forgetting the flesh pots of Egypt and the spaghetti of Rome will join open palms in honest cooperation to work and pray for a better, nobler, truer America.

· *21* ·

Hitler and the Negro (1942?)

This short essay was clearly written after 7 December 1941 because Pearl Harbor is mentioned. The file copy of the text lists Cooper as still associated with Frelinghuysen University, the Washington, D.C., school she served as president from 1930 (after her retirement from high school teaching) until 1942 when, in February, she delivered her farewell address as president. She did, however, continue to serve in the largely titular role of registrar after leaving the school's presidency. So the text may be later than 1942. But the unmistakable references to wartime sentiments about Hitler and Stalin suggest that the text was written during World War II.

$\mathcal{W}$ords have a quite human way of becoming besmirched by the company they keep. A case in point is the bad odor in which the damning epithet communist finds itself today after having properly and correctly characterized the simple life of not a few respected American Colonies as well as the early Christians when "neither was there any among them that lacked, for as many as were possessors of lands or houses sold them and brought the prices of the things and laid them down at the Apostles' feet, and distribution was made unto every man according as he had need (Acts 4:34).

This writer has no desire to whitewash the baby of the efficient propagandists who have so ably manipulated their job in collaboration with the March of Time. In the interest of clear thinking, however, and even more importantly to sweep the cobwebs from our own ideology, the issue between Stalin and Hitler with the basal motivation energizing each in the titanic struggle which threatens to engulf civilization and all humanity, should be dispassionately and intelligently faced.

The essay appears to have been privately printed as were many of Cooper's writings. We have been unable to locate the source of its publication or original printing. A file copy appears in the Moorland-Spingarn Research Center, Howard University, which graciously provided a photocopy of this and other previously printed materials. Archive locator: Cooper Box 23.5/Folder 64.

Let it be understood at the outset that the only "ism" for our breed, the only allegiance that challenges our loyalty, the only brand of social, economic and political ideas and ideals that carries our blank check endorsement is the American brand. Birth, training and tradition, willy nilly, have made us Americans. For better for worse, for richer for poorer, till death do us part. Here we stand and God help us, we can no other. The leopard cannot change his spots nor the Ethiopian his skin. We cannot afford the open Forum of pure academic reasoning about Nazism, Fascism, Communism or orientalism. The Japanese are a wonderfully progressive people. They are desperately in need of expansion for their rapidly multiplying population, and they are brown. Kagawa their great poet is one of the most saintly characters the world has ever known. All of which goes for nothing with us. Japan has attacked the U. S. A. She is at war with *us*. Admiration for her prowess, sympathy for her cramped natural limitation, even humane ties of Christian brotherhood must be held in abeyance while the war lasts, however painful the process. Altogether different is the case of Stalin against Hitler. Soviet Russia long ago declared war on capitalism, disfranchised its own aristocracy and enthroned the proletariat. So hateful does the whole Red ideology seem to most orderly minds trained under the American economic system of free enterprise that only the greater and more absorbing hatred of Hitlerism can render even a temporary and superficial alliance with Russia thinkable. We tolerate Stalin while and because he is pulling our chestnuts out of the fire. Even the least sympathetic must admit he is doing a magnificent job and invaluable service. One prominent columnist expresses it: "I'd love to have Stalin eat Hitler up raw and then die of cramp colic." Here again sentiment and abstract theories must give way before cold facts. However closely identified we may imagine ourselves to be with the bottom rail which the Russian Revolution put on top, it is undeniable that in our country the best brain and blood have followed consistently the Nation's conscience and that reforms have been wrought not by violent outbursts from below but by considerate conferences and adjustments between the more and the less privileged with a peculiarly American love of fair play and a willingness to look at things from the other fellow's view point. For capital it must be admitted, that any equal distribution of wealth "unto every man according to his need," could never have produced *for all the people* the Carnegie libraries, the Rockefeller foundations for the study and eradication of disease, the Mellon Art Treasures and the many Rosenwald benevolences. Our benefactors of great wealth need have no fear of a bolshevist invasion. Malefactors, great or small are being looked after by the F. B. I. and surely we of the less privileged will gain nothing by wishing camp colic on Stalin. Hitler, on the other hand embodies the one idea that threatens not alone our country's foundation principles but octopus like it would send its deadly tentacles into the vitals of every individual man and woman cutting adrift every racial variety of human form not answering "perfect" to his plans and specifications. Elimination of the unfit, ruthless and forcible elimination, ultimate annihilation or enslavement, not of Jews alone, but of Frenchmen, Italians, all Mediterranean races and nations and finally the now courted and applauded Japanese just so soon as they have served his purpose by closing the pincers around the democracies. Such is Hitler's ideal declared or implied and such his deliberate aim and purpose to make room for the supremely fit, the glorified progeny of Germanic kultu, the unadulterated Nordic breed, divinely appointed overlords and sovereigns of the earth. No need of a prophet to tell what would befall the darker races of this hemisphere should Hitler triumph. Nor would it take an orator's eloquence to persuade a racial minority wherein lies its only hope in the present struggle.

Negroes of unquestioned citizenship and unquestionable loyalty, realize all too keenly that law-allowed inequalities impeach the four freedoms enunciated by our great President and that injustice, not to speak of mob violence, still embarrasses this Land of the Free and Star of Hope for the oppressed of other lands. The right to work with its prerequisite, the right to opportunities for training in the arts of making a living is an essential element in the right to life, liberty and the pursuit of happiness. But most emphatically we realize further that responsibility to make the great American dream of Washington, Jefferson and Lincoln come true, rests alike upon every citizen of the Republic, high and low, rich and poor, black and white. In squarely shouldering his responsibility as a citizen and eagerly answering his country's call for service whatever the placement, the American Negro does not ignore abuses that exist through human imperfections, greed or selfishness in high places. He has learned, or is learning the difference between genuine and spurious Americanism and to discriminate between loyal and recreant Americans. No single individual in a democracy has a right to think of himself as on the receiving end only of its privileges and immunities nor can any even of the humblest minority group dare to nurse personal grouches when the country is in peril of attack on its most cherished ideals. In the language of the Council for Democracy: "If the world is to be a place where a free man can hold up his head, *We have to help make it so* with our own blood and sweat and tears," and by loyal and honest cooperation with the forces that make for righteousness at all times. This duty, responsibility and high privilege rests upon every mother's son without distinction of race, color, creed or condition.

And so, "We rededicate ourselves to the principles of American Democracy, to the perpetuation of our faith in human brotherhood, to the promotion of Christian manhood and womanhood, to the preservation of faith in ourselves under God and belief in the efficacy of Education; Christian Education, to make life livable as well as to make a living in America today under the Constitution."

· IV ·

World Politics, Race, and Slavery:
The Historical Studies

One of the common criticisms of Cooper's thinking is that she was too beholden to traditional values—those, perhaps, of true womanhood, but also those of her Christian belief. Lemert has tried in chapter 1 to demonstrate that Cooper's thinking, and indeed her life, were motivated always by a larger concern with the world of the poor and the world as such. There can be no argument that these concerns arose principally from Cooper's religious values. Not only was she the widow of an Episcopal priest, but she was also a lifelong practicing Christian. Many times, in A Voice from the South and through the years, she spoke openly of the centrality of Christian ethics and faith to her life (as in, among numerous examples, "The Ethics of the Negro Question," chapter 12). But, just the same, this did not prevent Cooper from being also a tough-minded student of both the dangers of real politics and the stark realities of world history.

Religious values are not always the blinders Marx and others believe them to be. As Lemert argues in the introductory chapter, the black feminist social theory of A Voice from the South is implicitly and explicitly a self-conscious facing-up to the social realities of a world divided by racial, gender, and class differences. Yet it is true that, in 1892, Cooper's social theoretical thinking was still somewhat implicit and not nearly so overtly sociological as it would become. In the work of the 1920s, principally that surrounding her doctoral thesis, Cooper comes out as the social historian whose sociology of the politics and economics of slavery and race is overt, daring, and well founded in fact.

The first two of the four chapters following (chapters 22 and 23) are from Cooper's doctoral thesis, "L'Attitude de la France à l'égard de l 'esclavage pendant la Révolution," which she defended at the Sorbonne on 23 March 1925. The remaining two chapters (24 and 25) are texts of Cooper's essays presented in defense of her thesis. The oral soutenance of a French thesis normally entails two written questions posed in advance by the faculty committee. The student prepares her response, though under extreme time pressure (a mere week in Cooper's case). The idea behind this gruesome practice is one central to French education—that, in addition to written work, the brilliant student must be able to express herself, virtually extemporaneously, in the finest spoken French. Chapters 24 and 25 are the prepared notes for the two questions posed in advance.

Chapter 22, "The Social Conditions of the French-American Colonies: The Class Structure," introduces Cooper as an astute sociologist of global politics as viewed from the perspective of France and her most wealthy Caribbean colony, Saint Domingue (present-day Haiti). Cooper's study is of the complex relations between the internal class structure of Saint Domingue in the late eighteenth century and the internal politics of its colonial power, France. In these few, startlingly clear pages,

Cooper explains that, in the colony, class conflict was a result of internal racial differences as well as competing economic interest. The latter were aggravated by the role of the white colonizers pursuing their advantages both in the colony and through the more global economic interests of France as they played out back home in Paris. At the same time, she explains, France's internal politics were affected by the economic and political rivalry between the radical Friends of the Blacks and the conservative, aristocratic Massiac Club, which was organized to oppose the white "friends" of the colonial blacks.

With very little fancy theoretical footwork, Cooper, writing in 1925, anticipates by nearly fifty years the key terms of today's dependency theory of global political economy—the school of thought associated with the work of the sociologist Immanuel Wallerstein. Cooper argues, as do many in the dependency or world-systems tradition today, that the economic fate of the colonies is due not to their "backwardness" but to the subtle ways the colonizing powers exert their influence within the very colonies from which they simultaneously extract natural and human-labor resources.

Chapter 23, "Black Slavery and the French Nation," illustrates the subtlety with which Cooper, writing a half century before the beginnings of dependency theory in sociology, wrote of the complex of interactions between the colonizing state and the colony itself. Chapter 23 combines material from the introduction and conclusion of Cooper's thesis. Though the selections of which this chapter is composed necessarily omit the main body of Cooper's evidence and discussion, they read well in sequence and suggest the details of Cooper's argument. Again, she reveals herself as a highly reliable sociologist of the interplay between the political and economic events in France and those in its richest colony, Saint Domingue. The resistance to the abandonment of slavery in France fed the discontent with the Old Regime and, thus, fueled the Revolution. Cooper concludes starkly: "So it was that the price France paid for her attitude toward slavery was disaster (p. 287). Chapter 22's analysis of the economic basis for France's refusal to abandon slavery is background to the strong argument Cooper makes in chapter 23 for the central contribution of race politics to France's political turmoil and much troubled Revolution.

Chapters 24 and 25, being Cooper's own translations of her notes for the questions posed in her oral exam, are different in tone and topic from the two preceding chapters. The questions posed in a soutenance *are meant to be in the general topical area of the thesis but can range quite far afield, as did those put to Cooper. In fact, early in her text, Cooper complains that the topic set by Professor Bouglé was "too vast, and too vague"—thus quoting the very words put to her the year before when the faculty committee rejected her original thesis topic. She did not miss a beat and cowered before no one.*

Though Cooper's "Equality of Races and the Democratic Movement" (chapter 24) is not as precisely argued as either the thesis itself or the second question (chapter 25), it is important nonetheless. Here Cooper returns to the voice theme with which she thematically organized her Voice from the South *some thirty-three years before in 1892. As Karen Baker-Fletcher has so well argued in* A Singing Something: Womanist Reflections on Anna Julia Cooper,[1] *Cooper took the speaking and singing voice seriously, much as, today, many write of the importance of the social or political voice of the excluded amid the discursive practices of social life. In this reply to the examination question, Cooper directly challenges the ideas of her most foreboding examiner, Célestin Bouglé (1870–1940). Bouglé was the most eminent member of the committee. In the era between Durkheim and Lévi-Strauss in French sociology, Bouglé was clearly one of the two or three dominant figures, as much for his power in the academic establishment as for his research and writing. Many years later, Cooper confessed that prior to the exam she was "frankly afraid of Bouglé" (see souvenir in chapter 28). Yet, and knowing that he was an atheist, Cooper faced up to him by attacking his rather reductionist and racist view of democratic civilizations by reference to the "Singing Something" within* all *human beings. She meant, obviously, that God's presence in all men and women is the origin of the democratic principle. She justifies her arguments with reference to the sources she consulted: Alexis de Tocqueville's (1805–1859)* Democracy in America *and James Bryce's (1838–1922)* Modern Democracies.*

Though the argument has all the earmarks of notes for an oral disquisition, Cooper nonetheless reveals herself as a courageous but disciplined thinker. She makes a persuasive case by referring not just to the historical sources but to her own religious idea of the Singing Something in the human spirit. This to refute Bouglé's claim that democratic culture is naturally limited to the more northern, and Euro-American, climatic regions. At the least, her argument must have impressed Bouglé, who was the one to pronounce her success: "Mademoiselle vous êtes Docteur" *(p. 329).*

"Legislative Measures concerning slavery in the Unites States," (chapter 25) is very much more straightforward, virtually a report on the major historical events appropriate to the topic. But, still, it is an impressive accomplishment, when one considers the short time Cooper had in which to sail to France, receive her questions, and prepare her answers under the pressure of the occasion and of the hostility of her school administrators in Washington, who had threatened (still again) to dismiss her for taking the leave in order to meet the examiners in Paris. She had but one week to prepare for the questions after they had been announced. In this light, "Legislative

---

1. (New York: Crossroad, 1994).

Measures," *if a little plain, reveals the level of her training in history—all the more because the topic was well outside that of her thesis proper.*

The writings in this part should put to rest all doubts that the less specific evidences of a theory of race and politics in A Voice from the South *were false notes. Cooper may have been a "Singing Something" herself, but she could sing with courage and intricate knowledge of the factual basis of the global politics out of which slavery arose in the very foundations of the world democratic movement.*

· 22 ·

The Social Conditions
of the French-American Colonies:
The Class Structure (1925)

This selection from the first chapter of Cooper's 1925 Sorbonne doctoral thesis has been translated from the French by Frances Richardson Keller. Keller translated the title of the thesis ("l 'Attitude de la France à l 'égard de l 'esclavage pendent la Révolution") as Slavery and the French Revolutionists: 1788–1805.[1] *Cooper's own French title might be more literally translated, "The Attitude of France toward Slavery during the Revolution." Keller does well to offer the more general description because Cooper's thesis was about very much more than what is conveyed by the English word "attitudes."*

On the other hand, Keller has made a surprising choice in translating "Saint Domingue" as "Santo Domingo." The latter is, first of all, the colonial name given to the geographic island of Hispaniola on which are found today's Dominican Republic and Haiti. Santo Domingo is also the name of the capital city of the Dominican Republic, a Spanish-speaking country. "Saint Domingue," being French, is of course the colonial name for present-day Haiti. Since Cooper's study was exclusively concerned with the French colony, we have taken the liberty of reintroducing the French name used by Cooper, Saint Domingue, where the translator has used the place name, Santo Domingo. Otherwise the text is the translator's.

$\mathcal{O}$n the eve of the Revolution the French colonies were extremely prosperous. Saint Domingue was especially well-off, for there, as in the other Antilles, the cultivation of cacao and of indigo was being progressively replaced by the raising of sugar cane to the point where not only the needs

---

The selection is reprinted here with the permission of Frances Richardson Keller and the Mellen Press. Most of Cooper's scholarly references to older French sources have been deleted. The section titles are supplied by the translator.

1. (Lewiston, N.Y., and Queenston, Ontario: Mellen Press, 1988).

of France but those of half of Europe were supplied, thanks to the labors of 200,000 slaves on approximately 3000 plantations, just for sugar alone.

With this prosperity came an unbridled waste of resources. The administrative system was especially cumbersome, a source not only of disorder and too many expenditures, but also . . . of oppression and excessive despotism. The one man who represented the King of France and who really governed was the Minister of the Navy; his edicts were law, and he appointed the high functionaries. Each one acted more or less as he liked. In Martinique and in many other colonies, embezzlements had become chronic. In Saint Domingue there were good reasons why the colonists, acting through their commissioner Gouy d'Arsy, were to bring charges of theft against their former Governor La Luzerne, who had become a Minister, and their tax collector, as well as several other administrators.

Saint Domingue was certainly the richest of the French possessions. Immense interests were at stake and this is without doubt one of the reasons why the struggle there would be so desperate.

The already considerable difficulties of the situation were further complicated, since in addition to the slaves and the white colonists who were landholders, the population was divided into three classes. These were "petits blancs," or lower-middle class whites, the mulattoes, and the freed blacks. All three of these classes aspired to play an important role in public affairs.

The "petits blancs" were not owners; rather they were artisans, shopkeepers, policemen, and former soldiers. Their ranks were swollen with fortune-hunters, come from all over. All these people were confirmed enemies of the blacks, whom they understood very little, and whom they never sought to understand. Nor did they wish to understand the mulattoes, whom they reproached with owning property and being rich. For the blacks they felt an extreme contempt, for the mulattoes an intense jealousy.

The mulatto class was restless and active; it was composed principally of landholders who were sometimes rather well educated and extremely desirous of affirming their equality with the whites; but the whites refused to have anything to do with them, obstinately opposing any reasonable sharing of their civil or civic rights. They pretended to many doubts, and either feigned or felt great fears of the possible results of any concessions. They would countenance not the least easing of the harsh laws then in force against the mulattoes; indeed they demanded stricter and more threatening measures.

The white colonist-proprietors and even the "petits blancs" took pride and pleasure in humiliating the mulattoes, in scornfully referring to them as dogs, ugly ones, big bellies, quarter-breeds, half-castes, and so on, further lumping all these odious implications together in the term "colored men." In the Antilles this name included not only those issuing from a mixture of the white race and the black race and their descendants but also the pure Negro natives of Africa or the colonies, provided that they actually possessed their liberty. There was thus no distinction between the emancipated and those who were born free; all were included in the term "colored men." The colonists never applied this term to slaves, even if they were slaves of whatever amount of mixed blood. The population of "colored men" increased rapidly, and in 1789 almost equalled that of the native whites.[2]

The white colonists, who certainly did not sin by excessive prudence in Saint Domingue, treated the mulattoes as outcasts. They did this, according to Boissennade,[3]

> even though [the mulattoes] possessed a quarter of the landed property, even though they rendered great services by their industry, their activity, their participation in land development, in military service and in the constabulary, even though they formed in a word the perfectible element of the inferior race and the germ of a future middle class; since the first third of the XVIIIth century the government, and above all the white colonists, had multiplied the measures of distrust and molestation against them. They forbade them to practice the liberal professions and a certain number of trades. They assigned them special sections in public places. They even tried to force them to wear a special dress; finally they prohibited marriage between them and the whites. The prejudice of the whites against the mulattoes was so deeply rooted that the least trace of black blood was carefully kept track of, even down to the remote descendants of colored men. At every opportunity the whites left no stone unturned to wound the pride of the mulattoes or to thwart their wishes. Without scruples, the whites committed against the mulattoes all sorts of denials of justice, and every kind of usurpation. They lost no chance to treat them as enemies. As one colonist put it, these men, who still bore on their foreheads the mark of slavery, had to be reminded constantly of their origin, through the weight of scorn and opprobrium and the breaking of their spirits. The whites refused them all rights of legitimate de-

---

2. Free men of color numbered about 26,000 at the period of which we speak, and whites 30,000. *AJC.*

3. Boissennade was the French author of a 1906 work on Saint Domingue.

fense, while for themselves they claimed the right to deal out justice without trial. One magistrate of the Superior Council of the Island even dared to propose taking property rights away from the mulattoes.

Finally, the third class was that of the freed men, who were generally poor, and who were almost as jealous of the mulattoes as of the whites. Through their easier approaches to their former comrades still under the yoke, they could not fail to be an active element of insurrection. It is significant that the colony had already experienced slave revolts in 1679, 1691, 1703 and finally in 1758; these revolts, however, were isolated uprisings, and they occurred at a time when the blacks were less numerous than in 1785.

White Colonists of Saint Domingue Approach the National Assembly of France: Geography and Conflicts

The question of whether to admit deputies from Saint Domingue to the National Assembly in Paris arose and attracted everyone's attention to the island at a time when, as in all the colonies where there was a slave-labor system, the condition of the blacks and of the "colored" men was absolutely pitiable. Even though they outnumbered the whites by a ratio of ten to one, the whites held them in subjection by fear, by torture and by cruelty. There were on this one island of the Antilles a half million human beings in slavery to a work which would come to fruition only for others, giving them no hope of recompense and debasing the poor blacks to the point of regarding them as mere beasts of burden. The situation presented an element of true tragedy; it portended the downfall of the whites who, with the most criminal obstinacy, refused to face the realities, and whose intoxication and ambition would finally succumb before that mute but eloquent suffering of the blacks. The previously unsuspected power of the free blacks, allied by blood and endowed with remarkable qualities of intelligence and dignity, would have been the only force capable of calming the tempest which was brewing in the heart of the unfortunate island. The French government failed to understand this fact soon enough.

In contrast to the rest of this astonishing population, the few white colonists of Saint Domingue, perverted by the scourge of slavery as much as by the detestable climate, which made them irritable and easily excitable, were extremely rich and often moved in the highest aristocratic circles.

These ties tended to create a middle class which resided in France more of the time than on its estates in the islands. These owners were satisfied to allow estate managers to gather their revenues; often the managers were cruel to slaves. It is clear that these absentee owners were out of touch with the situation on the island, though they could pretend to be knowledgeable when they wanted to be represented in the Assembly. They nonetheless exercised an important influence on the seats of power in Paris.

Without doubt all these elements contributed to misunderstanding, and created a considerable "conflict of colors" on the island. It is true, too, that from the beginning of its history Saint Domingue had known disorders as tumultuous as they were bloody, probable legacies of the Spanish domination and the violent conquistadors. This violent character seemed indigenous to the island, and for a long time Saint Domingue was considered a veritable pirate's den. This state of affairs had come to an end before the close of the reign of Louis XIV. Whatever their sins up to that time, the rulers of the island made some praiseworthy efforts toward taming some overly hot-blooded subjects. They attacked some subjects who turned out to be a little too hot-tempered. The mutinies were put down; since then the colony had steadily gained in wealth and importance. This development failed to stamp out the spirit of insubordination at the foundation of the social system. A governor of Martinique always had reason to complain of the great number of persons who were abandoning his island for Saint Domingue, where the action and the disorder offered an attractive prospect which was every bit as alluring as the hope of leading a licentious and unregulated life. The governors sent by France, who were subsequently so much criticized by the colonists, needed a good measure of tact and composure; they often encountered insolence rather than compliance with their orders. Rebellions had taken place in 1670 and again in 1723 when the authorities wanted to control certain commercial practices of the island, and from the beginning of the eighteenth century merchants and profiteers demanded exemption from taxes; they insisted on trading freely with all countries and enjoying republican liberty.

In 1789 the French part of Saint Domingue was divided into three provinces, which can be mentioned here by way of explaining the spread of the insurrections which will occupy us in a moment. There was the Plain of the North, with Cap-Française as its seat. This town was more commonly called Le Cap; it was the capital of the colony as well. The Plain of the North was the first area colonized; it was the most populous and the richest.

The Province of the West, in the center of the colony, was twice as large as the Plain of the North. It was less favored by nature for its climate was most unhealthy. A well-conceived irrigation had so improved it, however, that it had become prosperous by the period of which we are speaking. Its capital was Port-au-Prince.

The Southern Province was obviously the least important and the least developed. Social and economic conditions doubtless remained primitive there, yet possibilities for development were not lacking since there were some fertile valleys hidden in the mountains and even a small plain around the capital, Les Cayes.

Such was this colony—materially prosperous, but morally gangrenous, that at the moment news of the convocation of an Estates-General in France arrived, a very lively movement took shape to demand necessary economic reform and improved local administration.

Now the way to accomplish these reforms would be to send representatives to the Estates-General. But it was typical of the times to think of colonies as simple royal provinces, administered by the mother-country at the convenience of the mother-country. The French people of Saint Domingue thought, however, that under the circumstances they could ignore precedent.

By the term "French people of Saint Domingue" we refer to a considerable number of landholders, planters and merchants who lived in France as well as to those who lived more or less permanently on the Island. The movement would finally emerge from the narrowly-connected clique living in France. We shall see that their zeal was not surpassed by that of certain colonists remaining in the colony for whom they were commissioned to work as for themselves. Certainly they were well placed to act, finding themselves at the very sources of information and ideas.

From 1788 on the colonists in France had complained of the rapidly-spreading influence of the Society of the Friends of the Blacks. They raised a vehement clamor, uniting their objections with those of their Jamaican neighbors who were protesting against the Anti-Slavery Association of London. But the colonists remaining in Saint Domingue soon discovered that their brothers in France were acting rather precipitously. The hour was portentous, and they sensed danger. Disagreements arose between them and those who claimed to represent them in Paris. Is it any wonder that this opposition between the colonists in France and those in Saint Domingue should promptly divide France herself?

Out of this conflict the Massiac Club was born.

The Revolution Is Ushered in and Slavery Is Ushered into the Revolution: The Massiac Club and the Friends of the Blacks

The adversaries of the Friends of the Blacks were neither less well organized nor less dedicated than they, and it seems that their association was very much richer. This circumstance made an aggressive plan of action immediately feasible. We anticipate, for it was not until August, 1789 that they met regularly under the name of "Correspondent Society of French Colonists." Very quickly they became known by the name of the mansion belonging to one of their number; it was located at the Place de la Victoire in Paris. There they organized the Massiac Club.

The Massiac Club appears to have been a closely guarded precinct, not open to just anyone. The National Archives of France are rich in very precious manuscript-documents, which we have consulted without being able to exhaust them all; but it is clear that members gave a pass-word in order to attend meetings, since there was fear of spies from the other camp. The Marquis de Gallifet, landowner of the Plain of the North in Saint Domingue, was the founder and the first president. The list of members included the most famous names of the French aristocracy; all those colonists were rich and powerful through the influence they could exert. It is important to understand that their opposition stemmed not only from their colonial interests but . . . also from an overweening spirit of caste, which was more important to them than any new legislation. Above all else they appear before us as aristocrats.

The Friends of the Blacks had very quickly organized affiliated societies in the French provinces; in fact, they had organized a true Jacobin[4] system. It is not surprising that their adversaries at once thought of extending their influence to the maritime and commercial cities; these places were deeply interested in retaining slavery, in which all their material interests were involved. The voluminous correspondence which they left also shows that they were seeking a way to influence the Assemblies of Saint Domingue as soon as they were created. Propaganda in the colony was conducted through letters, but also through brochures. These brochures presented in a more-or-less true light, always shaded by inevitable prejudice, the events which were taking place so rapidly in Paris; soon it seemed necessary to act directly and several members of the Massiac Club betook themselves to the Island.

---

4. The Jacobins were the most extreme, radical revolutionaries in France.

As in most cases of this kind the society soon overstepped its prerogatives; it brought pressure on the French aristocracy and even on a minister to prevent blacks or mulattoes who had come to France from returning to the island. It also acted treacherously toward the Friends of the Blacks, since it wished to mold opinion, especially in France, and the influence of the rival society was strong within the Constituent Assembly. This is why the Massiac Club contested the election of the deputies from Saint Domingue, even before being officially constituted. To its way of thinking such an election attracted too much attention to their Island; this is why it later took steps to prevent the Assembly from taking decisions that risked its displeasure, attempting, for example, to impose a plan of Moreay de Saint-Méry's for the establishment of colonial Assemblies, and giving to certain orators the necessary documentation for their speeches at the Constituent Assembly. The Society even went so far as to try to control the municipalities.

In sum this would be a strongly organized pressure group serving class interests, and not noble principles, as the Friends of the Blacks intended to do. A great responsibility devolves upon the Massiac Club for the unfolding of the events which lost this fine colony for France, after having ruined even those who tried to use it. . . .

· 23 ·

Black Slavery and the French Nation (1925)

This chapter comprises selections from the introduction and conclusion to Slavery and the French Revolutionists: 1788–1805, *Frances Richardson Keller's translation of Cooper's doctoral thesis.*

Black Slavery: The Wheels of Power

$\mathcal{I}$n the European colonies of America, black slavery was an institution founded solely on the abuse of power. In all aspects created by a barbarous and shortsighted politics, and maintained by violence, ... it could, we shall see, be abolished by a stroke, a simple legislative measure when the people it dishonored felt that they could no longer violate moral laws. Precisely because of its artificial character, Negro slavery appeared more odious than any other, for it meant the exploitation of man by man. It was done without pretext and without excuse. And only in the name of the right of the strongest.

We have to look for the origins of this latest form of slavery in the customs of the Spanish and of the Portuguese, who were little inclined to manual work, and who were too indolent to do it for themselves. It was a slavery incomparably more cruel than that which was rampant in antiquity and which is still perpetuated in our day in Muslim countries. The Iberian peoples early found it profitable to combine the trade in slaves with all the other trade they engaged in along the length of the African coasts. For a long time they undertook this commerce on a small scale for their own colonies in the new world. They would voyage to the coasts of Africa to buy the blacks, then transport them across the Atlantic. But later they did

Reprinted with permission of Frances Richardson Keller and the Mellen Press. Many of Cooper's notes are omitted. Please see the introductory note to the previous chapter concerning the use of the colonial name "Saint Domingue."

this in order to sell the blacks to the English and French colonies. The notorious Prince Henri was already using his influence to protect a company that had been formed at Lisbon, and the market of that town had already become very important even before the discoveries of Christopher Columbus opened an unexpected new area of trade.

In 1503 several black slaves were first taken to Hispaniola;[1] it was immediately apparent that they were much more vigorous and very much hardier than the native Indians, especially for the exhausting work in the mines. The celebrated Bishop Las Casas, protector of the unhappy Indians who were perishing by the thousands because they were driven to excessive labor, then proposed to the Regent-Cardinal Ximenes that a black population be systematically organized to do the work of the mines—but Ximenes refused. Yet Charles the Fifth was to show fewer qualms: After 1517 he accorded to a Flemish gentleman formal permission to bring 4000 African slaves every year to the islands of Porto Rico, Hispaniola, Cuba and Jamaica, and the origin of the Negro slave trade can be traced to this concession. The commerce was very lucrative and it was to spread; the complement of slave ships promptly multiplied in European ports. England, France, and Holland took an active part in the trade, and, not satisfied to transport slaves only to their own colonies, they all fought for the trade of the Spanish colonies of Central and South America. It was estimated that at the time of the French Revolution 74,000 [*sic*][2] Negro slaves were transported each year to America; 38,000 were taken there by the English, 20,000 by the French, 4,000 by the Dutch and 2,000 by the Danes. This constant and terrible replenishment was necessary because of the excessive mortality of the slaves—almost three times their birth-rate.

At that, these 74,000 [*sic*] blacks who arrived in the colonies were but a negligible percentage of the victims of this barbarous commerce in human lives. For every one imported, four had already died, succumbing to the perils of the passage, during which the poor souls had been chained and penned like cattle. Above all they died in the course of the fearful man-hunts organized on the African continent to supply the demands of the African slave traders. As the devastation gradually extended the villages disappeared, and the populations were slaughtered in the resistance or sold. The slave trade was a catalyst for the plunder, the atrocious wars, and the

---

1. The colonial name for the island on which Saint Domingue, or Haiti, is located. Said to have been given by Columbus in 1492.

2. The "[*sic*]" is the translator's. It refers to the figure 74,000, which should be 64,000.

anarchy which for three centuries desolated western Africa, giving reign to savagery, and impeding the progress of all civilization.

Eighteenth Century Stirrings against Slavery: The Americans, the English, the French Listen

Despite some material gains, such crimes could only arouse a general condemnation. The humanitarian ideals of the eighteenth century were too flagrantly offended; indignant protests became current everywhere. A methodical campaign for the universal recognition of the most sacred human rights would be organized against this evil institution. The Revolution would finally bring about what even the principles of Christianity had been unable to achieve. The supremely philosophic century was to shake the conscience of all Europe.

The United States, where the principles of liberty were applied for the first time, above all the Southern States which had already suffered from the curse which slavery brought to them, had on several occasions demanded the abolition of the slave trade. At first the English mother-country turned a deaf ear: she profited too much from the traffic to be willing to suppress it. Then, when the independence of the English colonies of America was recognized and the new constitution was drafted, even the most honest and conscientious men of the nation felt fearful before the magnitude of the problem which they would have to solve if they took up such a burning question. Whether from excessive and mistaken patriotism or from moral weakness they allowed to persist an already established state of affairs which was to remain a living negation of their noble principles. A philanthropic movement favoring the emancipation of the Negroes nonetheless made itself felt throughout the United States, thanks to the Quakers, a sect which since 1774 had expelled from their society all those found interested in the slave trade, and thanks to such men as John Woolman, Benezet, and Warner Miflin.[3] This movement resulted in the enactment of certain measures against the importation of Negroes in nine of the newly recognized states, as well as the emancipation of all the blacks born in Pennsylvania after 1776.

In England the demand for abolition of the slave trade had been heard

---

3. It was the Quakers who began anti-slavery agitation in America as early as the end of the 17th century. In England, they were to present the first petition in favor of abolition of the trade to the House of Commons in 1808. *AJC.*

since 1780. And although the colonial slave-holders sought in 1784 to safeguard their interests from the consequences of this movement by the passage of the Consolidated Slave Act, William Pitt dared to speak openly in Parliament in 1788 for abolition of the trade. The English philanthropist Ransay, Granville Sharp, and especially Thomas Clarkson, the young and brilliant professor of Cambridge University, stirred up English opinion at that time by writing pamphlets exposing colonial practices. The abolitionists liked to buttress their arguments with that famous phrase uttered in 1772 by Lord Mansfield:[4] "The air of England has long been too pure for a slave, and every man is free who breathes it. Every man who comes into England is entitled to the protection of the English law."

In 1783 an association had been formed in London as much for the deliverance of the slaves of the Antilles as for the discouragement of the traffic on the coasts of Africa. Two years later Dr. Pinkard, the Vice-Chancellor of Cambridge University, proposed as a subject for the Latin prize "Is it proper to make men slaves without their permission?" Clarkson, who was then a student, won the prize, and the following year published a work titled *Essay on the Slavery and Commerce of the Human Species*. This book marked a turning point in the struggle against slavery. In 1787 Granville Sharp became president, and William Wilberforce and Clarkson the guiding spirits of the anti-slavery society formed in 1783; it reorganized on a serious basis with the aim of suppressing the slave trade.

Meanwhile, it was in France that the first flash of the philosophic ideal capable of awakening the entire world burst forth. Montesquieu, Rousseau, Voltaire, Filangieri and Raynal thundered the most forcefully against the odious traffic. It was in France that official acts striking a death blow to the most unjust of institutions would be announced for the first time. The honor of having voted the deliverance of the slaves in all the French colonies belongs to the National Convention of the French Republic. It did this at the meeting of the 16 pluviôse, year II. (February 4, 1794).

More than anyone else, Montesquieu sounded the knell of slavery in his book, *The Spirit of the Laws*. Half a century before the Revolution he pleaded for the abolition of slavery:

> It is not good by its nature. It is useful neither to the master nor to the slave; to the latter because he can do nothing virtuously; to the former because he contracts with his slaves all sorts of bad habits which accustom

---

4. William Murray, first earl of Mansfield (1705–1793): English barrister and statesman.

him imperceptibly to become wanting in all the moral virtues so that he becomes proud, hasty, hard, angry, sensual, cruel. . . . In a monarchial government where it is of sovereign importance never to abuse or defile human nature, there must be no slaves. In a democracy where the laws themselves must provide that everyone shall be as equal as the nature of government can permit, slaves violate the spirit of the constitution.[5]

It certainly is true that slavery has the most disastrous effect on intelligence and on customs, not only for the slaves but for their masters. Not simply the moral order but also the very economic order of civil societies is seriously damaged by it. Public welfare is corrupted at its sources. The exploitation of man by man, be it that of the weak by the strong, or of the poor by the rich, is always egotistical and thoughtless of others. Slavery is therefore a supreme crime against humanity; it is logical and just that it should carry its punishment in itself.

Moreover it is a mistake, and Montesquieu very correctly emphasized this, to imagine that black slaves are indispensable in certain climates and for certain work to which the whites, if we are to believe them, cannot adapt themselves: "There is perhaps no task on earth for which one cannot employ free men," he wrote. We need only consider the issue from the point-of-view of humanity and from that of good common sense to understand it. Furthermore the dangers of slavery are manifold, and those who do not wish to recognize them are indeed enemies of society.

What precautions it is always necessary to take to avoid disaster when that institution exists! Montesquieu warned his century about that too, indicating that only by treating slaves humanely could anyone hope to fend off the dangers inherent in the presence of large groups of them. He showed the Athenians treating their slaves with such gentleness that they did not trouble the state, as the slaves of Sparta did. The early Romans also lived the life of their slaves, working at the same level, even eating with them, showing them "much kindness and fairness" which permitted them to rely on the faithfulness of these good servants without needing special laws. Only when they wanted to make their slaves "instruments of luxury and pride" did laws become indispensable.[6]

If only the French colonies could have understood these words, and adopted this point-of-view! If only they had known how to appreciate the

---

5. The passage quoted is in book 15 of *The Spirit of the Laws* by Charles-Louis de Secondat, Baron of Montesquieu (1689–1755).
6. Ibid., book 16.

wisdom of Montesquieu's good counsel and profit from it! Warnings certainly were not wanting, for the Encyclopedists also sounded the same note of high reason and human justice. What bloodshed, what sufferings, what tragedies, what ruins and horrors could have been avoided! Unfortunately, we must relate a completely different story here; the colonists, the rich merchants, had too much to gain from the shameful traffic in slaves to be willing even to consider the possibility of suppressing slavery. Since the time of Colbert, too many French ports had been developed and enriched by the trade. Bordeaux, Saintes, Marseilles and Le Havre prospered. In the course of the conflict which was to erupt over slavery, these towns would side with the colonists against the blacks, aggravating a situation already fraught with perils. In the French Antilles work and profits had been organized in such a way that at first glance it could have appeared impossible to get along without the black man.

The Birth of the Friends of the Blacks

The coming struggle would be between the opposing interests of the colonists and the blacks; and in spite of the enormous number of slaves, it would have been very one-sided had not Brissot, Sieyès and Condorcet[7] founded in 1787 a society called the Friends of the Blacks, inspired by and modeled after the Anti-Slavery Society of London. Brissot had made a voyage to America, had returned full of compassion for the unhappy blacks, and resolved to defend their cause whatever the cost. Moreover, young and impassioned, he never proceeded by half measures; he had the reputation of always pushing ideas to the extreme. The strength of his opinions, his ardor and his energy rendered him a formidable adversary. Already closely allied with the Quakers, with Miflin and Saint-John Crèvecoeur[8] in America, he also profited from his frequent trips to England by studying the English philanthropic movement; he became especially friendly with Clarkson. In constant contact with that enthusiastic young group, he too was to consecrate all his energy to the defense of those who did not yet dream of claim-

---

7. Jacques Pierre Brissot (1745–1793), Emmanuel Joseph Sieyès (1748–1836], and Marie-Jean-Antoine Nicolas de Condorcet (1743–1794) were French Enlightenment philosophes and political figures in the Revolution.

8. Possibly, Thomas Miflin (1744–1800), a radical in the First Continental Congress (though, perhaps, the [to us] more obscure Warner Miflin on p. 282); but, assuredly, Jean de Crèvecoeur (1735–1813), a French essayist and farmer who settled in New York before the American Revolution.

ing anything for themselves. Brissot knew how to communicate that energy to his good friends, and how to organize them. They first installed their society at the Hotel de Lussan, Rue Croix-des-Petits-Champs, in Paris; later they moved to the Rue Favart and into the offices of the *Patriot,* a publication which became their official daily organ.

Mirabeau[9] became very much interested in the Society of the Friends of the Blacks. One of his pet projects at the time was *The Analysis of English Papers.* Not only did he take steps to persuade the government that it should give him the privilege of inserting translations of English anti-slavery works in the supplement of his publication; he even suggested that Brissot collaborate with him as Associate-Translator. This was an opportunity for publicity and influence that Brissot did not let pass. *The Analysis of English Papers* was a mere pretense by means of which Mirabeau intended to spread the boldest truths before the public, showing that they appeared inoffensive in England, and that they circulated freely there. Since Mirabeau did not know English, and basically understood nothing about the state of affairs in England, Brissot's collaboration was extremely valuable to him. For that matter it was precious to Brissot too. "If this paper of Mirabeau's had simply been subject to censorship," Brissot said, "I would never have dreamed of confiding to him the publication of works favoring the interests of the Negroes. But free of government interference, his writers could direct their energy to the public good."

Clearly Brissot is the dominant figure in the Society of the Friends of the Blacks. M. Boissonnade paints this delightful picture of him: "Imaginative writer, active reformer, spirited, unbiased and upright, and possessed of an intelligence more daring than safe, this little man of the pale face and the long straight hair, carelessly arranged, had the distant air of a dreamer, fell in love with all the humanitarian causes, and used his indefatigable energy as a polemicist and organizer in their service." But in addition Brissot knew how to assemble the most dedicated adherents about him. Besides those already mentioned, he chose them from the philosophers, the men of science, the journalists, who were at that time becoming more numerous and influential, and even from the great lords and the financiers. . . .

One can imagine that it was not easy to unify this array of men of good will. Brissot also had to endure more than one refusal, and it is apparent in his *Mémoires* that he sometimes felt discouraged. More than one man of

---

9. Honoré Gabriel Riqueti, count of Mirabeau (1749–1791): political leader and eloquent orator during the Revolution. Though not a radical, Mirabeau was wily enough to seek a middle course.

that period seemed naturally inclined toward prudent behavior, and seemed to feel a vague terror at the thought of stirring up subjects so fraught with menace for their own future security. Brissot wrote that Herault de Sechelles, quite a parliamentarian at the time, refused to take part. He was afraid to show himself an advocate of freedom for the blacks and to be taken as an accomplice of those who were planning the Revolution. . . .

We should note here that the society was often most unjustly calumniated by its detractors and that they sometimes accused the honest Brissot himself of serving English interests or of receiving money from the mulattoes of Saint Domingue. There was no evidence for these slanders. Neither Brissot nor the society grew rich from their ardent dedication; and if the Friends of the Blacks had been, as they were often reproached for being, one source of the insurrections that broke out in the French colonies, the fault was probably not theirs, but rather the result of circumstances in a difficult period and of the resistance provoked by their selfless efforts. The Constituent Assembly itself, overcome by tasks too heavy for it, would allow itself to be unhappily influenced by movements and changes in opinion, now for, now against emancipation. These fluctuations [would] have their repercussions on some difficult legislation, which in its turn [would] provoke both outbursts of enthusiasm and regrettable errors of judgment, but which [would] nonetheless lead eventually to the triumph of the ideas of the Revolution, unfortunately for France, at the expense of her most prosperous colony. . . .

The French Nation and the Slavery Experience

So it was that the price France paid for her attitude toward slavery was disaster.

We may wonder today [in 1925] whether she would not have been better off to follow the advice offered by some of the Friends of the Blacks, and by several members of the Constituent Assembly as well, from the very beginning of the Revolution, and immediately renounce her empire—at the very least Saint Domingue, since it could not in any case be kept if the new ideas of liberty, equality and fraternity were applied. Yet that was one of those extreme measures which it is difficult to decide upon; no patriot would have been willing, practically speaking, to accept the responsibility for such an action. The French legislators were certainly wrong to think as the American legislators did that time and future laws would provide an inoffensive and effective remedy. France had to suffer from this mistake much sooner than did the United States. But we should remember that the French faced the most difficult of tasks.

First they were presented with a serious economic problem. How could they ruin the planters and the merchants in Saint Domingue who had often invested considerable fortunes in their businesses, and who could not be compensated? And all this arose at a time when the country was on the threshold of bankruptcy, when the people of France did not have bread, and when the idleness of workers whose fate depended on the colonial trade was to be feared as much for a social evil as for an economic loss. It is certainly not difficult for us at our distance to indict the colonists, and to throw the responsibility for the events at Saint Domingue on them. They showed themselves as self-centered as they could possibly be. As P. de Vaissière[10] said, the admirable colonial effort of France for more than a century had only created a plutocracy incapable of seeing anything in Saint Domingue but a field for exploitation; it was totally ignorant of the needs, interests and aspirations of the colony. Be that as it may, no social body had ever been known to abandon its property lightly; instinct, and also a certain sort of justice impelled the slave owners to defend what they considered their rights. It is fair to recall here that, generally speaking, the colonists in Saint Domingue treated their slaves better than the Anglo-Saxon colonists did, this is even the opinion of English writers who have considered the question. Doubtless the colonists would not have refused to improve their methods and to make their slaves happier if the propaganda of the philosophes had not from the beginning made them fearful of an uncertain future.

After that it was a problem of race, the most difficult of all to solve. We are not speaking only of white and black here; that would have been relatively simple. Between the two there was the intermediate mulatto, who would singularly complicate the question, and compound an already insurmountable difficulty. In 1789 France found herself confronting here as elsewhere a state of affairs which she had no part in creating, but which she had inherited from the past. And these color prejudices, rightly abhorred by philanthropists, were easier to hate in theory when one did not live in the places where they had been perpetuated for centuries, and when one knew nothing of the life of the colonies, where they had grown so

---

10. Cooper cites Vaissière as the French author of a 1900 book on creole life in Saint Domingue before the Revolution.

deep that they were even stronger than all the other distinctions made between the free man and the salve since ancient times, to the point where a mulatto slave would have refused to obey a free Negro, even if the latter had [had] the audacity to buy him. And we are certainly obliged to recognize that in Saint Domingue the attitude of the mulattoes was even more cruel than that of the white colonists, and that the mulattoes resisted the emancipation of their still-enslaved brothers more than did the white colonists.

Finally it was a political problem. The change of regime was not accepted in these distant countries as it should have been, because it was not understood. The majority of the colonists remained royalists. *And so did the blacks.* A war of parties was added to a war of races.

When we study the question in depth we are therefore forced to conclude that for France the question was absolutely insoluble, from a political point-of-view, if an immediate solution was demanded. For this we cannot blame the men of the Constituent Assembly or those of the Convention.[11] Many contemporaries saw this, said it, and repeated it; we can understand it still better at a distance: it was impossible to reverse completely the regime of colonial slavery from one day to the next. All that could be done, for a time, was to mitigate its severity, and little by little, with caution, give the blacks their rights, along with the education necessary to exercise those rights and to become ready for democracy.

In fact, after the Constituent Assembly, which was freely accused of having been too moderate, and too vacillating on this point, we see that the Legislative Assembly was disposed to greater firmness, and that the Convention finally became too precipitous with its reforms. Composed from a group of extremists, the Convention did not know how to control those it liberated, and blood flowed in the Antilles as it did in Paris. It is not astonishing that Bonaparte[12] saw only this mistake, and that because the Convention had gone too far in many matters, he wished to back up. Unfortunately he forgot what he had so correctly thought at first, that it is

---

11. In France, after 1789, a series of national legislative assemblies were formed to represent the popular will against the king and the dominant classes. The Constituent Assembly was followed by the Legislative Assembly (formed in 1791), which was, in turn, replaced by the radical National Convention that provided legislative cover for the notorious Reign of Terror in 1794. In the next paragraph, Cooper captures the uncertainty of these successions and of popular rule in the Revolution.

12. Napoléon Bonaparte (1769–1821): consul and emperor of the Restoration in France after overthrowing the Directory, the political instrument of the leaders of the Reign of Terror, in 1799.

impossible to retreat on questions of liberty, and that a free man will not again take up the yoke. At the beginning of his career, this oversight cost him a fine army and an excellent general. In the other French colonies, he was to put off the general emancipation of the slaves for almost half a century.

But if the attitude of Revolutionary France does not at first appear to be sufficiently in accord with her principles, we shall see that [those principles] nonetheless triumphed less than half a century later—because, as A. Cochin put it, they are immortal principles.[13] By the generosity and the nobility of their doctrine, the Friends of the Blacks were to leave an indestructible legacy, and they remain benefactors of the African peoples whom they awakened to the knowledge of their individuality and their right to liberty. This remains true, however premature [the] demands [of the Friends of the Blacks] might have been or dangerous even, when considered from a strictly French point-of-view, since their doctrine was not always understood by others as they understood it.

In spite of the Napoleonic reaction, their effort and their work were therefore not lost, as some could have feared. At first exhausted, France little by little regained her reason. Years would pass but there would come a man, who, after Brissot, would deliver in a French Assembly the same eloquent message, consecrated to the same great cause, and who would show the same devotion. Indeed the hour always comes when progress resumes her march at the precise place where it was stopped. It would take another revolution, heir to that of [17]89, in order that Lamartine[14] can say:

> I had the rare good fortune for a statesman speaking for a people, to have been at once the philosophical spokesman for and the political executor of one of the most sacred and memorable acts of a nation and of an epoch, of one of those acts which clearly mark the history of a human race. Three days after the February Revolution, I signed the act conferring liberty on the blacks, abolishing slavery and promising the colonists indemnification. If my life were only for this moment, I should not regret having lived. . . . Crime and ruin were predicted. God thwarted these predictions, and all was compensated, free competition is established, and work begins again. The voluntary labor of free workers is more productive than the blood of insurrection.

---

13. A Cochin, *L'Abolition de L'Esclavage* [Abolition of Slavery], 2 vols., Paris, 1861. *AJC*.
14. Alphonse de Lamartine (1790–1869): French statesman and historian of the Revolution and the Restoration.

· 24 ·

Equality of Races and the
Democratic Movement (1925)

According to its cover page, this text was translated by Cooper in August 1945 for her students at Frelinghuysen University. It has been lightly edited to exclude several redundancies and remarks that seem to have crept in during the translation. (We have, however, left in one later emendation: her reference to "the Atomic Bomb [1945]" toward the end.) Among the deletions are two long quotes from Bouglé that appeared just after the first paragraph and that Cooper left in French. She summarized their main idea in the present text's second paragraph.

In his Thesis "Les Idées Égalitaires," Monsieur Bouglé declares quite decisively that the notion of Equality manifests itself only in our Western Civilization. "It is only in two parts of the glove, Europe and America, at points where Latin, German and Anglo Saxon Races have developed a certain culture known as Occidental Civilization that we discover a general evolution towards Democracy" (p. 37) . . .

In a word Mr. Bouglé's Thesis holds that Human Equality is a man-made concept resulting as a natural product of the transformations in Nordic Society. That his method in tracing its origin and growth must be purely realistic and dissociated from moral sanctions as to whether it is either right or realizable.

This decision is in my judgment as cold as the Russian Steppes and as bleak-barren as the peaks of the Himalayas. Can we—ought we to—analyze human society as if it were a question of minerals or of vegetation? Perhaps. But even so it is necessary in every case to beware of arbitrary preconceptions, and especially is it necessary to note well the importance of every exception which may vitiate the argument or falsify the conclusion.

So far as we have been able to learn, the text, having been privately printed, probably in 1945, is in the public domain and not under any copyright. We made our photocopy from the copy on file at the Moorland-Spingarn Research Center, Howard University.

The subject which has been imposed upon me is, as worded, too vast and too vague for a thesis. To do it justice would require the life work of a Grote and another of a Gibbon, not to speak of the modern democracies to which James Bryce has devoted two big volumes of more than a thousand pages in treating only six examples of [them]; nor of the classic work of Tocqueville who limits himself quite simply to the U.S.A. ending with 1830.

"Les Idées Égalitaires et le Mouvement Démocratique." (The Concept of Equality and the Democratic Movement.) Where? And at what Epoch?

It is necessary to set up some sort of metes and bounds for the terrain even if the flight contemplates only the stratosphere.

I have read carefully and with deep and lively interest the learned and scientific work of Dr. Bouglé of the Sorbonne Faculté and I would like if I dared such a liberty to place beside it some facts in actual life from a single one of the nations who bear aloft with assurance the banner of Equality in Democracy—nay, who are privileged as the most advanced to carry the torch of civilization for the enlightenment of the "Backward" races but who, to the world's amazement, show up some deplorable lapses away from the formula proposed by the philosopher. And right here may be the danger spot.

If one approaches the subject by pure reason it becomes necessary to accept the conclusion in its entirety without personal or local bias and without exception taken to suit any embarrassing fact. If for example the conditions for equality as defined by the author are achieved by some nations not included in the term "occidental," we cannot imagine some factitious lines in order to exclude the ones or to include the others. A case in point may be noted in the Franco-Japanese Treaty of August 4, 1896, which affirms:

> Among the legislative enactments of countries of the Orient, a place apart, a place of honor must be conceded to that of the Empire of Japan. Its most recent monuments bear the imprint of Western civilizations, the principles with which they are inspired are those of the most advanced codes of the Old Europe, and nowhere perhaps does this characteristic loom up more conspicuously than in the regulations which at the present moment govern the status in Japan of foreigners living there or who carry on business there. Equality of rights before the law between nationals and foreigners is openly and formally proclaimed, etc., etc.

Is it not reasonable to grant that if our theory regarding the elite of nations is not sufficiently comprehensive to include a nation with such a creditable recommendation, . . . we should either enlarge our definition to harmonize with the facts or else treat the subject of Equality not as an abstraction but as it manifests itself uniquely in Europe and in America? A better hypothesis it seems to me, would be the postulate that progress in the democratic sense is an inborn human endowment—a shadow mark of the Creator's image, or if you will an urge-cell, the universal and unmistakable hall-mark traceable to the Father of all, That

> In the mud and scum of things
> There alway, alway something sings

and it is that "Something"—that *Singing* Something, which distinguishes the first Man from the last ape, which in a subtle way tagged him with the picturesque Greek title *anthropos,* the *upward face,* and which justifies the claim to equality by birthright to the inheritance from a common Father for the "Backward" no less than the "Advanced" among his varying but undeniable progeny. The sense of "belonging" may seem to slumber more or less indefinitely here or there for racial groups and it may be blatantly denied and successfully ignored by aggressive usurpers who assert with conviction: "We are *the people!* Beside us there is none other." But the divine Spark is capable of awakening at the most unexpected moment and it never is wholly smothered or stamped out. Therefore the racial group or nation that undertakes the role to play God and dominate the earth, has an awful, a terrific responsibility.

To assume that the ideas inherent in social progress descend by divine favor upon the Nordic people, a Superior Race chosen to dominate the Earth, assuredly pampers the pride of those believing themselves the Elect of God. But one may as well anticipate Surprises. For example note the situation in Russia today (1925) little dreamed of 20 years ago, likewise in China, Turkey, in Egypt, the Gandhi movement in India.

"There are some instants," says Bryce, "when it would be wiser to bestow free institutions even if they are liable to be misused than to foment discontent by withholding them."

Might we not go so far as to say *a priori* that we ought to admit for all peoples the possibility of establishing these institutions without withholding them from any.

I trust my audacity may be pardoned in daring to take exception to certain conclusions of one of my judges, the learned Dr. Bouglé whose thesis [on] Egalité has been assigned me for questioning.

It is necessary, whatever the conditions to speak the truth as one sees it even if from a somewhat blurred viewpoint one is not able to follow exactly the shining pathway of the Master.

At page 44 the author [Bouglé] demands: "Would any one dare assert that in a given modern society there exist at the same time two different standards of justice fixing for the same act a heavy penalty if it has been committed by an artisan, a light penalty if it has been committed by a property holder?"

Two different laws inscribed as statutes? No. But custom which defies the law and makes of it a scrap of paper is so notorious that even for the nation where we love to picture the foyer of democracy, equality and justice, it is a common saying in advance of trials: "You can't put a million dollars in jail, or free a poor devil without a cent, particularly if the latter happens to be of a race proscribed."

In such circumstances Law, in the abstract founded on the unalienable Rights of Man and the indestructible value of Humanity makes sheer mockery of Equality. Lynching or the summary execution by a mob without judge or jury and often in a manner atrocious and barbarous, proclaimed at the start as necessary in order to forestall a horrible crime against women, has extended itself step by step from black men to black women and boys of 15 and 14 years of age and then, so contagious is the fever that one counts some white men and even quite recently a white woman among the victims of this travesty of Law. Defying the Law in certain states also is Peonage, a system under which prisoners from the State Penitentiary are farmed out to private landlords into worse than slavery and exploited without remedy. But lynching and peonage both are ugly excrescences on the body politic, a blot on the Scutcheon causing shame and embarrassment to intelligent patriots in all sections of a democratic country. A negation of Law thro unbridled passion and greed of individuals which let us hope with all true lovers of progress, is now on its way out.

Not so with the legalized inequalities such as the widely unequal provision for the education of youth, denial of the franchise in shameless contravention of the fundamental law of the land, the systematic exclusion from public libraries, recreation grounds and sources of amusement and mental improvement.

Mr. Bryce in his work *Modern Democracies* discusses the new problem of *Democracy Today* caused by the presence of races slightly advanced in close proximity with races advanced and impassioned with the ideology of Equality. He says:

The passion for Equality, civil and political, economic and social which having grown strong among the Advanced people, has not only spread among the more educated part—everywhere a tiny part—of the Backward peoples, but has disposed the Advanced to favor its sudden extension to the Backward thro the creation of institutions similar to those which had slowly developed themselves among the Advanced. This love of equality is not found in Europeans who live among colored races, who so far from treating the latter as equals, generally contemn and exploit them.

Again in discussing the tendency of the white race to exclude the black or yellow races from large portions of the earth, he says:

There is in Australia a general agreement that the continent must be strictly reserved for the white European races, excluding persons of East Asiatic or South Asiatic or African origin. The watchword, "A White Australia" is proclaimed by all parties alike. The philanthropic and cosmopolitan philosophers of the 19th century would have been shocked by the notion of keeping these races perpetually apart and warning black or yellow peoples off from the large parts of the earth's surface. Even now most large hearted Europeans dislike what seems an attitude of unfriendliness to men of a different color and a selfishness in debarring the more backward races from opportunities of learning from the more advanced, and in refusing to all non-European races, advanced and backward, the chance of expansion in lands whose torrid climate they can support better than white men can. Nevertheless, there is another side to the matter. Whoever studies the phenomena that attend the contact of whites with civilized East Asiatics in Pacific North America, not to speak of those more serious difficulties that arise between whites and colored people in large regions of America and in South Africa perceives that there are other grounds, besides the desire of working men to prevent the competition of cheap Asiatic labor, which may justify exclusion. The admixture of blood, which is sure ultimately to come wherever races, however different, dwell close together, raises grave questions not only for white men, but for the world at large. Scientific enquiries have not so far warranted the assumption that a mixed race is necessarily superior to the less advanced of the two races whence it springs. It may be inferior to either or the gain to the less advanced may be slighter than the loss of the more advanced.

And here is the horrible catastrophe! As if men and societies reacted like chemical atoms forming instantly a dreaded compound as soon as molecular action becomes possible. Human affinities and alliances are affairs of individual free will. Philosophic reasoning may overexcite but cannot obliterate either their attractions or repulsions. Surely we are intelligent enough to ride in common buses without flying into one another's arms for a mongrel progeny. Why not preach self control and practice the principles of the Christian Religion? Especially is it difficult to comprehend by what secret weapon these philosophers hope that they can hold back on coming tidal waves by wholesale persecution, inflicting vexation and humiliation on innocent individuals of their own generation. Besides, where, in their opinion, where on the terrestrial globe are the non-white races to go?

The white race of our day has a voracious appetite for the One World. It must have room—more room to expand and carry forward its good deeds.

The earth is the Lord's and the fullness thereof! And again: Blessed are the meek for they shall inherit the earth. Right! We are the meek! Bryce pretends that humility is an extinct virtue, but anyhow, we are the chosen of the Lord! His own children foreordained to inherit the earth, and so we enter Africa and forbid the natives to walk except in the middle of the road. We have preempted America—and Lo, the poor Indian! In Australia we say kindly but firmly to the aborigines: "I need the land. Here is abundance of it. But I am allergic to irritants in my sight. I do not like your complexion. It does not go well with my own. If you are submissive I can serve myself with your labor as a slave. If not, yonder is the exit. You will find spacious tombs over the mountains. Pity, really. But I am extremely apprehensive about my posterity. I have to keep the land 'White' for them!"

It is a curious fact that the nations calling themselves Christian under the banner of the Prince of Peace, devoted ostensibly to the progress of civilization, proudly named Christian civilization, Nations who adore the principles of Democracy, of Equality, of fraternity, who, among their congeners practice the noblest philanthropies, statesmen, philosophers, literati, preachers, teachers of the finest, most exalted ideas have to arraign themselves stoically against the simplest amenities of the Gospel, such as "a cup of cold water in the name of a Disciple," as soon as the question of color presents itself.

What is the trouble?

Is it that the Hand of the Potter has slipped? Must we blame God because He made of one blood all peoples that dwell on earth but went to sleep during the firing when some millions were tanned yellow, some brown and some even black. Or rather may we not rejoice that our civilization is to learn and finally apply this last and noblest lesson, the most difficult of all taught by the Master and so sacred that it should be studied, learned and inwardly digested till graven on the hearts of men and emblazoned on the suffering pathway of the Cross: "By *this* shall men know that ye are my disciples, *that ye love one another,*" and that so much the more because on receiving the least of my brethren ye are receiving Me.

The concept of Equality as it is the genuine product of the idea of inherent value in the individual derived from the essential worth of Humanity must be before all else unquestionably of universal application. It operates not between such and such places,—such or such shape of the cranium, such and such theories of civilization. In my opinion, which makes no pretensions to scientific sanctions on either sociological or psychological grounds, instead of being the Special product of any unique cult, the idea of human equality is the result of the final equilibrium of all the human forces of the entire world.

So far the civilization called occidental has attained partial equilibrium only of the physical and perhaps of the intellectual forces. The banner today is borne by the men or the nation who invents the most marvelous project of destruction, the most powerful and irresistible instrument of War. The Death Ray (1925)—the Atomic Bomb (1945)—is tops. But unless I am greatly mistaken, this poor world has need of a second incarnation of Divine Love to teach compassion, to erect anew the ideal already so ancient but so little comprehended even by the most advanced of today: To love mercy, to practice justice and to walk humbly before God. Then equality will become no longer the equilibrium of the jungle where one concedes the equality of another only when he cannot crush or exploit him. For equality, as I understand it, is objective, not subjective. It is not for the little fellow who swells up with the idea I am as good as the other fellow; but for the big fellow with all the power and all the controls to stop and consider: The other fellow is as good as I am. Both human, both mortal, both entitled to a place in the sun. The veritable equality will then be the harmony of a well tuned orchestra where each from the greatest to the smallest contributes at his best according to the part assigned by the conductor who can do no wrong, each player striving no longer to destroy but to serve the music of the spheres: and I have the assurance to believe that the contribution of the brother in black may be considerable in a normal world. He has the Heart Talent which perhaps the civilization "called occidental" might take on to advantage; and let not our world despise the one-talent man, and let him not despise himself and hide his lord's gift because he knows the Master is an austere man: Each at his best, reverencing the Self in the All. *The Master hath need of Thee!* Here you have my religion and my philosophy.

Mr. Bryce proves conclusively that a truly democratic government exists nowhere. Efficiency of performance requires that the ablest direct. The benevolent oligarchy in a democratic framework therefore is Bryce's ideal, and such is acknowledged to be the White Man's Burden wherever the two or the three races find themselves on the same terrain, and I accept it. But let the Ruler bear in mind that the Right to Rule entails the duty and the inescapable responsibility to Rule Right. Let him recognize the differences among men, in the Races of different pigment in epidermal cells, curl of hair and color of eye, length and breadth of cranium and facial angle not as obstacles to fulfillment of destiny of any so long as each can say: I am a man and no human impulse is foreign to me, these differences indicating precisely the providential contribution to that heterogeneity which offers the final test of our civilization, harmony in variety.

If the Christ who was despised and rejected of men nearly 2000 years ago, were making a second attempt to come to His own among the very men who build temples in His Name and magnify their civilization to give Him lip service, would He find Himself again rejected for choosing the humble of earth to confound the pride of the mighty?

Occidental Civilization in its Middle Age thrilled thro and thro in Crusades to deliver the tomb of its Lord from the hands of unbelievers. Today we see his living presence in some of the least of his children rejected, repressed and forced outside the pale for no better reason than that a certain pigment is not preferred by those who make up the books.

Inasmuch as ye have done these things to the least of these my brethren ye have done it to Me.

· 25 ·

Legislative Measures concerning Slavery in the United States: 1787–1850 (1925)

This text, Cooper explains on its cover page, was translated on 15 June 1942 "for her pupils in American History at Frelinghuysen University." It was privately printed at Cooper's direction and expense, possibly in 1942, though there is some reason to believe that it was printed later, about the time of "Equality of the Races" (chapter 24).

One day in May, 1619, (precisely one year before the Mayflower at Plymouth) there put in at the little port of Jamestown in the English Colony of Virginia, a Dutch trading vessel which carried in its hold 19 Negroes stolen from the shores of Africa. The captain was in need of supplies in return for which with a quantity of large leaf tobacco sufficient to cover a deal these 19 wretches were sold at auction among the inhabitants of the Colony, and the boat put to sea again, the crew well satisfied that they had done a good turn for the days record.

To tell the truth, it was a day's work big with fate, for this day marked the beginning of African slavery in the colonies which were to become the United States of America.

Thus, without the fanfare of trumpets or disturbance of the elements— neither thunder, lightning nor rumbling of earthquake—there entered into American life a fact, silent and unforeseen which was destined nevertheless to embroil the entire future, embitter friendly relations of brothers, of families, of states and finally to stir up a fratricidal war, the most bloody, the most devastating in all previous history.

We have been unable to find any rights-holder to the present text, but we thank the Moorland-Spingarn Research Center, Howard University, which provided us a photocopy from its files. The text has been edited to eliminate historical facts and events well known today.

And yet this fact at first was quite simply a local patriarchal custom, subject to the domestic regulations of the state or of the central power of the federated states. Thus we see that the custom soon disappeared in Massachusetts without opposition or discussion. They said quite simply that slavery was irreconcilable with their state constitution. Vermont never permitted it. Pennsylvania decreed that all children born after 1776 should be free. Other states likewise soon brought about the gradual abolition of a custom generally recognized as vicious and altogether antagonistic to generous principles. Thomas Jefferson [said] in . . . a letter . . . to Condorect . . . :

> "I am happy to be able to inform you that we have in the U.S., a Negro son of a native African, who is a mathematician of great ability. I have procured for him employment with one of our chief engineers who is drawing up the plan of the new federal city on the Potomac River: in his leisure moments he has written an almanac for next year which he has sent me in his own hand writing and which I enclose herewith. I have seen some of his solutions of extremely complicated geometric problems showing great mathematical genius. He is, let me say, a very worthy and respectable member of society and a free man. I shall be very happy to note similar cases of moral excellence so numerous that one might prove that the lack of talent observed in some individuals of this group is merely the effect of their degraded condition and not at all the result of any difference in the structure of parts on which depends the intellect and higher qualities of the soul.

In the same general tone, is a letter of George Washington to Phillis Wheatley, the African slave of a family in Massachusetts. President Washington thanks the young poetess for a copy of her book of verses and pays her a warm compliment upon her excellent achievement. . . .

In drawing up the Constitution in the Convention which met at Philadelphia from May 14 to September 17, 1787, the words "Slave," "Slavery" and "Slave Trade" were carefully avoided although evidently present in the conscious minds of all; further proof that the conception later alleged by the Supreme Court in the *Dred Scott* decision that the slave was a chattel (a "thing," not a person) was not from the beginning the conception of the fathers of the country. In the words of the Constitution the slaves were "persons held to service or labor under the laws of any state." The "Trade" was "the importation of such persons as any of the states already existing should think proper to admit." That is to say in according to the "states already existing" sovereign rights over their predetermined internal customs, the fathers of the Constitution had not the attitude of favoring slavery as an institution and very adroitly put upon it all the restrictions compatible with the leading idea of the day that the union of the 13 colonies was altogether voluntary and that the Federal government possessed only the powers granted to it by the states. However, *the fact* of slavery as a skeleton at the feast had already become an embarrassment to the fathers of the country, requiring and exacting many compromises, much confusion in trying to reconcile the convenience of the moment with those principles elaborated in the Declaration of Independence; and it was again Jefferson who said: "I tremble for my country when I remember that God is just." He was right. . . .

. . . Article IV, Section 2 [of the Constitution] makes . . . concession to the Slave power without using the word "Slave." "No person held to service or labor in one state under the laws thereof, escaping into another, shall, in consequence of any law or regulation therein, be discharged from such service or labor, but shall be delivered upon claim of the party to whom such service or labor may be due." We have seen that the foundation of such a fugitive slave law had already been voiced in the Ordinance of 1787, but it was only after 1850 that this principle became a burning question. The Constitution had provided for the extradition of fugitive criminals as well as of fugitive slaves; but in the case of criminals the action of giving them up [devolved] upon the governor of the state to which they had fled. As to slaves the constitution said nothing, but the Congress in 1793 decreed that this duty should rest with the Federal judges or upon local magistrates of the state. Then several states passed "Personal Liberty Laws" forbidding or restraining the action of their magistrates in such cases.

Now the Act of 1850, transferred the jurisdiction of these cases to the Federal courts and to the marshals of the United States, imposed penalties for failure to deliver and refused trial by jury. In consequence, the antislavery sentiment at the North flared out in white heat while slave hunting became more and more brutal.

Men said: "No longer are there any free states. We are obliged to be at the service of the Slave Power." . . . The immortal Lincoln cried: "The country cannot exist half free and half slave. The house divided against itself cannot stand." . . .

Now so long as the labor of the slave was altogether domestic and the relation between master and slave remained patriarchal, the only condemnation brought against slavery was purely philosophic from advanced thinkers at the South as well as the North. Nothing could be stronger in this regard than the words and ideals of Jefferson, who often refers to the slaves as "our brothers," and who reproved the notion of "beast of burden" as vigorously as the most ardent of Northern abolitionists did later. In fact, Jefferson in France, manifested great interest in the tenets and purposes of the "Amis des Noirs" society, explaining that as a representative of the United States, he was forbidden to take a more active part in cooperation with them.

In 1793, there was brought out an invention—that of Eli Whitney, for separating the seed from the fibre of the cotton boll; it was the cotton gin which produced an industrial revolution in the United States and the dream of a school teacher from Connecticut that riveted the chains of slavery more solidly than ever before. At the epoch of the Constitution, men did not believe that the cultivation could be made profitable for the South. The "roller gin" by slave labor could clean only half a dozen pounds per day. In 1784, eight bales of cotton unloaded at Liverpool from an American boat were seized in the belief that so much cotton could not be the product of the United States. Eli Whitney of Connecticut, who was teaching school in Georgia having observed from time to time the toilsome labor of the slaves, conceived the idea of a mechanical saw to pick the cotton by dredging it across metal combs too close to admit the seeds. One slave could now gin a thousands pounds per day. The exportation of cotton jumped from 189,000 lbs. In 1791 to 21,000,000 lbs. In 1801 and doubled itself again in three years more. Immediately, cotton was king! All of a sudden also, men envisaged the enormous wealth in the possession of one or more slaves and the profit of the slave trade became the most seductive lure in the world. Starting from this moment the slave power became the most important question in the politics of the United States. Having become now commercial and political, the system lost almost on the instant its patriarchal character. Here commenced the mad struggle for supremacy in the Senate, the battle to the death of the states who would favor slavery—a struggle that would not end till the bloody war of secession and all "the wealth piled up [by] the bondman's toil was sunk and every drop of blood drawn by the lash was paid by another drawn with the sword."

When Thomas Jefferson bought from Bonaparte the vast territory of Louisiana, slavery existed there already, supported by the laws of France and of Spain. It was the prudence of "laissez-faire" that Congress tacitly ratified existing laws and customs and slavery not only remained legal but extended itself more and more across the territory. The State of Louisiana, from this territory, was without question admitted as a slave state in 1812. But when Missouri, the second state carved from this territory, presented herself for admission likewise as a slave state, it was not without opposition on the part of the states of the North and Northwest, where labor was free. Seeing that the equilibrium between the number of antislavery and proslavery states was almost perfectly balanced, although the population of the free labor states as we have seen mounted far beyond that of the South, the proposed admission of Missouri was promptly authorized by the Senate representing states, but rejected by the House, which represented population. This deadlock continued several years until 1820 when the admission of Maine at the North, as a free state reestablished the threatened equilibrium and the famous "Missouri Compromise" seemed to calm for a moment the vexing question of slavery. . . .

The war with Mexico for possession of the territory of Texas, which had already declared herself independent, was fought (1847–8) solely for the purpose of giving to the Slavocracy, power of expansion in the Senate. Texas was admitted in 1845 as a slave state of course, but, on the condition exacted by the North that only a single state should be molded from its vast terrain. The Southern expansionists had figured out at least 4 new states affording 8 sovereign senators for their party. . . .

The Compromise of 1820, strangely enough, was not brought before the Supreme Court for the test of its constitutionality until 30 years after in the famous case of Dred Scott. Scott was a slave of Missouri, whose master had taken him into a free state. He brought suit for his liberty according to the law of the state where he found himself. In the meantime, having been sold to a citizen of another state, he transferred his suit to the Federal courts which have jurisdiction in cases between citizens of different states. By appeal, the case came before the Supreme Court from which the remarkable decision was handed down, Chief Justice Taney presiding, that neither a slave nor the descendant of slaves could have the rights of citizens; that they could neither sue in the courts nor be recognized under the law save as chattels, i.e. property or possessions of a master—*not* as persons or individuals. Furthermore, the opinion of the chief justice rendering the decision went on to attack the validity of the legislation in the Act of 1820, alleging that one of the functions of the Congress was the protection of property rights; that slaves had been recognized as property by the Constitution and that Congress was bound to uphold slavery in the territories quite the reverse of prohibiting it.

This decision quite frankly threw down the gauntlet between the two governmental theories in the United States. The North [held] that the Constitution regarded slaves as "persons held to service or labor" under the laws of certain states, and that the function of Congress was the protection of *Liberty* as much as the protection of property; and that Congress was bound to prohibit slavery in the territories, quite the reverse of protecting it.

The South on the other hand, maintained that the duty of Congress to protect slavery was not affirmed by the Supreme Court, that the republicans of the North were rejecting the only peaceable interpretation of the Constitution and that the South could no longer submit even to "Squatter Sovereignty" leaving it to the inhabitants to decide for territories. You see the impasse. Nothing but the arbitrament of arms could untangle the situation; after which, Amendment 14 of the Constitution was to define the law of citizenship in a manner so comprehensive and clear that it must settle for all time the question involved in the *Dred Scott* decision by establishing forever the *status* of citizens of the United States: "*All persons* born or naturalized in the United States are citizens thereof and of the States in which they reside."

· V ·

Reflections on Her Life:
Memoirs, Occasional Writings, Letters:
1925–1958

After retiring from public school service in 1930, Cooper began a decade's tenure as president of Frelinghuysen University, a group of schools for the working poor. She continued, thus, to work full-time to direct this struggling school against all financial odds. When it could no longer afford an independent building, Cooper turned over her large home at 201 T Street to the Frelinghuysen students.

Thus, well into her eighties she remained a vigorous worker and leader. Just the same, this period seemed also to mark the end of her work as an original essayist and scholar (with the possible exception of "The Negro's Dialect," chapter 18). Still, Cooper continued to write personal letters, letters to various editors, op-ed pieces and, most importantly, several valuable memoirs. The materials collected in this part (chapters 26, 27, and 28) show Cooper, in the years after the 1925 thesis, reflecting on her life while also keeping a hand in various public controversies.

Of her memoirs from the later years, one of Cooper's most valuable is her "Reminiscences" (chapter 26) of her early years in Washington, D.C. This essay appeared at the beginning of her last book, Personal Recollections of the Grimké Family and the Life and Writings of Charlotte Forten Grimké, *privately printed in 1951. Cooper had moved to Washington in 1887 and settled in her first year at the home of the Episcopal clergyman, Alexander Crummell (1819–1898), a national and international leader through his efforts to encourage American blacks to emigrate to Africa. Within the year, she established her own home at 1706 Seventeenth Street. About the same time, Francis Grimké, a gradu-ate of Princeton Theological Seminary, had settled his family in the nation's capital when he became the minister of the Fifteenth Street Presbyterian Church in Wash-ington, not far from Cooper's home. Grimké's wife, Charlotte Forten Grimké (1837–1914), the abolitionist and writer, soon became Cooper's closest friend in spite of a more-than-twenty-year difference in age.*

As she describes in this wonderful memoir, Cooper joined with the Grimkés in forming regular Friday and Sunday evening cultural soirees at their respective homes. These social and cultural gatherings were clearly a center of black cultural and social life. Cooper lists some of the noted visitors and regular members in her reminiscences. But Cooper and the Grimkés were the center of this circle of Washington's black intellectual elite. Though Cooper was closest to his wife, Charlotte, she maintained an honest relationship with Francis Grimké, who regularly lent his influence to her assistance, principally during the controversy that led to her dismissal in 1906. In the reminiscences, Cooper reprints one of her long poems, "Simon of Cyrene," and describes her friendly dispute with Francis over her liberal interpretation of the Bible passage from which she drew her inspiration for the poem. Later in life (see Cooper's letter to him in chapter 28), she continued to tease him for his moralism. These glimpses of Cooper's relations with Francis Grimké are among the few in which we see her formal, yet deeply felt, warmth for a man.

More broadly, "Reminiscences" provides a direct insight into the wondrous days at the end of the nineteenth century when Cooper and others, notwithstanding the constancy of racial struggles, enjoyed the promise of a shared social life that drew upon a common love of culture and high-minded human values. One can well imagine how much Cooper must have missed this experience during her exile in Missouri from 1906 to 1911, then again after the death of her dear friend Charlotte in 1914.

Chapter 27, "The Third Step," is Cooper's memoir of the long and difficult work toward her doctorate in 1925. It contains still other stories of the opposition she faced within her school district. She was, in the first instance, threatened with dismissal while she was in Paris in 1924 working furiously to complete the archival work during a leave from teaching. When friends alerted her to the possibility that she would be dismissed if she remained away longer than sixty days, she arranged to have the archives lent to the Library of Congress in Washington, then hastily returned home just in time to save her job. A year later, having finished the thesis in her spare time, she requested permission to return to Paris for the exam. This was denied, or at least not expressly granted. As she says, she went just the same, damning the threats to her livelihood. Nothing was to prevent her from making this third step (as she put it) beyond the undergraduate degree in 1884 and the master's (in mathematics) in 1887—both from Oberlin. It would seem, as Lemert suggests in chapter 1, that the third step was, in a more personal sense, a vindication of her quality as a teacher and scholar against the abuses to which she had been subjected beginning in 1906. We see in this memoir Cooper at her toughest, most determined best.

Chapter 28, "Selected Letters and Other Writings," is highly selective. Cooper left among her papers quite a large number of unedited writings, letters, cards, and journalistic essays. Those offered here represent several of the divergent strains in Cooper's approach to life and work. The first, for example, is an undated (but probably late) autobiographical fragment in which she delivers a famously sharp dismissal of her slave-owner father.

Thereafter in chapter 28, we include several representative letters. The first, from Francis Grimké (1910), surely concerns his attempts to broker the job that allowed Cooper's return to the M Street High School and, thus, to Washington in 1911. He is exceedingly formal at first, but his warmth toward Cooper is evident at the end. The next letter, from Cooper to the school administrator, Dr. Wilkinson (1926), is her defense of her record against the malicious attempt of the school administration to prevent her promotion in grade and salary. They claimed she had failed her written examination. Cooper's letter drips with indignation at the very idea that she could have failed an examination by local school board examiners.

Other letters reveal various and different sides of Cooper's attitude on the world. In one (to Mr. A. G. Comings, 1928) she refuses to join some Oberlin alumni in opposition to Democratic presidential candidate, Alfred E. Smith—an opposition based no doubt on his Catholicism but also vaguely confused with a fear that he would oppose the Eighteenth Amendment's prohibition of alcoholic beverages. The remaining few letters suggest something of the extent of Cooper's correspondence and activity: the note to Du Bois (1929) urging him to answer a viciously racist pseudohistory of Reconstruction; the letter to Cooper (1933) requesting permission for use of material from her translation of Le Pèlerinage de Charlemagne; *a rather snide rebuke from the editors of* Atlantic Monthly; *her own tender rebuke of Francis Grimké's moralistic preaching on Charlotte Perkins Gilman's suicide; and a very late note (written in uncertain hand in 1958), holding out hope for the eventual publication of two of her earlier manuscripts (Personal to the Afro, 1958— the "Afro" reference being obscure to us. We are happy to be able to fulfill this wish of Dr. Cooper's, made forty years ago when she celebrated her one hundredth birthday. The texts she mentions in this letter are chapters 12 and 18 of the present book.*

Chapter 28 continues with Cooper's privately printed "Souvenir" (that is, remembrance) of the occasion at Howard University when the Ph.D. was presented her. Next, the chapter offers a selection of two of Cooper's many letters to the editors of various newspapers and journals. It appears that she may have run a kind of informal column in the Washington Tribune, *a newspaper for the black community in Washington that was published regularly from 1925 to 31 December 1935. Some of the contributions are dated or otherwise identified; many are not. The greater number of them were pasted by Cooper into a kind of scrapbook that, unfortunately, was itself a magazine. It is very difficult, thus, to read some of them because the print of the host magazine bleeds through. The two newspaper articles we selected reveal Cooper as somewhat of a moralistic crank in her objections to a poem by Langston Hughes and to Richard Wright's* Native Son (1940). *We could have included others of a more gentle, less stern nature, but these qualities are already well in evidence in other of her writings in the collection.*

The chapter concludes, however, with a gentle, if otherwise unremarkable, poem that Cooper wrote on her birthday in 1940. In "No Flowers Please," Cooper gives instructions as to how she would like to be remembered—as "Somebody's Teacher on Vacation now. / Resting for the Fall Opening"! A bit sentimental perhaps, as some of her opinion pieces are moralistic, but, taken as part of a complex and long life, these selected writings together represent Cooper at her most human. They are, in their plain ordinariness, a fine concluding antidote to the heroic qualities of her character and life's work. That life and its work is summarized in the chronology of the final chapter.

· 26 ·

The Early Years in Washington: Reminiscences of Life with the Grimkés (1951)

*I*n 1887 I received, unsought, thro the kindly offices of my Alma Mater, an appointment to teach in a Washington High School. About the same time the Grimké Family returned to Washington, after a temporary sojourn in Florida, to resume [the] pastorate of the Fifteenth Street Presbyterian Church here. On the Branch, so to speak, for a year they had quarters in transit on Eleventh street in what was then facetiously called "Quality Row," while I made my home with Dr. and Mrs. Alexander Crummell, who were deep in the anxieties of constructing St. Luke's Church at Fifteenth and Church streets, northwest. In spite of absorbing cares and worries of house hunting and home prospecting for permanent anchorage on both sides, even in that first year *we met* we knew the meeting to be no chance acquaintanceship. Each saw and realized the "grappling hoops of steel" which clinched and finally stamped with the sacred seal of a permanent friendship the unspoken pledge: *Toute ma vie et au delá*. The very next year I had planted my little North Carolina colony on Seventeenth street where I immediately began, like the proverbial beaver to build a home, not merely a house to shelter the body, but a home to sustain and refresh the mind, a home where friends foregather for interchange of ideas and agreeable association of sympathetic spirits. The Grimkés also soon had their *Lares and Penates* comfortably ensconced on Corcoran street, their books and their pictures, their statues and flowering plants, the things they loved and would enjoy all the more by sharing with others of harmonious tastes and congenial minds. From that day till death began his inroads into that circle of kindred

Privately published by Cooper in 1951 as part of *Personal Recollections of the Grimké Family and the Life and Writings of Charlotte Forten Grimké*. We have been unable to find a rights-holder. The text has been edited for reasons of space.

310

spirits, I can safely say not a week passed for thirty years or more that did not mark the blending of those two homes in planned, systematic and enlightening but pleasurable and progressive intercourse of a cultural and highly stimulating kind. The week-ends were something to look forward to, Friday evenings on Corcoran street, Sunday evenings at 1706 Seventeenth street; and I think if there had been some "She-that-must-be-obeyed" to say to me, "If you don't watch your step you can't go to the Grimkés this week," I would have fallen into line pronto.

As may be supposed, it took a pretty stiff course of study to hold us so long. The Friday meets we called the Art Club. We never organized, had no officials, no constitution, no dues. Besides our two families and whoever chanced to be visiting either of them, Dr. Blyden, when on this side of the Atlantic, Richard T. Greener, Mrs. Frederick Douglass (we were too dilettante for the Honorable Frederick), Mrs. John R. Francis, Mrs. John H. Smyth, (known locally as "Smythe-Smith"), wife of the Ex-Minister to Liberia, and a few others met there. We drew no color line, in fact I believe we were not conscious of any. Visitors in my home such as Miss Alice M. Bacon of Hampton, Mary Churchill ("David Churchill" the author), when stopping over Sunday were pleased to meet my friends, the Grimkés, who were always in for music on that evening; likewise the denizens of "1706" had the pleasant privilege of meeting many choice New England spirits at Corcoran street on Fridays.

An amusing incident occurred in connection with the presence of Coleridge-Taylor[1] to conduct his "Wedding of Hiawatha" given by the Coleridge-Taylor Choral Society at Washington. Naturally and as a matter of course, when not busy with rehearsals, he made himself very much at home both with the Corcoran street coterie and with our circle on Seventeenth street. In fact, in a way, I may say I was responsible for his making the trip to Washington, and had to put forth no lion-hunting wiles to have him meet my friends when he came.

It happened this way. In the summer of 1900 I was on the program to speak in Westminster Hall at a Conference in London. Coleridge-Taylor furnished the music for that program, and afterwards he and his wife invited me to attend as their guest a presentation of "Hiawatha" in Alexandra Palace, at which time he received the greatest ovation my small-town "colored" experience had ever read or dreamed of. Mrs. Coleridge-Taylor took me at once right to her heart, and immediately began planning to come to

1. Samuel Coleridge-Taylor (1875–1912): Afro-English composer and musician.

"the States." I saw that she was just at the stage of love's lunacy, when you yearn for the sacrificial altar to prove by dying the undying attachment of conjugal devotion. I approved Mr. Taylor's coming but strongly opposed her making the trip with him. She argued. She knew all about the prejudice "over there." She "wouldn't mind it a'tall." She was sure that where Mr. Taylor went she would be only too happy to go. I argued that, however becoming the martyr's crown might be upon her pretty head, her friends should not be subjected to the pain of seeing it there; that what she knew about prejudice on the other side was hearsay, to moil through it was quite another thing. My argument finally prevailed, and Mr. Taylor came alone to "shed his sweetness" quite generously on "colored" America. Some whites bravely attended the concert given in a "colored" church. The Marine Band rehearsed faithfully under his baton and took orders quite meekly from the little brown Englishman. Not a ripple on the surface. The last goodbyes were said; colored Washington and neighboring boroughs were gloating over the triumph "for the Race." But Mr. White Man rarely gets left for long—that is, if he can get near enough to bribe the conductor and maul the engineer. As a few of us learned afterwards, a committee of "Bokkras" quietly boarded the train at Union Station, rode with Mr. Taylor as far as Philadelphia, brought him back as their guest, and banqueted him at the Shoreham! We were not invited. It was never noted in the papers, and we were left to imagine our friend at the time already en route to his native heath in Bonnie England. When we learned the truth, we had no regrets. Short'nin' bread fills the hungry soul more completely than caviar and champagne, and what is more to the point it leaves no hangover for the morning after.

I wish I could find in the English language a word to express the rest, the stimulating, eager sense of pleasurable growth of those days—eight to ten P.M. Fridays regularly at Corcoran street, Sundays at "1706" the same hours. The word study (Latin: *studere*) connotes zealous striving, suggests a teacher, competition, percentage marks, school, and inevitably some sort of promotion or reward of merit card at the end; and there is always an end to that sort of thing. You want it, and work for it, and hope for it. But here was just growth with the sheer joy of growing,—conscious, satisfying, complete, each hour of energized happiness sufficient unto itself, expecting no end and desiring none. Like the Tree that looks at God all day and lifts its leafy arms to pray, or the lowly cabbage that roots its way in the luscious bosom of mother earth and does no more than "head up," reveling all the time in the process. Here was activity, planned and purposeful, strenuous but joyous, not hunger-driven animal action to appease wants, rather spirit-driven by the inner spur and need for life—the more abundant life. Perhaps, in the way we went at it we may catch a figure from the war horse, quivering for the fray, with the smell of battle dilating his nostrils, the certainty of conflict sending quickening thrills into his hoofbeats. Or better still, perhaps, the Atlantean swimmer buffeting angry billows with affectionate strokes of leg and arm, rejoicing in the strength of the Universe as he feels it surge thro his tingling veins with every impact of the salt sea waves.

In the old college days my record was far from guiltless of faculty headaches for guiding professors, by reason of my insatiable craving for "more." Faculty business was interrupted to consider the case "of one 'Miss' Cooper, who asks permission to carry four subjects when three is the limit under the rules." On one such occasion, when differential calculus was the fourth pleaded for, Mrs. Johnston, Dean of Women, was asked, as authority on Woman psychology, to explain why this "Miss Cooper person" was clamoring for calculus. Mrs. J., her black eyes snapping, her thin lips drawn to a single line, informed the faculty in her deep sonorous voice that the only explanation she could offer for the phenomenon was, "Calculus is hard, and Mrs. Cooper likes to tackle hard things." That was not the whole story at the time, for I recall that, at a safe distance behind Lady Johnston's back, I retorted that with funds reaching just so far I had to crowd into the time I could pay for such subjects as needed the Professors' help. The "snaps" I could dig out alone. Be that as it may, I had the habit even then of grappling with difficulties and liking it. And I did enjoy my Math. . . .

. . . Mrs. Grimké was very fond of Raphael and the Umbrian School of Art. She loved Mrs. Browning and Mrs. Jamieson, and had herself contributed articles on Italian Art. And so it was soon decided we would study Art—not to practice but to enjoy it. *How to Judge a Picture, Art for Art's Sake, Taine's Italy, The Ideal in Art,* and *Lubke*—this last, two big volumes, we spent several successive winters on, taking a year's study for Architecture, another for painting, a third for sculpture, and so on; with collateral explanatory readings and talks, collecting scrap albums of things we wanted for keeps, and even picking up here and there plaster casts of classic models such as a three-foot replica of the *Venus of Milo* found in Toronto on one of our trips. The Perry Pictures were then obtainable of almost everything mentioned in the Art books and extremely low-priced, clear, and well photographed for mounting. Each of us had an individual book of preferences. Mr. Grimké joined in for the pure recreation of it, and he afterwards admitted seriously that he got a great deal out of it. I believe his favorite master was Michelangelo, a spirit most akin to his own for stern self discipline and unrelenting devotion to ideal perfection. His chosen masterpiece was Michelangelo's *Moses,* which he framed and kept on the wall of his study.

As already intimated, our reading was by no means desultory. The author to be studied was usually selected in the summer vacation by a representative appointed in June. The selection was made after several trips to the library and examination of publishers catalogues. The book chosen was purchased by each member and read aloud from cover to cover. As a test of thoroughness of work done, the task of bringing in a list of questions on the topics discussed was alternately assigned, and a field day of quizzing came after the completion of each major topic. A full hour at each meeting was given to the subject in hand, after which small talk and general conversation around Mrs. Grimké's tea table. I think I owe any cultivation I have now in the taste for teas to that acquired at Mrs. Grimké's hospitable board. Prior to my Corcoran street training in the flavors of oolong, Formosa, Salada, and the various India and Chinese brews, I confess the only conscious requirement I demanded was that it should be wet and sweet. Mr. Grimké changed all that, for he was the consummate miracle man who transformed water fresh from the spigot, brought quickly to the first bubble boil, into the brilliant amber-colored nectar that shed the delicate aroma of a tropical forest or a bouquet of tuberoses. He had a three-minute glass that came from Pisa, Italy. It took just so many minutes for its fine sands to flow from the upper to the lower bulb. Just so long, not a second longer, must the hot water remain on the tea leaves; and when the delighted ohs and ahs from his admiring audience announced that the performance was a complete success, Mrs. Grimké, whose wifely solicitude for his husband's spiritual graces far outweighed her satisfaction in such material achievements, would say, while her eyes all along had registered only the utmost gratification at her man's clearly foreseen triumphs: "Oh, don't inflate his vanity by too much praise. I assure you Frank is quite conscious already of his accomplishment, and indeed proud of the fact that he tops all competitors in the fine art of brewing tea. We shall have to call him the Champion Brewer."

A curious study in psychology, to my mind, is the contrast between Frank Grimké in the innocent, almost boyish, abandon of his home and the austere, almost painful-rigidity of Doctor Grimké of the pulpit. He could joke and take a joke at his own expense, provided, mark you, it did not cut across any "fundamentals" of his Calvinistic postulates. On one occasion, in Toronto, we met a young African prince, Momolu Massaquoi, a fine-looking, upstanding, well educated young man, who lectured on things African and exhibited pottery, basketry, and textiles of native weave. His tribe had a written language and he mentioned once, I recall, that his mother, the favorite wife, could both read and write Arabic and that he himself would succeed his father on the throne. We enjoyed his lecture *en costume,* a bolt of striped weave over his shoulder and an enormous spear in hand. I was both surprised and charmed at the purity of his English; and Mr. Grimké took delight in boosting the young prince as a great catch. One day Mrs. Grimké came to my room her eyes dancing with excitement, and informed me that the Prince was in the Parlor and wished to see me. I was not slow in catching her enthusiasm and all a-twitter she helped me into my prettiest frock and waited till everything was in apple-pie order. Ready with my most engaging smiles, I descended with her. When we entered the spacious parlor, there sat Mr. Grimké, his face somewhat in the shadow, a long flowered curtain draped across his shoulders, a curtain rod a-tilt ready to spear any ferocious beast of the desert, and fairly bursting with laughter over my complete discomfiture.

The tender solicitude with which he cared for Mrs. Grimké and the fond cheerfulness with which he served her slightest wants was beautiful, and to my mind unparalleled among the sons of men. She was older by several years than he and always, in the years that I knew them, an invalid. Yet he never tired, never seemed to settle into it as an old, old story. If one inquires after her health, he would answer as if he had never noticed it before: "Why she isn't at all well today. She is suffering with a dreadful headache." She was always chilly, and we Friday Nighters were sure he kept the house too warm. They had in both front and back parlors those huge latrobes that seemed in those days indigenous to Baltimore and Washington. They burned anthracite coal and Mr. Grimké never allowed them to fall below flaming heat. Once someone slyly remarked, apropos of his wonderful efficiency as a fire tender, that certain philosophers opined that we carry on to perfection in the world to come whatever attainments we have achieved here below. He was quick to see the implication and took good naturedly the joke at his expense. My mental observation was that there was no text of Scripture against it.

Not so my "Simon of Cyrene." I gave him a copy of the poem, as was always done by any member of "the Club" who broke into print—and most of us did sooner or later. He read my lines thro thoughtfully and silently at first. Then he came back over certain verses and fixing me with a disapproving glance he said: "But the Word has it They laid on him the Cross," and he quoted: *They found a man of Cyrene, Simon by name, him they compelled to bear His Cross.* "You make Simon a volunteer," and he read aloud:

> The human back was weary;
> The path was sharp and steep;
> A threefold load of sorrow,
> His Cross of anguish deep:
>
> The Cross of Love-rejected—
> "His own received Him not";
> *"How oft would I have gathered*
> *Your brook of hapless lot,*
> *E'en as a hen her chicken[s],*
> *To save—but ye would not."*
>
> The Travail-Cross of Service,
> On Heart that ached to give
> All of its soughing pulses
> That brother-man might live.
>
> And then, the thorny Wood-Cross,
> The nails of toilsome strife
> With earth's uncouth conditions,
> To give the lowly life.
>
> And so the Cross was heavy,
> Its threefold weight dragged hard;
> The feet were torn and bleeding
> That trod Judea's award.
>
> Beside the road to Calvary,
> A swarthy figure stood:
> One Simon of Cyrene,
> Alone amid the crowd.
>
> His brawny arms knew burdens,
> His big, broad shoulders, bent,
> To many a loving service
> A willing lift had lent.
> The Man of Sorrows halted;
> The man of Service saw
> The look of Love, exalted,

Triumphant over law
Of race or class proscription,
Of barriers high and low;
O'er narrowness of vision
That cannot see or know
A brother in the stranger;—
O'er drowsy ears that fail
To hear the needy calling;
O'er "slow of heart" that quail
At union in "One Father"
And kinship in "One blood."

Through all the dreary nothings
That keep mankind apart,
These Two, a look revealing
Shot forth from heart to heart.
Two Spirits met each other
At Nature's tidal flood—
Simon, the man of no caste,
Jesus, the Son of God.

A look, a thrill, a heart throb
Of comprehension clear,
To bind in one communion
God's children, far and near.
That look, divine stigmata
Graved deep in hearts for aye;
Sign of the mystic union
Of souls who serve the Way.

The African's broad shoulder
Beneath the Cross was thrust.
That Burden and its bearer
No more shall be accurst.

"We two went up together!
And they who love the Lord
Some day shall call me brother,
In mem'ry of His word."

In defending my point of view I was as illogical,[2] I suppose, as the girl in the play from the Bowery, who had suddenly become a Marchioness.

2. If indeed she was illogical, it was only because she felt so deeply about the connection between religious values, social service, and racial uplift. Karen Baker-Fletcher goes so far as to identify Cooper with the social gospel movement—an intriguing idea, well worth explora-

Her mentors kept telling her "That is not the way for a marchioness to behave," and she retorted, "Well, it's the way this marchioness behaves." St. Simon was not pictured in my mind as a slave, dumb driven, as an accidental beast of burden happening at the moment to be caught in the denouement of the greatest Drama of the Universe, but as one elect thru-out the Ages to play his part in that Drama when Asia betrayed and Europe crucified—Africa, predestined to come forward humbly and gladly to give Service, the peculiar contribution of "Ethiopia's blameless Race."

It was not my logic but my presumption, I think, that disturbed my friend's orthodox soul. As I argued for my Bill of Rights, including freedom of thought and freedom of expression, he got my tag with an epithet and put a quietus on further argument for that day. "That is rationalism," he said, "you are a rationalist." I shut up but did not give up after his bludgeon of name-calling. [The program at the] Sunday evening gatherings of the clans at "1706" . . . was less strenuous than the Art studies at the Grimkés', and bore in general an air of repose fitting the closing hours of the Sabbath day. We used to meet in my study, where there was a second piano, not to disturb or be disturbed by the youngsters of my household, who were frankly "bored" by music not distinctly of their generation. George Eliot says somewhere that we are blessed when our "theater" demands the best that is in us. . . .

And now I am going to utter a libel bringing, I fear, quick condemnation on my devoted head. I am glad today that Radio was not invented at the time of my long and patient struggle with classical music. Grateful I am for this miracle of the ages which comes just when I need it and find it to be indispensable. It relieves jaded eyes from poring over newspapers, it furnishes box seats free for Metropolitan Opera and numerous exquisite classical programs by the finest orchestras, from all of which, be it remembered, without Radio, the "segregated," whatever their qualifications, would be excluded by an adamantine American law for the most illiberal of the liberal Arts. So thank God for Radio! It has not yet caught on to the Jim Crow trick, and it still does the best it can for the aging and for shut-ins and shut-outs. I will not grudge to the young their swing and their jazz.

---

tion. The figure of Simon of Cyrene clearly had special meaning to Cooper. In 1931 Cooper commissioned Frank J. Dillon to design the glass window she gave to St. Augustine's College (her first alma mater) in memory of her husband who had died nearly a half century before. Louise Daniel Hutchinson has determined the year of the gift, as she has so many other biographical details of Cooper's life. See her *Anna J. Cooper: A Voice from the South* (Washington, D.C.: Anacostia Neighborhood Museum Smithsonian Press, 1981), p. 30.

I am glad that by a turn of the wrist, I can cut it out. I am wondering if it would not have made me lazy, carefree, and a bit reckless, if my youth had spent its energies on loose rhythm and commonplace melodies and that "let down" sort of music which lounges on its backbone and bangs the piano for sheer noise and motion. I am just as glad that most of the things I dug out for myself, laboriously and conscientiously because I liked them, have proven in the larger horizons of today worthy of being loved and kept alive by those more capable of judging than I. And I would not exchange the avid zest, the expectant delight with which I worked out for myself the beauty of these treasures, practicing every spare moment for my Grimké "Theater." And the reflected joy of their keen appreciation! For they, too, loved the Masters, knew details of their histories, often offered suggestions of their own impressions interpreting the mood of the music or the emotions aroused in themselves by its rhythmic beauties and elusive harmonies. An Opus of Schumann, I recall, the memory of which has haunted me for years. The album was thumbed to death and passed on to the trash man years ago but, like the Lost Chord, it remains to this day the object of eager expectancy whenever my radio favors me with a Schumann program, hoping the ether may bring it back. Vain hope! Such moments may be once but not twice. It began with arpeggios, sweet and tender, that make you think of Life's innocent childhood, of Mother play and baby songs, perhaps of babbling chords and harsh dissonances—conflict, hate, tough opposition, violent misunderstanding, hostile, ruthless force, and cruel injustice; then just the barest gleam toward the end of that first simple period of peace and tenderness. A lovely sunset emerging from black storm clouds after a turbulent, unsatisfying day.

· 27 ·

The Third Step: Cooper's Memoir
of the Sorbonne Doctorate
(1945–1950?)

Sometime after 1945, perhaps as late as 1950 or 1951, Cooper privately printed a booklet,
The Third Step. The booklet comprises this text, the talk Cooper gave when her French
diploma was formally conveyed in a ceremony at Howard University on 29 December 1925
(in chapter 28), and the written versions of her responses to the two oral questions at the thesis
defense (chapters 24 and 25). Although there is no date to establish with certainty when
Cooper brought these texts together in the booklet, it would have to have been after she
translated "Equality of Races" (chapter 24) in 1945. There are handwritten notes of the 29
December 1925 speech, so it is reasonable to assume that she had the speech printed after the
translations of the two thesis questions and may have written this memoir at the same time.
She would have been eighty in 1948, but she was still active at Frelinghuysen in the 1940s
and published the Grimké memoir (chapter 26) in 1951. It is entirely possible that she wrote
both this and the Grimké memoir when in her eighties. She would live nearly a quarter
century after her eightieth birthday.

> *Que Dieu vous protégé et bénisse vos courageux desseins.*
> *May God protect you and bless your courageous designs.*

𝒯hese are the words and this the prayer of M. l'Abbé Felix Klein,[1] French
author whose book, *Au Pays de la Vie Intense,* dedicated to President Theo-

---

We have been unable to locate a rightsholder. The text has been lightly edited.

1. Abbé Felix Klein was a friend of Cooper's going back to the early years in Washington
when in 1903 he visited the United States, toured the M Street High School, and wrote a
glowing report of Cooper's teaching and administrative skills. He also came to her assistance
in 1924 and 1925, when Cooper was in Paris for doctoral work, by arranging accommodations for her and by advising her on continuing the research in Washington when she was
forced to return home. Along with Francis Grimké, Klein was one of the two longtime male
friends with whom Cooper is known to have maintained a close friendship.

dore Roosevelt and containing a chapter on a visit to the M Street High School and an hour with a class in Vergil taught by its principal, caused a general raising of eyebrows in the United States and a few red faces in Washington, D.C.

The "Courageous designs" referred to were the audacious plan I had concocted to transfer my credits and thesis for the doctorate from Columbia University in New York to the University of Paris, France. It came about in this way. Following the Washington School Upheaval of 1906 in the reign of William the Chancellor, legal experts of D.C. found it expedient to promulgate a new doctrine, that reorganization of the school system involved the reappointment of all teachers—a thousand in a day. Thus it happened that the principal of M St. High School and several others were "overlooked"—not put out but left out in the shuffle, so to speak, just a simple little matter of "Move along, Joe!"

The next four school years I held the chair of languages (French, German, Greek, Latin) at Lincoln University, Jefferson City, Missouri. It was pleasant to spend the summers of these four years in Oberlin, the college of so many happy memories, and I promptly applied to President King to matriculate for my next degree, the doctorate. He informed me however, that Oberlin's charter did not confer the Ph.D. and I contented myself with stimulating courses in belles lettres.

The fall of 1910 Washington had had enough of "the Chancellor"[2] and Dr. Davidson, the new Superintendent sent for me to meet an appointment in his office on a certain hour and date. The formality of examination had already been passed and I was duly appointed teacher of Latin in the Washington High School.

The following vacation months of July and August 1911, 1912, 1913 were employed at La Guilde Internationale, Paris, pursuing courses in French literature, History, Phonetics. Provided with *certificats* for each of these courses and with honorable mention from Paul Privat Deschanel, the most brilliant and fascinating teacher of history it has ever been my good fortune to encounter, I matriculated for the long dreamed of Ph.D. at Columbia University, New York City July 3, 1914. . . .

Minimum residence! Ah, there's the rub. How was I to establish a year's residence in New York City from September to June without losing

---

2. The reference is to William Estabrook Chancellor, the district superintendent of schools who participated in the attack on Cooper in 1906. He was an associate of Washington's Tuskegee Institute, which no doubt explains his hostility to Cooper. Cooper referred to him sarcastically as "William the Chancellor."

my job and utterly abandoning several important irons I had in the fire? First there was the brood of five motherless children ranging in age from an infant of 6 months to the ripe age of 12 years. I had taken them under my wing with the hope and determination of nurturing their growth into useful and creditable American citizens. Then too I had been at some pains to find a place in Washington that would be a home to house their Southern exuberance—a place with room enough all around so that their "expansion" would not be as thorns in the side of our Washington public.

A place was found and with it was discovered a unique combination of the perfect gentleman with a Christ-like attitude toward little children "regardless of race, color, creed or national origin," General LeFevre, a truly great American, who sold me the place that had been his home in old Le Droit Park which in the historic past had been forbidden ground for colored people except as servants. The place had been used as a chicken yard by its white tenants and I immediately set about landscaping, threw an octagon sun room across the square cornered porch, changed the wooden pillars to graceful Italian columns and installed a concrete balustrade all around, none of which brought me any nearer the residential requirements at Columbia University.

With butter at 75 cents per lb. still soaring, sugar severely rationed at any price and fuel oil obtainable only on affidavit in person at regional centers, the Judge at Children's Court—on occasion I had to report there—said to me: "My, but you are a brave woman!" Not as brave as you may imagine, was my mental rejoinder—only stubborn, perhaps, or foolhardy, according to the point of view. . . .

Meanwhile for "Home Work" I started on the Glossary for *Le Pèlerinage de Charlemagne*. Dr. Alexander, Instructor in the Old French courses taken at Columbia thought it would be acceptable as a basis for research and the fact that it was one of the shorter old French epics rendered it acceptable to me. By courtesy of the University Library the rare Koschwitz edition was loaned the Library of Congress for my use and my photographer, Addison Scurlock was engaged to reproduce the whole edition complete with notes in German. Although the finished work did not reach Paris until two years later when I was there to defend my thesis it may be of interest to quote here the estimate put on this work then by a French author and critic.[3]

---

3. The identity of the French critic is unknown.

Whatever the faults or the merits of the Pèlerinage de Charlemagne, it was not easy hitherto to discover them. . . . Mme. Cooper in her preface says modestly that the present volume without pretense to erudition will render service perhaps to American students. It will be no less appreciated by French students and by their masters ("profs"), happy to be able, *grace à elle,* to peruse directly a work which does not fail to hold its own place in the history of our literature.

The two or three vacations of waiting were filled with out of town work as usual: War Camp Community Service in Indianapolis, Playground Director at Wheeling, when finally the hour struck. The answer to prayer came—but not according to preconceived plans and specifications. It was a "frowning Providence" readily diagnosed even by the unlearned as the "Flu"—the real thing truly that pointed a way for my year's residence abroad.

'Twas the night before Christmas. After a hectic day of last minute shopping and preparations, late at night I was busy sorting out gifts and filling the children's stockings, when suddenly, things began to swim before me and grow black. I left the stockings to the oldest girl and staggered off to bed. The next day and many after I was not able to raise my head above the pillow and when I did get back to school I realized I was not at my best and decided to ask for a year's sick leave. This ostensibly was granted but the string to which it was attached turned out later to have elastic claws. After much figuring, rearranging and refurbishing of rules to make the punishment fit the crime, it transpired that the substitute's compensation for every day of my absence was larger than my own per diem pay on the principle that the larger the divisor for a given dividend the smaller the quotient. This was a minor headache compared with the bomb shell that exploded when this cable reached me in Paris: "Rumored you will be dropped if not back in 60 days!" You've guessed it. I had posted to France after sending ahead my application and transcript of credits from Columbia University to the Sorbonne, University of Paris. It was astonishing and a bit amusing how earnest the Secretary to the Dean of Columbia became when I disclosed my intention to put in the year's residence in France. In anticlimax she argued it was impossible, unnecessary, undesirable. I countered for awhile and then ceased firing, yielding the palm to preponderance of vociferation rather than to conviction. This was the first summer session following the attack of influenza. I registered for repetition of Old French at Columbia not because I needed the points but to be on the spot for summing up the transcript. I took special examinations in Latin and Greek to be substituted for Italian and Spanish and submitted my glossary and notes on the *Pèlerinage*. It was then that I remembered to write my great and good friend the Abbé Felix Klein and received in reply his adorable prayer and blessing: May God protect you and bless your courageous designs.

I was on my way but far from plain sailing. Preliminaries of passport, photographs and identification assurances that I was I and a perfectly well intentioned American citizen going abroad for study etc. etc. etc. was not new, for I had been in Europe several times—4 summer sessions studying at [the] International Guild and one, my first back in 1900 as a mere Globe Trotter. But prelims to study officially documented Mss. at the Archives and to follow up special dossiers for the Bibliothèque Militaire and other libraries in various parts of Paris were quite another thing. First the United States Embassy for endorsement and request that Madame Cooper be granted etc. etc. etc. then the *Carte d'identité* to be obtained at the Salle des Étrangers in Hôtel de Ville. Here a new set of Photographs was demanded. The one brought from the United States did not picture "all the two eyes" *(tous les deux yeux)*. . . . Registration at the Collège des Étrangères whose charming Secretary arranged the necessary conferences, advised proper preliminaries and saw to the fulfillment of legal requirements such as the government revenue stamp on the application for authority to present "les épreuves du Docteur d'Université devant la Facultié es Lettres" all of which would have been a pretty puzzle for an unaided greenhorn *Américaine*. . . .

President Poincaré[4] had been making headlines that seemed to me significant of France's attitude towards Racial Equality. A monument had just been erected at Dakar, "Á la Gloire de l Armée Noire,"—"le patriotisme ardent des tirailleurs tombés sur tous les Champs de bataille de France." I had accumulated some notes and comments of my own on the Franco Japanese Treaty of 1896—The Naturalization laws of France: a) for Japanese, b) Hindus, c) Negroes, and of course the discussions in the National Assemblies during the French Revolution; the writings and speeches of and about La Société des Amis des Noirs—l'Abbé Gregoire and others. I subscribed to and read avidly such magazines as *Le Monde Noir* and such contributors to current thought as Franz Boaz, Jean Finot, Gobineau— Discourses of Lamartine before the Chambre des Députés 1835, 1836 on L'Émancipation des Esclaves, also at *Banquet à Paris pour L'Abolition de L'Esclavage* March 1842—his drama *Toussaint L'Ouverture* presented by Lemaitre

---

4. Raymond Poincaré (1860–1934): president of France, 1913–1920.

at Paris April 15, 1850 and lastly his thrilling words three days after the Revolution of February: "Je signai le liberté des Noirs, l'Abolition de l'Esclavage et la promesse d'indemnité aux colons. Ma vie n'eut elle eu que cette heure Je ne regretterais pas d'avoir vécu." . . .[5]

So after much priming and pruning my thought was trimmed down to proportions that won from the Conservateur des Collections: "21 Février 1924, Madame Cooper est informé que le sujet de Thèse choisi par elle a été inscrit le 20 Février sur la registre de la Faculté de Paris en ces termes: L'Áttitude de la France à l'égard de l'esclavage pendant la Revolution."

Followed another dossier aux Archives, more limited in time, deeper in content. I cannot speak too gratefully of the efficient and really sustaining service rendered me at the Archives. No sooner was my subject submitted and its limits known than a force, expert and specialized was put to listing all the material—documents, speeches, Acts of the Assemblée, at the Archives, the Arsenal and other special libraries in various parts of Paris that would have taken years and years to exhaust.

Not many days after the memorable 21 Février I was waiting at Bureau de Renseignements for some matters I had to look up, when I became conscious that I was being pointed out by a clerk at another desk in conversation with a tall gentlemanly person that had U.S.A. emblazoned on every inch of his consciously distinguished bearing. He approached me politely and asked in French if he might have a word with me. "Speak English, please," I said quietly and he continued in English that he was a reporter for the *Chicago Tribune* published in Paris, that he had learned I was there preparing a thesis for the doctorate and that I had already won acceptance of my subject by the Faculté des Lettres which last, he added pleasantly, was the hardest part of the battle. I marveled that he knew beforehand more or at least as much about my affairs as I myself, but begged him to keep it off the record at least for the present. "I don't see why," he said. "It is a most laudable ambition for an American woman to earn the degree of Ph.D. from the Sorbonne." "Tout le même, I am quite honestly on sick leave from school in Washington, D.C. And I have many misgivings about

---

5. Cooper translated Lamertine's words thus: "I have signed the emancipation of the blacks, the abolition of slavery and the promise of indemnity to the planters. If my life had had only this hour, I should not regret having lived."

The short section deleted is Cooper's account of the rejection of her first proposal for a thesis topic as "too vast and too vague," lines she played back to her examiners when they set a comparably vague and vast examination question in 1925.

the appreciation I shall receive for this 'laudable ambition' you speak of. I am not playing hookey. Quite the contrary, I am soundly convinced that every scrap of information I may gain in the way of broadening horizons and deepening human understanding and sympathies, means true culture and will redound to the educational value of my work in the school room."
"I believe you are right," he said earnestly and wished me the best of luck. Moreover, I think he meant it.

Nevertheless, it was not many days after the encounter that a friend close to authoritative sources at home cabled me: "Rumored dropped if not [back] within 60 days." Ouch! Just as I was settling down to work at the archives where you have to be checked to go in and double checked to get out!

On the credit side for my 50 days residence however they had prepared for me an exhaustive dossier of sources bearing on my subject and I would gladly have spent more than the promised year delving in so rich a mine. But 60 days! I began counting off my Saturdays and Sundays, the Christmas holidays, George Washington's birthday. Only 10 days remained for me to wind up my affairs and report "present" at Dunbar High School, Washington, D.C. A desperate Cinderella with no fairy godmother to turn to! But again yes; a friend in need, the friend indeed—my great and good friend Monsieur l'Abbé. A trip to Meudon to explain the situation. If I did not return at once, I'd lose not only my job as a present means of support but also all hope of future security on retiring. Would he recommend some colaboratrice whom I could employ to copy aux Archives the subjects I had already checked in the dossier and relay the same to the Library of Congress in Washington where I would work after school hours and week ends. I could arrange, I thought with the Doyen to continue my year's work in the Washington Library, returning to Paris for the *Soutenance* of my Thesis when completed. (Yes; come I would, I fiercely promised myself, "If I have to swim!")

When I walked into my class room 5 minutes before 9 on the morning of the 60th day of my absence, I did not sense the true inwardness of the gleeful applause that greeted me till sometime afterwards when I learned that these little friends of mine had had all the excitement of fans holding ringside seats at a race; for the substitute had confided to them "I'll be your permanent teacher if Mrs. Cooper does not get back by next Thursday."

Plugging away every leisure moment and putting in full time in summer vacation and holidays at the Library of Congress where a table in an alcove was graciously placed for me, I had my stuff fit to be typed by

Thanksgiving. This time I prostrated myself before the Throne and asked for leave under Rule 45 for "Emergency" stating the emergency to present my thesis before a Jury at the Sorbonne. I pulled every string I knew in Paris (and I had found several) for permission to send my MS. ahead to be reviewed, criticised and printed. (It must be in print before the *soutenance*.) *Absolument impossible!* replied the Doyen. Not even our men absent on military service would be allowed such a concession. My immediate supervisor wanted to know why the "emergency" could not be squeezed into the ten days of Easter holiday. Well we could not manipulate the Law of France to accommodate a High School in Washington. So again scrapping in Thanksgiving, Christmas, Easter and all Saturdays and Sundays, I took the bit in my teeth deciding "If they drop me this time it shall be for doing as I darn please. If I perish, I perish."

With my typed MS. in my hand bag I once again crossed the Atlantic, following the Beam; my colaboratrice, Mademoiselle C. who had faithfully kept in close touch all the year, sent a wire to my boat saying she would be at Madame L's by 10 the next morning to take my MS. to the Chairman of my Jury. My Washington typist had had no French accents on her machine, and I burned out a devastating number of Madame L's candles, sitting up all night to put in accents and make necessary corrections. When leave to print was finally obtained, I must see the members of my trial Board to learn the supplementary questions proposed by each for discussion at the *soutenance*. M. Bouglé wrote: "Madame Cooper pourrait être interrogé sur Les Idées Égalitaires et le mouvement Démocratique." M. Cestre, Professor of English Language and Literature at the Sorbonne, who said to me afterwards "Your success here will mean much to your countrymen" assigned the subject: "Les Mesures Législatives concernant l'esclavage aux États-Unis de 1787 à 1850." More sleepless nights and midnight candles. Electricity had not then been installed in Madame L's apartments. Recalling that my own subject had been rejected as "too vast and too vague," I wondered why something could not be done about Bouglé's[6] "Idées Égalitaires" with no fixed limit in time, space or human thinking. I had but one short week to think it through. Besides and most emphatically I was frankly afraid of Bouglé. My French ear seemed duller than ever when he spoke and my tongue stupidly stuck in my throat. Madame told me that he was Breton which explained his variation from the more accustomed Parisian. But to make matters worse, I found myself on the opposite side in some

---

6. On Célestin Bouglé, see the introduction to part 4.

pronouncements from his own thesis on *Égalité,* and when I gave out my opinion to Madame she said: "That will not help you. Bouglé is atheist."

As March 23 approached I tried to steel my nerves with the thought "It is a glorious thing to suffer and die for one's convictions." I did not dread the main thesis which I understood would be handled by Sagnac, and I felt quite at home on M. Cestre's subject. But for Bouglé while Bryce and Tocqueville were both familiar reading, I was apprehensive there would be the inevitable clash with the great Judge himself.

Somewhere off the quadrangle I had read in passing: "Thèse pour le Doctorate 23 mars à 9 heures Salle de Richelieu Mlle. Cooper." But the only directing I had received was "Tout près de l'Église" in very rapid and very careless French. As I entered for the first time the awesome portals of the Salle du Doctorat I was met by an elderly personage in black gown who addressed me as Mademoiselle and inquired what college was designated by my Master's hood of crimson and gold. He conducted me to a table at front on which a carafe of water, a goblet and a bowl of sugar for what purpose I was too painfully preoccupied to try to guess. I think I recall a painting of the great Cardinal and blurs of others high on the walls but too remote in consciousness to leave any impression today.

My good friend, the usher (can't say what his title should be in France, but he seemed to me most like a royal Major domo or perhaps a very intellectual court bailiff) rapped three times. The audience, which was behind me and did not disturb me in the least, rose and I stood up as the three judges filed in by a door at the rear of the high platform on which they seated themselves. . . .

The dreaded Bouglé gave a look in my direction that seemed to say in mushy Breton: "I didn't believe it was in her." The chairman proceeded with some criticisms of textual errors which I accepted and noted in the copy I held. He also took exception to my partisan pleading. He maintained that the *Gens de Couleur* were not unitedly fighting for the Rights of Man. That the mulattoes so far from espousing the cause of the blacks, narrowly sought only their own release and were not averse to holding slaves in their own right.

To me this discussion was both significant and informative. I realized, not unpleasantly that a *soutenance* was not a test "exam" to be prepared for by cramming and cribbing the night before and brazened through by bluff and bluster the morning after by way of securing a "passing" mark; rather and most emphatically a *soutenance* "sustaining," supporting, defending if need be, an original intellectual effort that has already been passed on by competent judges as worthy a place in the treasure house of thought, affords for the public a unique opportunity to listen in on this measuring of one's thought by the yard stick of great thinkers, both giving and receiving inspiration and stimulus from the contact. After about an hour on the main theme Sagnac passed the defendant over to M. Cestre who had to meet a class elsewhere at 11. In his kindly hands my fears ceased clawing at my heart. Without consciousness of the unusual I followed his lead as if in informal conversation when he mentioned John C. Calhoun, Thomas Jefferson, State Sovereignty, Nullification. When he rose to be excused I knew that I had at least one vote for "passing." . . .

From 11 to 12 the *Bête Noire*. My best bolstering boost was that Bouglé's Thesis, "Les Idées Egalitaires" had been carefully studied and I knew it almost as well as I knew my own. He could not trip me on that if once I caught his question. Only once did my ear stumble and it was on the word "densité." I hesitated "densité" *dans cité*—"Pardon, Monsieur, Je n'ai pas compris votre question." However, that was all straightened out and by the very irony of fate, when, after three solid hours of grilling questions and grueling fear, the mentor at my back rapped a third time for the audience to rise on the return of the judges, and I remained standing for the sentence to be pronounced, it was Monsieur Bouglé who delivered the verdict, of which all that I could make out or can now recall, was "bien satisfaits" and "que vous êtes Docteur."

As the two judges solemnly filed out by the same door at rear of the high platform through which they had entered three hours before, I could not realize that all was over till people from behind whom I had not seen before, took me by the hand or began saying things. Some just looked at me and smiled without saying anything. One woman speaking good old United States (How good it sounded!) said she had thought something of trying for the Doctorate but had not quite made up her mind. Wanted to buy a copy of my thesis. We went to the Secretariat together where she made her purchase.

Don't I get a diploma—or something? I asked meekly. Mais oui, bien entendu! Par les canaux diplomatiques, à l'Ambassade de la République Française aux États-Unis. The French government does not deal with individuals. Our ambassador will be pleased to entrust to the Mayor of your city de Diplôme de Docteur ès Lettres de la Faculté de Paris, honneur de votre obtention d'aujourd 'hui. I explained with what French I had left in me (it must have been lamely, for I was both tired and hungry, having eaten nothing before setting out for the Sorbonne at 8 A.M.) that my town was

Washington, D.C., that we had no Mayor but did business through three commissioners appointed by the President of the United States.

The only answer to my rather labored explanation was a French shrug and "Eh bien! Lex canaux diplomatiques, quelconque quel qu'il soit, Mademoiselle." This arrangement was fulfilled to the letter. The diplôme de Docteur ès lettres de la Faculté de Paris was in due time received at the Ambassade de la République Française aux États-Unis and presented to me by a delegate representing the Commissioners of the District of Columbia in a pleasing ceremony at Howard University under the auspices of the Xi Omega Chapter of Alpha Kappa Alpha Sorority December 29, 1925.

· 28 ·

Selected Letters and Other Writings
(1925–1958)

Autobiographical Fragment (n.d.)

I was born in Raleigh, North Carolina. My mother was a slave and the finest woman I have ever known. Tho untutored she could read her Bible and write a little. It is one of my happiest childhood memories explaining for her the subtle differences between q's and g's or between b's and l's. Presumably my father was her master; if so I owe him not a sou and she was always too modest and shamefaced ever to mention him. I was born during the Civil War and served many an anxious slave's superstition to wake the baby up and ask directly "Which side is goin' to win de war?" "Will de Yankees beat de Rebs & will Linkum free de Niggers?" I want to say that while it may be true in infancy we are nearer Heaven, if I had any vision or second sight in those days that made my answers significant to the troubled souls that hung breathless on my cryptic answers, such powers promptly took their flight with the dawn of intelligent consciousness. In the later struggle for existence I could not have told you how the simplest encounter with fate would end.

Letters

Washington D.C.
Nov. 19, 1910

Dear Mrs. Cooper:
   You have, doubtless, been wondering why you have heard nothing from this side of the line; we have also been surprised at the slow pace at

---

The autobiographical fragment, all the letters (except Cooper's to Du Bois), and "No

331

which matters have been moving. No action was taken at the last meeting of the Board. The matter did not come up at all. The alleged ground was that the examining committee had not, up to the time of the meeting of the Board, rendered a report. I have just had another interview with Mr. Bruce, and he assures me that matters will turn out all right in the end, and, he wished me to say that to you. The real cause of the delay, he now assures me is due to the fact that Supt. Stewart wanted first to talk the matter over with each member of the Board, before making the recommendation, in order to make sure that his recommendation would be sustained. It seems that the only member of the Board who has raised any objection, is Mr. Horner. Miss Barrier called me up a few days ago, and told me that she had also understood that such was the case. I went out immediately to Howard University and saw Tunnell, with whom I had talked before about the subject, and he told me to give myself no uneasiness about the matter, that he would see Horner and set him straight on the matter. So don't give yourself any uneasiness. Be a little patient, and soon everything will be all right. What Mr. Bruce said to me, of course, is confidential. Lottie is still quite poorly, and sends a great deal of love to you. We all wish to be kindly remembered, and with best wishes I am,

Yours truly,
Francis J. Grimké

*   *   *

201 T Street, N.W.
Washington, D.C.
May 24, 1926

Dear Mr. Wilkinson:

Once again I shall try (without offense I hope) to write you as a man rather than as an official.

The year 1927–1928 will mark my fortieth as a teacher in the High School of the District of Columbia, barring an interim of four years as college professor at Lincoln University. One year later (1928–9) I shall be retired automatically from the system by the age limit rule. I have therefore only about three years more of public school service before me, even if I

Flowers Please" are reprinted courtesy of the Moorland-Springarn Research Center, Howard University. The Du Bois letter is courtesy of the Du Bois Archive, University of Massachusetts. We assume that the newspaper contributions are to the *Washington Tribune,* which has been out of publication since 1935. The souvenir was privately printed by Dr. Cooper (see introductory note to previous chapter).

am not excluded before that time by some unforeseen disability. My ratings by officials immediately concerned have been uniformly "excellent" and "excellent superior." There has never been, to my knowledge, any question of my efficiency as a teacher or of my spirit of willing cooperation in all the deepest concerns of our school population. Much of my aims, ideals and principles of action is personally well known to you and many of my achievements have been consciously aided, inspired and abetted by you. I believe I have had many evidences of the sincere esteem and appreciation with which my service is regarded by the humble laity whom I serve, and yet it is to be admitted that official recognition still seems tardily and grudgingly accorded and pecuniary emoluments, so eagerly sought by most persons, are stubbornly withheld while every opportunity is seized in some quarters to excuse this material injury by detraction and misrepresentation.

Now I should utter no word of complaint for all this were it not my firm conviction that nothing vitiates the morale of any educational system more completely than a sense of unfairness in the distribution of rewards. Once let the conviction take root that merit does not count, that service, however long and faithful and efficient can be outstripped any day by sheer pull or flimflam, and no administration would be secure. The strength of the head rests on those loyal hearts that respond to a sense of justice and fairplay and on that support that goes out spontaneously always to unselfish devotion.

It may be that you can without jeopardizing your own interests prevent the perpetuation of those studied attempts at persecution and humiliation which have been so patent in my case. I do not ask you to say or do one thing to embarrass yourself. But as it seems to me now and as it has seemed all along to a few very thoughtful friends of mine, it could only strengthen your hold on the community and give real significance to your position in the eyes of the country, if you would take a firm stand for justice and fair play in the bestowal of those favors that involved the taxpayers' burdens. You, if any one, can say that neither N. E. Weatherless nor Marion P. Shadd can convince one who has ever been a student under Anna J. Cooper that she does not know her subject. Surely the testimony of Oberlin and Columbia and La Sorbonne should not be allowed to be discredited by any factitious "board of Examiners" in the Washington Public Schools.

A report from Mr. Hine dated May 11, 1926 *in re* my appeal before the Committee on Complaints contains this paragraph: "The Committee is impressed with Mrs. Cooper's attainments as a scholar and student and takes pride in the recognition which her work has lately received. But a 'passing mark' on the written examination is required for promotion and as Mrs. Cooper at the hearing held before the Complaints and Appeals Committee did not claim that she should have been given a passing mark on the written examination it is therefore impossible for the appeal to be granted."

The whole ground of my complaint and appeal to the Board was from the first that several candidates were given the promotion over my head [altho their] educational claims were admittedly below mine, [and] their written examination papers . . . had been marked below the required passing mark [by the first set of judges], as had my own presumably. I have never raised a question of those markings. I think I could show if I were allowed to see my papers that I have a fairly good account of myself. I have never in my life failed in a written test and I have taken on an average I am sure one at least for every year of my teaching experience. The quantity of work required in these Washington examinations is purely arbitrary and the questions themselves designed rather to "stump" the candidate than to test his ability to teach the subject. In this case the questions had been carefully mimeographed or typed and were full of errors that had to be unravelled in order to give any sort of intelligent answer. The translation was wholly sight work and as I recall it the first question had five or six subheads for comments, mythological, historical, or interpretative, on certain lines of a poem that must first be scanned to mark the rhythm, show the caesure and classify the meter. There may have been ten or could have been fifty questions after this—I never knew. I think I answered something like two or three after the first which had consumed most of the forenoon. Then since as you know there is no hostelry near the Franklin where a colored person can procure a glass of milk, I had to walk all the way to the "Y" [at] 9th and R.I. for lunch. Caught a cab coming back but was not so fortunate going. When I returned the others were already under way, but I put in the time remaining as best I could, on the afternoon work consisting of principles and methods, conduct of department, etc. etc.

I mention these trifling details to show why I employed a lawyer to plead for the "merging" of the written and "oral" marks in giving the final standing [as the law of Congress provides]. . . . Fixing the entire weight of eligibility exclusively on the written test papers is in the opinion of my lawyer wholly extra-legal. Indeed the law nowhere says that the written examination shall even be passed or any defined standard shall be met therein. The teacher is promoted for "superior work" only [as the law states] "*after oral and written* examinations." Now the word "oral" as interpreted in practice by the Superintendent of Schools sums up the whole arc of personal efficiency in the work of the schools and should if anything be made the *sine qua non* of a "superior" teacher's claims for promotion. Yet strangely enough I was excluded from consideration under this head until the Board of Education at the instance of my lawyer ordered first that the Oral be given me and later than that ratings be affixed to the several items. It was on this so-called oral test that my complaint rested and still rests. The law was clearly violated in promoting to Group B a teacher who had not reached her maximum in Group A; it was violated only by implication in promoting those whose test papers in a written examination were rated below 210. Again all the more was it violated in my case in altogether disallowing the "oral examination," just as legally necessary as the other, and insisting on an arbitrary standard of 210 on the written examination before any other claims could be considered. . . .

The Superintendent's circular had estimated 300 points for written, 300 for oral and 400 [for] Personal characteristics and Teaching Ability. My 700 superior points as elements of actual teaching service were discredited for the first 300, a purely arbitrary element of written examination.

I wish distinctly and unequivocally to disclaim responsibility for any disrespectful remarks concerning either the Superintendent of Schools or any member of the Board of Education made by David A. Pine who was employed to present my appeal to the Board. He may not have been tactful; he certainly was not successful in representing my own attitude of mind regarding the question at issue. But the Administration cannot be willing to play the role of persecuting a faithful servant who has from the beginning been innocent of any intention to offend.

And may I not at least hope, Mr. Wilkinson, that you with your usual judicial mind will see this somewhat from my point of view and that your natural love of justice and fairness will not rest till due consideration is given where it deserves.

Very respectfully yours,
[Anna J. Cooper]

★   ★   ★

201 T St. N.W.
Washington, D.C.
October 1, 1928

Mr. A. G. Comings, Treasurer
Authorized Oberlin Committee
    Campaign Fund of 1928 of the
    Anti Saloon League of America.

Dear Mr. Comings:
    I am sorry I cannot enter wholeheartedly into the Campaign for downing Governor Alfred E. Smith. My own vote, it is true, if I had one, should go to Hoover as, of the two, the man coming nearer to representing the best in American ideals. But, speaking personally, the 14th and 15th amendments to the Constitution are just as precious in my sight as the 18th and I am unable to warm very enthusiastically with religious fervor for Bible "fundamentalists" who have nothing to say about lynching Negroes or reducing whole sections of them to a state of peonage worse than slavery. I do not at all question the sincerity of the little band of Oberlin workers for those ideas which Oberlin, as I know it, has always championed and which I most heartily endorse. But Al. Smith has the same right to his opinions that I have to mine and even if elected could not carry the country any further than our representatives in Congress will allow.

Very sincerely yours,
Anna J. Cooper.

★   ★   ★

AJC
201 T. St. N.W.
Washington, D.C.
December 31/[19]29

My dear Doctor Du Bois:
    It seems to me that the *Tragic Era* should be answered,—adequately, fully, ably, finally, and again it seems to me *Thou* art the Man! Take it up seriously thro the *Crisis* and let us buy up 10,000 copies to be distributed broadcast thro the land.
    Will you do it?
    Answer.

Faithfully,
Anna J. Cooper

★   ★   ★

Northwestern University
College of Liberal Arts
Evanston, Illinois
November 7, 1933

Mrs. Anna J. Cooper
201 T Street, N.W.
Washington, D.C.

My dear Mrs. Cooper:

Professor William C. Holbrook and I, both of Northwestern University, are preparing, for early publication with D. Appleton-Croft Co., an anthology of medieval French literature in modernized versions, and should be very grateful to you for permission to reprint certain excerpts from your translation of *Le Pèlerinage de Charlemagne* (Paris, Lahure, 1923).

The passages which we should like to use are as follows, p. 2, pp. 23–32 *passim,* 27–43 *passim.* Unfortunately I have not the text at hand at the moment, but if there is any question about the extent of the material we wish to use, I should be glad to give you the exact lines.

Apparently the book is not copyrighted in the U.S., but we have hesitated to use even the brief passages indicated without your authorization. Needless to say, we shall make full acknowledgement of the source upon which we have drawn.

We are indebted to Professor Jameson, of Oberlin, for obtaining your present address.

Very truly yours,
Thomas R. Palfrey

★   ★   ★

Office of the Editor
The Atlantic Monthly
8 Arlington Street
Boston, Mass.
31 January, 1935.

Miss Anna J. Cooper,
201 T Street, N.W.,
Washington,
District of Columbia.

Dear Miss Cooper:—

Anyone who knows the *Atlantic* would not think that we meant to insult the Negro race or any other. Dr. Zinsser, in the course of his scientific studies, did take lice from the head of a poor Negro, but he might have borrowed them from the heads of Americans of a dozen races of other descent. Nothing that you imply was intended by the article.

Yours faithfully,
The Editors

★   ★   ★

AJC
201 T St., N.W.
Washington, D.C.
April 9, 1936

Mr. dear Doctor Grimké:

I have read with great pleasure the brochure you so kindly sent me. I always appreciate your letting me see whatever you publish and hear whenever you are preaching one of your special sermons. I wish in the leaflet on Frances [Charlotte—that is] Perkins Gilman you had given your readers more of the life of your subject. The poem you quote there is so very beautiful and lofty in its tone. I am sure the facts in that life, leaving out its tragic end, would have been full of inspiring interest and stimulating encouragement. But you are always *the preacher* you know, and *must* draw your moral for the benefit or the confusion of the rest of us poor sinners.

I forgive you and wish you all the joy and happiness of the blessed Easter season.

Sincerely yours,
Anna J. Cooper

⋆　⋆　⋆

Personal to the Afro

It is my wish that Two Hundred Seventy Nine Dollars 65 cents contributed in honor of my hundredth birthday be deposited at interest in Savings Dept. at National Savings and Trust Company to be used later in publication of my work ["The] Ethics of [the] Negro [Question"] and ["The Negro's] Dialect."

With thanks and appreciation to all concerned I appoint my Niece Madeline Beckwith and my friend West A. Hamilton Joint Trustees and administrators of this fund.

Signed Anna J. Cooper
201 T St. N.W.
Washington, D.C.
September 2, 1958

⋆　⋆　⋆

Souvenir

No nation, no race, no individual, in any clime or at any time can lay claim to civilization as its own creation, or invention, or exclusive personal possession. The impulse of humanity toward social progress is like the movement in the currents of a great water system, from myriad sources and under myriad circumstances and conditions, beating onward, ever onward toward its eternity, the Ocean. And though at one time or another there may be little pools or eddies of stagnant "shut ins" or "shut outs" that have lost by the accident of separation the onward sweep of the mighty torrent, these segregated *arriérés,* these units less instructed than their age demands, cannot, must not be disinherited or denied their birthright to civilization, the *de facto* right to claim and appropriate to capacity, as part of the human family, all the several, the attainments of human progress. This RIGHT TO GROW is sacred and inviolable, based on the solidarity and undeniable value of humanity itself and linked with the universal value and inalienable rights of all individuals.

Civilization has been likened to a divine torch that passes with the alphabet of self-expression from age to age and from race to race. Phoenicians passed it to Greeks, Greeks to Romans, and Romans to the barbarian forebears of the modern world. But who gave it to the Phoenicians, and who to him and who to him? No one knows. The beginning of things is always shrouded in mystery, and the guess of one is as good as another. The

Greek myth has it that Prometheus in the service of men stole the spark from Heaven, paying the penalty for his audacity by deathless torture in an immortality of suffering and pain. The myth does not intimate, however, that Prometheus ever repented of his daring deed. Suffering is not seldom the reward for service:—even so, the privilege of having helped the car of humanity along its toilsome journey, ever so slightly, is too precious to heed its cost in pain.

Of all the nations that have been torchbearers in the vanguard of human enlightenment, none, it seems to me, can claim a more liberal spirit, a more cosmopolitan good-will in the *realness* of fraternity, equality and true liberty, than the one to whom we offer a tribute of gratitude tonight, splendid, great-hearted, suffering, glorious France! In no land or country whether of the past or present time, is the marvelous culture of the nation, so fully and so freely broadcast for the enlightenment and the enjoyment of all people and tribes and kindreds that on earth do dwell.

I sat not long since in the *Salle des Étrangers* at the Hôtel de Ville, waiting with others to secure the *carte d' identité* required of all foreigners who intend to spend an extended time in Paris. I was struck by the concourse, a motley crowd from Europe, Asia, Africa, North American, South America and the isles of the sea; and as this stream of humanity filed past the different clerks charged with examining their passports, photographs, pedigrees and references, I was amazed when my own number was called to find the individual cost of it all was just 10 francs—a little less than half a dollar! Here truly it may be said: "Tros Tyriusque mihi nullo discrimine agetur."

Whosoever will, let him come; let him that is athirst, come! Yea, let him come and partake freely of the knowledge, the inspiration, the achievements and the glory of French civilization and French unparalleled culture and refinement.

And now, if I may be pardoned a personal word on an occasion so provocative of pride and vainglory, I may say honestly and truthfully that my one aim is and has always been, so far as I may, to hold a torch for the children of a group too long exploited and too frequently disparaged in its struggling for the light. I have not made capital of my race, have paid my own way and have never asked a concession or claimed a gratuity. Nor on the other hand have I ever denied full identification in every handicap and every limitation that the checkered history of our native land imposes. In the simple words of the Master, spoken for another nameless one, my humble career may be summed up to date:—"She hath done what she could."

And surely no deeper joy can come to anyone, no richer reward than the pure pleasure of this moment from the expressions of appreciation in this assembly on the part of the community in which the best service of my life has been spent. In the language of our beloved Cicero: Nothing dumb can delight me. I ask no medal in bronze or gold. There is nothing in life really worth striving for but the esteem of just men that follows a sincere effort to serve to the best of one's powers in the advancement of one's generation.

I take at your hands, therefore, this diploma, not as a symbol of cold intellectual success in my achievement at the Sorbonne, but with the warm pulsing heart throbs of a people's satisfaction in my humble endeavors to serve them.

With all my heart, I thank you.

★   ★   ★

Contributions to the *Washington Tribune*

Strut and wiggle
Shameless gal
Wouldn't no good fellow
Be your pal?
Hear dat music—
Jungle night
Hear dat music
And the moon was white.
Sing your Blues song,
Pretty baby
You want lovin'
And you don't mean maybe.
Strut and wiggle,
Shameless Nan
Wouldn't no good fellow
Be your man.

DR. COOPER DOESN'T LIKE THE HUGHES POEM

To the Tribune Editor:

I think it a pity that the high note of your editorial page should be vitiated by a selection that presents the very opposite ideal from the one you so ably advocate.

That so serious minded a paper as the *Tribune,* which condemns *Amos 'n' Andy* as pernicious propaganda and a vicious caricature of the race, should allow "Midnight Nan" to "strut and wiggle" through the same page where-on we find earnest advice for "Children's Reading" must surely have been an oversight. A full survey of Langston Hughes' poetry ought to furnish, I am sure, some samples of his genius more in keeping with the high standard announced by the *Tribune* than this nauseating portrait of a colored prostitute. My criticism is not against Hughes for writing about whatever he sees and happens to know; but I do object to pictures of the gutter and sewer being culled and paraded by preference from all the ennobling and inspiring examples of art that present themselves—examples that are just as true to life, just as humanly appealing, and just as artistically acceptable.

Walt Whitman did much that was coarse and vulgar in his poetic creations, but one has to wade through his unexpurgated works to find it. You will not be confronted with the filth of "Leaves of Grass" on the editorial pages of a cosmopolitan newspaper, and this is not from race squeamishness either, but a mere matter of literary taste and fine selection according to the eternal fitness of things.

Anna J. Cooper.

$\star$ $\star$ $\star$

WRITER FLAYS "NATIVE SON"; WOULD LIKE STORY ON VICTOR HUGO THEME

To the Tribune Editor:

When the nation is facing a crisis that threatens to undermine and disrupt the most sacred principles of its historic structure and traditions, it is well for racial minorities to pipe down on specialized counter irritants, however important they may seem to be locally and specifically, if they do not serve to promote the general welfare and thus tend toward harmony in adjusting internal differences in the body politic.

Like a burr under the saddle of a turbulent steed or sand in the spinach for an exasperated dyspeptic, racial differences with minority rights and privileges clamored for at such a time can only result in snapping over wrought tempers and upsetting the entire applecart.

Conservative thinkers will view with some misgiving the announcement that Paul Green, who holds the Pulitzer Prize for his production, *In Abraham's Bosom,* has offered his expert service as playwright in collaboration with Richard Wright to dramatize *Native Son,* the sensational problem study of the year.

By way of accentuating the agony and crowding out the mourners they intend, I believe, to have Orson Welles and John Houseman parade their product in New York next season.

I have not read and shall not read Mr. Wright's novel. Even to live through a dramatized hour of it before footlights would equal the torture of ten nightmares. No overflow of presumption, however, could tempt me to criticize it.

By the yard stick of "success" it is undeniably tops. As a money getter and as towntalk it displays a startling preview of what the public wants, and every pencil pusher is hot on the trail of another Bigger Thomas.

The type is etched in lurid lines and no delineator of Negro character has a Chinaman's chance who essays to depart from it. Added to a morbid taste for dirt in the realism of today which sends camera men snooping around moral cesspools and social garbage cans for available "copy," there is the more subtle, more persistent urge of the propagandist who knows how to inject the virus of social unrest and hide-bound antipathies into what seems a bold reproduction of reality.

The clash between law of organized society and human frailties and individual appetites is an unfailing source book for creative genius; and the tragedy of it has been portrayed in immortal pictures of classic literature.

I have often wished that another Victor Hugo might conceive "The Brute" of Negro life, comparable to the "Wretch" in Jean Valjean. It will be a masterpiece for all time if ever we get it. It will not be a novel with a purpose, nor a "Problem of Today."

It will be Life As Is—Life in the raw, struggling, failing, falling, battling the hardships, buffeting the onslaughts, accepting the handicaps, but toiling on and up, irrepressibly up and always human—always understanding by every other human, not a monster of race, color or creed.

Nor will this novel, if truly great, undertake to establish a thesis, prove a point and fix the norm of human relations contrary to nature and subversive of the Gospel rule.

Peace among men of goodwill is both sane and safe. Society does not need the fiery Cross of a lynching to further terrorize victims of long injustice, nor hooded nightriders to prevent an orgy of interracial tolerance and American fair play.

Anna J. Cooper.

★　　★　　★

No Flowers Please (August 10, 1940)

Oh, just a rose perhaps, a few violets
Or even a handful of wild honeysuckle
Or Star of Bethlehem and sweet alyssum
Which says you remember kindly.

For this I shall thank you, Wherever I am.
And more for the courage and strength
You gave in the Struggle we call Life.
By the touch of your shoulder to shoulder
And the Understanding glance of your eye
And the hearty Pull together of a sympathetic heart.
Priceless and undying these as God's gracious bounty.
And I shall thank you, Wherever I am.

But *please, please,* don't pass the hat for big florist's offerings
Or take up a collection to crowd the room and cover my poor bier
With mute withering symbols of God's eternal love and Christ's
   unspeakable Prayer
Agonizing that we all should be one and love one another
Even as He and the Father are One in Love.

No flowers please, just the smell of sweet understanding
The knowing look that sees Beyond and says gently and kindly
"Somebody's Teacher on Vacation now.
Resting for the Fall Opening."

The Life of Anna Julia Cooper: A Chronology

The most controversial date in Cooper's life is that of her birth year. We believe that the year 1858 can be reliably used even though Cooper recalled late in life (see the autobiographical fragment in chapter 28) that she was born during the Civil War. It would not be unusual for anyone, lacking a birth certificate (which, given the circumstances of her birth, Cooper surely lacked), to confuse the dates of birth and early infancy. We take her August 10th birth day at face-value, on the assumption that birth days are usually correctly remembered even when the year is uncertain. Based on her application for a marriage license (dated 11 June 1877), where Cooper represents her age as nineteen, it seems reasonable to conclude that she was born 10 August 1858.[1]

1858?	Born in Raleigh, N.C. (10 August)
1865?	Begins school at St. Augustine's College, Raleigh
1868?	Tutors older students (her first teaching experience)
1877	Marries George A. C. Cooper (21 June)
1879	Husband dies (27 September)
1881	Completes schooling at St. Augustine's College
	Applies to Oberlin College in Ohio (27 July)
1884	Graduates with B.A. in math from Oberlin
	Teaches college at Wilberforce in Ohio
1885	Returns to St. Augustine's College as teacher
1886	Speaks to black clergymen on womanhood in Washington, D.C.
1887	Receives M.A. (for college teaching) from Oberlin
	Moves to Washington, D.C.; begins high school teaching
1890	Speaks to educators on higher education of women
1892	Publishes *A Voice from the South* at Xenia, Ohio

This chronology is taken from various sources, principally the archival records, Cooper's own records of her life, and various secondary sources, of which the most thorough is Louise Daniel Hutchinson's *Anna Julia Cooper: A Voice from the South* (Washington, D.C.: Anacostia Neighborhood Museum and Smithsonian Press, 1981). Each entry has been checked against a second source.

[1] The application is reprinted in Hutchinson, *Anna Julia Cooper*, p. 29.

1893   Speaks for black women at the Chicago World's Fair
1894   Cofounds Colored Women's League, Washington, D.C.
1900   Attends Pan African Congress in London
1901   Appointed principal of M Street High School, Washington, D.C.
1902   Addresses Quakers on ethics and race in New Jersey
1905   Booker T. Washington visits M Street High School
1906?   Dismissed from position at M Street High School
        Supervises Colored Settlement House in Washington, D.C.
1906   Moves to Missouri; teaches at Lincoln University
1911   Returns, after five years, to M Street High School
1912   Makes first study trip to Paris (summer)
        Resumes work with poor in Washington, D.C.
1914   Begins doctoral studies at Columbia University
1915   Becomes guardian of five infant children (25 December)
1916   Buys house at 201 T Street, N.W. (28 January)
1917   Translates *Le Pèlerinage de Charlemagne*
1919   Works at War Camp in Indianapolis (summer)
1920   Supervises playground in West Virginia (summer)
1923   Becomes ill (24 December); takes sick leave from teaching
1924   Begins doctoral work in Paris while on leave
        Job threat; hurries home from Paris to Washington (February)
1925   Completes doctoral thesis on France and slavery
        Defends thesis at the Sorbonne in Paris (23 March)
        Presented with doctoral degree at Howard University (29
            December)
1930   Retires from M Street (now Dunbar) High School
        Becomes president of Frelinghuysen University (15 June)
1931   Frelinghuysen moves to Cooper's T Street home (October)
1941   Leaves presidency of Frelinghuysen; continues teaching
1945?   Publishes *The Third Step*
1951   Publishes *Personal Recollections of the Grimké Family*
1958   Celebrates 100th birthday (10 August)
1964   Dies at home (27 February); buried in Raleigh (4 March)

Index

About the Editors

Charles Lemert, Professor of Sociology at Wesleyan University in Connecticut, is the author of many books, including *Social Things: An Introduction to the Sociological Life* (Rowman & Littlefield, 1997) and *Sociology After the Crisis*. **Esme Bahn** has been Director of the African American indexing Project at the Smithsonian Institute and is former principal curator at the Moorland-Springarn Research Collection at Howard University.